GOLF MAGAZINE'S
Complete Book of
GOLF INSTRUCTION

GOLF MAGAZINE'S
Complete Book of
GOLF INSTRUCTION

*By George Peper, James A. Frank,
Lorin Anderson, and John Andrisani*

HARRY N. ABRAMS, INC., PUBLISHERS

Project Director: Margaret L. Kaplan
Designer: Liz Trovato

Library of Congress Cataloging-in-Publication Data

Golf magazine's complete book of golf instruction / by George Peper . . . [et al.].
p.   cm.
Includes bibliographical references (p.   ) and index.
ISBN 0–8109–3393–4 (clothbound)
I. Golf.   I. Peper, George.   II. Golf magazine (New York, N.Y. : 1991)
GV965.G524   1997

796.352—dc21   97–6088

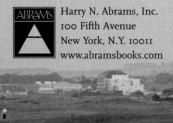

Harry N. Abrams, Inc.
100 Fifth Avenue
New York, N.Y. 10011
www.abramsbooks.com

CONTENTS

INTRODUCTION
PAGE 8

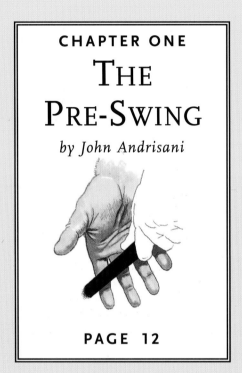
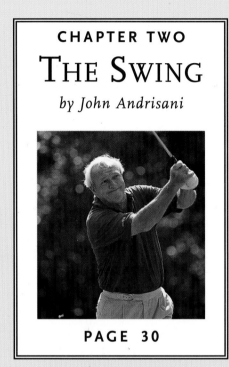
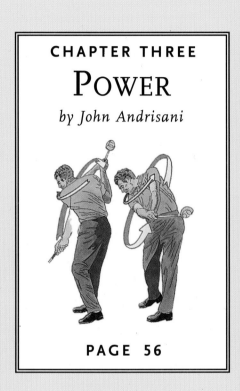
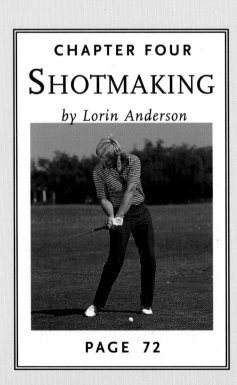
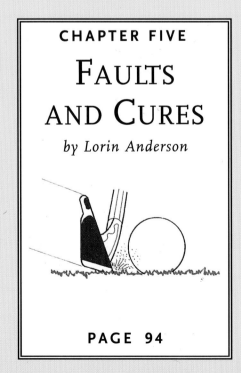
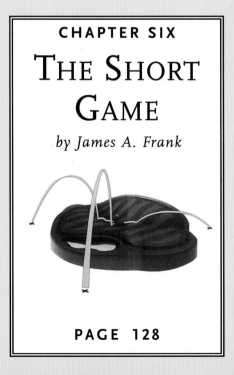

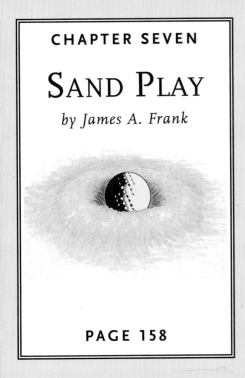
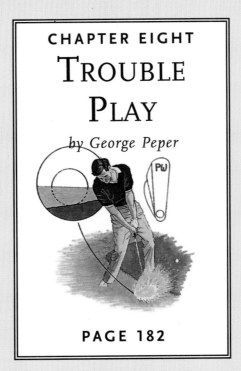
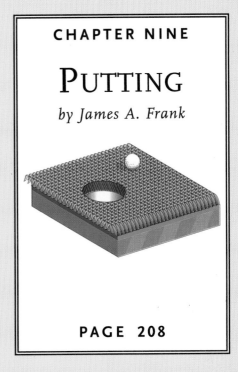

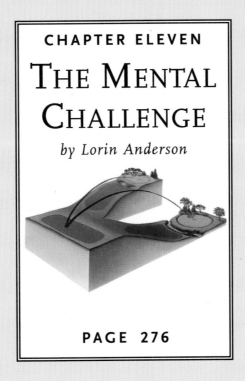
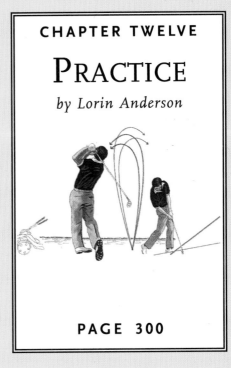

INTRODUCTION

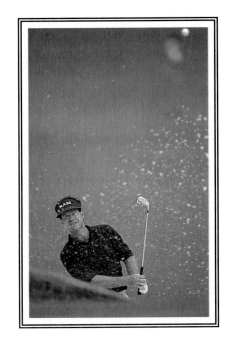

SINCE THE FIRST GOLF INSTRUCTION MANUAL WAS published in the United States—100 years ago—thousands of "how-to" books have followed. Each one has tried to make its mark by putting forth a particular method for hitting the ball.

A century later, this book breaks the mold. *GOLF Magazine's Complete Book of Golf Instruction* was born from our firm belief that there is no single correct way to play golf. Since no two golfers are exactly alike in size, athletic ability, or temperament, what works for Player A almost certainly will not work for Player B.

For five decades, *GOLF Magazine* has been dedicated to this philosophy—we are a forum for all reasonable ideas on how to play the game. Thus, the book you are holding is not solely an instruction book at all, but also a book *about* instruction—its history, traditions, practitioners, and, most of all, its best ideas.

This is the ultimate reference for anyone who is serious about improving his—or her—game. Four of *GOLF Magazine's* editors have spent the better part of two years researching, analyzing, and distilling the thoughts and techniques of the top teachers and players, from Old Tom Morris to Tiger Woods. The result is a compendium of 12 chapters, each one on a different area of the game—a dozen definitive distillations of golf know-how.

The main section of each chapter is built around what we've called the "Prevailing Wisdom," a compilation of the ideas currently favored by most teachers and players. But since we know that sound instruction often differs from the orthodox, we also have presented a host of alternative methods and "Different Strokes" throughout the text. Our objective was *to be* objective—to present every sane and sensible theory, every method with the capacity to help you play better golf. At the same time, we rejected dozens of unreasonable methods, just as we do each month when editing the magazine.

Collectively, the four authors have 60 years of experience in golf writing and instruction, and have written all or part of more than 25 books. Background and experience like this could come only from *GOLF Magazine,* the game's leader in golf instruction.

However, we did take a few liberties that we'd like to explain. First, we have assumed that the reader already knows a little bit about the game, so we didn't explain terms over and over again; if there's one you don't understand, it will be found in the Glossary. Second, the instruction is written primarily from a right-handed golfer's point of view, because more than 90 percent of the world's golfers are right-handed. However, we tried to use "directionally correct" references like "back foot" and "high shoulder" whenever possible.

It has been a most absorbing and, at times, consuming project, but having completed it, we feel we are both more knowledgeable and more skilled in the game we love. We hope, having bought it, you'll feel the same way.

GEORGE PEPER, EDITOR-IN-CHIEF, *GOLF MAGAZINE*

JAMES A. FRANK, EDITOR

LORIN ANDERSON, SENIOR EDITOR

JOHN ANDRISANI, CONSULTING EDITOR

MARCH 1997

GOLF MAGAZINE'S
Complete Book of
GOLF INSTRUCTION

CHAPTER ONE

THE PRE-SWING

WHEN IT COMES TO THE IMPORTANCE OF THE SET-UP POSITION, ONE STATEMENT by Jack Nicklaus, the greatest golfer of all time, says it all:

"If you set up correctly, there's a good chance you'll hit a reasonable shot, even if you make a mediocre swing. . . . If you set up incorrectly, you'll hit a lousy shot even if you make the greatest swing in the world."

So wrote Nicklaus in *Golf My Way* in 1974. By that time, at age 34, Nicklaus had won two U.S. Amateur titles, 50 PGA Tour events, and a dozen major championships. He knew what he was talking about.

Faithful adherence to the fundamentals was a key to Nicklaus's quick rise to stardom after turning pro at age 21, and helps explain how he has sustained good play for so long. Beginning at age ten, under the tutelage of Jack Grout at the Scioto Country Club in Columbus, Ohio, Nicklaus practiced the building blocks of address until they became second nature. Day after day, Grout drummed into Nicklaus that the set-up was the most important position in golf, and the only part over which he had 100 percent control. These lessons taught Nicklaus never to hit a shot until he was sure all the elements governing his set-up—grip, stance, posture, body alignment, clubface alignment— were correct. This same discipline is vital to the amateur who wishes to repeat a good swing, hit crisp, on-target shots, and shoot the lowest possible scores.

One hundred years earlier, although golf was well entrenched in Scotland, there were no universal guidelines for addressing the ball.

One of the most popular ways to stand was with the feet spread far apart, stance closed, ball well back, and knees deeply bent. This set-up produced the flat St. Andrews swing used by that town's top golfers, including Mungo Park and Young Tom Morris—winner and runner-up, respectively, in the 1874 Open Championship. Like the other top players from the "Cradle of Golf"—Willie Park, Willie Dunn, James Anderson, Thomas Dunn, and others—they were influenced by two local legends, Old Tom Morris and Allan Robertson, who hit the ball low to get the most roll on the hard turf of the town's windblown links. The around-the-body St. Andrews swing also was well suited to the long-shafted clubs made by local artisans.

But this was not the only style of play. Away from St. Andrews, some golfers stood in a square or open stance, their feet closer together. In other towns, the ball began farther forward in the player's stance, the body aiming to the left of target. No matter where the game was played, however, nearly every golfer held the club in the palms of both hands, because this allowed him to grasp firmly the thick, leather-wrapped handles.

There were several reasons for the wide variety in set-up and swing. Golf was mostly self-taught, so players learned and played by instinct. Few people outside St. Andrews had seen the Morrises, Parks, Dunns, or other

local talent, so they were not influenced by them; according to Horace Hutchinson, most amateurs mimicked the set-up and swing of their local club champion.

Conditions varied by locale, and if the course was not by the sea, like St. Andrews, players would not need a low draw to handle the strong winds common to a links. And not all club-makers made brassies, spoons, and baffies the way the St. Andreans did: Many clubs were shorter and lighter, allowing the golfer to stand closer to the ball and make a shorter, more upright swing.

Golf came to the United States in 1888, and in no time was being played around Chicago, Philadelphia, New York, and elsewhere. The more enterprising pros from Britain came to the New World to teach the game to a new audience. At the same time, changes in equipment led to standardization: American companies such as A.G. Spalding and Bros. started using modern manufacturing techniques to mass-produce clubs, creating a uniformity that encouraged uniformity in instruction.

In 1897, H.J. Whigham wrote the first comprehensive instruction book published in America, *How to Play Golf*. Whigham was a Scot who had captained the Oxford University golf team before moving to the United States, where he won both the 1896 and 1897 Amateur championships. His impetus for writing a self-help text was to clear up the confusion about swing technique that he had seen in his homeland.

"By far the largest class of golfer includes men and women of all ages

and temperaments," Whigham wrote in the Introduction, "who by accident or intention have taken an interest in the game of golf sufficient to inspire them with a desire for improvement, and yet find a difficulty in acquiring any accuracy or form or execution on account of lack of practical information upon this subject."

Whigham emphasized the importance of grip, ball position, stance, posture, body alignment, and clubface position. He realized what every teacher and fine player does today: How you set up to the ball determines the swing you make. The New World's new golfers were hungry for instruction, and Whigham's book, reprinted

several times, laid out a mostly modern set of principles they could use.

In one of his few borrowings from the St. Andrews method, Whigham instructed golfers to spread their feet two to two-and-a-half feet apart. This wide base gave the early golfer firm footing, so he remained in balance during what was still a fairly brutish swing.

Whigham's other suggestions showed that he was influenced by a new breed of golfer on the other side of the Atlantic, most particularly one Harry Vardon, who would win six British Opens and one U.S. Open between 1896 and 1914. Like Vardon—and unlike the St. Andrews school—Whigham told golfers to play

Jack Nicklaus in a perfect address position. He looks both relaxed and ready to begin the swing.

from a square or slightly open stance, distribute their weight evenly between each leg, and place the ball more toward the front foot (all positions much like those taught today). The resulting shot would be a controlled fade, rather than a draw that easily could turn into an untamed hook.

The overlap grip is almost always credited to Vardon, and still bears his name. But Vardon did not invent the overlap. It is said that John Henry Taylor, another great British player and a contemporary of Vardon's, developed it simultaneously but independently; and top Scottish amateur John E. Laidlay employed it in winning the 1889 British Amateur, a year before Vardon played his first tournament round. But there is no question that Vardon popularized the overlap, most notably during 1900, when he came to America, played numerous exhibition matches, and won our Open championship.

Before Vardon, the golfer gripped the club like a baseball bat, with eight fingers on the leather and the thumbs across the fingers. Vardon placed his thumbs on the shaft and let the right pinkie overlap the left forefinger. There are other grips in use today, but Vardon's remains preeminent.

Bobby Jones was among the first to eschew a wide stance. "With the feet spread wide apart," he wrote in *Bobby Jones on Golf,* "the lower part of the body is almost completely locked, and even the shoulder movement is made more difficult."

In his books and Hollywood-produced instructional films, Jones counseled golfers to stand the most natural way possible: "When one stands natu-

DIFFERENT STROKES

JOHNNY MILLER'S NO-DUCK GRIP

If you can't stop the right hand from overpowering the downswing, creating a duck hook, follow Johnny Miller's lead. He lets his right forefinger dangle away from the club, as though holding a trigger, instead of gripping the club the conventional way— right forefinger draped under the handle, with its tip pinching the right thumb. Jack Nicklaus, Lee Trevino, and John Daly also use this trigger-finger grip.

Johnny Miller dangles the right forefinger down the club. This "trigger-finger" position weakens the power of the right hand, reducing the possibility of hitting a duck hook.

rally erect, with feet approximately twelve inches apart and each in a natural position as in walking, there is a perfect balance of the body, and a complete facility of movement in either direction without destroying that balance. . . . This is what we are striving for in addressing a golf ball. . . . The more like a natural standing posture the thing can be made, the better off we are." From Jones came the idea of standing with the feet shoulder-width apart when playing the driver, then narrowing them slightly as the clubs get shorter and more lofted.

Vardon, like Whigham, recommended fanning both feet outward, the left more than the right. The thinking was that splaying the right foot allowed for a bigger hip coil on the backswing, and turning out the left foot promoted the clearing of the left hip through impact. Many pros play from this stance today, but a substantial number set the right foot perpendicular to the target line, a position introduced by

Opposite: *H. J. Whigham was an early proponent of the modern swing utilized by Harry Vardon. But he played most of his golf before Vardon popularized the overlap grip, so, like most golfers of his day, Whigham (shown here in 1897, the year his How to Play Golf was published) held the club in the palms of both hands, his thumbs off the shaft and resting on the forefingers.*

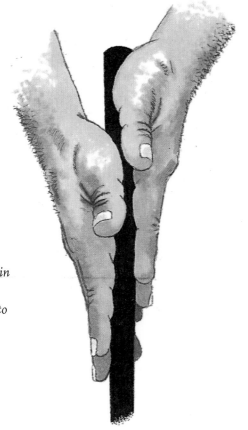

No matter what grip you choose, begin with the palms parallel, then keep them parallel as you adjust the grip to produce different ball flights.

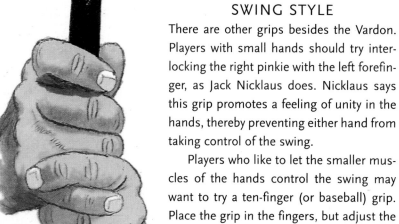

DIFFERENT STROKES

GEAR YOUR GRIP TO YOUR HAND SIZE OR SWING STYLE

There are other grips besides the Vardon. Players with small hands should try interlocking the right pinkie with the left forefinger, as Jack Nicklaus does. Nicklaus says this grip promotes a feeling of unity in the hands, thereby preventing either hand from taking control of the swing.

Players who like to let the smaller muscles of the hands control the swing may want to try a ten-finger (or baseball) grip. Place the grip in the fingers, but adjust the hands so the side of the right pinkie is touching the side of the left forefinger.

In the interlock grip, the right pinkie and left forefinger hook together. It is a popular hold for players with small hands because it forces the hands to work together as a single unit.

Ben Hogan in *Five Lessons: The Modern Fundamentals of Golf* (1957). Hogan believed this stance "acts as an automatic governor on the amount of hip turn the golfer can take (and should take) on the backswing."

Clubface alignment followed the rest of the set-up. The St. Andrews swingers aimed to the right of the target to allow for the draw (as do modern golfers with pronounced right-to-left ball movement). Early golfers like Vardon often aimed left of the target to allow for the fade. It wasn't until Jones showed that great shots could be hit with a square stance and square clubface that golfers believed this set-up could be good for them.

With the advent of instruction books, movies, videos, and television, more and more golfers can see and hear—and copy—the pros. Teachers, too, take their cues from the great players. But the astute instructor gives some leeway, particularly in the set-up. Jim McLean, having observed Tour pros placing their hands behind, ahead of, and in-line with the ball, permits students to work within parameters. He teaches keeping "the hands and the club's handle between your body's center and the crease in the slacks of your front pant leg." He calls these parameters "corridors of success."

As you read the "Prevailing Wisdom" section that follows, remember that, as the pros prove, there is some room for personalization. However, the pros have spent hours getting where they are and spend many more working to stay there. If you cannot devote that kind of time to perfecting an unusual address position, be prepared for a checkered career.

PREVAILING WISDOM

GRIP

"The simplest way to understand the proper grip is to clap your hands. Stand up, bend slightly from the waist, and let your hands hang naturally at your sides. Now, bring your hands flat together as if you were clapping."

Greg Norman's advice may be a bit simplistic, but it does make one important point: The grip, like everything else in the golf swing, should be more natural than most people make it.

Before putting your hands on the grip, sole the head of the club on the ground, its face close behind a ball and pointing directly toward a target. Set your body parallel (square) to an imaginary line running from the club, through the ball, and to the target. Let your arms hang naturally at your sides, so the palms of both hands face each other. This is the "palms-parallel" position, the first fundamental for a good grip. The palms must stay parallel as you set each hand on the club.

Left Hand: Lay the handle diagonally across the base of the fingers and partially into the palm; the butt of the club should rest under the muscle pad of the hand's inner heel. Stretch your thumb straight down the shaft as far as comfortably possible. This flattened, "long thumb" position closes the gap between the palm and fingertips, so the grip doesn't loosen during the swing. Once the hand is closed around the club, check that the back of your left hand faces the target, and that two to two-and-a-half knuckles (not counting the thumb) are clearly visible.

Right Hand: The handle rests along

 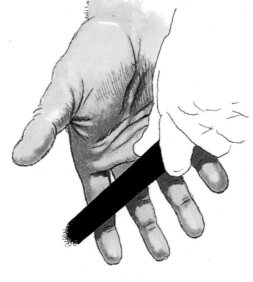

In the left hand, the club lies diagonally across the base of the fingers. The butt of the grip just makes it into the palm and rests under the fleshy pad in the heel of the hand.

In the right hand, the club lies along the bottom of the fingers (where they meet the palm). When closing the hand around the grip, the fleshy pad under the right thumb covers the left thumb.

DIFFERENT STROKES

VARY YOUR PRESSURE

Teacher Butch Harmon believes the hands work best as a team when the degree of pressure is equal in all fingers. On a one (lightest) to ten (tightest) pressure scale, the grip should be about a seven.

Harmon also says that grip pressure should change for certain shots. For example, if you're trying to hit a low punch shot into a strong wind, calling for the hands to lead the clubhead through impact, tighten your hold on the club to a pressure of eight or nine. But if you're trying to loft a soft lob over a bunker and stop it quick, you need light pressure, maybe a three. In general, tighten your grip for low shots, lighten it for high.

TAKE YOUR GRIP OUT OF NEUTRAL

Look at the longest, most accurate players on Tour and you won't see a neutral grip among them. Most of them take either a very weak or very strong grip, usually turning the right hand more than the left.

John Daly, Fred Couples, Bernhard Langer, and Tom Kite take a strong grip—with the right-hand V pointing at the right shoulder—to exaggerate the releasing of the hands at impact. This closes the clubface, imparting right-to-left drawspin on the ball for added power and distance.

Corey Pavin, Curtis Strange, and Ernie Els assume a weak grip—the right-hand V pointing at the chin—so they hit a more controlled left-to-right fade that sits down fast.

The "strong" grip promotes a strong release of the hands through impact. It helps long hitters like John Daly, Fred Couples, Bernhard Langer, Tiger Woods, and Payne Stewart stay long. It gives shorter hitters like Tom Kite hope of more yardage.

Among those using a "weak" grip are Corey Pavin, Curtis Strange, Ernie Els, Johnny Miller, Brett Ogle, and Steve Jones. They use it to hit a more controllable left-to-right fade that does not roll very far after landing.

From left to right:

In the Vardon (or overlap) grip, the pinkie of the right hand rests on top of the left forefinger. This is the grip usually prescribed for most golfers with average-size hands.

Starting in the "neutral" position— with the Vs formed by the thumb and forefinger of each hand pointing just right of the player's chin—should return the clubface at impact to the position it was in at address.

Two popular images for applying the right amount of grip pressure: 1) Think of holding the club as you would a small bird; 2) Use as much pressure as you would to squeeze a tube of toothpaste.

the bottom of the fingers, where they meet the palm. Close your hand so that the big fleshy pad beneath the right thumb covers the left thumb. Curl the fingers around the grip, with the tip of the right forefinger just touching the front side or touching the tip of the right thumb.

In the overlap (Vardon) grip, the pinkie of the right hand covers the left forefinger. This is the most common type of hold, used by all but a few pros.

To give yourself the best chance of swinging the club on the correct path and plane, and hitting a straight shot, check that the Vs formed by your thumbs and forefingers point midway between your chin and right shoulder. This is called the "neutral" position because it should return the clubface to impact the same way it points at address.

In a "strong" grip, the Vs are pointing farther to the right, closer to the right shoulder; this promotes rolling the hands toward the target on the downswing, closing the clubface for more distance or to stop slicing. A "weak" grip begins with the Vs pointing directly at the chin, and inhibits the closing of the club, so the clubface is more open at impact.

The consensus among teachers and players is that you should hold the club just tightly enough to be able to feel the clubhead, but not so firmly as to create tension in your hands, wrists, and arms. Sam Snead's famous image was to hold the club as you would a small bird; another description is to apply the same pressure you would use to squeeze a tube of toothpaste.

Jim Flick teaches his students the proper amount of grip pressure by

DIFFERENT STROKES

TO TEE OR NOT TO TEE

Only five-foot-seven and 130 pounds, Chi Chi Rodriguez has always hit the ball much longer than one would think his small size would allow. His secret is a low, running draw off the tee, which is set up by using extra-long tees that perch the entire ball above the top of the clubface. This high tee promotes a very flat backswing and a powerful sweeping action through impact. You may have to special-order these tees from a golf-supply store.

From a small man with tall tees to a big woman with no tees. Laura Davies, long-hitting queen of the LPGA, sometimes tees the ball on a tuft of grass, passing on a wooden peg altogether. By purposefully allowing blades of grass to get between the clubface and ball at impact, the shot flies 10 to 20 yards farther than normal.

Lee Trevino sometimes goes tee-less when hitting irons on par-three holes. His rationale is that since he hits most iron shots during a round off fairway grass—without benefit of a tee—he can better judge the right club for the shot if he views the teeing ground as another piece of fairway.

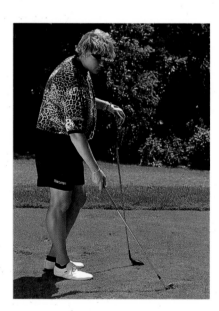

Arnold Palmer positions the ball off his left heel for the driver, then moves it progressively back in his stance as the clubs get shorter.

All fingers do not grip equally. The greatest pressure should come from the last three fingers of the left hand and the middle two fingers of the right.

Long-driving Laura Davies sometimes forgoes a tee. She kicks up a little mound with another club, places the ball on it, and tries to catch some grass between the head of the driver and the ball to produce a hot, low "flyer."

having them hold the club straight out in front of them horizontally, when the clubhead feels the heaviest and grip pressure must be greatest to keep the shaft parallel to the ground. Then he has them hold the club vertically and feel none of the headweight, meaning that they can reduce grip pressure almost to nothing. He's looking for the happy medium, so he has students hold the club halfway—at a 45-degree angle with the ground. The relatively light grip pressure they feel then is what they should strive for throughout the set-up and swing.

Certain fingers of each hand should be doing most of the gripping. Specifically, hold on tightest with the last three fingers of the left hand and the middle two fingers of the right. A good test of your grip pressure would be to have someone try pulling the club from your hands: They should feel only slight resistance.

BALL POSITION

When it comes to positioning the ball, there are two schools of thought:

Arnold Palmer leads the camp that says to play the ball opposite the left heel when using the driver, to encourage an upswing hit; then move it back gradually to promote a more downward blow as the clubs become shorter and more lofted.

Jack Nicklaus and Greg Norman play all standard full shots with the ball off the left heel. These players prefer sweeping shots off the turf, even with short irons, rather than digging into the dirt and taking the chance of hitting an uncontrollable flyer.

BEND FROM THE HIPS, NOT THE WAIST

Power hitter Mike Dunaway ignores two basics of posture—bending at the waist and flexing his knees. This is how he describes his posture in *Hit It Hard*:

"Once I'm confident that my body and club are square, I bend over from the ball-and-socket joints of the hips while keeping my knees relatively straight, but not locked. As I bend to the ball, I let my buttocks extend out a bit to counterbalance the weight of the upper body, which is now a little further forward since I'm bending over more. This allows me to set my weight into my hips, not my knees.

"If you assume this posture, then look in the mirror, you'll see a vast difference between this new position and the classic address. By keeping your legs straighter and bending more at the hips, you create a sharper angle between the legs and spine—it should be about 30 degrees. This position ensures that you stand the right distance from the ball, and also enables the body to turn more freely going back and coming down into the ball."

Whether he's swinging a driver or a short iron, Greg Norman plays all normal full shots with the ball positioned off his left heel.

DIFFERENT STROKES

PRE-CLEAR THE LEFT HIP

One of the most important movements in the swing is the rotation of the left hip around and to the left on the downswing. "Clearing" the left hip opens a space for the hands and club to come down into the ball from inside the target line. If the left hip doesn't get out of the way, the clubface approaches impact wide open, which creates a slice.

To promote the clearing of the left hip, many pros pull the left foot a few inches back from the line, opening their stance. This lower-body shift points the left hip slightly to the left, in a "pre-cleared" position. With this head start, the hip should clear even faster, producing solid shots.

To encourage a fast, full clearing of the hips on the downswing, some pros set up at address with their left foot and/or left hip slightly open. Various combinations of left foot/hip positioning are used by Lee Janzen, John Daly, Fred Couples, Curtis Strange, Seve Ballesteros, and Jay Don Blake.

To help his students determine where to position the ball, British teacher John Jacobs has them swing each club. Wherever the club hits the ground is where the ball should be positioned.

TEE HEIGHT

Most professionals and low-handicap players tee the ball so half of it is above the top of the clubface. This encourages a shallow backswing plane and a clean hit, catching the ball on the upswing.

As you move through the bag toward the higher-lofted clubs, the backswing becomes more upright and the downswing more descending. There is less chance of catching the ball on the upswing, so the ball must be teed lower. Very simply, as the club gets shorter, the tee goes deeper into the ground.

STANCE

When setting up to drive, your stance should be slightly wider than the width of your shoulders, measured from the insides of your heels. Both feet should be turned out slightly: the left 30 degrees, the right a little less. This position facilitates a free hip turn on both the backswing and downswing.

As the clubs get shorter and more lofted, narrow the stance slightly. A narrower stance leads to a steeper backswing and downswing, which is what you want with the shorter clubs.

As noted above, Ben Hogan recommended placing the right foot perpendicular to the target line. He said the

For a normal drive, half of the ball should be above the top of the clubface. When you want extra distance, tee the ball about an inch higher to promote a more powerful sweep through the ball.

back foot would serve as a brake on hip turn during the backswing. When the right foot is turned outward, the hips can turn too far, so the club swings on an overly flat plane. Then it's difficult to deliver the clubface squarely to the ball without spinning the hips back toward the target on the downswing. Spinning is a good way to lose balance.

Although Hogan didn't say this, it has since been proven that limiting hip turn on the backswing is one way to generate more power. Letting the shoulders turn freely while restricting the hips builds more torque, storing more power at the top of the swing to be released as the club whips through the ball. (See "The X-Factor" in Chapter 3 on Power.)

The feet should be at least as wide as the shoulders (measured at the heels). Turn both feet out slightly, the front foot a little more than the back.

POSTURE

Flex the knees slightly before bending over at the waist. Distribute your weight evenly over the balls of each foot. Tilt your right ear slightly toward your right shoulder; this will give you a sense of being behind the ball.

DIFFERENT STROKES

BACK TO ST. ANDREWS

One of the key elements of the old St. Andrews swing was an extremely wide stance. Today, Greg Norman, the amazingly long Tiger Woods (both of whom worked at one time with teacher Butch Harmon), and a few other players are widening their stances again as a way to widen the swing arc and sweep through the ball. Woods's heels are nearly outside his shoulders, creating a stable base and limiting hip turn. (More on this in Chapter 3.)

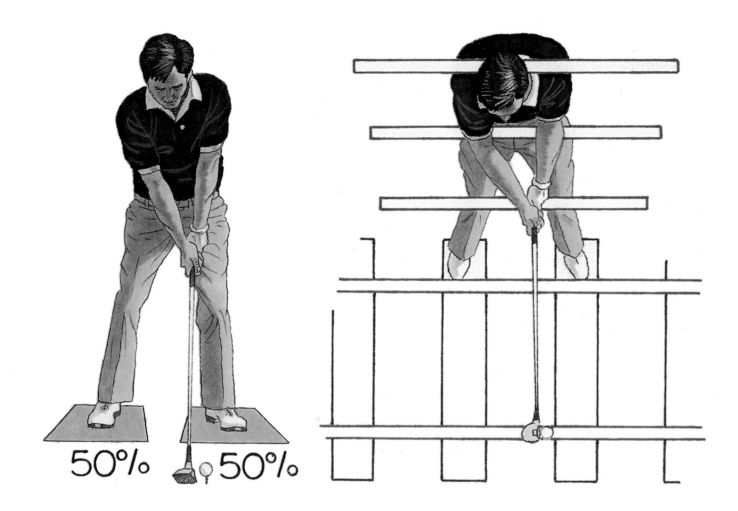

50% ♀ 50%

DAY-TO-DAY BALL POSITION

Seve Ballesteros believes that always using the same method of position leads to trouble. He says some days the body is sluggish, other days it's supple, and how you feel on a particular day should be the determining factor on where the ball begins.

"Some days my body and the club move more slowly than on others, in which case I'll position the ball farther forward to give my sluggish body more time to square up the clubface at impact. Conversely, on mornings when I feel extra supple and my swing speeds up, I compensate by positioning the ball a little farther back, which helps me to stay behind it through the hitting area."

Left: *Flex your knees slightly to help balance your body weight evenly on the balls of both feet.*

Right: *One way to assume perfect, parallel alignment is to imagine standing on a pair of railroad tracks, the ball on the outside rail, your body on the inside one.*

BODY ALIGNMENT

No matter how well you swing the club, if your body isn't properly aimed, the ball has no chance of finding the target. The best shots begin with a square set-up, in which the body is parallel to the target line—the imaginary line running from the clubhead, through the ball, to your ultimate target. Think of imaginary lines drawn across your feet, knees, hips, and shoulders, and set them parallel to the target line.

One of the most-used images in the game is that of a set of railroad tracks, the two rails parallel: The body stands

HOVER THE CLUB

Neither Greg Norman nor Jack Nicklaus soles the clubface of either a wood or an iron. They feel hovering the club just above the ground encourages a more athletic set-up, standing taller with weight split equally on the balls of each foot. It also keeps the club from catching a patchy bit of turf in the takeaway, which could throw the club off plane.

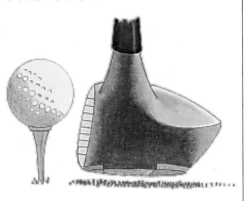

Even the best swing in the world won't hit the ball in the right direction if your body is not properly aligned, Greg Norman takes a "square" set-up, the lines of his shoulders, hips, knees, and feet all parallel and aiming slightly left of his target.

on the outside rail, the ball on the inside one. The ball should be on the rail pointing at the target; your body, because it's to the side of the ball, must be aimed just slightly to the side of the target.

Teaching pro Jim Flick has his students imagine a rolled-up umbrella lying on the target line a few feet in front of the ball. During playing lessons, he actually lays an umbrella on the ground to help ingrain this positive image in the student's mind.

Your hands should be even with the ball when playing woods, as well as

WORDS OF WISDOM

Good golf begins with a good grip.
Ben Hogan

Before they ever begin swinging, I can improve nine out of every ten typical amateur golfers.

At least that proportion—probably higher—have stances that don't give them a chance to do their best. They're ruined before they start.

Tommy Armour

I have the feeling when I'm taking my stance that someone has just pulled a chair from behind me and I'm waiting for him to put it back.

Arnold Palmer

The only way to ensure a proper aim is by aligning your body around the position of the clubface. Work around it. Assuming the leading edge of the clubface is at 90 degrees to the target line, allow everything else to simply follow its lead. I advocate aligning your feet, knees, and hips parallel to the target line.

The shoulders must be a little open at address. This helps your unit of club, hands, arms, and chest work away from the ball together.

David Leadbetter

In addressing the ball, your arms should be comfortably flexed, and tension-free. That way, they are poised to swing the club at maximum speed.

Sam Snead

Too many people, I believe, feel so uncomfortable and off balance at address that it's almost impossible for them to get the swing started, let alone finish it.

Mickey Wright

long and medium irons. Angle the hands slightly ahead of the ball for short irons and wedges, again to encourage a more descending blow.

You may notice some touring pros beginning with the hands slightly behind the ball at address. They feel this stops the wrists from hinging too early in the takeaway, a fault that promotes a steep backswing plane and sliced drives. Fred Couples also says it leads to a strong upswing hit.

CLUBFACE ALIGNMENT

When the club is soled, it should be almost flush to the ground (assuming a level lie), with only enough space for a dollar bill to slip under the toe. If you can't set up naturally with the clubhead soled this way, your clubs may not have the proper lie angle (the angle at which the shaft comes out of the clubhead) for your size and shape. Incorrect lie angle can produce poor shots, as well.

To aim the clubface at the target, visualize the target line and set the club's leading edge perpendicular to it. Be careful not to use the top of the club for alignment: On irons, the topline usually is set slightly open as a result of the club's loft.

DIFFERENT STROKES

HEEL OF AN IDEA

If you want to make contact on the sweetspot—the meat of the clubface—start with the ball directly in front of it, right? Not necessarily. The Tour pros shown here address the ball off the heel of the club. Their reasoning is that at address the arms are relaxed, the hips and shoulders parallel to the target line. But at impact, the left hip and, to a lesser extent, left shoulder have moved slightly farther from the ball. This means that the club is pulled slightly toward the body on the downswing. So, playing the ball toward the heel means impact will occur closer to the center of the clubface.

There are other advantages to teeing off the heel at address: 1) It lets the player stand closer to the ball, which makes it easier to be relaxed, with the right posture and weight distributed evenly on both feet. 2) Should a mishit occur, it's better to make contact toward the heel, which is closer to the shaft and produces better results than hitting out toward the toe.

Since the upper body is slightly farther from the ball at impact than address, many pros tee the ball between the center and heel of their club. Corey Pavin, Fuzzy Zoeller, Jack Nicklaus, Andrew Magee, Tom Kite, and Billy Andrade know this body shift means contact ultimately will be made off the sweetspot.

THE SWING

GOLF HISTORIANS ARE NOT SURE WHETHER THE GAME EVOLVED FROM A ROMAN PASTIME called paganica, kolven in Holland, or perhaps a sport played in the Chinese court nearly 1,000 years ago. They *are* certain that the Royal Burgh of St. Andrews, Scotland, is the "cradle of golf." There, on linksland situated near the North Sea, enthusiastic sportsmen first popularized the game, and the St. Andrews swing was born.

Because St. Andrews hangs on the lip of the sea, golfers then (and now) played at least half the course into the wind. Through trial and error, they learned that a flatter swing produced a low, right-to-left shot that stayed below the breeze and ran a long way on the hard ground. The typical St. Andrean swept the club back swiftly inside the target line and around his body. Breaking his left arm and allowing his right elbow to fly away from his side, he made a long, loose backswing, the clubhead dipping well beyond parallel at the top. The downswing action, controlled mainly by the hands and wrists, swept the ball cleanly off the turf or a sand tee.

Climate is not the only explanation for the St. Andrews swing. The wooden shafts of early driving clubs were so long that the player could do little else but swing it around his body. Players also found it impossible to make anything

The early St. Andrews golfers started in a closed stance, and took a long, mighty swing. They let the right elbow fly on the backswing, swung the club well beyond parallel at the top, and whipped the club through with the hands and wrists while lunging forward on the downswing.

other than a flat swing when wearing a long, buttoned overcoat, the sporting attire of the day. The St. Andrews swing truly was born of necessity.

As golf grew in popularity in Scotland and throughout the British Isles, different swings evolved. The most successful came from the cricketers, who played from their sport's open batting stance. They employed even more wrist action than the typical St. Andrean, swung the club on an upright plane, and contacted the ball on the upswing. Their shots flew higher, curved slightly left to right, and carried farther, all of which gave them an advantage on downwind holes and helped them stop approach shots on the firm greens. The open set-up also generated extra clubhead speed, making the technique useful when playing into the wind. Both John Ball, the sensational English amateur, and the great Harry Vardon were influenced by the cricketer's swing.

Yet some stuck to the original tech-

nique. Horace Hutchinson, a leading amateur and author of the influential volume of golf instruction for the *Badminton Library* (1890) as well as other golf books, believed wholeheartedly that the St Andrews swing remained the method of choice. Preaching the hegemony of golf's birthplace, he wanted to preserve the flat swings of Old and Young Tom Morris, Willie Dunn Sr. and Jr., and of Willie Park Sr. and Jr. Needless to say, Hutchinson disdained golfers who played from the cricketer's open stance (back foot closer to the target line), and criticized it whenever he could.

"One golfing instructor actually advises that the right toe be placed in advance of the left," wrote Hutchinson. "He claims for this position a gain in power, and points to certain gifted players who, with, or in spite of this style of stance, are of the very foremost rank. Yet these partake rather of the nature of the exceptions which go to prove the rule." Hutchinson expressed his frustration with the bastard swing styles. He was particularly angry with those who wrote that, "provided you hit the ball, the manner is of no importance."

The same year Hutchinson wrote *Badminton Library*, Ball won both the British Amateur and British Open Championships using the cricketer's swing. Four years later, John Henry (J. H.) Taylor—another exemplar of the open stance and upright motion—won the first of five British Opens. Vardon won the British Open Championship six times (1896, 1898, 1899, 1903, 1911, and 1914) using much the same. The St. Andrews swing was all but dead.

H. J. Whigham, who wrote the first definitive American instruction manual, *How to Play Golf* (1897), was strongly influenced by Vardon's swing. So much so that he warned: "Don't, above all, as you value your golfing future, adopt a full St. Andrews swing. . . . It is better to miss the ball in the right way than to hit it in the wrong."

In a book titled *Great Golfers: Their Methods at a Glance*, by George W. Beldam, Vardon described his technique:

"I feel both hands taking the club back, and both wrists working in unison. My wrists start turning away from the ball the moment the clubhead leaves it.

"The wrists should drag the arms after them, and when the arms reach a point in the swing when they could go back no further, the left knee at once commences to bend in towards the right toe to allow the body to turn until the left shoulder is opposite the ball. The head, being kept still and in the

Harry Vardon was among the first to prove that golf could be played well from an open stance, with the ball forward and a wristy, upright swing. His method is not that different from what is preferred today.

"Long Jim" Barnes, winner of the first PGA Championship, wrote an instruction manual in 1919 that was richly illustrated with photographs of him at key points in the swing.

same position as when the ball is being addressed, is now looking over the left shoulder at the ball. This bending of the left knee and consequent turn of the body from the hips has allowed the wrists to take the arms still further back, till the club is in a position slightly past horizontal.

"There is a distinct pressure on the left toe, and very little more weight should be felt on the right leg than there was when the ball was addressed.

"In the swing back, the clubhead leaves a straight line behind the ball about three inches from it, and the club, though taken round the right leg, is taken up more uprightly than is usual.

"There is no perceptive pause at the top of the swing. The clubhead should be evenly gaining speed from the time it leaves the ball, until at the moment of impact it is travelling at its highest velocity. For this reason, slow back at the beginning of the swing is a good maxim."

"[On the downswing] I try to feel that both hands and wrists are still working together. The wrists start bringing the club down, and at the same moment, the left knee commences to resume its original position. The head during this time has been kept quite still, the body pivoting from the hips. When the left knee has turned, I find I am standing firmly on both feet, and the arms are in position as in the upward swing, before the left knee started to bend. From this point the speed of the wrists seems to increase, and the impact is thus made with the clubhead travelling at its highest velocity.

"Almost simultaneously with the

impact, the right knee slightly bends in the direction of the hole, and allows the wrists and forearms to take the club right out in the direction of the line of flight, dragging the arms after them as far as they will comfortably go, when the clubhead immediately leaves the line of flight, and the right foot turns on the toe. This allows the body to turn from the hips and face the hole, the club finishing over the left shoulder."

Note how similar this is to today's preferred swing. The biggest difference is Vardon's exaggerated wrist action, which was necessary to handle the whippy wooden shafts of his day.

Golf's growth was helped in the early 1900s by the success of other Vardonesque swingers, including Willie Anderson, winner of four U.S. Opens between 1901 and 1905 (he missed in 1902). Walter Travis, who was born in Australia but learned the game in America—and not till the age of 30!—prodded things along by stunning the British with a victory in their amateur championship of 1904.

But the biggest boost was provided by the 20-year-old American amateur Francis Ouimet, who beat Vardon and English pro Ted Ray in a playoff for the 1913 U.S. Open at Brookline, Massachusetts. Suddenly, everyone wanted to play. To fill the need, American golf magazines began publishing regular instruction articles, while big-name publishers began printing highly technical golf books.

In 1916, the Professional Golfer's Association was founded to help the masses learn the game. However, few courses had practice areas, and there were but a handful of good teachers. That would quickly change, and with the new instructors came many new theories about the swing.

Alex Smith was one of the first qualified teaching pros to emerge. Known for building on a player's natural tendencies, his students included national champions Jerry Travers, Glenna Collett Vare, and Walter Hagen. He referred to golf as a "science," teaching how the swing and clubhead positions influenced ball flight. It was Smith who introduced a shorter, more controlled swing, while encouraging golfers to become creative shotmakers.

Around this time, a young Atlantan named Bobby Jones was learning the game. His model was his teacher, Stewart Maiden, a son of Carnoustie, Scotland, who came to America in 1908. Maiden abhorred mechanics, ingraining in Jones the simple thought to take the club up, down, and through with the hands.

By 1919, America's enthusiasm for golf had reached fever pitch, with pros writing books and new teachers arriving on the scene. That year, *Picture Analysis of Golf Strokes,* by PGA champion "Long Jim" Barnes, became a best-seller. It featured full-page photographs of Barnes at key points in the swing, along with descriptive text. Like Vardon before him, Barnes played from an open stance and swung on an upright plane. But his swing was less wristy, and featured a unique "late-hit" action through the impact zone.

Three years later, Seymour Dunn wrote *Golf Fundamentals,* with visuals of flat and upright swing planes, plus advice on who should use which: He thought short players should swing flatter, tall players more upright.

In 1923, Ernest Jones, a pro from England, moved to New York and set up the first indoor golf school. Jones believed the club should be controlled with the hands, while the bigger muscles made "admirable followers." On the backswing, the hands swing the club inside the target line. Coming down, they return the club to a square impact position. As the club fans open on the backswing, the wrists hinge slightly. On the downswing, according to Jones, the clubface closed while the wrists unhinged, much like a swinging door.

To teach students to feel the swinging clubhead, Jones attached a handkerchief to a penknife: Swinging the knife back and forth like a pendulum, the hanky stayed taut; but trying to swing the knife with a pulling action, the hanky moved and the knife remained still. Jones was the first to teach a deliberate releasing of the club with the hands and wrists.

In 1923, Bobby Jones won his first U.S. Open. He won it again in 1926 and 1929, and in 1930 captured the "Grand Slam"—the Open and Amateur championships of the United States and Britain. Americans were hungry for instruction from the red-hot Bobby. Retiring from competitive golf after the Slam, he satisfied their appetite with short films and books. Describing his technique, Bobby explained that he played from a slightly open stance, depended on a solid weight shift from the right foot to the left, and delayed the unhinging of his wrists to the very last possible moment (like Barnes's late hit).

Nothing out of the ordinary until

Seymour Dunn thought the swing plane was key to determining success. In Golf Fundamentals, *written in 1922, he explained how they differed: flat (club well below the shoulders); upright (club well above the shoulders); and on-plane.*

Ernest Jones used a penknife attached to a handkerchief to prove the merits of swinging the hands to move the club.

Bobby Jones, who swung the club beyond parallel, was an early proponent of keeping the left arm straight, a precursor to the one-piece takeaway.

Jones described his takeaway, in which the left arm remained straight. This was the beginning of the one-piece takeaway and left-sided technique. Coincidentally, it was the end of an era: Unpredictable hickory shafts were being replaced by the more consistent and reliable steel, which would contribute to the next big swing change.

Another proponent of left-sided golf was teaching pro Alex Morrison, who taught a swing powered and controlled by the muscles of the left arm, hip, and leg. His model was a young pro named Byron Nelson.

"Byron Nelson," wrote Dick Aultman in *Masters of Golf,* "dominated his peers as no one ever has or will and who did it with a swing that departed dramatically from the norm. Nelson set a new standard of shotmaking excellence, and quite naturally some ingredients of his unusual technique became the model for those that followed. In fact, it can be safely said that if there is a watershed between the classical stroke spawned eighty some years ago by Harry Vardon and the swing method employed in large part by the top players of the world today, it was the one-piece, upright, left-side dominant, flex-kneed swing of John Byron Nelson.

"Nelson's role as a pioneer of the golf stroke is most apparent when one studies movies of tournament professionals in the 1940's. . . . The finest players of that generation were all 'hitting against a firm left side,' a phrase that was to remain part of the golf-instruction lexicon for at least another quarter of a century. Just prior to impact these players' left legs would straighten and remain all but immobile while their arms continued swinging forward. Of the dozens of players filmed, only Nelson retained some left-knee flex throughout the entire swing as he drove forward with both legs. Instead of hitting against his left side, Nelson hit *with* his left side. . . .

"The metal shafts that began to appear around 1930 did not twist and bend as much, required less hand-wrist manipulation, and thus allowed players greater use of their legs as a source of power. While all great players, even as far back as Vardon, had used their legs to some extent, none had done so to the degree that Nelson

In the early 1930s, Alex Morrison taught a left-sided technique that would prove popular as whippier hickory shafts were replaced by steel.

CHAPTER TWO

Byron Nelson, considered the first modern swinger, adapted the left-sided swing to the new steel shafts.

did. In short, the metal shafts created a new golfing 'environment.' Byron Nelson adjusted to it first and best."

Left-side theory remained popular until 1953, when it was challenged by Tommy Armour. The "Silver Scot," who parlayed one U.S. Open and one British Open into fame as an instructor, believed right-sided action was more natural. Furthermore, because the right hand was closer to the clubhead, he felt it should control the swing.

In 1957, the quietest champion, Ben Hogan, wrote *Five Lessons: The Modern Fundamentals of Golf.* It became a classic, influencing teachers

and students long after the author stopped playing.

Hogan was quick to disagree with Armour's right-side theory, citing rotation of the left hip as one of the swing's most important power sources. Hogan believed the faster the left hip cleared on the downswing, the more clubhead speed was generated. Hogan also argued against Armour's idea of hitting only with the right hand.

Said Hogan: "On a full shot you want to hit the ball as hard as you can with your right hand. But this is only half the story. Hit the ball as hard as

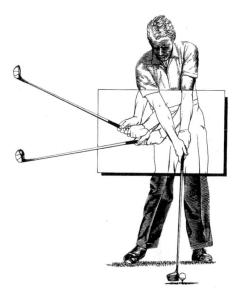

Going against the popular trend, Tommy Armour preached a right-sided swing. He felt it was more natural for right-handed golfers to depend on their dominant side.

you can with both hands. The left is a power hand, too. If you hit hard with only the right and let the left go to sleep, you will not only lose much valuable power, you also will run into all the errors that result when the right hand overpowers the left. You must hit as hard with the left as with the right."

Hogan also described a move that he guaranteed would turn a hook (a problem common to good players) into a power-fade. It involved rolling, or twisting, the hands to open the club-face on the backswing. This "prona-tion" had been taught by the early Scottish professionals who emigrated

to the United States at the turn of the century. It worked, Hogan said, because no matter how hard he tried to "supinate" his wrists on the down-swing—rolling them back to close the clubface—it could never close fast enough to be square at impact. It would always finish slightly open, pro-ducing a powerful, controlled, left-to-right shot.

Perhaps Hogan's most enduring contribution to golf instruction was the image of the swing plane as a pane of glass. At address, he visualized the pane tilting down from his shoulders to the ball. At the top of the backswing,

Creating one of the most enduring images in golf history, Ben Hogan compared the swing plane to a pane of glass that ran from the golfer's shoulders down to the ball.

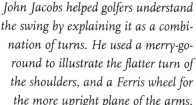

Jack Nicklaus's original teacher, Jack Grout, emphasized keeping the head steady on the back-swing. Grout's assistant would hold young Jack's hair so the head could swivel without moving—swaying—off the ball.

John Jacobs helped golfers understand the swing by explaining it as a combination of turns. He used a merry-go-round to illustrate the flatter turn of the shoulders, and a Ferris wheel for the more upright plane of the arms.

he said "the left arm should brush against the glass pane and incline at the exact angle of the plane.

"The golfer gets on the downswing plane once he turns his left hip to the left. The plane for the downswing is inclined at a shallower angle than the plane of the backswing, and its lateral axis points slightly to the right of the golfer's target." For those who mastered it, this image led to a shallow, in-to-out swing.

Hogan's methods were not being practiced by an Ohio teenager named Jack Nicklaus. His teacher, Jack Grout at the Scioto Country Club in Columbus, emphasized the fundamentals and taught Jack to forget Hogan's hands and hips. Instead, Nicklaus followed his teacher's instructions to drive the legs on the downswing.

When Nicklaus became the dominant force in the 1960s and 1970s, it was only natural that weekend golfers would copy his slightly open stance, upright swing, and powerful leg drive. They all wanted to launch drives into the sky and hit high, soft-landing long irons like the Golden Bear. But many amateurs confused leg drive with leg lunge, turning America into what British teacher John Jacobs called "a nation of slicers."

New teachers and new theories emerged as the game grew.

Bob Toski told students to "swing the arms." A Toski disciple, Jim Flick sounded like Ernest Jones when he said that "the hands should swing the body and club . . . the big muscles play a supporting role."

John Jacobs advised golfers to "swing the arms up as the body turns and swing the arms down as the body swings through." He used imagery to get his points across. One of his favorites, suggested to help students understand the different motions of the swing, was to "imagine a merry-go-round to swing on a flat plane; a Ferris wheel to swing on an upright plane."

Carl Lohren believed the "one move to better golf" was turning the left shoulder to the inside. (It also became the title of his best-selling book.)

Paul Bertholy had students swing a piece of heavy pipe, stopping at key points along the way and holding those positions to train the muscles.

Jimmy Ballard's star rose in the 1980s after the success of two students—Hal Sutton, who won the 1983 PGA Championship, and Curtis Strange, who captured the 1988 and 1989 U.S. Opens. Ballard isolated "common denominators," movements he said could be seen in the swings of Sam Snead, Ben Hogan, Byron Nelson, Jack Nicklaus, and Seve Ballesteros.

According to Ballard, generating maximum power through the creation of a wide swing arc requires the big muscles of the arms and shoulders to control the takeaway. Moreover, the arms have to stay "connected" to the body. For example, during the first part of the swing, the upper part of the left arm should hug the player's chest; let the left arm "run away" from the body and the club swings outside the target line on an overly steep plane. At the start of the downswing, the right elbow must stay hinged and close to the right side, so the club drops into a shallow plane; if the elbow moves away from the side, the club comes over the top and the plane becomes too steep. To

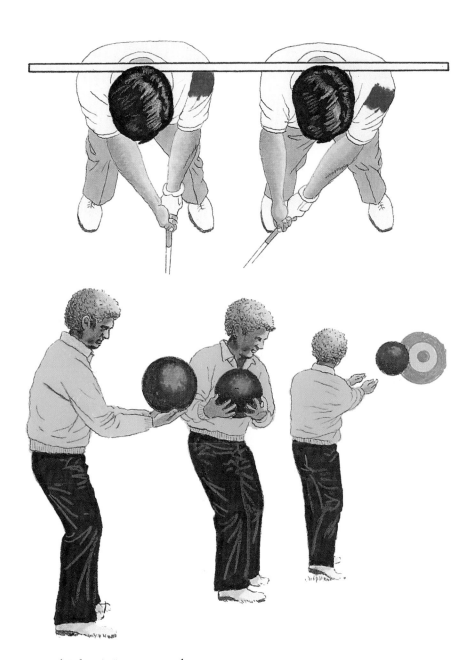

Top: *Carl Lohren's "one move to better golf" was swinging the left shoulder inside to begin the swing.*

Above: *Jimmy Ballard's theory of "connection" relies on keeping the arms close to the body going back and through. He prescribed tossing a medicine ball to ingrain the proper feeling.*

Ballard's "connection" theory grew out of earlier teaching by Percy Boomer, who advised students to "swing in a barrel" as a way of keeping the motion "tight."

teach the feel of connection, Ballard has students make side-arm tosses of a medicine ball: If the left arm or right elbow strays, distance and direction are affected.

Jimmy Ballard was influenced by teaching pro Percy Boomer, who wrote *On Learning Golf* in 1946: "There are a number of connections in the swing, and should any of these connections be broken, should our swing become disjointed, then the feeling of the clubhead cannot be transmitted back to the force—the center." Boomer's way of explaining connection (and making what today's teacher calls a "tight" swing) was to have pupils imagine that they were swinging in a barrel.

The 1980s and 1990s have been the age of the teaching pro, with many instructors gaining notoriety, usually for their work with Tour pros.

In 1985, South African David Leadbetter began teaching Nick Faldo a new swing, one that emphasized pivoting around the right leg on the backswing and the left leg on the downswing, and generating clubhead speed through acceleration of the arms, rather than Nicklausean leg drive. Faldo, an up-and-coming star on the European Tour, spent two years grooving this highly technical action. It paid off when he won three Masters and three British Opens between 1987 and 1996. As the Englishman became golf's number one player, his teacher became the number one instructor.

Other teachers in ascendance include Jim McLean, Rick Smith, and Claude "Butch" Harmon, one of four teaching sons of 1948 Masters champion Claude Harmon Sr.

McLean, who coached 1992 U.S.

DIFFERENT STROKES

CROSSING THE LINE

What do John Daly, Bobby Jones, and Jimmy Demaret have in common? All three let the club cross the line, letting it point to the right of target at the top. Reaching this position means your right shoulder has gotten so far behind the left that you can be aggressive on the downswing, really going after the ball without fear of coming over the top and slicing.

Crossing the line with the club at the top—so it points slightly right of the target—is the sign of a big upper-body turn. It also means the golfer can be aggressive, like John Daly, on the downswing without worrying about a slice.

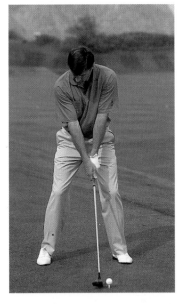

The dominant swing of recent years is owned by Nick Faldo. But it didn't come easily. Under the tutelage of David Leadbetter, Faldo spent more than two years revamping his action and learning the two-pivot swing—turning over the right leg on the backswing, over the left leg on the downswing.

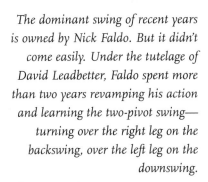

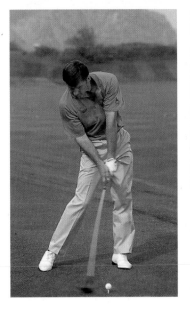

Open champion Tom Kite, was instrumental in isolating the "X-Factor," the gap between the size of the shoulder and hip turns, and its influence on power (see Chapter 3). In the December 1992 issue of *GOLF Magazine*, McLean and fellow pro Mike McTeigue, developer of the computer-driven SportSense Motion Trainer, used the device to prove that the key to power was increasing the gap—turning the shoulders farther than the hips to increase the resistance between them.

Rick Smith, who worked with 1993 U.S. Open champion Lee Janzen and helped Nicklaus after he started playing the Senior PGA Tour, coordinates hip rotation with arm swing—his answer to employing a more rhythmic swing.

Butch Harmon gained notoriety by revamping the swings of Greg Norman, Davis Love III, and Tiger Woods. Harmon promotes clubhead feel through a light grip and swinging on a more rounded plane.

In the next wave is Mike Adams, who launched a teaching system based on an individual's body shape, strength, and flexibility. His LAWs System—for Leverage, Arc, and Width, the names he gives to the three swings—was introduced in *GOLF Magazine* in March of 1996.

So who is right, Hutchinson or Hogan? Jones, Jones, Jack, or Jim? All have had their adherents, disciples who would swear by the teachings of the great man (or woman—women are making an ever-greater mark on golf instruction today). What is important is that it work for you.

"You don't need to have a textbook swing to play good golf," notes Rick Smith. "On the other hand, your swing can't be totally devoid of fundamentals. There has to be something that you 'must' do to arrive in the practically identical impact position of the pros, and to hit the ball solidly and accurately."

Indeed, there are "musts."

DIFFERENT STROKES

RIGHT-SIDED ACTION IS MORE NATURAL

While almost all teaching pros talk about a left-sided downswing trigger— "replant the left heel"; "shift weight onto your left foot"; "clear the left hip"— teacher Jimmy Ballard, pros Seve Ballesteros and Johnny Miller, and power hitter Mike Dunaway all believe that a right-sided downswing feels more natural and yields better results.

All these golfers, like Tommy Armour before them, begin the downswing by pushing the right hip downward and inward, setting off a chain reaction. First, the knees start sliding toward the target. Second, the arms, hands, and club fall virtually straight down, into the perfect hitting slot. Third, the right shoulder dips downward, keeping the upper body behind the ball through the hitting area.

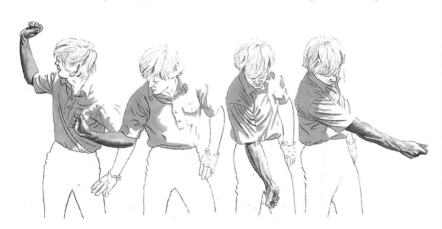

Johnny Miller depends on the right side, particularly the right arm and wrist, for power.

According to Mike Adams, golfers of different sizes need different swings that make the best use of their strength and flexibility. The Leverage Swing (top) is flatter and depends on more hip turn and hinging of the wrists; the Arc Swing (center), for taller, more flexible players, gets the hands high and drives the legs on the downswing; the Width Swing (bottom), for golfers with less flexibility, is characterized by a wide stance, strong grip, and big shoulder turn.

The moment of truth. Ray Floyd, Ben Crenshaw, Fred Couples, and Seve Ballesteros have very different swings, yet look very similar where it matters—at impact.

DIFFERENT STROKES

MATCH YOUR HIPS TO THE TOP

In *GOLF Magazine*, David Leadbetter described how to match the downswing motion to a backswing position.

From a laid-off position at the top (the club points left of the target): "You have to flatten the downswing arc, such that the club approaches the ball on a shallower angle and on more of an inside path. So, make your first move down a lateral shift of the hips. Keep your hips square to the target line until the momentum of the follow-through forces them to open. Also, think of straightening the right arm sooner in the downswing, promoting an earlier release of the clubhead. The combination of these two adjustments will get the club moving on a shallower, more inside path, setting up a clubface-to-target position just prior to, and right through, impact."

From cross-the-line at the top: "A quick rotation of the hips will clear the lower body out of the way and cause the upper body to follow automatically. The right elbow will release outward along the right side of the ribcage into the correct delivery position, instead of being trapped behind the body. Concentrate on having the hips approximately 45 degrees open at the moment the ball is struck. The clubshaft can work its way back along the target line into a good downswing path as the hands approach the hitting zone. This allows the club to release and the clubface to be square at impact."

PREVAILING WISDOM

PRE-SWING

To make a smooth transition from the set-up position—when you're standing almost stock-still over the ball—to the takeaway, most pros recommend a forward press. This action of the hands, legs, or other parts of the body unfreezes the muscles and ignites the swing with rhythm and flow rather than a jerk and a bang.

The two most common forward press actions are:

1) Pushing the hands slightly toward the ball, then swinging back, a la Tom Watson.

2) Kicking the right knee inward and toward the target, then rotating it away again, as Gary Player and Johnny Miller do.

Then there's Jack Nicklaus, who combines two actions to ease the transition from address to backswing. Just before starting the club away, he increases his grip pressure slightly and swivels his chin to the right, a move Sam Snead used throughout his long, successful career.

wrists stay firm (no hinging!). During this stage of the swing, the player wants to have the sensation that the club is being pushed away by the large muscles of the body.

Many players trigger a one-piece takeaway by forgetting the hands, thinking instead about turning the left shoulder toward the chin. The shoulders and hips rotate, but the head remains relatively still.

Once past the first 18 inches of the takeaway, you're into the backswing. Weight starts shifting to the right foot and the body continues turning. The arms, hands, and club are pushed upward as a result of the upper body's turning. As weight moves away from the front side, the left heel can lift slightly off the ground.

At the top of the swing—when the arms and club have swung as far as they can without going past parallel to the ground—the player wants to feel most of his body weight pressing into the right instep and heel. The right elbow must be relatively close to the player's side and pointing down at the

Gary Player starts his swing with a kicking in of the right knee. Like all good triggers, it relaxes the muscles, allowing for a smooth transition from the address into action.

THE BACKSWING

The first foot or so of the backswing is called the takeaway. It's crucial because it sets the tone and direction for the entire swing. The club should swing back smoothly, begin coming inside the target line, and stay close to the ground. It's vital that the takeaway be performed with a one-piece motion, meaning that the hands, arms, and shoulders move in unison while the

DIFFERENT STROKES

KEEP YOUR LEFT FOOT DOWN

The next time you watch Nick Faldo or Nick Price—both students of David Leadbetter—note the position of their left foot. Instead of letting it rise off the ground during the backswing, they keep it firmly planted. From lifting the foot it's easy to lift the whole body, which weakens the upper-body coil. In true Leadbetter fashion, both strive for a big turn over a braced right leg.

Amateurs who feel they aren't making the most of their turn, and their shots, should look at their left foot and concentrate on keeping it planted throughout the backswing.

LET THE RIGHT ELBOW FLY

Blame Nicklaus. Before he came along, one of the worst things a golfer could do was let the right elbow fly away from his body at the top. Even after he won a few Opens and other titles, the skeptics were still predicting Jack's career wouldn't fly as far as that elbow.

Today, Ernie Els and Tiger Woods are just two of the many golfers who have had success letting the right elbow fly. It strengthens their turn and helps them reach the cross-the-line position—the club pointing slightly right of the target—that they prefer at the top.

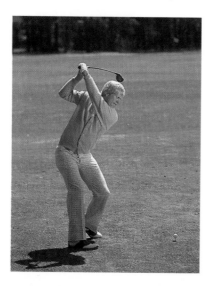

Jack Nicklaus made the "flying right elbow" famous. Many players—including Nick Price, Fred Couples, and Corey Pavin—let the elbow come away from the body at the top of the backswing as a way of enlarging the swing and getting the club to "cross the line" at the top.

ground. The left wrist is flat, the left arm relatively straight.

For years, teachers told students that the shoulders should rotate 90 degrees (left shoulder fully under chin), and the hips 45 degrees. Those are ideal numbers, difficult for most golfers to achieve. But the shoulders should turn much farther than the hips, building power in the resistance between the two turns. Many experts have credited the relationship between the two turns as the secret to Tiger Woods's powerful, yet smooth, swing.

Here are some helpful checkpoints for the backswing. The clubshaft should be parallel to the target line both at waist level and at the top. At waist level, the toe of the club should point at the sky; at the top, it should point toward the ground.

THE DOWNSWING

As soon as the club reaches its topmost position—parallel to the target line or well short of that—the downswing begins. There should be only the slightest pause as the transition is made, begun by replanting the left heel and rotating the hips back the way they came.

The head stays behind the ball as the lower body shifts and rotates, and the weight shifts to the left foot. The player wants to feel as if he is waiting for the club in the time it takes for the hands to drop down into "the slot."

"If there is any such thing as a Magic Move in the golf swing," wrote the plain-spoken teacher Harvey Penick, "to me it is an action that I stress over and over on the practice tee: To start your downswing, let your

LET YOUR
LEFT ARM BEND

Nick Price, Bernhard Langer, Ray Floyd, Pat Bradley, Betsy King, Chi Chi Rodriguez, Nancy Lopez, Curtis Strange, Lee Trevino, and Lee Janzen are among the leading pros who ignore the often-repeated tenet, "Keep your left arm straight."

Keeping the left arm stiff during the golf swing is nearly impossible for all but the double-jointed. Even if you could keep it straight, it would make the upper body tense and constricted, cutting clubhead speed and power.

"Keep the left arm straight" is meant to maintain the radius of the swing, creating the widest possible swing arc. The only time you truly want full extension of the left arm is at impact, and it isn't something you can control: If your arms are relaxed and moving at full speed on the downswing, centrifugal force causes the left arm to straighten so it lines up with the clubshaft at impact for maximum power.

There's nothing wrong with bending the left arm on the way back. In fact, letting it hinge naturally promotes less tension, a freer swing, and longer shots.

From left to right: *Not only is it physically impossible to keep the left arm straight during the backswing, it's also harmful to the swing. Letting the left arm bend—like Curtis Strange, Nick Price, Nancy Lopez, Lee Janzen, Bernhard Langer, and Chi Chi Rodriguez—keeps the swing loose and free-flowing.*

weight shift to your left foot while bringing your right elbow down to your body. This is one move, not two."

There is no conscious pulling on the club with the hands. Instead, the force of the weight shift, coupled with the change of direction, prompts the right elbow to fall in close to the body. The club should drop onto an angle of attack slightly shallower than its path on the backswing.

The left hip turns out of the way—clears—which opens a passageway for the arms and hands to swing the club

---

DIFFERENT STROKES

LET THE HEAD MOVE

Jim McLean disagrees with traditional teaching, which holds that a steady head encourages a strong backswing turn, good balance, and powerful shots. McLean thinks the head should have a swing of its own—swiveling or moving a few inches to the right on the backswing to accommodate the rotation of the upper body and shoulders. Says McLean: "The stronger the turn, the more power you generate."

In worrying about the arms and the club, many golfers overlook the importance of the feet in the swing. Greg Norman demonstrates ideal footwork and balance as the club moves through the hitting area, providing a solid base of support for the power of impact.

OUTSIDE/INSIDE TAKEAWAY

Fred Couples begins his swing by starting the club slightly outside the target line. Then he sets his wrists and folds his right arm. This combination of movements puts his left wrist in a slightly concave, "cupped" position at the top.

"I prefer the slightly cupped position (which indicates a slightly open clubface) because I know that on the downswing I can really let my wrists whip into the ball with no fear of hitting a wild hook. I think, therefore, that the cupped position ultimately results in a more powerful golf shot."

Ray Floyd drags the club well inside the line to encourage a strong hip turn on the backswing and prevent a reverse pivot, in which his weight would be moving the wrong way during the swing. Once his hips coil, Floyd reroutes the club on a steeper backswing plane.

Seve Ballesteros gets his swing going by pulling the club away gently with his right hand. He says, "This sets off a positive chain reaction in which my body coils smoothly and fully and my rhythm is excellent."

From left to right: *As soon as his swing begins, Fred Couples takes the club outside the target line. Ray Floyd's takeaway brings the club back on an exaggerated inside path, which leads to a powerful hip turn. Seve Ballesteros depends on the right hand to set his swing in motion.*

THE IMPORTANCE OF TEMPO

One of the most important aspects of any swing—and nearly impossible to teach—is tempo. For one thing, tempo is difficult to define. Some call it rhythm, others swing speed or timing—it's never the same thing to any two people. Sam Snead said, "Rhythm is the speed that you swing, and timing is the coordination between all the different elements of the swing." Jack Nicklaus said tempo is "a pace of swing at which you can best swing efficiently and consistently," while rhythm "means that the speed of each portion of your swing must blend into a smooth, effective whole."

In *GOLF Magazine*, teacher Bill Moretti offered another definition:

"Tempo is...according to Webster's, a smooth rate of motion or activity.

"Tempo is...when your backswing and downswing feel as if they're moving at the same speed.

"Tempo is...when your arms and body work in harmony during the swing.

"Above all, tempo is the great equalizer. It compensates for mechanical flaws in your swing, and will reduce your slices, hooks, and inconsistent contact."

Tempo is highly individual. A teacher can look at your swing and say it seems that you're moving too fast or too slow. But ultimately, your perfect tempo is whatever is comfortable and works. So if you swing fast and hit the ball well, great; if not, slow down.

Personality has a lot to do with tempo. If you're hard-charging, high-strung, and thrive on tension, it's unlikely your swing can ever be loose and leisurely. (Do you think Lanny Wadkins, who has one of the fastest swings on Tour, is ever mellow?) And if you naturally walk slowly, speak slowly, and take things as they come—like Nancy Lopez—you're more likely to have a slower, more easygoing swing. Neither one is right. What is wrong, however, is trying to mismatch your personality and your tempo.

"Whatever your tempo," explains Judy Rankin, "slow, fast, or somewhere in between—the secret is to make it the same, day in and day out. This will take some of the variables out of your game."

Jim Flick equates tempo to feel for the clubhead: If you can't feel the clubhead throughout the swing, it's too fast. (Of course, you must maintain a grip pressure that *allows* you to feel the clubhead, as described in Chapter 1.) It's something Nicklaus also believes in, having written in *Golf My Way*: "Feeling the weight of the clubhead against the tension of the shaft helps me to swing rhythmically."

Ken Venturi, who said, "It's difficult to exaggerate how important good tempo is to the golf swing," suggests taking cues from players whose rhythm you admire. He modeled his swing speed after Snead's, saying, "I always found that my tempo was better when I played with Sam."

Once you find your tempo, time it with a metronome. If you feel later on that your tempo isn't right, use the metronome to help you get back in sync.

And swing slower; it almost always helps.

down and through the ball. The club begins the downswing well inside the target line, but swings back to square at impact. The rotation of the right hip increases the acceleration of the arms and club.

In the hitting area, both arms extend as a result of the force generated on the downswing. The head should be behind the ball. As the clubhead approaches the ball, the player should feel the "release," the right hand and forearm rotating over the left, the left wrist holding firm at impact.

It's important to realize that hitting the ball isn't the end of the swing. The idea is to swing through to the target, not to hit the ball. One instructional bromide worth remembering is that the ball is simply getting in the way of a good swing. And a good swing continues to a full follow-through, accelerating until the clubshaft is over the shoulder.

A few more checkpoints to watch for. At waist level in the follow-through, the clubshaft is again parallel to the ground, the toe of the club pointing upward. In the finish, the player is balanced and poised; nearly all his body weight has moved to the left side, so on the right side, only the right toe is touching the ground. Finally, the player's chest (some teachers say belt buckle) is facing the target.

WORDS OF WISDOM

Professionals take every pain to see that the learner gets the upward swing correctly, knowing by experience that a correct downward stroke will naturally follow.

Horace Hutchinson

Driving is entirely a matter of swing. As soon as the golfer begins to hit "at" the ball he is hopelessly ruined.
H. J. Whigham

It is utterly impossible for any golfer to play good golf without a swing that will repeat.
Ben Hogan

You can't start a car from a dead start and put it immediately up to 70 miles an hour. No matter how powerful your engine, you must have a gradual acceleration of speed. So it is in a golf swing.

Mickey Wright

Naturally you have to learn the various parts of a golf swing. But once you get it, don't think about your swing anymore.
Sam Snead

A great many players turn their shoulders and think that their hip action is correct. What they don't realize is that you can turn the shoulders while keeping the hips fixed, but when you turn the hips, the shoulders go along.
Tommy Armour

You must try to keep the golf swing as simple as you can. That is why I'm so adamant about fundamentals.
Kathy Whitworth

When we have entirely broken down in our swing it will be found in some cases beneficial to leave off the game for a time.
W. G. Simpson

CHAPTER THREE

POWER

JOHN JACOBS, ONE OF EUROPE'S PREMIER TEACHERS, SAID, "POWER IS CLUBHEAD speed correctly applied." Ask most amateur golfers and they would say something like, "Power is what I want!"

Hitting the ball a long way has a lot to recommend it. For one thing, it gives the golfer a distinct scoring advantage: The farther you are down the fairway, the shorter your next shot. And if you can hit a more lofted club into the green, you are more likely to stick the ball close to the hole.

Just as important—maybe more so—crushing the ball feels good. Listen to golfers at the 19th hole and you will hear more bragging about long drives than low scores. And why not? It is hard to beat the sensation of flushing the ball, hitting it "on the screws" so it sails past your opponent's measly efforts.

There is not much on record about the long-hitters in golf's earliest days, but there can be no doubt that among the games played by the shepherds hitting rocks with their crooks was "Who Can Hit It Farther?" When golfing societies formed in Scotland in the seventeenth and eighteenth centuries, the requisite long coats and ties must have made it difficult to really pound the ball (especially a ball that was prone to burst open or fall apart if struck too hard).

In the game's next era, numerous references can be found to the prodi-

The ball changes shape at impact, flattening against the clubface. This compression contributes to the length of the shot.

gious driving of Young Tom Morris, who broke clubs with the force of his swing, and Old Willie Dunn, one of the first to combine grace and power. Two-time British Amateur champion Horace Hutchinson was one of the first to comment on the exhilaration of a long drive: Among his "supreme delights of the game," the best was "to hit a gutta percha ball 200 yards."

The Great Triumvirate of James Braid, J. H. Taylor, and Harry Vardon, which dominated golf for two decades before World War I, did so in large part with long-hitting. Braid was a big man, who, as expected, hit a big ball. Taylor was small, but capable of "catching" it. Vardon was the master, generating great clubhead speed with an effortless swing—the Victorian Fred Couples.

"The outstanding impression of watching Vardon play," *The American Golfer* reported in 1924, "is that of utter ease and lack of physical effort.

His hands, arms, body and legs appear to work as a well-oiled machine, and there is always present that element denoting complete coordination, ordinarily referred to in golf matters as rhythm."

Golf captured America's fancy during the Roaring Twenties, and power was one reason why. Among the idols was Walter Hagen, the swashbuckling son of a blacksmith who swayed and lunged into the ball, hitting it long if often wild. Gene Sarazen, small in size, used a strong grip that helped him take the club on a shallow plane and hit through the ball with an extra-powerful sweeping action.

Then there was Bobby Jones, whose natural, graceful swing never looked to be working hard, but hit the ball hard. "Many shots are spoiled at the last instant by efforts to add a few more yards," Jones wrote in 1938, after retiring from competitive play. "This

As balanced and graceful as he was throughout the swing, Bobby Jones was one of the longest hitters of his day. His secret was a lack of tension that let him whip the club through impact.

KEEP YOUR HEAD STILL

Gary Player has always been firmly against letting the head move. He feels it's important to keep the axis formed by the head and spine fixed in place, turning the body around it to generate more power from a compact coiling of the upper body.

Like many veteran teachers, Player believes that head movement leads to a sway on the backswing, which can cause you to straighten up and lose your coil. Swaying also makes it harder to time the downswing, which results in inconsistent contact.

Above: *In the 1930s, crowds started coming out to see long-hitters like Jimmy Thomson. He left nothing in the bag when going after the ball.*

Opposite: *Mike Souchak played football in college, then harnessed his strength for an attack on the Tour in the 1950s. His record four-round score of 257 in the 1955 Texas Open was accomplished, in part, by having nothing but short irons into most of the greens.*

impedes rather than aids the stroke. Muscles tensed in making this sudden effort must hold the clubhead back. I like very much the concept of a free-travelling clubhead at impact and left arm acceleration through the ball."

Jimmy Thomson, who wowed the public in the late 1930s with long-drive exhibitions, and fast-swinging Craig Wood led the next generation of power hitters. They were followed by Byron Nelson, whom many consider the father of the modern swing. Nelson's powerful left-sided action (described in Chapter 2) rocketed the ball far—and straight—down the fairway.

For power with rhythm, few have been better than Sam Snead. Many have commented on his syrupy tempo, but Snead relied on agile footwork to help make a powerful shift onto his right foot and leg on the backswing, then an equally strong shift onto his left foot and leg on the downswing. He was a long hitter for a long time, continuing to amaze crowds with distance well into his 60s. His advice to older golfers, in a book called *Golf Begins at Forty,* summarized his thinking on long-hitting: "You will hit the ball farther more frequently when you don't try to hit it far."

Snead's mantle was worn for a while by George Bayer, all six-foot-five,

A FIRM STANCE ON GRIP PRESSURE

Going through their pre-swing checklists, both Jack Nicklaus and Tom Watson make sure they take firm hold of the club—with all fingers. This guards against the grip coming loose at the top of the backswing. If the grip opens up, the tendency is to release the club too early, casting (throwing it out away from the body) on the downswing. Casting means that the wrists have uncocked too soon, throwing away power long before impact.

250 pounds of him. Passing up a career in professional football in the 1950s, he turned pro and awed galleries with drives that averaged 300 yards. There are numerous tales of him hitting the ball 400 yards and more, but few tales of him winning: He had four PGA Tour wins, compared to Snead's unofficial total of 135 worldwide.

Mike Souchak, another barrel-chested ex-footballer, is remembered today for his four-round score of 257 in the 1955 Texas Open. At the time, he was also known for hitting a long ball.

One of the first pros to harness raw power as a tool for winning was Arnold Palmer. Beginning in the late 1950s, he beat courses into submission week after week, swinging for the fences and going for broke on every shot. Palmer muscled the ball off the tee, from rough or trouble, and into the hole. He cemented his reputation in the 1960 U.S. Open at Cherry Hills near Denver, when he opened the final round by driving the first green—350 yards away. He followed that with 64 more shots, won the Open, and inspired an army of followers (many of whom are still marching with him).

Close on Palmer's heels came Jack Nicklaus, who swung the club beyond parallel at the top, triggered the downswing by replanting his left foot, and thrust his legs toward the target. Booming the ball high and out of sight, Nicklaus regularly won with the 300-yard drive.

But Nicklaus was no carnival act. A thinking golfer, his words influenced an entire generation of golfers who hoped to copy his style. Among his pearls were these thoughts on long-driving:

"There are really two ways of increasing your distance," he wrote, with collaborator Ken Bowden, in *Golf My Way* (1974). "You can learn to swing the clubhead faster. Or you can learn to deliver it to the ball more accurately. Which you choose, I suggest, must depend on your physical make-up, age, present level of skill, and other such personal factors. The best advice I can offer has to be general. If you swing slowly or easily, but think you could swing the club faster while still making contact with the ball, then that's your way to go. If you swing the clubhead fast already but don't deliver it accurately, then it is control you need to work on, not speed."

The success of Arnie and Jack encouraged other long-knockers, men like Tom Weiskopf, Tom Watson, Seve Ballesteros, Craig Stadler, Fred Couples, and Greg Norman—and most recently, John Daly and Tiger Woods. All captured the public's imagination by hitting the ball long while winning.

Add to that list of heroes two lesser-known Englishmen. Alastair Cochran and John Stobbs, a scientist and a writer, respectively, conducted in-depth research on the game that proved a few extra yards off the tee lowered one's score, even if those longer drives did not always find the fairway. They legitimized "swinging out of one's shoes"— as well as spending a small fortune for a new miracle driver.

Power surges among amateurs usually followed changes in club design. Jones, Hagen, and Nelson were saddled with clubs and balls built for precision; the ball had to find a tiny sweetspot on the club. And that was fine for the pros, who hit hundreds of

Opposite: *For 40 years—since coming on Tour in the mid 1950s until today— Arnold Palmer has attacked golf courses. His swashbuckling, go-for-broke style endeared him to galleries the world over.*

Above: *Jack Nicklaus redefined the power game, using a mighty thrust of his legs to hit 280-yard drives followed by high, soft irons into the greens.*

SWING SHORTER FOR DISTANCE

Some pros, and many amateurs, are finding that less is more when it comes to the backswing. Rather than living by the command to "swing to parallel," many golfers, including 1996 PGA Tour Player of the Year Tom Lehman, increased their distance by shortening their swing to three-quarter length. They found that a shorter swing is a tighter, more efficient swing. The wrists don't overhinge at the top, so there is less chance of casting, unhinging too early, during the downswing. Furthermore, an individual's tempo and rhythm might be better suited to a swing that's a little shorter, which guarantees it is still accelerating at impact. A shorter swing also can be easier to keep in balance and under control.

A long swing is not a prerequisite for power. Many pros and amateurs actually increase their distance with a shorter backswing. In the 1960s, Doug Sanders (top left) never got his hands above his shoulders. Among today's players who stop short of parallel are Ian Woosnam, Paul Azinger, Davis Love III, Gene Sauers, and John Cook.

balls a week while tuning up for weekend paydays. For the rest of us, however, playing once a weekend and practicing even less was not nearly enough to groove a swing capable of power and consistency.

That began to change in the late 1970s. No, amateurs did not start practicing. They started buying metal woods, cavity-back irons, and two-piece balls. These "game-improvement" products took the premium off precision; we could swing harder with less worry about shots sailing sideways.

Encouraged by heroes who drive the ball nearly 20 yards longer than they did 25 years ago, playing courses that demand longer shots, and wielding equipment that makes it easier to hit longer, is it any wonder we are obsessed with power?

Absolutely not. And that obsession has not been lost on today's teachers, who capitalize on our quest for power by offering special schools, books, videotapes, and teaching aids.

But is there really anything new being added to our quest? Compare two lessons, one from H. J. Whigham, circa 1897, the other from David Leadbetter in 1970.

Whigham: "At the top of the swing every ounce in the body almost rests on the right leg. As the club comes down, the balance is restored and the weight is almost evenly distributed as the ball is struck, but is moving forward all the time until at the finish of the stroke it rests entirely on the left leg. And yet, although the weight changes, the body does not appear to alter its position to any great extent; the shoulders revolve upon an almost immovable axis. There must be no forward movement of the whole person as there is in baseball. The weight certainly moves, and that is where the strength of the stroke comes from, but it must be transferred almost invisibly, and the momentum must be applied to the ball chiefly through the medium of the right shoulder and forearm."

Leadbetter: "Acceleration in the golf swing stems from the turning or pivotal motion of the torso—the power base or engine room of every athletic swing.

"Rotating around your right axis point, then your left, will encourage what I call a 'turning weight' transfer in both directions. Your body weight, from a fairly even start at address, moves to your right heel on the backswing and toward your left heel on your downswing.

"Even the most efficient pivot motion could not generate a great deal of clubhead speed operating alone. Your hands, arms, and shoulders must react to the movement of your body."

As these two instructors from two generations prove, power comes from pivoting and shifting weight. Build power on the backswing, release it on the downswing. Make a swing that is flatter, fuller, and faster than our normal one. And, then, practice!

The secret to power has not changed all that much.

MOVE THE BALL BACK

Many long-hitters, including Nick Price, Davis Love III, and Ernie Els, place the ball back in their stance, a few inches *behind* the instep of the front foot. They believe playing the ball farther forward than that actually leads to lunging into impact, either driving the legs too vigorously toward the target (and getting ahead of the shot), or leading the downswing with the upper body and coming over the top (resulting in pulls or slices). Playing it back helps them time body movement with club movement and make a freer swing through impact.

Setting up for the power-swing, play the ball forward in your stance, off the instep of your front foot.

Tiger Woods achieves tremendous length by taking an extra-wide stance, then making an extremely wide swing arc that pushes his hands way above his head. This extension is a prime factor in his ability to deliver the club with power.

PREVAILING WISDOM

SET-UP

At address, tee the ball off the instep of your front foot. Make sure your hands are in-line with the ball; this discourages breaking the wrists too early and shortening the arc of the swing.

"The forward ball position will encourage you to 'chase' it with the clubhead through impact," explains teacher Jim McLean, "promoting a desired 'flat spot' that's common among power-hitters. In turn, you will keep the clubface on the ball a moment longer, which increases the compression and power of the shot."

Teeing the ball slightly higher than normal promotes a shallower backswing, more around the body than up-and-down, which ultimately encourages the hands and forearms to rotate more vigorously through impact. As Ken Venturi says, "This action allows the toe of the clubface to lead the heel, thereby imparting right-to-left spin on the ball."

You can't generate extra power without a wide swing arc: A longer swing going back means a longer, faster swing coming down. And a big arc begins with keeping the club low to the ground as long as possible. Sequence photographs of John Daly's swing show that the sole of his driver brushes the grass for the first 18 inches.

The first key to a extra-wide arc is an extra-wide stance, several inches beyond the shoulders (measured from the insides of the heels). You can see for yourself that standing with the feet close together causes you to pick up the club quickly in the takeaway, hinging the wrists, which narrows the swing arc.

Other easy adjustments include pulling your back foot a few inches away from the target line, which closes the right hip, and fanning the right foot out about 30 degrees. These moves flatten the plane of the backswing; on the downswing, that means a strong release of the forearms, and a lower, longer-running, right-to-left draw.

"Whenever I want to hit a drive with a little more power," says Tom Weiskopf, "I close my stance by keeping my left [forward] foot in place and moving my right foot back a couple of inches from its normal square position, so my feet are no longer parallel to my target line.

"This automatically closes the hips and shoulders slightly, enabling you to create a more inside-out swing path. This will allow you to hit the ball more solidly and squarely, thus producing a slightly right-to-left power-packed shot."

A stronger grip further encourages the flatter swing. Once the club is soled—with its face aimed slightly right of target to allow for the draw—check that the Vs formed by your thumbs and forefingers point up at your right (back) shoulder. Lighten your grip, as this will lessen tension in the hands and arms, allowing for more release through impact.

THE BACKSWING

To make a big turn and strong weight shift, don't be afraid to let your head and body shift slightly away from the

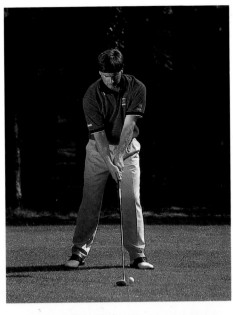

One of the Tour's longest hitters, Fred Couples achieves great distances with an effortless-looking swing.

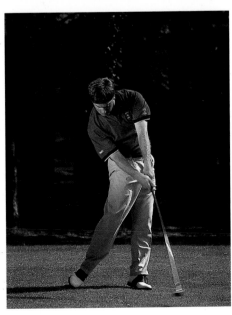

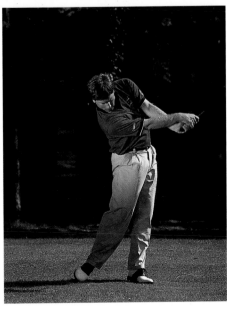

LIETZKE'S LOW TEE

Bruce Lietzke fades all his shots. When he wants to crank up his drive and hit a power-fade, he tees the ball unusually low—only a small portion of the ball is atop the clubface—and sets his hands behind the ball at address. This combination of adjustments makes his swing more upright and out-to-in across the target line, two keys to hitting left to right.

The shoulders and arms swing on two different planes: The shoulders go back on a flatter plane than your arms, setting up a shallower plane for the downswing.

BELLY BALL

Long-hitting Roberto de Vicenzo, the greatest player ever to come out of South America, fired his shoulders and hips into the downswing by rotating the center of his body toward the target. At the top of the swing, his thought was to get his belly button facing the target. It cleared his hips and drove his club into the ball. It was what de Vicenzo meant when he said, "I hit the ball with my stomach."

target—"off the ball"—in the backswing. David Leadbetter says, "It is quite normal for your head, especially on the backswing, to move a little laterally as you turn. It should certainly be free to swivel. Keeping your head overly still can only restrict your motion." Numerous other teachers note that the average player's attempt to "keep the head still" creates so much tension that the shoulders are restricted from turning. Don't exaggerate the head turn, but let it swivel naturally back and through to help keep the upper-body muscles loose.

A body shift is especially important for shorter players, says Chi Chi Rodriguez, because "it increases the distance the clubhead travels, thereby lengthening the swing arc. . . . Using this method, you'll hit the ball much farther down the fairway than you would if you kept your head perfectly still and turned around the axis of your spine."

Exaggerate the turning of your shoulders and hips, keeping the upper part of your left arm close to your chest: The clubhead will fan open as it swings well inside the line. The lower body should be so tightly wound that you feel slight pressure in your right hip.

Unless you are extremely flexible, allow your left heel to lift more than normal. This will help push your hands high above your head at the top and maintain a wide arc. Letting your right elbow fly away from your body will exaggerate the turn and get the club to cross the line at the top; as explained in Chapter 2, these "faults" lead to an aggressive downswing while limiting the possibility of hitting a slice.

To encourage a more powerful turning action, think about turning your back to the target. It's a key for Helen Alfredsson, one of the longer hitters on the LPGA Tour: "Rather than thinking about the shoulders or hips, I find the best thought is 'Turn the back to the target.' You can't get your back that far around without turning everything else. Thinking 'back' gets all the elements—shoulders, arms, hands, hips, etc.—working together."

Another reason the pros and even many Seniors are able to make strong turns is daily flexibility exercises. Gary Player, who is past 60, still adheres to a regular workout of stretching the hip, back, neck, and hamstring muscles. It helps explain how he can make a strong turn without lifting his heel and risk losing balance. Regular exercise also enables Tour players to swing hard without hurting their backs.

However you can, strive for a powerful windup in the backswing, so the body feels compelled to unwind with force toward the target.

THE DOWNSWING

Although the downswing happens in the blink of an eye, there is time to consciously initiate clearing of the hips and a hands-arms swing. (If there isn't, you are swinging too fast.)

Once you reach the top, start the downswing by turning your left hip to the left (back toward the target) as quickly as you can. At the same moment, try to whip the club into the

---

DIFFERENT STROKES

BUYING POWER

Looking for more yardage? Try looking in your pro shop for the latest in equipment.

Start by having your clubs custom-fitted. Buying clubs, particularly irons, with the proper shaft flex, lie, grip size, and other specifications for you will help make the most of your swing. You also might consider some subtle adjustments for power: Smaller grips encourage releasing the hands and arms on the downswing; reducing loft hits the ball lower and longer; whippier (more flexible) shafts can give the ball an extra "kick."

One of the easiest ways to buy more distance is to buy a longer shaft. A few years ago, the standard driver was about 43¹/₂ inches. Now it's closer to 45 inches as everyone wants to buy a longer game. When the shaft is longer, the clubhead moves faster, even if you don't speed up your swing. But be careful: Longer shafts are harder to control, so along with a few extra yards, you might be buying more shots from the rough—or worse trouble. Many players find the best swing for their new, longer clubs is a slower swing.

Other options from the pro shop include oversized heads, exotic materials in heads and shafts, harder-cover balls . . . the list goes on and shows no signs of stopping.

Hey, it's only money: Aren't a few extra yards worth a few extra bucks?

---

ball. As the left hip and knee rotate, the arms extend outward, gradually increasing speed. The force of this dual action—one part of the body moving out to the left, the other to the right—creates torque that forces the left leg to straighten, providing a firm brace to hit against.

"I think of only two things on the downswing," reported Ben Hogan, "starting the hips back and then hitting the ball as hard as I can with the upper part of my body, my arms, and my hands, in that order."

Speed creates a powerful chain reaction: The faster you clear the hips, the faster weight shifts to your left foot, the faster the right side releases, and the faster the hands and arms sling the club into the ball.

Says Phil Ritson: "This rotary movement of the left side—what I call

THE X-FACTOR

Until the discovery of the X-Factor by teaching pros Jim McLean and Mike McTeigue, golfers believed the secret to distance was turning both the shoulders and hips on the backswing. But in the December 1992 edition of *GOLF Magazine*, McLean and McTeigue reported the findings of a lengthy study in which they strapped a device called the SportSense Swing Motion Trainer to the backs of pros and had them swing. The SMT sent information to a computer, which yielded, among other things, data on each player's shoulder and hip turns.

Comparing the data with video of the swings, McLean and McTeigue discovered that lines drawn across the shoulders and hips at the top of the swing converged to form an "X." Furthermore, the longest hitters were not those with the biggest turns, but those with the biggest gap between the two turns. The greater the differential between the size of the shoulder turn and the size of the hip turn, the greater the resistance between the upper and lower body, creating torque that translates to added clubhead speed and power coming down.

The data also showed that not one big hitter turned his shoulders 90 degrees and his hips 45 degrees, previously thought to be the ideal power-generating combination. John Daly *(below)* turned his shoulders 114 degrees and his hips 66 degrees from address, creating a gap of 48 degrees (114 minus 66 equals 48). Daly's gap was the largest measured, which makes sense, since he was the PGA Tour's longest hitter at the time.

The discovery of the X-Factor, by teaching pros Jim McLean (above) and Michael McTeigue, proved that power is the product of the resistance between the shoulder and hip turns.

"Grip It and Rip It" are the words John Daly lives by. Not since the days of the St. Andrews swing has a player taken the club so far back that it points down to the ground. And no other player—except, perhaps, Tiger Woods—has as great an "X-Factor."

'rotation power'—automatically brings your hands, arms, and the clubhead out and around so that the clubhead is delivered powerfully into the ball on a shallow path."

Fast rotation of the hips is the direct cause of a fast clubface on the downswing. If you keep the arms loose, the right arm turns over the left, rotating the clubface and putting drawspin on the ball; this accounts for the right-to-left flight and yards of added roll. And as long as the club falls onto the proper shallow path, contact will be made slightly on the upswing off the high tee. If you block the ball to the right or hit it high in the air, chances are tension is keeping you from releasing and sweeping through impact.

As with any swing, the ball is not your ultimate goal. Think about accelerating into the follow-through and the finish. Planning to finish "low and around" before you begin the swing can lead to a shallower power path.

DIFFERENT STROKES

KEEP YOUR EYES OFF THE BALL

Watch the young stars Annika Sorenstam and David Duval and you'll notice that both swivel their heads past the ball through impact. In fact, they are looking up at the ball as soon as it begins streaking off the tee.

Jim McLean says this swiveling action "helps clear the left hip more quickly and generates faster arms-hands-club speed." So forget keeping your head down and watching the club hit the ball. Instead, let the head move toward the target on the downswing and look up off the ball *before* you hit it!

WORDS OF WISDOM

The beginner should not strive for distance until he has cultivated a good swing.

Jerome Travers

Trial and experiment demonstrated to me that the necessary powerful whirling motion of the club was produced only when the force activating the club had its origin in the center of the body.

Bobby Jones

When looking for added power, the hips can't go too fast.
Ben Hogan

No power hitter ever swings as hard as he can; that is, he doesn't throw everything at the ball. Rather, it's a matter of timing, not overpowering the ball.
Arnold Palmer

What I've learned—even as a relatively long hitter—is that, first, there'll always be someone who can knock it past you occasionally; and, second, that power becomes a real asset only in ratio to your ability to hit straight as well as long.

Jack Nicklaus

Controlled power off the tee allows you to control the course.
John Daly

My first rule is, "Distance without direction is worse than no distance at all."
Nancy Lopez

CHAPTER FOUR

SHOTMAKING

Watch any golf telecast and two phrases you will hear used to describe the professionals are "great ballstriker" and "great shotmaker." Is there a difference? The practical definition of a ballstriker is someone who can consistently move the ball from point A to point B, usually using the same right-to-left or left-to-right flight pattern. A shotmaker is a player who can reliably move the ball from A to B in any number of different ways—high, low, fade, draw, high spin, low spin—whatever it takes. And he can hit these shots in the heat of competition.

Nick Faldo, Moe Norman, Hal Sutton, and Johnny Miller are wonderful examples of ballstrikers: They spent their careers aiming at or near the hole and hitting it there. Sam Snead, Bobby Jones, Lee Trevino, and Seve Ballesteros are the consummate shotmakers: They have produced every conceivable shot with championships on the line.

In a physical sense, shotmaking is simply controlling the spin, curve, and trajectory of a shot to handle the conditions present and hit the intended target. Mentally, it is much more.

"Imagination is what separates the great players from the good players," says shotmaking wizard and 1964 U.S. Open champion Ken Venturi. "The great

Sam Snead was considered the consummate shotmaker by his peers. They would never look in his bag to see what he was using, knowing he could vary the distance he hit each club.

Ken Venturi believes that the best shotmakers don't win every week because there are so many talented players on Tour. Usually, the one who can put together four solid rounds of ballstriking and outstanding putting wins.

Opposite: A series of instructional films made in the 1930s proves that Bobby Jones was a shotmaking virtuoso. His abilities were even more remarkable considering the inconsistencies in clubs and balls in his day.

ones see more options, more ways to solve the problems a hole presents. That's the essence of being a shotmaker."

Interestingly, shotmaking may be the only aspect of the game that many of the game's critics believe was more skillfully handled by yesterday's stars. But if shotmaking is truly a dying art, what is killing it? Opinions include the proliferation of high-tech equipment, modern course architecture, and new agronomic practices.

Most of today's irons and metal woods are designed to minimize curvature on poorly struck shots. To do this, the clubheads have a greater percentage of their mass distributed around the outside edge. This "perimeter weighting" minimizes clubhead twisting and side spin on off-center hits. It is good for the weekend golfer because it minimizes his hooks and slices. It is bad for the shotmaker because it minimizes hooks and slices.

Many of the high-profile courses built during the past few decades are laden with water hazards and greens fronted by deep bunkers. The only way to attack such courses is to fly the ball all the way to the hole, which stifles creativity.

Courses today also are watered from tree line to tree line, dramatically limiting shot selection. Heavily watered fairways and greens minimize roll, so courses play longer and approach shots must fly all the way to the green, since the ball won't run up the lush fairways.

Put these factors together and many courses become paradise for ballstrikers hitting from A to B with one soft, high shot after another.

"If I came out here today with the

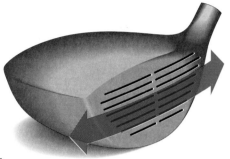

The shaping of today's metal woods is designed to minimize shot curvature. This is great for the beginner, but reduces the shotmaker's arsenal.

Opposite page, above: The Country Club, Brookline, Massachusetts. Below: The Old Course, St. Andrews, Scotland. Lush fairways and greens—common across the United States—may eliminate the shotmaker's advantage. Fairways are effectively wider because balls don't roll as far; approach shots from the rough are easier because the ball stops on softened greens. Firm fairways, like those on British links courses, put a premium on choosing the correct option on every shot.

game I played in '67, I'd be back selling tacos in El Paso," says Lee Trevino. "Course conditions have taken a lot of accuracy out of the game. By watering the fairways like they do now, you make the fairways play wider because a poor drive won't run as far. By making the greens soft, you make the rough less of a penalty because the ball will stop anyway. Get these courses firm, fast, and running and you'll see some shotmaking."

But despite these significant changes, shotmaking is far from dead. European professionals, who play in a wide range of course and weather conditions; many PGA Senior Tour players, who retain the wide variety of shots they learned on the dry, fast courses of the 1950s and 1960s; and current American stars including Phil Mickelson and Corey Pavin prove that shotmaking genius still can translate into tremendous golf success.

If shotmaking is so admired, why do the players who have all the shots not win every week? Venturi believes there are so many talented players on Tour that many times it is the one who can put together four solid rounds of ballstriking and outstanding putting who wins. He also notes that some of the best shotmakers are less than outstanding putters, which keeps them from capitalizing on their superior abilities.

To develop shotmaking skills, a golfer must create an inventory and understanding of:

Swing factors that affect ball flight. These include clubhead path, face angle, angle of attack, swing speed, and centeredness of contact. (All of these fac-

Best known for his left-to-right fade, Lee Trevino is a canny shotmaker who can work the ball with any shape or trajectory necessary.

tors are explained in detail in Chapter 5, Faults and Cures.)

Environmental factors that affect ball flight. These include the lie, type of grass, wind, weather, and slope.

Architectural factors that affect shot selection. These include placement of the hazards, green shape, topography, and course boundaries.

Having learned the basics of how and when to play various shots, one's trust in shot selection and swing mechanics comes only from experience. It's no coincidence that many great shotmakers, including Chi Chi Rodriguez, Seve Ballesteros, and Lee Trevino, learned to play with only a couple of clubs with which they manufactured every conceivable shot.

Jack Nicklaus adds that a strong mind is a huge asset to shotmaking. "Your powers of observation are your first strategic weapon," he explains. "Second is your imagination. There is an ideal way to play almost every shot in golf. The better you can identify and imagine it, the greater your scoring chances become.

"I have always felt that the sheer intensity Ben Hogan applied to shotmaking specifics was one of his greatest assets. It left no room in his mind for negative thoughts. The busier you can keep yourself with the particulars of shot assessment and execution, the less chance your mind has to dwell on the emotional 'if' and 'but' factors that breed anxiety."

Eddie Merrins, who taught Corey Pavin and other Tour stars while golf coach at UCLA, agrees that shotmaking is enhanced by proper observation

Modern shotmaking is personified by Phil Mickelson's crafty wedge play and courageous recovery shots. His seemingly fearless attitude allows him to pull off shots other pros won't even attempt.

Corey Pavin is the perfect example of how sharp shotmaking skills can level the playing field against players who hit the ball 50 yards farther off the tee.

Chi Chi Rodriguez believes shotmaking has declined because today's beginners start with a complete set of clubs. "If I were teaching a young player today," he says, "I would insist he or she play nine of every 18 holes with a maximum of four clubs."

During the 1980s, Seve Ballesteros was the king of the shotmakers. His swashbuckling attitude, coupled with amazing touch, demonstrated the importance of improvisation and imagination to an entire generation of golfers.

and organized thinking. He offers the following four-step process for choosing the best shotmaking option and then executing it with precision.

Step 1. Assess the lie. When approaching any shot, the first consideration should be the ball's position. Is it sitting up on a tee or down in a hole? Is it a good lie in the fairway or a poor lie in the rough? Is the ground sandy or wet? Is the lie level or is the ball above or below the feet? Is the lie angled uphill or downhill?

Using your understanding of swing mechanics, appropriate adjustments must be made to accommodate the lie. For example, if the ball is on a downhill slope, set the body perpendicular to the slope for solid contact and set more weight on the forward foot to maintain balance.

Step 2. Fix the target in mind. Once you've assessed the lie's effect on the shot, select a specific target: That is the distance and direction you want to achieve. Never make a swing without choosing and focusing on a target. The target may differ depending upon your confidence level, standing in the match, or swing performance.

Step 3. Imagine the shot. With a target in mind, mentally play the shot you want to hit. The shot can be a fade or draw, high or low, whatever you deem necessary to reach the target. Remember previous shots you hit on the course and practice tee to create a clear mental picture. Don't make the shot more difficult than necessary: If the situation allows for either a fade or draw, always go with your natural tendency. Once

you have a clear image of the necessary shot, stick with it as you go through your pre-swing routine.

Step 4. Use a single swing thought. The final key is to focus on a thought that triggers the swing you need in order to hit the chosen shot. During the two seconds it takes to make a swing, the mind cannot comprehend more than one thought. The more swing thoughts, the worse the result.

The remainder of this chapter offers a guide to maneuvering the ball in the direction and trajectory of your choice, plus a comprehensive list of environmental factors and explanations of how each will affect a shot.

Ben Hogan is remembered as a very mechanical and accurate player, but those who saw him play witnessed an almost magical ability to stick the ball close to his target.

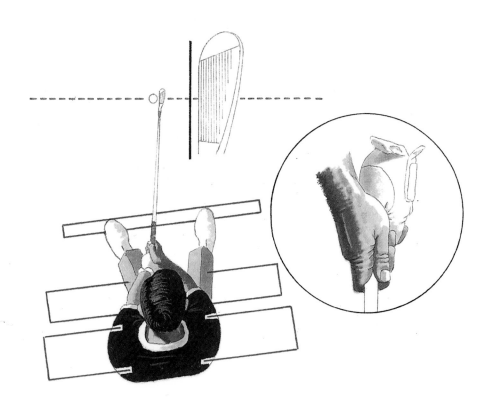

Grip and set-up for a fade.

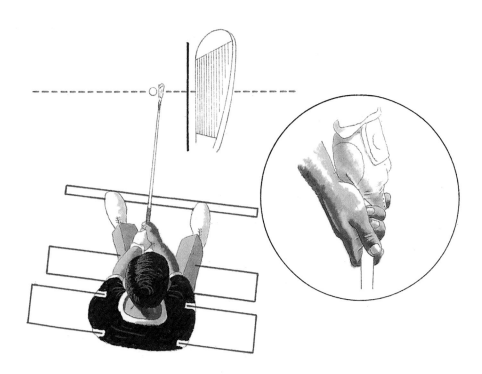

Grip and set-up for a draw.

THE BASIC SHOTS

To become a shotmaker requires mastery of the four basic shots: The left-to-right fade, right-to-left draw, high shot, and low shot. Once the golfer is able to call up these curvatures and trajectories at will, more subtle variations can be crafted to fit the lie and conditions. With one proviso: Curving the ball becomes easier as loft is reduced. If a shot requires an 8-iron or less to reach the target, don't expect the ball to curve very much.

The Fade. To hit a controlled left-to-right shot that starts straight and then curves, begin by setting up with your stance, knees, hips, and shoulders aligned to the left of the target line and the clubface aimed directly at the target. The farther the body aims left, the bigger the curve back to the right. Swing back and down along the stance line so the clubface is effectively open at impact and imparting left-to-right cut spin.

Producing a fade means not letting the toe of the club pass the heel until after impact. Johnny Miller increases the grip pressure in his left hand and loosens his right to prevent the right hand from rolling over the left at impact. Ken Venturi sets his hands higher at address, believing this makes it more difficult to roll the right hand over the left.

Jack Nicklaus suggests weakening the grip—rotating the hands counterclockwise on the club at address—as another way to keep the clubface slightly open at impact, insuring a fade. He also suggests matching the pre-swing waggle to the intended swing path to ingrain the proper takeaway.

The Draw. To hit a controlled right-to-left shot that starts straight and then curves calls for a mirror image of the set-up and swing used for a fade. Aim the stance and body to the right of the target. Aim the clubface directly at the target and swing along the stance line both back and down. The clubface reaches impact closed to the target line, producing right-to-left spin.

For a draw, the toe of the club must pass the heel through impact. Miller promotes this rotation by softening his left-hand grip and increasing right-hand pressure on the club. Setting the hands lower at address, like Fuzzy Zoeller, promotes a draw by flattening the backswing plane and making it very easy for the wrists to cock. On the downswing, it's easier to cross the right hand over the left, which helps close the face slightly at impact.

Strengthening the grip at address—rotating the hands clockwise on the club—can also promote an earlier rotation of the clubface through impact. Nicklaus tries to slow his hip rotation on the downswing to allow the hands and arms to rotate sooner.

The High Shot. Adding height to a shot requires moving the ball forward in the stance, which increases the effective loft of the clubface. Stand taller at address to promote a more upright swing path and play the ball about an inch closer to the body. Make sure the clubface is square to the target after adjusting it forward and closer. Tom Watson recommends setting the left thumb straight down the shaft or even a little bit left to promote a more open clubface at impact, which sends the ball higher.

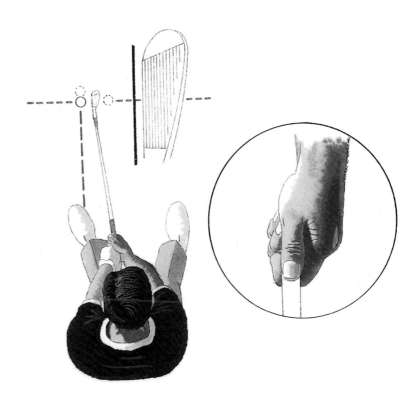

Grip and set-up for a high shot.

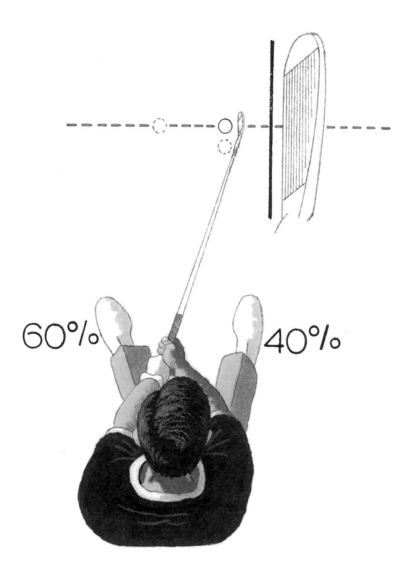

60%   40%

Grip and set-up (including weight distribution over the feet) for a low shot.

When hitting for height, take one more club than usual—for example a 5-iron instead of a 6-iron—because the shot will have a shorter carry.

Focus on holding the upper body back during the downswing, finishing with the hands high above the head.

The Low Shot. To hit a full shot lower than normal, move the ball back in the stance at address while keeping the hands in their normal position. This lessens the effective loft of the club because contact is being made earlier in the swing. Be aware that as the ball is moved back in the stance, the club-face must be hooded for it to remain square to the target.

Weight distribution should slightly favor the left side (60 percent left/40 percent right). Complete the set-up by moving the ball an inch or two farther from the body to promote a flatter swing path.

During the swing, focus on a low finish, the hands stopping at approximately shoulder height.

ENVIRONMENTAL
CONSIDERATIONS

Grasses. The playing surface can have a substantial effect on a lie and the club-head's behavior through impact. If you want maximum control over your shots, you must factor in the tendencies of the grass on which you are playing. There are times when the ball ends up in a lie that isn't typical fairway or rough and the keys to handling those special lies are covered in Chapter 8, Trouble Play.

The following are playing charac-

teristics of the most common types of golf-course grass, the regions where they are found, and how they are likely to affect full shots. If unsure as to the playing surfaces, ask the club professional to identify the predominant fairway and rough grasses and explain their characteristics.

Bentgrass. A fine-bladed, cool-weather grass usually found in fairways in the northern half of the United States, portions of Europe, and Japan. The lush fairways of championship venues like Winged Foot, Medinah, and Baltusrol are bentgrass. Bent lies are tight, so shots have more backspin, which means they normally carry shorter distances. Bentgrass is not found in rough areas, since the plant usually

doesn't grow more than an inch high. Because bent must be watered heavily to remain green, expect less roll when the ball lands on bentgrass fairways.

Bermuda grass. A warm-weather grass commonly found across the Southern half of the United States, throughout the Caribbean, and most/other tropical climates. PGA National in Palm Beach Gardens, Southern Hills in Tulsa, and Colonial in Fort Worth all have Bermuda fairways. Common Bermuda has coarse leaves while new hybrid Bermuda species have finer leaves. As a fairway grass, Bermuda allows the ball to sit up above the ground, so there is little clubhead resistance at impact and the ball usually flies farther than normal. When grown long in the rough,

The bentgrass fairways at Winged Foot Golf Club in Mamaroneck, New York, are manicured to perfection. This type of care provides golfers with tight lies and maximum backspin.

Southern Hills Country Club in Tulsa, Oklahoma, has firm Bermuda grass fairways and wiry Bermuda grass rough.

Bermuda becomes stiff and wiry and tends to grab or twist the clubhead at impact, making control difficult. Because Bermuda needs less water and grows on sand-based, easily drained soil, play for extra bounce and roll when the ball lands in the fairway.

Bluegrass. A cool-weather grass with moderate-size blades that can thrive in most regions with proper care. Shots from bluegrass fairways will travel a little bit shorter because of the tight lie. Bluegrass rough, like that at Valhalla in Louisville, holds a great deal of moisture and will grab the club through impact, causing a substantial loss of distance. The need for heavy watering

also means the soil is usually soft, which limits roll even when cut short.

Fescue. A cool-weather grass with a variety of blade sizes. Most commonly found near salt water, it is standard issue on British links courses. The thinner-bladed version, called fine fescue, offers minimal clubhead resistance from the fairway and, like other cool-climate grasses, produces tight lies. Fine Fescue rough is easier to get out of than bluegrass, but thick-bladed Tall Fescue, when used for rough, is tangly and one of the most difficult grasses to play from. The club will have great difficulty contacting the ball before being grabbed by the tall blades.

Kikuyu grass. Found in mild climates such as California, this grass has thick and wiry blades. Maintained at fairway height, it will promote shots similar in length to those hit from bent or fescue. But when allowed to grow—and kikuyu grows very fast—the strong blades will firmly grab the clubhead, making escape a crap shoot. Riviera Country Club near Los Angeles is well known for its kikuyu rough.

Poa Annua (Annual Bluegrass). This grass is found in many parts of the United States in the cooler spring months before dying out in the summer heat. Poa Annua grows quickly and in clumps, producing patchy fairways and rough, and a variety of lies that can pose problems on shots around the greens. On full shots the grass performs similar to bent, with fairly tight fairway lies.

Ryegrass. Like poa, this is another cool-season grass that dies under intense heat. Ryegrass is often used to overseed Bermuda grass fairways in the winter in the southern United States to provide a healthy-looking playing surface. Grand Cypress in Orlando and Doral in Miami overseed with ryegrass, which has playing properties similar to bluegrass. Shots from the fairway travel a little shorter, while its ability to hold moisture makes ryegrass rough a challenge because it is prone to causing substantial clubhead resistance at impact.

Zoysia. A warm-climate grass with a very coarse blade, zoysia can handle extreme temperature changes. It thrives in mid-South states such as

Top: *Valhalla Golf Club in Louisville, Kentucky, is covered with thick bluegrass rough that holds moisture and severely limits recovery options.*

Below: *Hard, tight fescue fairways, such as this one at Royal Lytham and St. Annes in St. Annes on Sea, England, are the norm on Britain's links courses.*

DIFFERENT STROKES

FADE VS. DRAW

While you may have noticed many Tour pros playing a high-flying fade, amateurs at almost all handicap levels should learn to play the lower, longer-distance draw. Otherwise, most courses will play too long for them. Tests conducted by Titleist, the equipment company, found that a draw hit by a driver travels substantially farther than a fade. Their robot was set to swing a driver at 90 miles per hour, approximately that of most single-digit handicappers. One-third were hit with the clubface 1.5 degrees open (producing a fade), one-third were hit with the clubface 1.5 degrees closed (draw), and one-third with the clubface square to the target.

Hit into a slight head wind, the draw averaged 233 yards total distance, the fade 216 yards (both groups finished an average of 18 yards left or right of center). The straight shots traveled the same overall distance as the draws.

Frank Thomas, Technical Director of the USGA, explains the results: "When the clubface is open to the swing path at impact, loft is added to the club, the ball is launched at a higher angle, more backspin is added, and the aerodynamic effects of lift and drag on the ball in flight are increased. So the ball sails higher, tailing to the right because of the initial clockwise spin imparted by the open clubface, but it does not go as far.

"When the face is closed at impact, the opposite happens. The club's loft and the launch angle are decreased, less backspin is created, and lift and drag are decreased. The ball flies lower and because of the counterclockwise spin created at impact, curves to the left. While backspin is necessary to keep the ball in the air, apparently the effect of less backspin is more than offset by the increase in forward speed, so the ball carries farther."

At 109 miles per hour, approximately the average driver speed for men on the PGA Tour, draws averaged 275 yards while fades averaged 265 in dense air and wet turf. At those lengths, giving up a few yards isn't as critical as the 17 yards or more amateurs give up when they don't hit the draw or straight ball.

Tennessee, Arkansas, and Missouri. Bellerive in St. Louis has zoysia fairways. It is also common in Japan under the names *korai* and *noshiba*. Fairway lies on zoysia are similar to Bermuda grass, the ball sitting up above the ground with little clubhead resistance. Most golfers will find that they hit their approach shots farthest when playing from zoysia. In the rough, zoysia's playing characteristics are similar to Bermuda grass: The ball usually sits down and the clubhead is grabbed through impact, causing difficulty with direction control.

SPECIALTY SHOTS

The High Drive. Sometimes hitting a driver a little higher than normal can carry the ball over a stand of trees at the corner of a dogleg or take advantage of a tailwind. Greg Norman, who is known for towering drives, plays this shot by moving the ball from its normal position—inside his left heel—one inch forward (toward the target), approximately even with the ball of his left foot. This set-up change moves his head behind the ball and keeps it back at impact, slowing the release of the hands, keeping the clubface slightly open until after impact, and launching the ball higher than usual.

The Low Drive. To keep a drive under the wind, Greg Norman moves the ball slightly back in his stance so that contact is made before the clubhead reaches the low point of the swing arc. He also tees the ball one-quarter to one-half

inch lower than normal. During the swing, keep more weight to the left to further promote making early contact.

Big Slice with the Driver. Corey Pavin, one of the shorter hitters on Tour, likes to hit a big, high slice with his driver on very long par threes. (The driver's minimal loft makes curving the ball relatively easy.) To hit the intentional slice, align your feet, hips, and shoulders well left of the target while aiming the clubface at the flag. Grip down one inch and tee the ball a bit higher than normal. Take the club back along the stance line so the shaft points left of the target at the top of the backswing. On the down-

swing, the club should come down along the stance line, traveling on an out-to-in path, imparting slice spin and a higher than normal trajectory.

Driver Off the Ground. To have any chance of successfully hitting a driver off the deck, conditions must be favorable. You need a nearly perfect fairway lie, and because the shot will travel on a low trajectory, the landing area should be dry and hard. Even a topped driver off the fairway can roll a long distance. Most important, according to Tom Watson, is a smooth swing. Don't try to help the ball into the air, but hit down slightly. A perimeter-weighted,

Riviera Country Club in Pacific Palisades, California, is renowned for its ferocious kikuyu rough that can make controlling shot distance nearly impossible.

Above: *Poppy Hills Golf Club in Pebble Beach, California, has Poa Annua fairways.*

Below: *Like many courses, Grand Cypress Resort in Orlando, Florida, overseeds its fairways and rough with ryegrass during the cooler half of the year.*

metal-headed driver, with its low center of gravity, will get the ball airborne more easily than a solid, wood-headed club. Pavin suggests setting up as if hitting a fade, your body open to the target. This increases the effective loft at impact, making it easier to get the shot airborne.

The Punch (a.k.a. The Knockdown). To play a punch shot, move the ball back slightly in the stance, approximately two inches behind your normal position. Hood the clubface so it aims directly at the target and move your hands forward. Tighten grip pressure a bit in both hands to keep the wrists quiet. As in a controlled slice, don't let the right hand rotate past the left until after impact. Shorten the follow-through so the club finishes pointing at your intended target.

The common mistake is to move the weight too quickly to the left side—a sway—which results in the head and right shoulder moving forward, throwing the club outside the intended path, so the ball either is pulled left or sliced right. Keep your head steady and let the hands and the clubface do the work.

The Floater. The floater is a bit like a baseball knuckleball, a shot with very little spin. Sam Snead was the master of this shot and often used it either to get the ball back to the hole on a long green or to confuse opponents watching his club selection. To hit a floater, take two clubs more than you would normally hit for the distance, e.g., a 4-iron instead of a 6-iron. Set the clubface square to the target, the hands slightly ahead of the ball, and keep the grip pressure light. Make a slow, lazy swing, letting the clubhead do the work. The ball will seem to float through the air, then sit fast upon landing.

The Low, Running Long Iron. This is a super shot in very windy conditions or when the greens are hard and won't hold a high approach. Move the ball back in your stance to an inch inside the right heel. Make a wide, shallow swing, going back to three-quarter length. Instead of hitting down, try to sweep the ball off the ground holding your head behind the ball until after impact. In heavy winds, lower the ball flight further by gripping down an inch on the club and closing your stance slightly while keeping the club-face aimed at the target. This setup creates right-to-left hook spin, lower trajectory, and additional roll.

The Low Fade. The low fade is an advanced player's shot because left-to-right fade spin usually propels the ball upward. Properly executed, it can work for most golfers using a club with no more loft than a 6-iron. Norman plays this shot by moving the ball back an inch and widening his stance an inch with each foot to lower his center of gravity and promote a shallower swing arc. To create the fade, align the body to the left of the target, keeping the clubface aimed at the target. Swing back along the stance line, trying to hold the clubface open to the target. Do not let the toe pass the heel until after impact. The backswing is very short, perhaps no more than half a standard full swing, for more control over the clubface. Don't shift too much weight toward the target on the downswing. Finish

DIFFERENT STROKES

SHOTMAKING IS SPIN

The combination of backspin and sidespin controls a ball's behavior after it leaves the clubface. Backspin gets the ball airborne; sidespin makes it curve left or right. Both spins affect trajectory and allow a shot to stop abruptly or release forward upon landing.

While many golfers won't find the study of spin exciting, it's important information that takes some of the mystery out of the game. Understanding spin lets you determine why your bad shots behaved the way they did. Understanding spin also makes it easier to choose the proper modifications in technique and strategy.

What happens at impact? During the .0005 of a second the ball is touching the clubface, it dramatically compresses against the club, so much so that a large portion of the face is covered by the ball. The ball then slides up the clubface a tiny amount, creating friction. This friction causes the ball to begin spinning backward as it rebounds into the air. With a 5-iron, this collision will launch the ball spinning at approximately 80 to 120 revolutions per second, depending upon clubhead speed and other impact conditions.

The aerodynamic principles of lift and drag take over, and while the explanation can become overly technical, the result is that backspin causes the air above the ball to move freely over its surface, reducing downward pressure. So the ball rises: In physics, this is called the Bernoulli Effect (an airplane wing works much the same way). How important is backspin to a golf shot? Without it, Tiger Woods would still be waiting for his first drive to carry more than 200 yards.

Four factors are primarily responsible for maximizing backspin:
- Additional clubhead speed at impact.
- Additional loft on the club.
- A steeper clubhead angle of approach at impact.
- Squareness of clubface contact.

A ball's construction (two-piece or three-piece), cover material, and the pattern, size, and depth of its dimples all affect backspin and flight. Many companies make balls designed for maximum and minimum backspin.

Sidespin is created whenever the clubhead path is moving in a direction other than how the clubface is pointing. For example, the clubhead approaches impact from outside the target line with the clubface square to the target. Because there is an angle formed between the path and the clubface's alignment, the impact creates sidespin. In this case, the spin is clockwise, opposite the direction the clubhead is moving. (Newton's third law of movement: For every action there is an equal and opposite reaction.) This spin causes the shot to curve from left to right. The opposite conditions would create a right-to-left shot. The greater the angle between the swing path and the clubface, the greater the amount of curvature, provided the backspin is the same. Backspin overrides sidespin, which is why short irons don't hook and slice as much as long-iron and wood shots.

It is impossible to impart backspin on any shot unless the ball is struck below its equator. Shots that fly low and hit the ground quickly do not have overspin, just less backspin than normal owing to poor contact. Any shot that becomes airborne at all has some backspin.

Zoysia fairways thrive in the mid-South such as at Bellerive Country Club in St. Louis, Missouri.

the swing low and left, pulling your arms across your body.

The High Draw. The high draw, like the low fade, is a combination of opposite spins. To hit a high right-to-left shot, move the ball forward in your stance (toward the target) so your head is behind the ball at impact. Set your weight more over the right foot, increasing the trajectory. To create the draw, align the body right of the target, aiming the clubface at the target. Take the club away along the stance line. On the downswing, keep the head steady and finish with the hands high. The shot will start right of the target with plenty of height.

The Intentional Mega-Slice. This shot demands the right equipment, lie, and mechanics. Johnny Miller suggests starting with a long club—no less than a 5-iron—even though the distance to be covered may be no more than 140 yards. Your ball must be sitting in light rough, fairway, or on bare ground; thick grass will eliminate most of the sidespin. Aim the clubface open to the target, setting your body well left of the target. Increase grip pressure in the left hand while decreasing it in the right. The swing should parallel the stance. Most important, don't close the clubhead until after the ball is struck. The ball will climb higher than usual because of the open face and out-to-in clubhead path.

The Intentional Mega-Hook. Launching a big hook requires the same equipment and lie as the big slice. Align the clubface left of the target, the body and stance well right. Firm up the right-hand grip, relax the left, and be conscious of letting the arms rotate so that the right hand rolls over the left. Although the face of the club is closed, the ball will start right of the target and very low.

Maximum Backspin Approach Shot. This shot is useful when faced with a short iron to a narrow green or when a hole is cut directly behind a bunker. To put extra spin on the shot, stand a little taller and an inch or two closer to the ball than normal. Make a steep backswing and hit down hard on the back of the ball.

Minimum Backspin Approach Shot. This is the shot when you've got a mid- or short-iron into a long green and the hole is well back and hard to get to. Widen your stance and stand about an inch farther from the ball. Make a three-quarter backswing and strike the ball with a sweeping blow. The ball will fly lower with less spin.

WORDS OF WISDOM

It is always the player who takes the most into consideration who comes up a winner.

Johnny Miller

Shotmakers have the ability to play shots that vary from the straight and normal trajectory to fashion something that's different. Sadly, that sort of thing is rarely called for anymore, so it's disappearing. Now the golf swing has evolved into a machine-like action—an endless repetition of the same shot.

Peter Thomson

I always believed that you should be able to hit three or four different clubs from wherever you are. That was the only real fun I ever got out of this game. I loved figuring out which shot I wanted to hit and pulling it off.

Dave Hill

I'd rank the top five [shotmakers] as Ben Hogan, Sam Snead, Lee Trevino, Tommy Bolt, and Jack Nicklaus. It would be very, very close between Ben and Sam, but I think if you went right through the bag and rated each player by club, Ben would come out slightly higher.

Tom Weiskopf

CHAPTER FIVE

FAULTS AND CURES

THE PREVIOUS CHAPTERS EXPLAINED HOW THE GOLF SWING IS *SUPPOSED* TO FUNCTION. But most golfers are not able to build a perfect swing, so they spend their golf careers trying to determine why the last shot didn't fly to the target.

Curing individual faults has been the essence of golf instruction for as long as the game has been played. Nearly every magazine article, book, and video tape about the swing discusses specific faults and their cures. As far back as 1905, when Harry Vardon wrote *The Complete Golfer,* he included a section on faults and their cures. He even noted that the slice was "the trouble from which the player most frequently suffers." Some things never change.

This continual search for remedies fuels the golfer's eternal quest for improvement. The player has another reason to be hopeful: While there are many ways the body can make a poor swing, there are only ten possible outcomes for a single shot. If it doesn't fly relatively straight, the ball can be sliced, pushed, hooked, pulled, chunked, topped, skied, smothered, or shanked. While the bad news is that nine of the ten results don't put the ball close to the target, the good news is that all nine mishits can be traced to the same few components.

Numerous instructors over the years hinted at the underlying causes of all golfers' distress, but it took John Jacobs to pull together all the pieces of the ball-flight puzzle.

Jacobs, one of Europe's finest players in the 1940s and 1950s, and its best-known instructor since the 1960s, centered his teaching on identifying and fixing swing faults. In 1972, this "cause and effect" instruction became available to all with the landmark publication of his *Practical Golf.*

"The *only* purpose of the golf swing is to move the club through the ball square to the target at maximum speed," wrote Jacobs. "How this is done is of no significance at all, so long as the method employed enables it to be done repetitively.

"Technically, golf is a much simpler game than most people realize," he went on. "If you are consistently mishitting and misdirecting the ball, it should cheer you to know that there are only two basic causes. Either you have an open clubface at impact, or you have a closed clubface at impact. By the same reasoning, if the swing path is not on target at impact, it can only be either out-to-in or in-to-out. The perfect impact occurs only when the clubhead travels exactly along the target line and exactly faces the target. This is your goal—the total objective of all you do with a golf club. You should never forget it."

No less an expert than Jack Nicklaus agrees with Jacobs's fault-based teaching. "In my mind one acquired trait to becoming a good golfer stands out well ahead of all others," said Nicklaus. "It is a total understanding of golfing cause and effect: A precise knowledge of exactly what is required in terms of club and ball impact to make a golf ball travel in a particular manner."

Developing the skills required for diagnosing faults and determining their correction begins with understanding the elementary physics of a golf shot, the relationships between the clubhead path and clubface angle. These are called the ball flight laws. In this sense, "laws" refers to the physical forces that influence the ball's flight. They are identical for every golfer and every swing.

Unlike the lightbulb or the telephone, the invention of ball flight laws can't be traced to a single moment or person. Books from the late 1800s discussed the importance of the club's path and face position for hitting the ball in the desired direction. Teachers throughout the first half of the twentieth century pondered various ball

The club and ball are in contact for only one-half of one-thousandth of a second.

flight laws, but never addressed the entirety. Jacobs was the first, popularizing the concept through frequent clinics, books, and magazine articles both in Europe and in the United States.

Also in the mid 1960s, a research team headed by physicist-author Alastair Cochran spent five years experimenting and analyzing the game's elements under the auspices of the Golfing Society of Great Britain. They conducted the most in-depth study to date of what happens when ball and club meet and how impact conditions affect the shot. The resulting book, *Search for the Perfect Swing*, by Cochran and John Stobbs, confirmed Jacobs's theories and established scientific proof for the ball flight laws.

While Cochran's search for a perfect golf swing did not find one, it did lay the foundation for American instructor Dr. Gary Wiren to author *Laws, Principles and Preferences* in 1973. Beginning with the ball flight laws, Wiren built a complex model of principles that must be adhered to within the swing's framework to create the ideal impact conditions. These principles are the fundamental considerations in the swing that have a direct bearing on the golfer's application of the ball flight laws. These principles include: grip, aim, set-up, swing plane, arc width, arc length, wrist position, levers, timing, balance, and swing center. Once established, these principles and their corresponding preferences— the nearly endless variety of possibilities that are functional and do not violate physical law—were detailed to show how seemingly very different swings such as Ray Floyd's and Arnold

Above: *Englishman John Jacobs spread the gospel of ball flight laws to instructors around the world during the 1960s. Jacobs knew that if he understood the laws of impact he could make more accurate diagnoses of the golfer's problems.*

Below: *Jack Nicklaus was taught "a total understanding of golfing cause and effect" at a very young age by his teacher, Jack Grout (shown here in the middle watching Nicklaus practice at Scioto Country Club in Columbus, Ohio).*

Right: Alastair Cochran was hired by the Golf Society of Great Britain to make a scientific analysis of the game. His five years of research were published in 1968 as Search for the Perfect Swing. *Thirty years later, parts of the book are slightly dated but it is still the bible for many teachers.*

Below: Dr. Gary Wiren expanded on ball flight laws, building a complex model of principles and preferences that explains how golfers could have different swings yet hit the same shot. His document became the framework for the first PGA Teaching Manual in 1990.

Palmer's can both create consistently solid impact.

In 1990, when the PGA of America published its first *PGA Teaching Manual,* also edited by Wiren, ball flight laws and their corresponding swing principles and preferences were the cornerstone of the entire volume. Today, nearly every instructor uses these ball flight laws to diagnose swing faults.

THE BALL FLIGHT LAWS

The Ball Flight Laws are fairly straightforward: Two factors affect a shot's direction: clubhead path and clubface angle. Three factors affect distance: Point of contact on the clubface, clubhead speed, and the clubhead's angle of approach.

By understanding how each influences a particular shot, anyone is able to see a shot and determine what conditions existed at impact. With all else being equal, here are the effects of each of the five factors:

Clubhead path. The path of the clubhead—in conjunction with the clubface angle—influences the shot's initial direction. The faster the clubhead is traveling, the more influence path has on initial direction.

Clubface angle. Where the clubface points at impact indicates the direction the ball will curve during flight. Clubface angle also influences the shot's starting direction.

Point of contact. The ball will travel farther and straighter when struck closer to the center of the club's sweetspot.

Clubhead speed. The faster the clubhead is traveling at impact, the farther the ball will travel.

Angle of approach. This is the steepness of the clubhead path approaching impact. The greater the angle, the more backspin is generated, creating additional lift, reducing overall distance, and counteracting any sidespin on the shot.

All of these factors are at play on every shot. But because they are more consistent, angle of approach, clubhead speed, and point of contact generally have less effect. Clubhead path and clubface angle, which can vary significantly from shot to shot have greater influence on the shot's results.

The illustrations on pages 100–101 shows the nine ball flights and the combinations of path and face angle that are responsible for each.

Other factors can influence shots. Clubface loft, ball construction, and clubface material contribute to the amount and direction of spin imparted to the ball. Environmental conditions including the lie, air temperature, humidity, wind, and altitude also have some effect on ball flight and are discussed in Chapter 4, Shotmaking, and Chapter 8, Trouble Play.

But more than any other factor, the clubface—whether open or closed to the target—determines the shot's direction. That is why an out-to-in swing path can send the ball in one of two different directions—a pull (a shot that starts left of the target and continues in that direction) when the clubface is aimed in the same direction as the path, or a slice when the clubface is aimed right of the path at impact. Similarly, an in-to-out path can cause either a push (a shot that starts to the

THE FIVE BALL FLIGHT LAWS

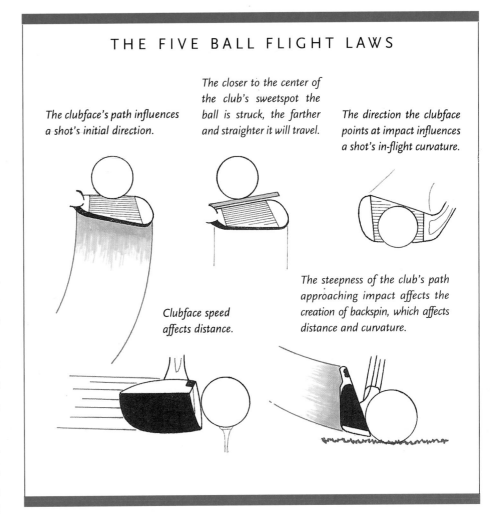

The clubface's path influences a shot's initial direction.

The closer to the center of the club's sweetspot the ball is struck, the farther and straighter it will travel.

The direction the clubface points at impact influences a shot's in-flight curvature.

Clubface speed affects distance.

The steepness of the club's path approaching impact affects the creation of backspin, which affects distance and curvature.

Before being able to build and maintain a sound swing, golfers must understand why the ball goes where it does. Nine ball flights can occur from the two factors that affect shot direction: clubhead path and clubface angle. The clubhead can approach impact moving directly along the target line, from inside the line, or from outside the line. The clubface points directly at the target, to the right of the target, or to the left. The nine combinations create the nine shot-shapes shown here.

Path to left of target line, clubface closed at impact

Path to left of target line, clubface at target at impact

Path to left of target line, clubface open at impact

TARGET LINE

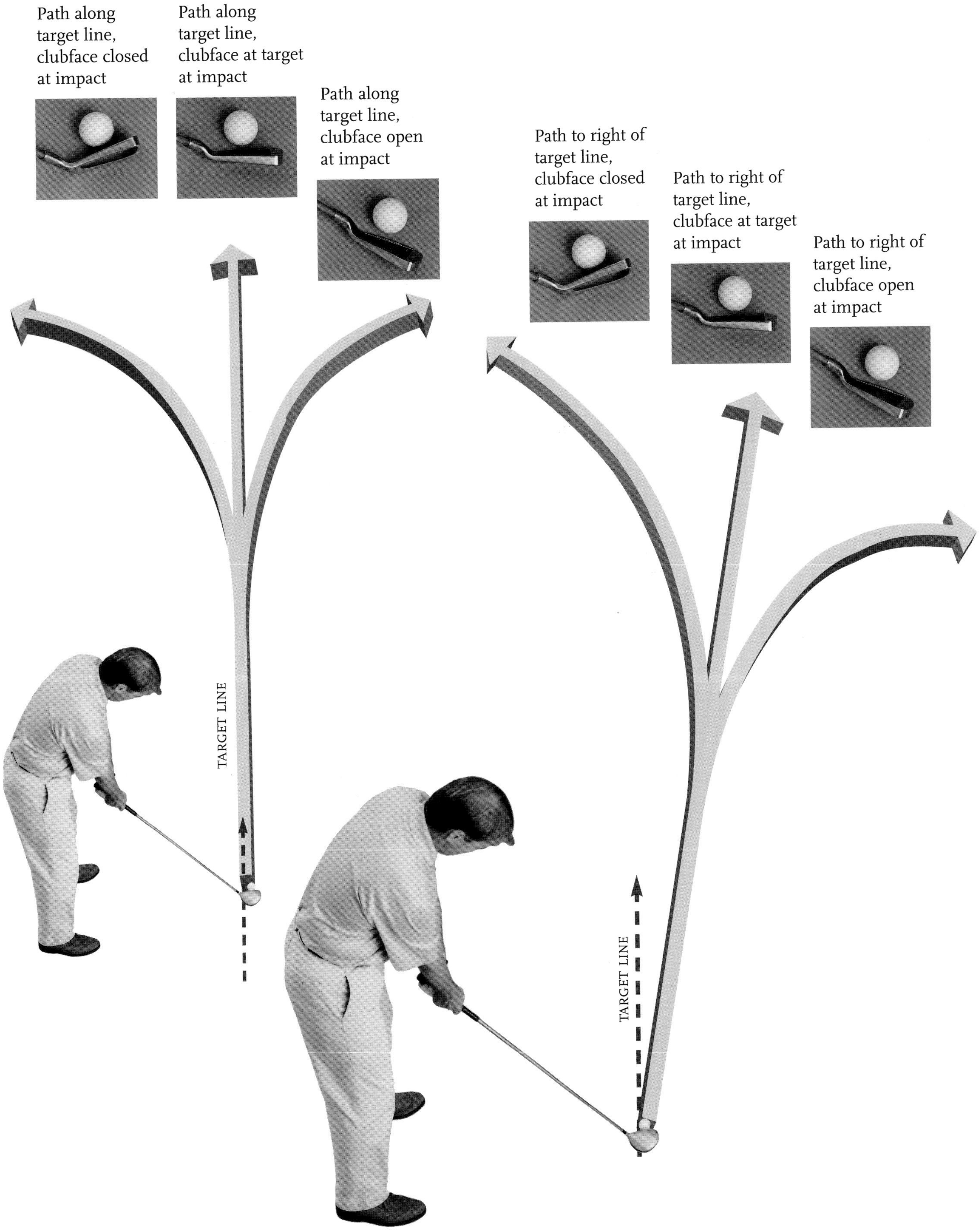

Path along target line, clubface closed at impact

Path along target line, clubface at target at impact

Path along target line, clubface open at impact

Path to right of target line, clubface closed at impact

Path to right of target line, clubface at target at impact

Path to right of target line, clubface open at impact

TARGET LINE

TARGET LINE

right of the target and continues in that direction) when the clubface is aimed along the clubhead path, or a hook when the clubface points left of the path at impact.

The combination of backspin and sidespin also helps determine ball flight. More loft on a club means more backspin on a shot, and backspin overrides sidespin. For example, pulls and pushes are very common with a 9-iron since it has a lot of loft, which creates a lot of backspin. Slices and hooks are more common from woods and long-irons, which have relatively little clubface loft, create little backspin, and are heavily affected by sidespin.

Even a rudimentary understanding of ball flight laws provides the insight necessary to identify impact condi-

Lee Trevino (below) and Canadian great Moe Norman (opposite) have two of the more unusual swings among golf's champions, but both deliver the club properly through the impact area, moving it along the target line and facing the target for twelve inches. If the ball is contacted at any time along that span, the shot will fly toward its intended target. Most amateurs keep the clubhead on line and facing the target for less than two inches.

tions. For example, to determine clubface position at impact, hit a few drivers or 3-irons: If the ball slices, the face is open; if it hooks, the face is closed. To identify swing path, hit some 9-irons or pitching wedges: If the shots are pulled left, the path is out-to-in; if they are pushed right, the path is in-to-out.

Even with this information readily available, most golfers' problems derive from either not understanding or ignoring the fact that the only thing the golf ball knows is what the clubhead tells it. "The ball does not care what the player's body is doing as it swings the club," adds instructor Jim Flick. "The ball responds only to how those actions cause the clubhead to strike it."

Study the unorthodox swings of champions such as Lee Trevino, Moe Norman, Miller Barber, Isao Aoki, Jim Furyk, Calvin Peete, Nancy Lopez, and Chi Chi Rodriguez and it becomes obvious that there are many ways to hit shots consistently to the target. All of these great players have trained themselves to deliver the club along the target line and facing the target during the one-half of one-thousandth of a second that matters.

No matter what your current swing key or theory, the fact is that the irrefutable laws of physics control every golf shot ever hit and every one that will ever be hit.

GOLF'S NINE BAD SHOTS AND THEIR CURES

Golf's Nine Bad Shots was the title of a 1947 instruction book by Jim Dante and Leo Diegel. Fifty years later it remains a blueprint for the causes and cures of each of golf's less-than-perfect results. Each is documented in detail on the following pages, with drills to help correct the faults and create the feeling of a correct swing.

SLICE

Aliases: Banana, Block

The Result

A slice is a shot that curves dramatically to the right. Slicing is the most common fault in golf, according to John Jacobs, the predominant flight path for three-quarters of all golfers. There are three types of slices: The Straight Slice starts at the target and then curves to the right. The Pull Slice takes off heading left of the target and then begins to curve back to the right. The Push Slice starts right of the target and curves still farther right.

Why It Happens

Straight Slice: The ball starts fairly straight, but flies too high and falls to the right at the end of its flight. This is the most common slice because, says

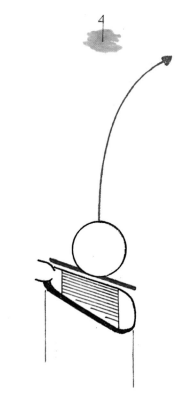

A straight slice starts at the target and then curves right.

Jacobs, Jack Nicklaus was too successful. The better Nicklaus did, the more average golfers tried to copy his upright, straight-line swing. But to win with this motion requires tremendous lower-body strength, something Jack has that most of us do not.

This swing results from bending the body too far over the ball at address. A bent-over posture steepens the clubhead path. A higher handicapper also may drop his head too far down onto his chest, restricting shoulder turn. On the backswing, the golfer lifts his right side and his shoulders rock underneath, taking his arms and club on too straight a path. The right arm is unable to fold, producing a "flying" right elbow. This is a classic reverse weight shift with the body moving over the left leg rather than the right at the top of the backswing. On the way down, the left side of the body catches up, but the hips can move only laterally left and their rotation is squelched. Because the hips can't turn, the arms can't rotate and the hands are "blocked" from releasing and the club returns to impact pointing right of the target. (Jacobs refers to this shot as the "rocker blocker.")

The angle of attack also is too steep owing to the upright backswing created by the reverse weight shift. This results in a higher than optimum trajectory. Because the hands can't release, the clubface points right of the target (open) at impact, causing a slice.

Two additional but less common causes of blocking are a lack of body motion and a stiff left arm at impact.

A swing that is almost all arm motion usually results in little more than a slapping of the club at the ball, which leaves the clubface open at impact.

When the left arm becomes too stiff on the downswing, the hands are prevented from rotating the clubhead and the clubface remains open at impact.

CURES

To correct the "rocker blocker," stand more erect at address. A taller posture helps the shoulders turn on a flatter plane, taking the arms, hands, and club more inside the target line. At the top of the swing, the clubshaft will be positioned over the right shoulder rather than the neck. The shoulders turn going back and coming down, and the hips can rotate more easily. This allows the arms and hands to rotate fully from inside the target line to directly along the line at impact and back inside the line after impact. The resulting angle of attack is shallower and produces a lower ball flight.

When the arms become overactive, the big muscles don't give much support because they can't keep up; the torso and lower body don't completely rotate away from the target. Incorporate additional hip and shoulder turn into the backswing to lengthen and smooth out the motion. Think of turning the belt buckle directly away from the target to get both the hips and shoulders to make a more complete turn.

For straight slicers who take the straight left arm to the extreme, relax the left arm and extend the right arm through impact. After impact, let the left arm fold, to promote the necessary rotation of the clubhead so it is square at impact.

Pull Slice. Most pull slicers start out hitting a straight slice, then try to fix it by aiming the club to the left of the target.

That causes the following chain reaction, which creates an out-to-in clubhead path and a closed clubface at impact:

When the body is aimed left, the ball is more forward in the stance. As a result, the right shoulder moves forward, opening shoulder alignment and producing an outside-to-in swing path that starts the ball left of the target. The forward right shoulder also leads to weakening the grip (hands turned to the left), and an even bigger slice than before.

The open alignment/ball forward set-up also causes the golfer to swing the club to the inside and around the body. Therefore, the arms are swinging too flat with the clubface fanning open. The arms and shoulders then try to compensate by lifting the club at the start of the downswing; coming from outside the target line, it drops steeply on the ball with the clubface open.

Two other potential contributing factors to an out-to-in clubhead path are setting the hands behind the ball at address, or starting the downswing with the shoulders instead of the hips.

When the hands begin behind the ball, the clubhead trails the hands and is forced outside the target line during the takeaway, leading to an outside-to-in clubhead path through impact.

If the downswing becomes too quick, the upper body and hands take over, causing a spinning action of the shoulders that also forces the clubhead into an outside-to-in path.

Because of his steep angle of attack, the pull slicer is terrible with woods and long irons (which require a more sweeping swing), and has more success with high-lofted irons, which pro-

duce backspin that overrides the sidespin caused by the out-to-in path. Still, short shots tend to be pulled.

CURES

To cure the pull slice, the club must be aimed at the target and the shoulders must be square to the target line so the club can travel on an inside-square-inside path. Move the ball back in the stance so it is no farther forward than just inside the left heel. Your shoulders may feel closed to the target line when actually they are square; after a bit of practice, this sensation will disappear. Adopt a stronger grip (both hands turned farther to the golfer's right) and position the hands slightly ahead of the ball at address for iron shots; position them even with the ball for woods.

Start the forward swing by unwinding the hips before the upper body begins uncoiling.

Push Slice: Golfers who push slice are fighting both poor swing path and poor clubface alignment. Consciously or otherwise, they have tried to cure the curve to the left by aiming the club or body to the right of the target.

Aiming right has the effect of moving the ball back in the stance and aligning the shoulders right of the target. This combination creates an inside-to-out swing path, which starts the ball right of the target line. Positioning the ball farther back also leads to a stronger grip (hands turned more to the player's right), so the gentle draw is gone, replaced by a big hook.

At this point, the swing path is so in-to-out that the angle of attack at

A pull slice starts left of the target then curves right.

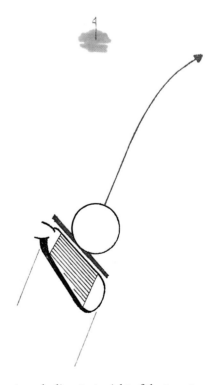

A push slice starts right of the target then curves farther right.

impact is very shallow. This swing may hit the occasional good drive with a hook, but shots with other clubs are usually fat or thin.

The golfer aims the clubface still farther right until the ball is so far back in the stance that the hands have no time to release and the clubface is open in relation to the inside-to-out swing path. The ball starts right, then curves farther right.

CURES

The first step to curing a push slice is to move the ball forward, but not past the inside of the left heel. This allows the clubface to aim at the target, keeps the shoulders square to the target line, and creates a swing that moves down the target line through impact.

The hips probably are spinning too quickly around to the left. Proper lower body action allows the hips to open naturally through impact. Practice slowly sliding body weight toward the target, moving it from the inside of the right foot to the inside of the left foot to start the forward swing. This restricts body rotation and gives the hands and arms a chance to square the clubface to the target at impact.

EQUIPMENT NOTE

Slicing can be caused by a lack of clubface rotation through the hitting zone. Some golfers reduce their tendency to slice by switching to thinner grips on their clubs. A thinner grip promotes quicker arm and hand rotation at the bottom of the swing.

REGARDING HEELED SHOTS

Shots hit on the heel (that portion of the clubface between the center of the face and the hosel) are caused by the same set-up and swing conditions as a slice. Because the clubface is open and coming across the target line from out-to-in, the heel of the club leads at impact. If the slice set-up and swing motion are corrected, the golfer will no longer hit shots in the heel.

Drills to Cure Slicing

Drills are an important component for improving one's golf swing. They are the most efficient way for the body to incorporate and ingrain a new motion into the swing. Good drills are simple to understand, easy to repeat, and proven to work.

Comb Drill: To keep the clubface from opening during the swing, slide a comb (or a pencil) under the watchband on the target side of the left wrist. This promotes a flat wrist at the top of the backswing while eliminating any cupping between the wrist and the back of the left hand. This drill is most effective with a three-quarter swing. NOTE: Make sure the back of the left hand presses against the comb at the top of the backswing.

Heel First Drill: To keep the clubface from fanning open during the backswing, draw a target line on the ground and place a ball on the line. Begin the takeaway by moving the heel of the club along the line. Put a dot on the heel to help the eyes focus on this part of the clubface. This over-compensation helps break the habit of rolling the face open on the takeaway.

Right Foot Back Drill: To promote an inside-square-inside swing path, address a ball with the right foot drawn back and lifted so only the toes touch the ground. From this position, make half swings. Angle the grip end of the shaft toward the target at impact to promote a descending blow.

Head Cover Drill: To increase clubface rotation through impact, place a headcover in your left armpit. Swing trying to keep the headcover in place back and through. The left arm will have to fold at the elbow in the follow-through, forcing the arms and hands to rotate the clubface, rather than the body.

Knee Swing Drill: To flatten out the steep swing path associated with a slice, practice hitting shots while kneeling on a towel. Any up-and-down motion will cause the club to hit the ground well behind the ball. This drill also promotes fuller upper-body rotation.

Shadow Drill: Another way to flatten the swing path is to put a shaft in the middle of your shadow at address and make a weight shift that moves the shadow just to the right of the shaft at the top of the backswing. This weight transfer over the right foot will flatten the swing plane.

Sidehill Lie Drill: Flatten the swing path by hitting shots from a sidehill lie with the ball a few inches above the feet. This lie forces the golfer to stand farther from the ball and guarantees a relatively flat plane.

PUSH
Alias: Block

The Result

A shot that starts to the right of the target and continues relatively straight along its initial path.

Why It Happens

Despite the fact that the ball goes to the right, the push is closely related to a hook—their clubhead paths are identical. Only the clubface alignment at impact is different. A push occurs when the club swings on an exaggerated in-to-out path and the clubface is square to the path. The push usually feels good since it is struck solidly in the middle of the clubface with a square blow. In general, the swing that causes a push is nearly sound, but one which probably has moved the body ahead of the ball at impact. This stifles clubface rotation and leads to an open face at impact. It happens because of one or more of the following:

• Swaying to the left on the downswing, which slows arm rotation.
• Addressing the ball too far back toward the right foot, which gives the club less time to square up to the target before impact.
• Aiming right of the target.
• Keeping the head too close to the chest during the swing, which inhibits arm rotation.

CURES

For a sway: Load most of the body's weight over the right leg at the top of the backswing. On the downswing, try to return the clubhead to the ball while keeping the lower body stable and your head behind the ball until after impact.

For ball-back position: This produces the same effect as swaying to the left, because the body is too far out in front at impact. Moving the ball position more toward the target allows the club more time to square up before impact.

For poor aim: Place a club on the

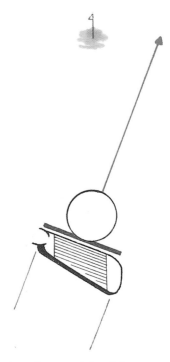

A push starts right of the target and continues along that initial path.

Like the slice, there are three types of hooks.

ground along the target line and address the ball with a slightly open stance (the left foot pulled farther back from the target line than the right) and a square clubface. If this address position is duplicated at impact, the hands and arms will be free to move the clubhead along the target line.

For keeping the head down: If the head remains buried against the chest on the downswing, shoulder and hip rotation are hindered so the clubface can't rotate back to square. The head should be allowed to swivel and turn naturally with the follow-through. By avoiding a rigid head-down position, the body is given the freedom it needs to square the clubface at impact.

Drills to Cure Pushing

Split Grip Drill: Train the hands and arms to rotate correctly and square the clubface at impact by taking a grip on a 7-iron with at least three inches of space between the hands. Make swings with the hands reaching only hip level during the backswing and on the follow-through. Through impact, feel the right hand cross over the left. During the backswing, stop when the clubhead reaches hip high on the backswing to check that the toe points to the sky, then continue to swing until the arms reach hip high. When the clubhead reaches hip high in the follow-through, the toe should again point skyward.

Bow-Legged Drill: To minimize excessive lateral motion during the downswing, which causes the swing center to move ahead of the ball at impact, tee up a driver and take address with your legs bowing outward. (This is opposite

of a normal swing, where the knees point slightly inward.) During the swing, remain flat-footed to condition the lower body to move less and provide a stable base for the upper body.

HOOK
Aliases: Wounded Duck, Snap

The Result
A shot that curves dramatically from right to left. As with the slice, there are three hooks delineated by their starting direction relative to the target: The Straight Hook starts at the target, then curves to the left; the Push Hook takes off heading right of the target then curves back to the left; the Pull Hook starts left of the target and curves farther left.

Why It Happens
All three hooks result from a closed clubface (pointing left of the target) at impact. These are the opposite combinations of errors that cause the slice. For a hook, the clubface is closed at impact and the angle of attack is too shallow, the result of swinging too much around the body.

The three hook shots are caused by different clubhead paths through impact. If the clubhead is traveling along the target line, the ball starts at the hole. If the path is moving in-to-out along the target line, the ball starts to the right of the target. If the path is traveling out-to-in, the ball starts to the left.

The corrections for an outside-to-in or inside-to-out path can be found under Push (inside-to-out) and Pull (outside-to-in). The corrections here are for eliminating a closed clubface, and pertain to all three hooks. If the clubface is closing at impact, one or more of these faults is to blame:

- The grip is too strong (hands are turned too far to the golfer's right, away from the target).
- The ball is too far from the body at address.
- The stance is aligned too far right of the target.
- The left-hand grip is loose or out of position at the top of the backswing.
- The swing's tempo is too quick.

CURES

Strong grip: Starting with the hands turned too far to the right at address (right palm pointing right of the target and upward), the arms and hands naturally attempt to return to neutral (right palm facing the target) at impact. Instead, take a neutral grip at address with the right palm facing the target and the V formed by the thumb and forefinger of the right hand pointing between the right shoulder and chin. The hands will return to this position at impact and square up the clubface.

Ball too far from body: Standing too far from the ball flattens the swing path, causing an around-the-body swing. This shallow arc makes the clubhead rotate—and close—more quickly. Stand more upright (less bending from the hips and knees) and let the arms hang straight down from the shoulders. From this set-up, the swing will become more upright and the clubface won't roll over as quickly.

For poor alignment: No matter the root cause, almost everyone suffering from consistent hooking instinctively aims right of the target to allow for the shot's leftward bend. Instead, make sure the feet, knees, hips, and shoulders are all aligned parallel to the target line at address.

For a loose left-hand grip: At the top of the backswing, the club slides up into the fingers of the left hand. The right hand takes control on the downswing, causing the wrists to uncock too early and shut the clubface before impact. Shorten the backswing so the shaft doesn't dip past parallel. The longer the backswing, the greater the chance the left hand will lose control. Exercises that strengthen the left hand and fingers also will help; squeeze a tennis ball or commercial grip strengthener.

For a quick tempo: An overly fast tempo can kill an otherwise fine swing by ruining the proper sequence of motion, increasing the rotation of the clubhead and shutting the face before impact. The easiest way to better time the rotation of the clubface is to set-up with the stance, hips, and shoulders slightly open to the target. This shortens the backswing and promotes a slightly slower clubface rotation through impact.

EQUIPMENT NOTE

Hooking can be caused by the hands' exaggerated rotation through impact. Some golfers find thicker grips place the club farther into the palms, slowing hand and arm rotation.

REGARDING TOED SHOTS

Shots hit on the toe (the portion of the clubface between the center of the face and the outside edge) are caused by the same set-up and swing conditions as a hook. But because the clubface is closed and moving in-to-out across the target line, the toe reaches the ball first. If the hook set-up and swing motion are corrected, the golfer will no longer make contact in the toe area.

Drills to Cure Hooking

Divot/Line Drill: To steepen the angle of approach, hit balls off a painted line perpendicular to the target line. You want to take a divot on the target side of the line. To do this, the swing will have to be steeper, the hands and shaft farther forward at impact.

Sidehill Lie Drill: To steepen the swing plane, hit shots with the ball a few inches below your feet. This lie forces you to stand closer to the ball, which promotes a more upright path.

Address the Toe Drill: For a golfer who has a relatively flat swing and hits hooks off the heel of the club, practice lining up with the ball off the toe. This promotes a taller address and a more upright swing plane.

No-Right-Hand Drill: Take your normal stance. Place the right hand directly on top of the left hand so your right fingers cover the left fingers. Make full practice swings, concentrating on making a wide clubhead arc and maintaining control of the club. This drill promotes a controlled swing tempo and slows the rotation of the clubface through impact.

7-Iron Divot Drill: Tee a ball about one inch off the ground. Take a 7-iron and hit the ball, taking a divot after impact. To take a divot, you must hit down on the shot on a steep angle, which pre-

vents the clubface from turning over too quickly. This drill helps train the hands and arms to delay the rotation of the clubface.

Right-Hand-Let-Go Drill: Using an iron, make full swings and let go with the right hand at the moment of impact. Start with slow swings and work up to longer, full-speed efforts. This drill also can be used to hit balls: Hold on with the right hand until a split second after impact. This drill prevents the right hand from closing the clubface at impact.

Aim Left Drill: Many hooks result from a dramatically in-to-out downswing path. This drill forces the golfer to swing from out-to-in during the downswing. Stick an old shaft in the ground about 10 feet in front of you directly on the target line. Make a swing that starts the ball left of the shaft. This promotes an earlier rotation of the left hip so the hips are aligned well to the left of the target by impact.

PULL
Alias: Yank

The Result
A shot that starts left of the target and flies straight on that line.

Why It Happens
The pull, like the push, usually feels good since it is struck solidly in the middle of the clubface with a square blow. But because the clubface is traveling on an out-to-in path at impact, the ball starts left of the intended target and continues straight.

The path of the pull is identical to that of a slice. Only the clubface alignment at impact differs. Pulls are usually rooted in one or more of the following:

• Swaying back to the right during the backswing.

• Too much weight over the left side at the top of the backswing.

• Right elbow moves too far from the body on the downswing.

• Clubshaft points well left of the target line at the top of the backswing.

• A downswing where the arms and hands get ahead of the lower body rotation.

CURES

For a sway: On the backswing, coil the body around a fixed axis. Imagine a pole running from inside the right foot, up the inside of the right leg, and through the top of the head. Make sure the head, shoulders, and hips rotate around this pole on the backswing. The result will be a better coiling of the shoulders and back, which moves the clubhead inside the target line during the takeaway and promotes an inside-square-inside path through impact.

Too much weight over the left side: Failure to shift enough weight to the right side often causes shifting to the right during the backswing or falling back on the downswing. This forces the clubhead outside the target line. Create a proper weight shift by allowing the majority of the body's weight to move over the inside of the right foot until beginning the downswing. As the club starts down, the weight should immediately return to the left side.

Flying right elbow: When the right elbow moves away from the body before impact, the clubhead swings outside the target line. Keep the right elbow tucked as near as possible to the right side. Think of starting the downswing by moving the right elbow toward the right hip.

Laid-off clubshaft: This is a hands and arms mistake. Halfway back, the left wrist bows, which drops the clubhead well behind the hands. Move your left arm closer to and more across the body. At the same time, the hands should feel that they are more underneath the shaft. At the top of the backswing the club should be supported by the right hand. The right wrist should be directly above the right forearm.

Rushing the downswing (hitting from the top): On the downswing, let the upper and lower body move to the left in unison—in a smooth, unhurried motion. There should be no sensation of forcing the clubhead to the ball. The wrists will uncock automatically as centrifugal force builds prior to impact.

Drills to Cure Pulling

Feet Together Drill: To train the arms to swing freely and with an inside-to-square-to-inside swing path, hit 7-iron shots with the feet together. This forces a free arm and hand swing that promotes squaring the face at impact. While doing this drill, make a point to swing the arms on a more upright plane than that of the shoulder turn. Think: Turn the shoulders level around the spine while swinging the arms up and down.

Baseball Footwork Drill: To promote a better weight transfer back to the left side on the downswing, tee a ball and address it with a 7-iron. Before swinging, draw the left foot back (away from the target) so it is touching the right shoe. Make a backswing. As the back-

A pull starts left of the target and continues along its initial path.

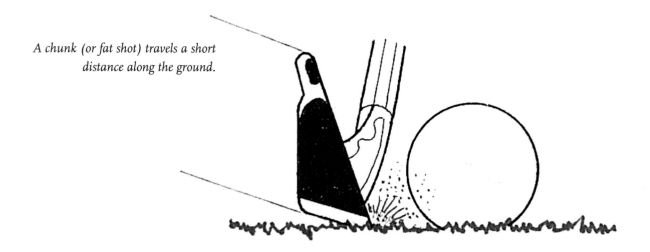

A chunk (or fat shot) travels a short distance along the ground.

swing is completed, stride forward with the left foot just as a baseball player does stepping into a pitch. To make solid contact, it will be necessary to swing smoothly, with weight shifting to the left side slowly but emphatically.

CHUNK
Aliases: Fat, Heavy, Sclaff, Fluff, Scuff, Stub, Dunch, and Lay the Sod Over

The Result
A shot that usually travels a very short distance along the ground.

Why It Happens
The clubhead strikes the ground before the ball on the downswing. Or as some teachers like to say, the golfer "hit the big ball before the little ball." Common causes include:

• Crouching too far over at address.

• Lowering the swing center on the downswing (dropping the head, dipping the right knee, or dropping the right shoulder).

• Increasing the angle formed by the left arm and clubshaft during the swing.

• Transferring weight in the downswing from left-to-right rather than right-to-left.

CURES
Crouched address: Bending too far over causes the clubhead arc to reach the ground before the ball. Either grip down on the club to shorten the arc (and shorten the shot's distance), or stand taller at address. Standing more erect creates a larger swing arc, which most likely will increase distance.

For a swing center that moves lower: Even from a good address, it's possible to crouch during the swing. To stop dipping, practice swinging without a club, with the forehead pressed against a wall. This will keep the head from lowering. Duplicate this feeling while on the course.

For increasing the angle between the left arm and clubshaft: The result of arching the wrists during the swing, this is stopped by maintaining constant grip pressure. Also, make sure the arms are hanging straight down from the shoulders at address.

Incorrect weight transfer: Start the backswing in one piece without dipping the left knee or dropping the head. Let the weight flow to the inside of the right foot as the body turns. At the top of the backswing the majority of the body's weight should be over the right foot.

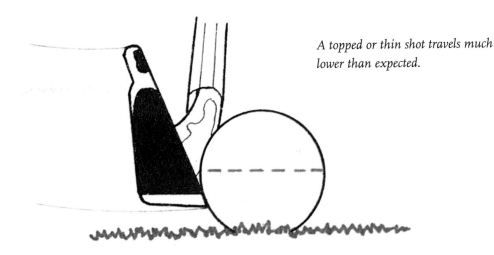

A topped or thin shot travels much lower than expected.

Drills to Cure Chunking

Head Cover Behind Drill: To promote a better weight transfer, stick a tee (without a ball) in the ground. Place a head cover 12 to 18 inches behind it. Make a swing, trying to miss the headcover while clipping the tee. To succeed means making a good weight transfer back to the left foot during the downswing.

Halfway Down Drill: To delay the release until impact, practice a mini-move. Starting at the top of the back-swing, bring the club to halfway down. The arms should be even with the ball, the left arm nearly straight, and the right arm bent. The clubshaft is parallel to the ground, and, most impor-tant, the wrists are hinged and ready to release their stored energy. Repeat 10 times or until the feeling of delay-ing the release becomes automatic.

TOPPING

Aliases: Blade, Skull, Thin, Grass Cutter, Worm Burner

The Result

A shot that travels much lower than expected, usually bounding along the ground.

Why It Happens

The club makes contact above the ball's horizontal equator. Topping often accompanies slicing (particularly when the shots are topped to the left), and is common to beginners, but accomplished players occasionally hit the ball along the ground.

A less severe version of the top is the thin shot, where the club contacts the ball between the ground and the ball's equator. On the professional tours this is a common mistake, but one that the pros don't mind because thin shots usually end up going at least as far as a properly struck shot. In fact, there is a saying on Tour "thin to win" that points out their much greater dis-taste for a chunked shot.

Topping and thinning can be caused by a variety of mistakes, including:
• Standing too far from the ball.
• Positioning the ball too far forward in the stance, so that the club makes con-tact after it has begun to rise on its upward arc.
• Holding the club in the palm of the right hand—instead of the fingers—causing the left arm to shorten and the clubhead to come up at impact.
• Using a grip that is too strong (turned

to the golfer's right), causing the club-face to be severely closed at impact.
- Lifting the head during the downswing, raising the bottom of the swing arc.
- Moving the body laterally right or left during the backswing, then countering with a slide in the other direction during the downswing. This often results in the clubhead hitting the ground too soon; it then bounces up into the top half of the ball.

CURES

Standing too far from the ball: At address, let the arms hang straight down from the shoulders. Standing closer to the ball creates a more upright swing plane and improves the chances for solid impact.

Poor ball position: Set up with the ball slightly behind the left heel for woods and at least an inch inside the left heel for irons.

Poor grip: Make sure the club handle is resting against the fingers of the right hand and that the V formed by the crease between the thumb and forefinger of each hand points somewhere between the right shoulder and the chin. This grip position should eliminate premature closing of the clubface and will preserve the club's full loft through impact.

Excessive head or body movement: Both upward and lateral movement of body or head can be eliminated if the weight is moved correctly to the right side on the backswing. Stand erect at address with only a slight bend at the knees. Keep the right knee bend constant as the weight moves over the right leg dur-

ing the backswing. This will keep the head in place and minimize swaying.

Drills to Cure Topping

Shaft by Face Drill: When the body slides too far toward the target during the downswing, a topped shot is a likely result. This drill promotes a stationary swing center and requires having someone stand in front of the golfer (in the direction the golfer's body is facing) holding a shaft or yardstick against his left ear. If he slides forward on the downswing, he will feel the increasing pressure of the shaft against his head.

Leaning Shaft Drill: To keep the body moving upward during the swing, practice hitting shots with a club leaning against your rear end. The grip should rest on your back pants pocket. Swing back and through, trying to keep the club steady. If you can reach impact without the club falling, you won't top the shot.

SKYING
Alias: Pop-up

The Result
A shot that travels much higher and much shorter than anticipated.

Why It Happens
The club makes contact at the bottom of the ball. Skying is most common when the ball is hit from a tee. The usual cause is picking the club up sharply on the backswing, taking it outside the target line, then chopping down across the ball from outside-to-in. The clubhead goes under the ball and contact is made near the top of the clubhead. Attempting to hit the shot harder than

normal is a common trigger for picking the club up abruptly on the backswing.

Skying can also occur if too much body weight remains on the left foot at the top of the backswing. This causes the left shoulder to dip, resulting in a steep downswing.

Teeing the ball high does not necessarily cause a pop-up. A chronic skier will hit pop-ups no matter how high or low he tees the ball. He'll continue to sky shots even when teeing the ball lower than normal to prevent this shot.

CURES

Don't overswing. Let the clubhead rise gradually during the takeaway. Drag the club along the ground for the first six inches of the takeaway, creating a smooth, controlled tempo.

Trying to hit the ball hard also causes the hands to become overactive. Start the downswing with hip rotation, letting the upper body follow. If the hands move too early on the downswing, the clubhead will pass before impact, creating extra loft and a very high (and short) shot.

If the problem is too much weight on the left side at the top of the backswing, start at address with weight evenly distributed over both feet. Swing the clubhead on as large an arc as possible while maintaining balance.

Drills to Cure Skying

The Air Swing Drill: To combat overswinging, tee a ball and hover the driver directly over it about six inches above the ground. Make a swing, breezing the club over the ball. Concentrate on keeping your head behind the ball throughout the swing. Repeat 10

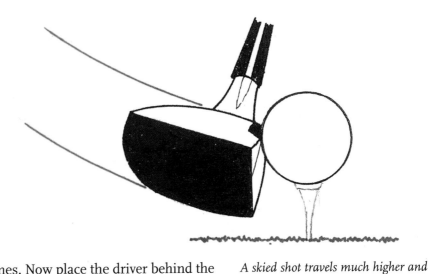

A skied shot travels much higher and shorter than expected.

times. Now place the driver behind the ball, still off the ground. Make a full swing while staring at the back of the ball throughout as you focus on sweeping it off the tee.

Baseball Swing Drill: To shallow out the clubhead angle at impact, practice making baseball swings with a driver. Take a normal address, then straighten up until your back is upright and the clubhead is a couple of feet above the ground. Turn the shoulders on a horizontal plane as if trying to hit a baseball. After repeating 10 times, hit shots trying to repeat the feeling of this level shoulder turn.

SMOTHER
Alias: Dying quail

The Result
A shot that becomes momentarily airborne before diving quickly to the ground, usually heading well left of the target.

Why It Happens
The clubface is extremely closed at impact, usually owing to one of four reasons:

• The grip is too strong (hands rotated too far to the golfer's right).

A smothered shot dives quickly to the ground, usually heading well left of the target.

- The ball position is too far back (toward the right foot) in the stance.
- The head and shoulders move excessively forward (to the left) on the downswing. (This can be related to tilting the shoulders on the backswing.)
- The left hand loosens or moves under the club at the top of the backswing.

CURES

Strong grip: Address the ball with a neutral grip. Place the club in the fingers of both hands—not the palms—and align the V formed by the right thumb and forefinger between the right shoulder and the chin.

Ball position too far back: At address, move the ball toward the target, but no farther forward than off the inside of the left heel.

Head and shoulder movement: This motion usually is a defensive mechanism developed after hitting pushes or slices to the right. Unconsciously, the player compensates by moving the head and shoulders forward and to the left on the downswing. If the player is a pusher/slicer, he should work on curing those afflictions first. Once the push or slice is eliminated, confidence returns and the movement diminishes.

Poor left-hand position at the top of the swing: Make sure the last three fingers of the left hand grip the club firmly. If the left hand has a firm hold, the club will rest properly above the right wrist at the top of the backswing. A loose left hand gets under the club, which results in rotating the left hand forcibly on the downswing, causing a quick closing of the clubface.

Drills to Cure Smothering

Thumbs Under Drill: Stop at the top of the backswing and check that both thumbs are directly under the shaft.

Mirror Drill: To stop body slide, place a six-inch piece of tape vertically on a full-length mirror at the height of your head. Take your normal address, positioning the center of your head even with the tape. Make practice swings, watching the mirror to confirm that the head remains steady until after impact.

SHANK
Aliases: Socket, Hosel

The Result:
A shot that travels sharply to the right (but sometimes goes sharply left, depending upon where the ball contacts the club).

Why It Happens
The shank occurs when the ball is struck on the hosel (where the clubhead attaches to the shaft). It is the most demoralizing and feared shot in golf, because it produces the worst result—a ball shooting off at nearly a right angle to the target—and creates tension, even in skilled players, making it nearly impossible to correct during the round.

Many instructors recommend waiting until after the round, on the practice tee, to work out a solution.

In most cases a shank results from one of these mistakes:
• The swing plane is extremely flat.
• The body straightens up during the swing, flattening the swing plane.
• The shoulders and head move forward and to the golfer's left on the downswing.
• The ball is too far from the body at address.
• The hands and arms roll the clubface open during the backswing.

CURES

Flat swing plane: This often begins with addressing the ball with the shoulders open to the target, then swinging back on an inside plane. This produces a flat swing, which leads to an outward movement of the right shoulder at the start of the downswing. The club is thrown forward, with contact on the hosel. To correct, align the shoulders, hips, and knees square to the target at address and think about swinging the club up and over the right wrist. The more upright the swing path, the more difficult it becomes to shank.

Straightening the body: This flattens the path, increasing the chance of hitting off the hosel. Keep the base of the neck stable during the backswing: It should not move forward, back, up, or down during the swing. Keep the hip bend and right knee flex constant and the swing plane will move on a more upright path.

Shoulder and head movement: This causes the hands and club to move outside the target line on the down-

swing. During the backswing, make a fuller hip and shoulder turn while letting the club set above the right wrist at the top of the backswing. Feel the chin pointing at the ball throughout the downswing until after the ball is struck.

Standing too far from the ball: This is often the first reaction after hitting a shank. But it actually flattens the swing path, increasing the chance of hitting another. At address, stand closer to the ball. During the backswing, lower the left shoulder and raise the right shoulder to promote a more upright swing path.

Rolling the clubface open: Opening the face excessively during the takeaway makes the club "laid off," moving on a very flat path. The club is out of balance and loops outside the target line on the downswing, causing impact between the ball and the hosel. To feel a proper wrist cock—rather than a wrist roll—stand at address, then bend the wrists upward, moving the clubhead up in the air until it can go no higher. This is a good wrist cock. Duplicate this position at the top of the swing and the "laid off" path will be fixed.

Drills to Cure Shanking

Back to the Wall Drill: To eliminate an overly flat swing plane, practice making swings with your rear end approximately six inches from a wall. To avoid hitting the wall with the club, the swing will have to become more upright.

Quiet Hands Drill: To prevent rolling the hands and arms during the backswing, they must remain in the same position relative to the shoulders that they were in at address. Practice by pretending your hands and wrists are

A shank usually travels sharply to the right, but can go left depending exactly where on the hosel contact occurs.

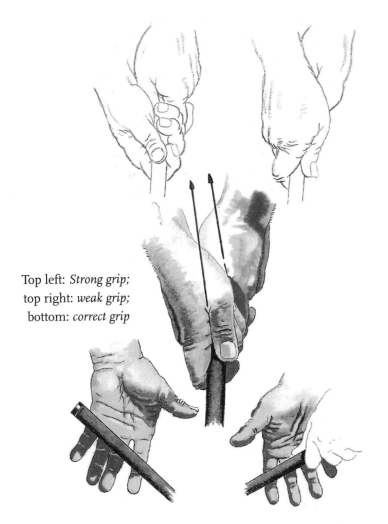

Top left: *Strong grip;*
top right: *weak grip;*
bottom: *correct grip*

tance. When the left hand is turned too far to the golfer's right, it promotes a hook; placed too far to the left, it promotes a slice.

Cure: Place the club so that the grip runs diagonally from the base of the little finger through the middle of the index finger. This position will promote maximum wrist cock. To make your left-hand grip neutral, rotate it until you can see two knuckles on the back of the hand at address or until the V formed by the thumb and forefinger points between the chin and the right shoulder.

Fault: Poor right-hand grip
Problem created: If the right hand holds the club too far into the palm, the golfer will pick up the club on the backswing, destroying the swing's rhythm and narrowing its arc. A right hand rotated too far to the golfer's right at address promotes a hook; too far to the left promotes a slice.

Cure: Run the grip diagonally through the joints of the second and third fingers and across the middle of the index finger. The V formed by the right thumb and forefinger should point between the chin and right shoulder.

Fault: Poor posture
Problem created: Stooping from the waist, hunching the back, or overly flexing or straightening the legs make a fluid swing and big clubhead arc nearly impossible. Poor posture ruins the swing's balance and costs distance and accuracy.

Cure: In the set-up, flex the knees just enough to feel the body's weight mov-

in a plaster cast until they reach waist high on the backswing, then simply cock the wrists straight up until the backswing is complete. Done correctly, the club will feel very light and the swing path will become more upright.

ROGUE'S GALLERY

Here are 25 common swing errors, the unwanted shots they cause, and their corrections.

ADDRESS

Fault: Poor left-hand grip
Problem created: When the club is held too far in the palm rather than the fingers, the wrists can't hinge on the backswing, resulting in a loss of dis-

ing over the arches of both feet. Let your rear end stick out to create a counterbalance and keep the lower back straight. Keep your chin up, let the arms rest lightly against your chest, and tilt your left shoulder slightly up and your right shoulder slightly down.

Fault: Misaligned clubface

Problem created: When the clubface points left of the intended target, the shot is likely to be pulled or hooked. When the clubface points right of the target, the shot is likely to be pushed or sliced.

Cure: To check that the clubface is square at address, hold the club in front of you at waist height. Look to see that the leading edge is exactly vertical. Lower the club to the ground and the clubface will be pointing at a right angle to your stance.

Fault: Poor ball position

Problem created: Playing the ball toward the back foot promotes a hook or a push (depending upon clubhead path and alignment at impact). Playing the ball toward the front foot promotes a slice or a pull.

Cure: The general guidelines for ball position are opposite the instep of the front foot for woods; approximately two ball-widths behind that point for irons. Better players must usually guard against moving the ball too far back; higher handicappers must guard against playing the ball too far forward. For a solid iron play, ball position should promote a descending blow; with woods, you want a slightly ascending arc at impact.

Poor posture and its correction

Fault: Stance too wide

Problem created: This is a common mistake among high handicappers, inhibiting maximum body rotation and limiting weight transfer. As a result, there is no coordination between the upper and lower body, leading to a herky-jerky swing and inconsistent contact.

Cure: The stance should be wide enough to create a stable base and, at the same time, narrow enough to allow for maximum weight shift and

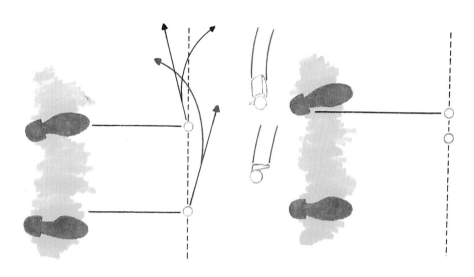

Poor ball position and its correction

body rotation. Normally this is best accomplished when the heels are approximately the width of your shoulders for the woods and long irons, then gradually closer together for the shorter irons and wedges.

Fault: Stance too narrow
Problem created: A narrow stance promotes a loss of balance and loose, whippy upper-body rotation during the backswing that can turn into an overswing. The result is a loss of accuracy.

Cure: Follow the corrections outlined above for "Stance too wide."

Fault: Excess tension
Problem created: When the muscles tighten, the swing's rhythm is ruined before the club starts moving away from the ball. Tight muscles also are slow muscles, which means tension reduces distance and the lack of rhythm reduces accuracy.

Cure: At address, keep a firm grip on the club but relax the arms. (Some players refer to this as "soft arms.") If the arms are relaxed, you should be able to feel the weight of the clubhead at address while maintaining a firm grasp of the club.

BACKSWING

Fault: Picking the club up abruptly
Problem created: Picking the club up rather than letting it swing gradually to the top of the backswing means the hands are too active. This creates a narrow, power-robbing swing arc and a steep downswing.

Cure: Start the backswing by turning the triangle formed by the arms and

---

DIFFERENT STROKES

WHY SLICES SOAR AND HOOKS DUCK

Anyone who plays golf has noticed that curving shots have different trajectories: Hooks tend to fly lower and roll significant distances after landing; slices fly higher and stop more quickly after landing.

According to *Search for the Perfect Swing*, by Cochran and Stobbs, the answer lies in the asymmetry of the golf swing and the club. The shaft comes into the head at about a 55-degree angle to the ground, and the golfer swings the clubhead along a path inclined from 45 to 60 degrees. With these conditions, turning the face of the club to the golfer's right (for a right-hander) increases the loft, increases the launch angle, and increases backspin.

Exactly the opposite conditions occur on a hook. Turning the face to the left of the target reduces the effective loft at impact, creates a lower launch angle, and reduces the amount of backspin applied to the ball.

shoulders away from the ball in one smooth motion. Keep the triangle intact until the hands pass the back leg. This is referred to as a "one-piece takeaway."

Fault: Pulling the club too far inside
Problem created: This usually results in a very flat swing path or lifting the arms in an attempt to get the club to the top. The result is a poor body turn or an out-to-in loop on the downswing that produces a pull or a slice.

Cure: During the takeaway, don't let the clubhead come inside the hands until the clubshaft is past parallel to the ground. It may help to think about starting the swing with the butt end of the club rather than the clubhead.

Fault: Closing the clubface
Problem created: If the clubface rotates closed during the backswing, compensations must be made on the downswing to square it by impact. But usually the clubface remains closed and, depending upon the path, the ball is pulled or hooked.

Cure: Use a neutral grip (refer to earlier grip items), then concentrate on rotating the clubface with the body turn. Don't let the hands turn the face faster or slower than the body movement.

Fault: "Laid-off" backswing
Problem created: "Laying the club off" means the clubhead path has become too flat, causing inconsistent club-to-ball contact. Swinging the hands around the body, standing too far from the ball at address, or collapsing the left wrist during the backswing are all possible causes.

Too wide/narrow stance and its correction

Picking the club up abruptly and its correction

Pulling the club inside and its correction

Laid-off backswing and its correction

Reverse weight shift and its correction

Cure: Check the club's path when the arms reach parallel to the ground on the backswing. In this position, the grip should be at a spot a couple of inches inside the target line (behind the ball).

TOP OF SWING

Fault: Reverse weight shift
Problem created: When the weight stays over the left side at the top of the swing—usually the result of a player's efforts to keep his head down and right arm straight—the downswing loses power. Depending upon the hand action, the result is a big hook or slice.

Cure: Allow the head to rotate to the right as the club swings back, with the left shoulder turning beneath the chin. This encourages the body's weight to move over the inside of the right foot at the top of the backswing. At this point, the chest should be directly over the right knee.

Fault: Incomplete body turn
Problem created: If the hips and shoulders are restricted from making a full turn away from the ball, the arms become too active and lift the club to the top. Without a full body coil, power is reduced and the swing's rhythm is ruined.

Cure: Practice dragging the clubhead away from the ball along the grass for the first six inches to create the largest backswing arc possible. Allow the spine to coil so the left knee points inward and the body's weight is set over the inside of the right foot at the top.

Fault: Right-side sway
Problem created: Letting body weight sway to the outside of the right foot limits

upper-body turn and causes inconsistent contact, since the body must sway back to the left to meet the ball.

Cure: Focus on retaining the flex established in the right knee from address to the top of the backswing. The left knee should move back toward the right knee during the backswing rather than jutting out toward the ball.

Fault: Overswinging

Problem created: Overswinging usually occurs when the left arm breaks down at the top of the backswing, the left hand grip becomes loose, or the swing is too quick.

Cure: At the top, the right elbow should form a right angle, with the upper portion of the right arm parallel to the ground. In this position, the left arm won't bend and the grip will remain firm.

Fault: Clubhead path too flat

Problem created: A very flat clubhead path usually begins with a too upright posture. The shoulders rotate on a shallow plane and bring the arms across the chest. The clubhead then returns to the ball on a shallow, inside track, leading to heavy or thin contact and a substantial loss of power.

Cure: The angle of the spine at address determines the overall path of the swing. It is the axis around which the shoulders turn. In front of a mirror, swing to the top of your backswing. If your swing is on the proper path, the arms will be at a 90-degree angle to the spine.

Fault: Clubhead path too upright

Problem created: A very upright clubhead path usually begins with a bent-

Right-side sway and its correction

Overswinging and its correction

Overly flat plane, overly upright plane and correction

Not enough downswing weight transfer and its correction

Too much downswing weight transfer and its correction

over posture. The shoulders tilt rather than turn, bringing the arms above the head. The resulting downswing path is nearly vertical, often outside-to-in across the target line. The resulting shots include skies, chunks, pulls, or slices.

Cure: Stand more erect at address. Check in a mirror that your arms at a 90-degree angle to the spine at the top of the backswing.

DOWNSWING

Fault: Premature release ("Hitting from the top")

Problem created: When the change of direction at the top of the backswing occurs too quickly, the hands often take over and uncock immediately to start the downswing. The hands jerk toward the ball, causing a steep swing that approaches the ball from outside the target line. The result is a big pull or slice, depending upon clubface direction at impact.

Cure: Initiate the downswing with the lower body moving toward the target; the arms and hands follow the lower body's lead. Focus on a smooth rhythm throughout the swing. The hands should feel as if they are falling with gravity to begin the downswing.

Fault: Insufficient weight transfer

Problem created: If the body weight remains over the back foot at impact, the lower body becomes rigid. Clubhead speed is reduced, and the hands scoop at the ball, resulting in weak blocks and slices.

Cure: Think about moving the right knee toward the left so they touch when the club meets the ball. In reality they won't, but the sensation of getting the right leg moving left early in the downswing will help move the body's weight back to the left side, insuring maximum clubhead speed through impact.

Fault: Excessive weight transfer

Problem created: When the body's weight moves too aggressively to the left side, the upper body slides toward the target. The swing's balance is upset, and the arms and hands must try to catch up to the lower body. When they don't, the clubface is open to the target, causing a slice. After fighting the problem for a while, the arms and hands often overcompensate, creating hooks. Overactive legs also can cause a "reverse C" finish, with the back arched. This is hard on the spine and can cause back injury.

Cure: Think of the lower body as a stable base for the arm swing. Instead of letting the legs slide laterally during the downswing, firm up the left side through impact and into the follow-through. Visualize a wall placed just outside your front foot and try to finish with your entire body flat against this wall. The left side must be firm enough to support the upper body's rotation through impact. The result is more solid contact and a finish with the back nearly vertical.

Fault: Casting or early release

Problem created: While better golfers retain the angle created between the clubshaft and the left forearm until the last moment before impact, poor players usually release this angle on the downswing. The result is a substantial

DIFFERENT STROKES

THE DISTANCE EFFECT OF OFF-CENTER CONTACT

At impact, the ball strongly resists the clubhead's attempt to launch it at speeds up to 150 miles per hour. This resistance is strong enough to flatten the ball against the clubface. With a driver, the pressure between ball and club exceeds 1,000 pounds per square inch.

When this force is applied to the middle of the clubface, the clubhead will slow up substantially without twisting. This is the impact condition of a perfectly struck golf shot when maximum distance is obtained.

But when the contact is more toward the toe, heel, top, or bottom of the clubface, the impact not only slows *the* club, but causes it to twist toward the point of impact. Any shot hit off-center wastes power by leaving the clubface with less initial speed than a shot struck on the center of the clubface.

While the distance lost varies by club and player, tests conducted in the 1960s for Cochran and Stobbs's *Search for the Perfect Swing* showed that a scratch golfer using wooden clubs and forged irons, contacting the ball 1/4 inch toward the toe or heel, loses 3 yards; 1/2 inch toward the toe or heel costs 12 yards; and 3/4 inch nearer the toe or heel deducts 30 yards.

Testing conducted by Titleist in the mid-1990s produced percentages of overall distance lost with a perimeter-weighted driver, 3-, 5-, and 8-iron. The test results were that contact 3/8 inch higher than the center of the face cost 2–4 percent of the shot's overall distance. A shot hit 3/4 inch low cost 4–5 percent. For heel shots 3/4 inch from center, deduct 3–4 percent; 3/4 inch toe shots, deduct 6 percent.

Titleist's tests with drivers found that a hit 1 inch closer to the heel reduced overall distance by 14 percent. A 1-inch toe hit cost 7.5 percent. Contact 1/2 inch high cost only 2 percent, while contact 1/2 inch low cost 9 percent.

Casting from the top and its correction

Excessive head movement and its correction

loss of power and a scooping action at impact.

Cure: The simplest and most natural way to keep this angle intact is to pretend you're chopping down a tree with your club. When the goal is to produce a powerful blow, you control the "ax" with the larger muscles in the back and legs rather than the smaller muscles of the arms and hands. You will also find that you hold the angle between the ax handle and the left forearm.

Fault: Loss of balance

Problem created: Balance is critical to consistent ballstriking. Most balance problems are in the lower body. The hips, knees, or feet become overactive, and the resulting severe weight shift moves the body's center of gravity. The intended swing path is changed, producing inconsistent contact.

Cure: During the swing, maintain the distance between the knees until just before impact. On the downswing, keep the right hip, knee, and foot from moving toward the target. This forces the lower body to work as a stable base under the swinging arms.

Fault: Excessive head movement

Problem created: The head must move during the swing to facilitate a good weight transfer, but not a lot. A couple of inches to the right on the backswing, or an inch or two up and down before impact is fine. But excessive motion in any direction moves the swing's center and often causes fat or thin shots.

Cure: A steady head is the result of a steady spine angle during the swing. To feel a steady spine, practice making swings (without a club) first with your head propping a pillow against a wall, then with your butt against the wall. You should feel the spine angle remaining constant until after the point where impact would have occurred.

Fault: Poor tempo

Problem created: Tempo is the body's pace during the swing. When it becomes too fast or slow, the proper sequence of motion throughout the swing (rhythm) is thrown off. There is no one proper tempo; it varies based on individual preference and personality. When you are swinging well, no doubt you are using your preferred tempo.

Cure: A swing that is too fast or slow usually is the result of a herky-jerky start. Don't worry about taking the club away from the ball slowly. Instead, think about swinging the club smoothly on the backswing. Try a backswing trigger, a small physical motion that triggers the body to start the swing. It may be a gentle squeeze with the left hand, a waggle of the club, or a slight inward press of the right knee. Whatever small motion gets the swing going is fine.

WORDS OF WISDOM

The most important consideration of all is to get firmly registered on the player's mind a correct mental pattern of the swing.

Jim Barnes

You can talk to a slice, but a hook won't listen.

Lee Trevino

The fault with much of the golf teaching of today is that the teacher tries to eradicate specific faults by issuing specific instructions… the good tip system. This is fatal, mainly because it is no system at all but just a conglomeration of golf patent medicines.

Percy Boomer

In golf, when we hit a foul ball, we got to go out and play it.

Sam Snead to baseball great Ted Williams

If I had to boil down my entire philosophy of golf instruction to one simple piece of advice, this would be it: Let ball flight be your teacher.

John Jacobs

The shank is the skeleton in golf's closet.

Dai Rees

Golf is a game requiring an enormous amount of thought, and unless the player can always ascertain exactly what is the reason for his faults and what is the reason for his method of remedying them he will never make much progress.

James Braid

Without recognizing the scientific basis of a successful swing, it is impossible for anyone to distinguish essentials from individual mannerisms.

Alex Morrison

I think it is safe to say that all good golfers have fought a hook at one time or other.

Johnny Revolta

CHAPTER SIX

THE SHORT GAME

AMATEURS THINK GOLF SUCCESS CAN BE SUMMED UP IN SIX WORDS: "Drive for show, putt for dough." But the pros know where the money is. More than 50 years ago, Tommy Armour said, "The pros master the short game because they want the money." In the last 15 years, Dave Pelz statistically studied the pros' games and proved that the skill most closely correlated with money earnings was the wedge game. Not driving, not putting, but the ability to stick the ball close to the hole from inside 100 yards.

The short game usually refers to four skills: pitching, chipping, sand play, and putting. The last two are covered in later chapters, leaving the two shots that Byron Nelson called the "most valuable" in the game.

Many golfers do not understand the difference between chipping and pitching, and while there is no universally accepted set of definitions, here is a simple rule of thumb: If the ball spends more time in the air than on the ground, it is a pitch shot; if it spends more time rolling than flying, it is a chip. Therefore, Tom Watson's shot from the long greenside rough at the 17th hole during the 1982 U.S. Open at Pebble Beach was a chip, despite the fact that the ball flew fairly high: What's important is that it dropped quickly on to the green and rolled a longer distance before falling into the hole.

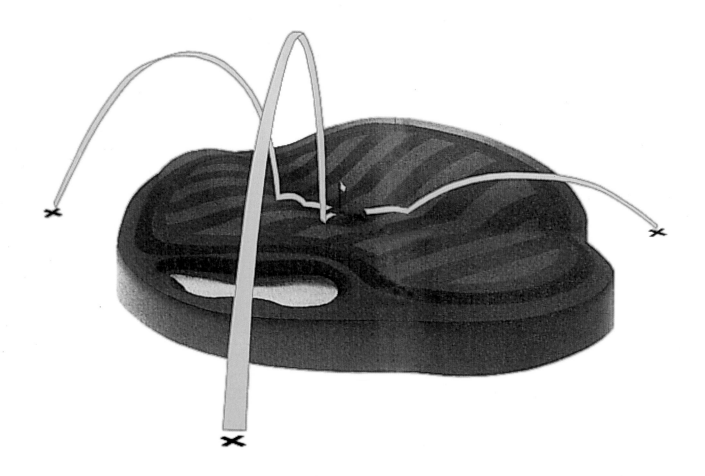

A good short game gives the golfer options near the green: Play it high so it drops and stops; run it in low; spin it back or let it roll a long way; play the break or carry the break, and so on. A good short game also is the best indicator of success on the professional Tours.

Another critical difference is that the chip was being played hundreds of years before the pitch was developed. On the early Scottish golf courses it was almost impossible to tell where the fairway ended and the putting surface began. But at some point the golfer was too close to make a full swing, too far away to putt, and the ground up to the hole too bumpy and unpredictable to allow for rolling the ball. Furthermore, until the end of the nineteenth century, most greens were too hard to accept a high-lofted shot; it would bounce hard and long. So players had to be adept at the low "run-up" shot, which also had the advantage of staying below the wind that was a nearly constant presence on the original seaside links. The run-up is the original chip.

The pitch did not evolve until the end of the nineteenth century, when a number of factors came together. First, greens began to receive maintenance and watering, a minimal amount but enough to make them softer and more receptive to lofted shots. Also at this time, clubs with metal heads began replacing those of wood; it was easier to shape metal with the loft necessary to shoot the ball high in the air and make it stop quickly upon landing. Simultaneously, improvements in golf balls—notably the deliberate use of dimples and brambles on the cover—gave them more aerodynamic lift.

Finally, at the turn of the century the game came to the United States, where most of the land is far from the sea. The inland courses built here did not have weather to confound players, so architects found other ways to "protect" par, notably by making greens

more inaccessible, raising them or tucking them behind bunkers and water hazards. Suddenly, hitting and holding a green meant either throwing the ball in from on high or sending it lower but with a new element—backspin.

A century later, the common wisdom remains that Europeans are more proficient than Americans at weather-resistant pitch-and-runs, "bump" shots, and other low approaches. Americans, for their part, are more successful at "target golf," launching the ball and making it stick on the green.

Golfers today have a wide selection of weapons for attacking the green, their choice dependent on the situation and conditions. One hundred years ago, the sentiment was very different. "It is hardly necessary to state," wrote H. J. Whigham in 1897, "that it is advisable, as far as possible, to employ only one club for all the approach shots within a hundred yards of the hole."

The first club used for bumping the ball in was the baffing spoon, or baffy, from the Scottish word for "a blow made with something soft." The baffy was the shortest, stiffest, and most lofted club in the early golfer's arsenal, making it well suited to a shorter, more precise shot that rose just a few feet off the ground. As soon as iron clubs came into use in the late 1800s, the baffy was replaced by the "lofter," or lofting iron, then the mashie and mashie-niblick, all shorter, iron-headed clubs with enough loft to get the ball into the air.

On the early British courses, like Muirfield in Scotland, flat, open areas around large greens put a premium on the short game.

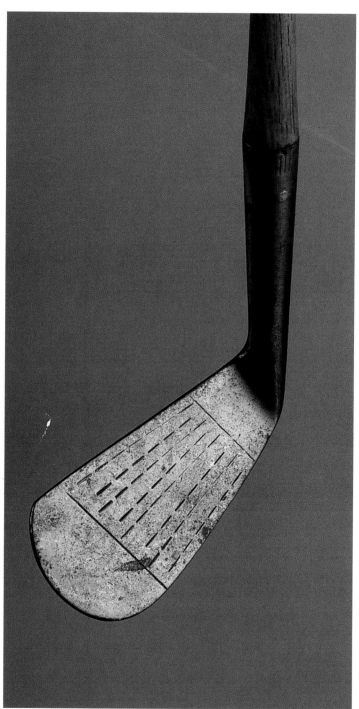

Left: *The first chipping club probably was the wooden-headed baffing, or baffy, spoon. Short, stiff, and well lofted (for its time), it was effective hitting short, accurate shots.*

Right: *As metal replaced wood, it became easier to build clubs for specific purposes. By the turn of the century, the niblick was the short-game club of choice, available with a choice of loft to suit any situation.*

The refinement of the mashie helped spur the development of the short game. According to Robert Browning's *A History of Golf*, the mashie was the most lofted club in the normal set: Depending on whom you believe, it was somewhere between a modern 5- and 7-iron. In 1890, Horace Hutchinson wrote, "The mashy [*sic*] may be said to be a hybrid growth. But a few years ago it was almost unknown. Now its use is universal."

For many, the mashie was the chipping tool of choice for decades, "clearly the club to use for such a simple emergency," wrote Roger Wethered in 1931. Bobby Jones, stating a more modern viewpoint, believed it was but one choice: Writing well after his competitive days were done, he said, "I used anything from a three-iron to a nine-iron for shots that could properly be called chip shots."

The mashie was also the first pitching club. Findlay Douglas, 1898 U.S. Amateur champion, wrote a year after his victory that this club "was only intended to be used in approaching a hole which was up close behind a hazard. In this case, the ball had to be pitched a certain distance, and yet not run off upon falling, as it would do if played with an 'iron.'" That same year, Willie Tucker, a golf instructor at America's seminal golf club, St. Andrew's, wrote, "The mashie will pitch a ball high, so that it will stay within a few feet of where it falls, allowing better judgment when you have a bunker, rough ground, or a hazard quite close to the green, and a hazard beyond the hole."

Within a few years, the mashie was replaced by the restyled niblick. Once

Perhaps the most dramatic chip of all time was Larry Mize's 35-yard hole-out on the second hole of a sudden-death play-off to win the 1987 Masters. Mize's shot never got as high off the ground as he did.

Bobby Jones's chipping method was the epitome of perfect balance and smooth, unhurried motion.

the name given to a wooden-headed trouble club, the turn-of-the-century niblick was metal and had as much loft as today's 9-iron. As golfers realized the importance of sticking the ball close, niblicks appeared in all shapes and sizes, with a choice of lofts, and with assigned applications for rough, bunkers, and other hazards. "Pitching niblicks" were offered for sale by the late 1920s, and in 1934, a year after Gene Sarazen's R99 sand wedge reached the market, Wilson Sporting Goods produced the companion R9 Sarazen pitching iron: "For distance up to sixty yards," said the catalogue, "it is ideal."

The short game no longer requires dedicated clubs. Although a few stalwarts use a single club when chipping, the prevailing sentiment in golf instruction—and the preference of most Tour professionals—is to chip with whichever iron best handles the length of the shot and the terrain to be carried. The pitching clubs today include all the short irons—usually 9-iron to most lofted wedge—with the desired distance in the air the determining factor.

From the baffy to the modern investment-cast iron, the clubs used for chipping have changed dramatically. The method of wielding them, however, has not. It seems there are only a limited number of ways to hit the ball consistently low with control.

In *The Complete Golfer,* first published in 1905, Harry Vardon said that "the feet and body are further in front" of the ball and the hands farther down the grip. His stroke was straight-back and straight-through, with the swing stopping "when the shaft of the club is pointing a little to the left of the direction of the ball that is speeding onwards, the blade being on a level with the hands." That is not too different from what is taught today.

However, Vardon counseled turning the right hand over the left, saying, "This is the kind of stroke that the skilful golfer loves most, for few others afford him such a test of calculation and judgment." Closing the clubface through impact would keep the ball lower and produce more roll. But it demanded precise touch and timing, making it better suited to the better player.

There was a little more variation in pitching technique. In *Travers' Golf Book* (1913), four-time U.S. Amateur champion Jerome Travers suggested playing the ball off the front heel, maintaining a firm grip, taking the club straight up and down with the wrists and forearms, and keeping the rest of the body "rigid except for a slight turning of the shoulders in the back swing." Travers finished his lesson with two sentences that could appear in a present-day instruction manual: "Many players make the mistake of trying to assist the ball to rise, instead of letting the lofted face of the mashie accomplish the desired result. The important things to remember when playing the mashie are to keep the body and head still, and to follow through well and take turf."

Bobby Jones was one of the great short-game practitioners of his, or any, day. In *Golf Secrets of the Masters,* Scott and Cousins described him as "a very good player of short approaches for the very reason that he was a good golfer in other respects—perfect balance. His feet were so close together for chip shots that they almost touched, yet the only sign of movement below the waist was a very slight twist and bend of the knees as the clubhead came on to the ball." In his own book, Jones described his pitching swing as "leisurely, of ample length, and with a perceptible crispness as the ball is struck." Today, the only difference might be that the swing would be a bit less leisurely, not as long going back: In Jones's era, the wooden-shafted clubs and rougher course conditions would have demanded a little more oomph on the shorter shots.

A final thought from Jones, one that golfers should keep in mind when reading the following instruction and, more important, when setting up to a short shot on the course: "In playing a pitch, chip, or shot from a bunker near the green, there is one significant difference to be noted between the method of the expert player and that of the duffer; in one case, the swing is amply long, smooth, and unhurried; in the other, it is short and jerky, because the club has not been swung back far enough."

Remember, it is called the short game, not the short swing.

PREVAILING WISDOM

A firm advocate of firm wrists in both chipping and pitching, Ken Venturi went so far as to put his hands and arms in casts for a cover of GOLF Magazine.

CHIPPING

Making an effective chipping stroke is fairly simple as long as you meet the ball with a descending blow. Nothing is more important than dropping the clubhead down, being sure, as Dave Pelz puts it, "to hit the little ball before the big ball [the earth]."

Jack Burke, winner of the 1956 Masters and PGA and a very influential teacher, explained the importance of the descending blow when he described the chip as "in essence, a billiard shot. I don't care if the pin is ten feet away or a hundred, the ball still must be hit down upon. This imparts spin to the ball, and spin means control. Without a downward blow you are not taking advantage of the loft, which is built into each iron for a purpose."

Yet many golfers do not trust either their own skills or the clubface to lift the ball off the ground, so they try scooping, which usually results in hitting the ground behind the ball first. These "fat" chips barely move at all, which means the next shot usually is either another chip or a very long putt. It cannot be emphasized enough that everything about the set-up and motion of chipping must promote hitting down on the ball.

THE GRIP

Place your hands as far down the grip—close to the shaft—as possible. This maximizes your feel for the clubhead while encouraging a more upright, and therefore descending, swing. Place the club in the fingers of your right hand, the right palm facing the target. The last three fingers of your left hand should hold the club a bit firmer than the others, to keep the clubface from turning over through impact.

Most golfers use either their normal full-swing grip (overlap, interlock, 10-finger) or their putting grip. The choice is yours; experiment to see which feels better and is more suited to producing a downward blow.

One of the most arresting images ever to appear on the cover of *GOLF Magazine* was Ken Venturi with his hands, wrists, and forearms in plaster casts. The point Venturi was making was to freeze the wrists when chipping, counteracting the tendency to get "flippy" and try helping the ball in the air. This is a powerful image to conjure up if your chips are feeling wristy. (Just remember that putting wrists in a cast does not mean creating unwanted tension; they should be firm, not stiff.)

TWO MORE CHIP GRIPS

Phil Rodgers, a former Tour player who gained recognition in the early 1980s for working with Jack Nicklaus on his short game, proposes an alternative chipping grip borrowed from a short-game wizard of the 1930s, Paul "Little Poison" Runyan. Both Rodgers and Runyan set the hands in opposition, each restraining the other from moving, with the wrists hinged so the forearms are at right angles. That position is maintained throughout the stroke.

Just before placing all 10 fingers well down the grip, Rodgers turns the right hand one-quarter turn away from the target while rotating the left one-quarter turn toward the target. The tips of the last three fingers of each hand should form a straight line along the top of the handle. Grip pressure should be firm enough for the hands and wrists to feel locked in place during the stroke.

Teacher Jim McLean used to give students a good feel for solid chipping by making them practice with the club held "cross-handed"—left (forward) hand below the right (trailing). According to McLean, this method eliminates unwanted cupping of the left wrist while keeping the right wrist properly cocked. He noticed that many of his students were using the practice grip on the course with success, so he began prescribing it for real play. It is especially good for golfers who have trouble getting the ball in the air, or whose chips tend to run left.

Right: *In chipping as in putting, a "cross-handed" grip—left hand below the right—can help cure a most destructive fault: letting the left wrist break down during the swing.*

Below: *Teaching pro Phil Rodgers taught Jack Nicklaus a chipping method he adopted from old-timer Paul Runyan. Sharply hinging the wrists keeps the hands from moving on their own; the sharp wrist break is maintained throughout the stroke.*

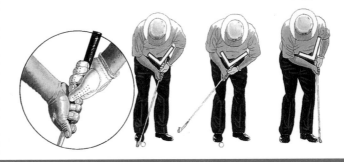

Near left: *For accurate, controlled chipping, the clubface should be square to the target. Opening and closing the face increases sidespin, making shots react erratically. Chart distances show what happens to the same stroke with the clubface square, 20 degrees open, and 20 degrees closed.*

Far left: *Playing the ball back in the stance assures crisp contact—hitting the ball before the ground. It also lowers ball flight, promoting more predictable roll. However, as this chart shows, it has little effect on overall distance.*

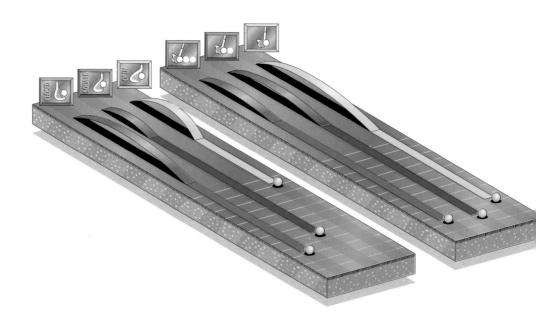

Good chipping demands good feel. Seve Ballesteros, one of the game's great short-game players, waves his right hand back and forth while sizing up a shot to help him gauge just how much stroke is necessary.

THE SET-UP

Stand relatively tall and close to the ball. As in putting, you want to have the sensation that your eyes are directly over the ball. Let your arms hang naturally and relaxed.

Take a very narrow stance, the heels about six inches apart, and shift your body weight so it favors the left (front) side. Aim your body—shoulders, hips, knees, feet—square or slightly open to the target line: This is another matter of personal preference, with many golfers preferring to be slightly open, as it improves their view down the line and seems to promote a more flowing stroke.

Don't sole the club flush on the ground: It could snag on a clump of grass going back or force you to get too wristy in the takeaway. Instead, hold the club slightly off the ground to preserve the feel for the clubhead in your hands. Or angle the clubhead so only the toe touches the ground: The shaft becomes more vertical, like a putter, and your wrists lock into position so you make a smooth, arms-and-shoulders stroke.

No matter which club you use, for the best combination of distance and accuracy Dave Pelz has proven that the clubface should be square to the target line. Opening and closing the face creates sidespin that kicks the ball off-line and out of control. Opening the face can be especially harmful because it creates higher shots with more backspin that may bounce erratically on the green.

Pelz's research also proves that the most effective ball position is well back in the stance, on line with the right (back) ankle. This assures hitting the ball before the ground, producing solid contact and no fat shots. However, the farther back the ball begins, the lower its flight: This is good because the ball won't bounce too erratically upon hitting the green; it also means you must take a club with enough loft to be sure of carrying whatever grass or other obstacle is between the ball and the green.

Experiment with ball position, but don't place the ball farther forward than the middle of the stance. Varying position influences loft and roll—the farther forward the ball begins, the higher it flies, with more air time and less roll—while overall distance remains roughly the same.

Another variable to consider when sizing up a chip is the lie. As the ball gets deeper in long grass, position it farther back in your stance: You want to avoid letting too much grass get between the clubface and ball at impact, minimizing your control of the shot. When the ball sits on top of long grass, take a less-lofted club and run the ball up rather than taking a lofted club and trying to hit a delicate, difficult flop shot.

DIFFERENT STROKES

ONE CLUB OR MANY?

Without a doubt, the most commonly asked question about chipping is, "Do I use one club or several?" There is no one answer for every golfer; evidence supports both opinions.

Jack Nicklaus heads the "one club" school. He uses a sand wedge on all chips except those that require unusually long roll. Nicklaus says he prefers a single club because he "can become more expert and confident in an hour's practice with one club than by giving. . . six clubs 10 minutes practice apiece."

Leading the "many" camp is the late Bobby Jones, who, as noted earlier, used anything from a 3- to a 9-iron. He said, "it has been found far simpler to change a club than a swing. Varying lofts . . . in very short approaches [removes] the need for clever little cuts and delicate backspin shots that introduce so much difficulty."

"Club selection is the critical factor in chipping success," says Raymond Floyd, one of the game's best chippers. "I use as many clubs as are necessary, everything from the 4-iron to the sand wedge . . . . Club selection and length of the stroke will vary with your distance from the green, the location of the hole on the putting surface, and the speed of the green."

Research conducted by Dave Pelz, GOLF Magazine's Short Game and Technical Consultant, found that the lower the angle a chip lands on the green, the straighter it will bounce and the tighter the dispersion pattern around the target. This supports the idea of using many clubs, choosing the one in any situation that will provide the lowest possible trajectory while still landing the ball safely on the green.

Chipping with many clubs also means practicing with many clubs to know how each will perform. As you practice from the wedges down through the mid-irons, note the height, carry distance, roll, and overall distance created by each club so you can choose the best one in each situation.

Is one method right and the other wrong? Not necessarily, although "many" is more widely taught today. Still, most instructors recommend using whichever method gives you a more positive attitude and confidence. Because if you believe you're a better chipper using one method instead of the other, you probably are.

Jack Nicklaus is nearly alone in his reliance on a single club for chipping. He feels specializing with the sand wedge makes him more expert with one club than he could become with half a dozen.

The chip shot. Begin with the hands ahead of the ball, so they lead the club-head through impact, producing a downward blow. Maintain the triangle formed by the arms and shoulders, and accelerate through impact. The follow-through should be at least as long as the backswing.

No matter what club and shot you choose, test your choices by waggling a few times while staring at the line. Try to see and feel the shot with the club in your hands; if you can't, try another club. Watch Seve Ballesteros sizing up a chip and you'll see he waves his right hand back and forth several times, trying to get the feel for the shot.

THE STROKE

Keeping the wrists firm, swing the clubhead back with your arms; the club should arc inward and upward. Don't rush the swing or make it too short; you need enough backswing to create momentum for an accelerating downswing and crisp contact.

Every good chipper—Tom Watson, Raymond Floyd, Seve Ballesteros—begins with his hands ahead of the ball and then lets them lead the clubhead through impact. This is one more way to create a descending blow and keep the wrists quiet while helping the clubhead accelerate through impact.

While most of the work is being done by the arms, the lower body is contributing. The knees move slightly toward the target in response to the natural acceleration of the downswing. But don't let the legs get too active; their movement should be gentle. If you still feel too stiff from the hips down, rotate your right knee toward the target as the club swings down.

Be sure to finish the swing, with the club continuing well out in front of the body. The follow-through should be longer than the backswing to ensure acceleration through the ball. Claude Harmon was the rare teacher

who wanted the through-swing to be shorter than the backswing, which created a lower, punched chip.

STRATEGY

Where to Land the Ball. Although the hole is your ultimate goal, it is not your target when chipping. A simpler, more dependable idea is to pick a spot on the green for the ball to land and envision it rolling the rest of the way. Thinking "spot" instead of "hole" reduces tension, allowing you to make a better swing. Tom Watson says "spot-chipping" is the "best way to develop feel and consistency."

When picking a landing spot, give yourself a healthy margin for error: Trying to drop the ball one inch onto

---

DIFFERENT STROKES

"CLUB, CARRY, ROLL"

In *GOLF Magazine*, Phil Rodgers proposed a way to figure how much carry and roll each club creates:

"In chipping, your major concern should be distance. If you take three from the edge, it's usually because you hit the shot too far or too short. With that in mind, my method of chipping is based on what I call 'the rules.'

"'The rules relate to the amount of carry and roll you get when chipping with various clubs. The rules are:

CLUB	CARRY	ROLL
Pitching Wedge	1 part	2 parts
9-iron	1 part	3 parts
8-iron	1 part	4 parts
7-iron	1 part	5 parts
6-iron	1 part	6 parts

"So, for example, if you're chipping with a pitching wedge and you carry the ball five feet, the ball will roll 10 feet for a total of 15 feet. These distance are approximations, but the carry versus roll ratios are accurate."

Note: Rodgers said these ratios apply only when using his chipping grip (see page 137), with the wrists out of the stroke. They should hold true with any wristless chipping.

the green is difficult, nerve-wracking, and unnecessary. Aim to land it two to three feet onto the green, so if you hit a little short, the ball will still finish on the putting surface. Floyd's words are gospel: "Land the ball safely on the green in all cases."

Phil Rodgers sees an imaginary, six-foot-long "landing strip" that begins six inches onto the green and is broken into three two-foot sections. With proper club selection, landing the ball in the two-foot section closest to the edge of the green will get the ball close to, but short of, the hole; landing in the middle section will roll the ball snug to the pin; landing a little farther onto the green means the ball will get to the pin, and probably a foot or two past.

If your landing spot will be on a hump in the green, plan another shot, with another club, to be sure of hitting a flat area. Landing the ball on a hump magnifies any error you might make in executing the shot: Hit short and you'll hit the upslope of the hump, making the ball bounce up at twice the angle of the slope, slowing it down considerably, so it finishes well short of the hole; hit long and the ball hits on the far side of the hump, so it kicks forward at twice the angle of the downslope, sending it well past the hole.

However, if you can plan a shot that will land in the middle of a hollow, or dip, in the green, go for it! If you land short, the downslope kicks the ball forward, making up for your lack of carry. Hit a little too long and you'll catch the upslope on the far side of the hollow, slowing its progress. Total distance for all three shots—landing in the middle, short, or long in the dip—will be about

the same, providing the largest possible margin for error.

GRAIN

One factor many golfers overlook is the grain of the green, the direction in which the grass is growing. They don't realize that on certain grasses common in the United States, grain can affect the speed and break of chips. Pelz found that on a flat, dry, medium-speed green planted with Bermuda grass (a coarse, fast-growing type found throughout the South and West), a wedge shot that carries 45 feet rolls an additional 45 feet when moving with the grain. When the same shot lands across the grain, it rolls only 33 feet, and when hit into the grain, only 21 feet.

Golfers who play on the finer-bladed, lusher bentgrass of the northern states don't have to worry about grain. Pelz's tests found no measurable difference in roll when the direction of bentgrass grain changed.

Here are the basics of grain, with tips on how to handle it:

Chipping into grain. This slows the ball and tends to exaggerate any break as the ball rolls across the green. Use a less-lofted club for a lower trajectory shot that lands a bit hotter than your normal chip.

Chipping down-grain. Chips run faster and break is minimized. Take a more lofted club than normal and hit a higher shot that lands more softly.

Chipping cross-grain. On a flat chip, expect the ball to break in the direction of the grain. If the slope goes in the same

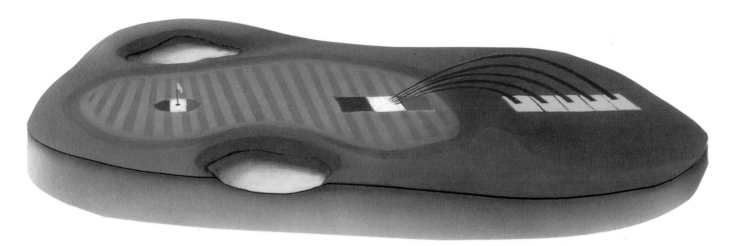

Land chips on the green with a healthy margin of error. Teaching pro Phil Rodgers recommends visualizing a six-foot-long "landing strip": Aim for the blue to be assured of being long enough; the white to finish within one-putt range; the red when you want to play defensively.

Avoid humps, aim for hollows. The chart to the left shows how short, per-fect, and long chips finish on a flat green. The middle chart shows that if the ball hits a hump, a short chip becomes much shorter, a long chip much longer. But hitting into a hollow (far right) reduces the margin of error on misplayed chips, so they all roll about the same distance.

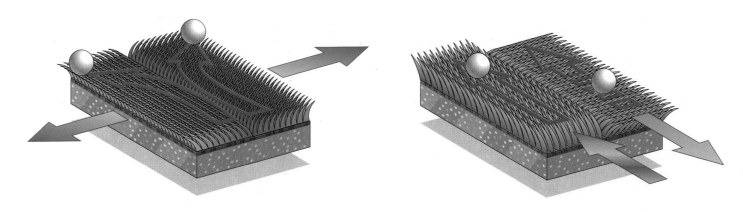

Left: *When chipping cross-grain, the ball will be affected by the growing pattern of the grass. Account for that when picking a landing area.*

Right: *Chips will roll shorter when hit into the grain, longer when running with the grain.*

direction, play for additional break; if the slope is in the opposite direction, play for less-than-normal break.

Late in the day on slow Bermuda grass, cross-grain chips could have their break doubled or halved, depending on their correlation to the green's tilt. As the ball's momentum decreases, grain's effect becomes more pronounced, so the grain closest to the hole will have the greatest influence on the chip.

PIN IN OR OUT

Perhaps the second-most-asked question about chipping is, "Should the flagstick be in or out?" In 1990, *GOLF Magazine* asked Dave Pelz to conduct a test. Using a device he invented called the TruRoller, and helped by PGA Tour veteran Tom Jenkins, he measured how the pin affects the odds of holing chips.

Running the test on perfectly flat greens as well as ones that sloped, Pelz rolled the ball at different speeds and at different parts of the hole: dead center; left- and right-center of the pin; left and right edge of the pin. Jenkins and the TruRoller launched thousands of shots, an equal number with the pin in and out, on different greens, at different speeds, to all the different parts of the hole.

What was the result? Says Pelz, "Without question, you should leave the pin in the hole when chipping from off the green." There were only three situations when the pin should not be left in: 1) If it is leaning decidedly toward an incoming chip, leaving no room for the ball; 2) If the wind is blowing the flagstick, moving it around in the hole so it might knock an incoming ball away; and 3) If your course uses larger-than-standard steel flagsticks.

In the TruRoller tests, 33 percent more chips were made with the pin in than out. In the human test, Jenkins made 18 percent more chips with the pin in. Two other highlights:

1) The faster the ball is rolling, the greater the advantage of leaving the pin in. That means it's most important to leave it in on longer chips, those from difficult lies, and downhillers.

2) Even if you don't hit the pin dead-center, it still helps to leave it in the hole. On off-center hits, the pin absorbs energy from the ball, reducing its speed.

THE MENTAL SIDE

What should the golfer's mind-set be when chipping? This one is easy, best stated by the wizard Ballesteros: "My philosophy for chipping is and always has been 'knock it in.'"

WRISTY CHIPPING

Japanese star Isao Aoki taught himself the game, and as a result developed an extremely wristy chipping method. His stroke travels straight up and down, chopping down on the ball. He begins very bent over at the waist, steepening his swing, and plays the ball off his right (back) heel. With the body aimed slightly open (left of the target), he lets his elbows bend and wrists cock on the backswing. The right hand takes control on the downswing, dropping the club on the ball so it pops up with lots of backspin.

Wrist action was more common when fairways and greens were not as well manicured. Some teachers and players still advocate adding a little wrist cock for extra distance on chips. This method demands lots of practice, yet ultimately will succeed or fail based on your feel for how much wrist action is right.

Jack Nicklaus uses his hands to hit a variety of finesse chips. He hits what he calls a "hot" chip, one that runs a long way, by rotating his hands clockwise as the wrists hinge on the backswing, then giving control to the right hand and turning the clubface open to closed through impact, imparting some hook spin. For a "dead" chip that stops quickly, he rotates the hands counterclockwise going back, then swings the club slightly from closed to open, with the left hand in control.

Compare Isao Aoki's (dark sweater) wristy chipping with the more conventional style used by Gary Hallberg. Despite Aoki's many deviations from traditional teaching, he is an expert around the greens thanks to many hours practicing his method.

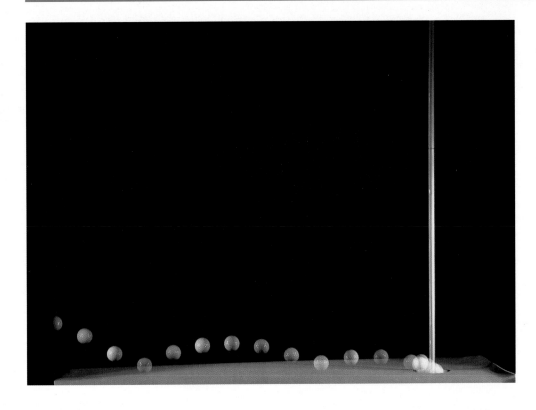

Extensive testing proved that a chip is far more likely to go in the hole if the flagstick is in the hole.

SPECIAL CHIP SHOTS

Pop Wedge. Often hit from a tough lie off the green but close to the hole, the idea is to loft the ball a little higher in the air so it drops and stops quickly. Widen your stance to keep the lower body still, and grip the club as lightly as possible. Cock the wrists and make an upright swing, taking the club slightly outside the target line. With the hands very soft, drop the club gently into the grass behind the ball. It will pop out with cut spin so it doesn't roll after landing.

Cut Shot. When the lie is strong, wiry grass, this shot lets you catch the ball cleanly and put some cutspin on it to negate the "flyer" effect. Open your stance, so the arms have room to swing back and through, and play the ball back in a narrow stance. On the backswing, tilt your head slightly toward the target, which causes the shoulders to tilt, shutting the clubface. Tilting also ·leads to a deliberate reverse weight shift—weight on the front foot going back, on the back foot coming down. Staying more on the back foot makes the club swing from shut to open, nearly scooping the ball at impact. The open face imparts the spin, so the ball rolls quietly to the hole after coming out cleanly.

Hooked Chips. Nick Price says he owes much of his success at Turnberry in 1994, when he won the British Open, to a low, running chip with a little hook spin. Address the ball with the face of the club "toed in," slightly closed to the target. Angle the hands ahead of the ball, with the body leaning into the left foot. Swing the club back low to the ground and to the inside. Coming

down, make an in-to-out swing, consciously trying to hook the shot. The ball will come off the clubface low with little to no backspin, so it will roll.

Bare Lies. Take a low-lofted club, like a 5- or 6-iron; you may want to use a putter (then the shot is called the "Texas wedge"). Play the ball back in your stance, angle your hands ahead, and make clean contact with the back of the ball. If you need more loft, use a wedge, lifting the shaft so only the toe of the club is on the ground. This eliminates the effect of the bounce (the metal hanging beneath the sole). This shot also works from a low-lipped bunker if there is little to no sand.

Bump-and-Run. You're off the green, a bank looms between your ball and the putting surface, and the pin is close to the near edge. Popping a delicate wedge shot over the bank is a low-percentage shot. The smart play is to take a mid-iron (4- to 7-iron) and bump a low shot into the hill so it bounces over the top and rolls onto the surface and to the hole. Set up for a normal chip—ball back, hands ahead—then use a little more arm action so the shot doesn't die in the hill. Aim for a spot on the bank where you want the ball to hit. Again, don't be shy: Hit the ball hard enough to get it over the hill, but not so hard it shoots over the other side of the green.

Downhill Chip. Hitting along a downslope delofts the club, so once you have the right one for the distance, open the face: The steeper the slope, the more you open the face. Play the ball well back in your stance with your hands well ahead, ensuring you make contact early in the downswing. You may have to flex your right (back) knee to level your stance a bit. Use your basic chipping stroke, but be extra careful to keep the wrists quiet so you don't flick the club and top the ball. Swing back to about knee height and control the action with your arms. Let the hands lead the clubface through impact.

Uphill Chip. The mistake you want to avoid is leaving the ball short, very possible because an uphill lie adds loft and subtracts distance. Either plan to make a longer swing or take more club (an 8-iron instead of a pitching wedge, for example). No matter which method you use, check that the ball is in the middle or back of the stance; on an uphill lie, the tendency is to let the ball get too far forward, since your weight is falling back.

In the Fringe. The ball has rolled just off the green into the fringe grass. If the ball is a little too deep in the grass to allow for conventional chipping, try chipping with a 5- or 7-wood: Choke down a bit and sweep through the grass and the ball. (Chipping with a fairway wood also works for long chips.) Or else take your most lofted wedge, play the ball way back in your stance, choke down almost to the bare shaft below the grip, and make a sharply descending blow. Hit just below the middle of the ball, taking care not to let too much grass interfere with impact.

Very Short Chip. You're in the fringe, just a few feet from the pin, but the lie won't let you putt. Choke well down on a wedge, onto the shaft if necessary, and make a normal chipping stroke.

Choking down shortens the club, killing its power, so you can make a good swing without worrying about the ball going too far. (Choking down also means the clubface is likely to close; grip firmly and aim a little right.) Practice this shot to see how far down you can place the hands and retain control.

Bellied Wedge. When the ball rolls up against the collar of grass around the green, clean contact with either a putter or wedge is difficult. Ray Floyd is one of many chipping experts who suggests putting with the leading edge of the sand wedge: His technique is to take your normal putting grip and stance, rest the sole of the club lightly on the top of the fringe, make your normal putting stroke, and hit the equator of the ball with the leading edge. The ball will come out rolling.

No rule says you have to use a wedge around the green. From deep rough, a lofted wood will have no trouble sweeping through the grass and the ball.

There's no easy shot when the ball rests against the collar. Try the bellied wedge, hitting the middle of the ball with the leading edge of the sand wedge.

PITCHING

The Grip. The club you use for pitching should be handled with deftness and finesse. Using your normal full-swing grip, keep the pressure light. This will help you make a smooth, accelerating swing.

Another reason to take a light grip is to feel the clubhead throughout the swing. If you can sense where the club is at all times, you eliminate harmful tension and are swinging at a good pace.

For precise shotmaking, the clubface must be square at impact. Therefore, the right-hand grip is critical. Lay the club along the middle of your fingers—not down near the palm—so the grip doesn't get too strong and the right hand can't take control and turn over the clubface.

Don't choke down, but grip near the end of the club. Choking down shortens the club so it feels lighter, which encourages a faster swing. Choking down also leads to crouching over; gripping at the end of the club makes you stand tall.

The Set Up. Just as with chipping, the fundamental action of the pitch is hitting down on the ball—not scooping or in any other way helping it into the air. Unlike the chip, once the pitched ball hits the green, it is supposed to stop fairly quickly.

To get higher flight and more backspin than the chip, position the ball in the middle of your stance, centered between the heels. (Don't use your toes, because most golfers turn their toes toward the target on short shots. The heels don't move.) By centering the ball, you're assured of hitting down on it as the club approaches the low point of its swing. If you aren't making crisp contact with the ball in the middle of the stance, then your body is swaying during the swing, shifting the position of your low point.

Do not move the ball forward in your stance to hit shots higher. You'll either top it or subconsciously move your body forward during the downswing in an attempt to reach it.

Move the ball back in your stance if you're looking at a bad lie, particularly down in long grass. Moving the ball back will minimize the amount of grass getting between it and the clubface at impact, a condition that lessens your ability to control distance. Moving the ball back also delofts the club, so take one with more loft to compensate.

To create an upright swing, take a narrow stance and stand tall. Resist the temptation to get close to the ball by crouching or widening your stance. These moves restrict lower-body action while giving control to the hands and arms, leading to inconsistency.

Do not stand too far from the ball. Your arms should not reach out at address but be hanging almost straight down from your shoulders, remaining loose.

Stand square or slightly open to the target, whichever feels more comfortable. As you near the target, open your stance, which produces a more out-to-in swing, lifting the ball higher and shorter. But always keep your clubface aimed square at the target; don't open

As the lie gets worse, move the ball back in your stance. And choke down on the club to steepen the angle of attack.

DIFFERENT STROKES

LEG ACTION

The legs are vital to a good pitch, both as support for the upper body and to help produce a smooth, rhythmic swing. To help the legs participate in the motion, keep your knees slightly flexed.

Ray Floyd: "If I asked you to take a ball and pitch it 20 feet into a trash can, you wouldn't stand stiff-legged and straight and just make an arm movement. You would be very rhythmic. You would rock back and forward with your legs, at the same time swinging your arm back and through and up, and you would toss the ball high so it would fall into the can."

Ken Venturi: "Leg action is the key to pitching the ball well. The faster you move the right knee toward the left leg in the down-swing, the more spin you will put on the ball. You'll get softer shots, too. With no leg action, you work your hands and hit a lot of shots with less spin or bite on them."

There may not be a lot of leg drive on a short shot, but there's some. Make sure the knees begin flexed and move with the upper body back and through.

---

it for more height and less distance.

At address, your hands should be in-line or just slightly ahead of the ball.

The Swing. One of the most common mistakes golfers make is thinking the pitch is an arm swing. It is a full-body motion. Begin the backswing by turning the legs, hips, and upper body away from the target. Let the arms and hands move in response to the turning of the shoulders. If you are swinging outside the line, as on a sand shot, then the arms are working independently of the body, which leads to trouble.

Begin the downswing by turning the lower body back toward the target. Be very careful to keep the arms and hands from starting the downswing, trying to "hit" at the ball.

Don't rush the downswing. Play the shot, as Armour put it, "without haste." Trying to speed things along inevitably leads to throwing the hands, arms, and club at the ball.

From a slow start, accelerate through the ball. The club should be speeding up, not slowing down, at impact, to assure crisp contact with the clubhead firm, on the target line, and square to the target. Forget the theory that you only swing as far forward as you swung back. Strive for a full finish, swinging the club up to shoulder height or beyond even on short pitch shots. This forces you to accelerate down and through.

To get the feeling of acceleration, envision a roller coaster as it negotiates a large dip. Starting downhill slowly, it gradually picks up speed and accelerates through the bottom arc, gradually slowing as it climbs the next hill. Forget about the ball and

The pitch shot. Stand tall and close to a ball centered in your stance, your arms hanging loose. Turn the legs, hips, and upper body together away from the target, letting the wrists set naturally. Start the downswing by turning everything back toward the target. Accelerate through the ball and continue to a high, full finish.

swing the clubhead with that same rhythm.

Be sure you're hitting down on the ball, not scooping or lifting it in the air. Force yourself to hit down by imagining a small wedge of wood behind the ball. Aim to drive the wedge under the ball with the leading edge of the club. You'll get the ball in the air while eliminating bladed and skulled shots.

THE RIGHT DISTANCE

There are a number of ways to regulate the distance of your pitch shots. One way that does *not* work is changing the tempo of your swing, swinging harder to hit it farther, softer to hit it shorter. As Bobby Jones wrote, "It has been found to be a far simpler matter to change a club than a swing."

Most good short-game players vary distance by relying on feel and experience, consciously or unconsciously changing elements of their swing while keeping their tempo constant. Watch the pros and you'll see some choke down the club when they want to hit it shorter, others shorten their follow-through, while many change the length of their backswing.

Tom Watson says, "You must feel how far to hit the ball, and feel is the most elusive part of golf."

Ray Floyd, who uses a sand wedge for all pitches inside 60 yards, widens his stance, uses his legs, and lengthens the swing as he gets farther from the green. But he never resorts to a full, hard swing.

Seve Ballesteros categorizes pitches as long (80 to 110 yards) or short (inside 80 yards). He uses a pitching wedge for the former, a sand wedge for the latter. On long pitches, he opens his stance only slightly, keeps his shoulders square, and swings back to three-quarter length. On short pitches, the body is more open, more weight is put on the left (front) foot, and the swing is shorter.

Nearly every golf instruction book advises practicing pitch shots from different distances, getting the feel for how much swing each one needs.

GRAIN

Grain can make a big difference on a wedge shot. If you're hitting into the grain (the grass on the green is growing toward you), even from 100 yards away the ball tends to stop quickly or draw back a little after it lands. Shots hit downgrain will bounce a few times and roll before stopping. The end result is a big difference: From 100 yards, a 99-yard shot hit into the grain will bounce forward once and then check up and leave you about a six-footer; the same 99-yard shot downgrain bounces forward twice, then rolls to a stop 20 feet past the hole.

You must be perceptive to determine the grain in advance and from the fairway. If greens are Bermuda grass, keep in mind that grain runs toward the setting sun. If there's water around the green, the grain on both bent and Bermuda grass generally will run toward it. The best way to tell is with sharp analysis of the land: If you dumped a lot of water on the green, where do you think it would go? That's the usual direction the grain runs. (Be sure to take into account subtleties such as the slopes created by bunkers, etc.)

Also consider the grain of the grass you're hitting from. If it's growing away from the target and into you, swing as if the distance is five to 10 yards farther than its true measurement. If it's growing toward the target and away from you, take five to 10 yards off the yardage.

THE MENTAL SIDE

From 40, 70, or 100 yards, you want a pitch shot to finish close. If you've practiced the wedge game, know how to produce shots of varying distances consistently, and can make a repeatable, smooth swing, there's one more step you can take to help the ball roll to the pin: visualize.

"The proper order of procedure," wrote Bobby Jones, "is to visualize the shot, to determine where the pitch should drop and how much roll it should have; then to select the club and attempt the shot that should produce this result."

"Visualization gives you a feel for what you want to do" is how Ray Floyd explains it. "Then you let your body reproduce that feel. It's amazing how many times I visualize pitching a ball a certain height and see it land on a specific spot, then have it happen exactly as I imagined it." (Note: Floyd doesn't just see the ball stopping near the pin; like all the best short-game players, he sees it in the air, how high it flies, and exactly where it hits the green before rolling to its finish.)

Floyd also notes that visualization puts a positive picture in your mind, rather than the image of a bunker or water hazard lurking between you and the green.

SPECIAL PITCH SHOTS

For More Height. The easy way to produce a higher shot is to swing a more lofted club. But for still more height, hit a cut shot. Weaken your grip, turning your hands toward the target so they won't turn over and close the club through impact. Take a very open stance, pulling your left (front) foot back from the target line about 30 degrees and setting most of your weight on the back foot. To swing without hitting your right hip, which is now in the way, take the club on a more outward and upward path, and think about trying to slide it under the ball. Break the wrists quickly in the backswing. This methods works on a long (full swing) or short (partial swing) shot, but you must practice to see how shots come off different clubs. (For still more loft, open the clubface and tilt the club back.)

DIFFERENT STROKES

WRIST WORK

If you make a full-body swing and keep your wrists relaxed, they will hinge naturally as a result of the arms swinging. Be careful not to force the wrists to cock or let them break prematurely; this produces inconsistent contact.

Other teachers have had different roles for the wrists. Tommy Armour was a big advocate of wrist action in pitching, calling for more wrist cock and less arm swing. He wanted the player to choke down, play the shot with the hands, and keep the body out of the action. Therefore, the wrists were needed to provide speed and power.

Ken Venturi's view is the opposite of Armour's, believing the wrists should be absolutely quiet, in the same plaster casts he imagines wearing when chipping. He also advocates widening the stance, increasing the flex in the knees, and choking down the shaft, three adjustments that make it easier to get the feeling of slipping the clubhead under the ball.

Ray Floyd widens his stance and lengthens his swing as he gets farther from the green. But the tempo of his pitch swing remains the same—smooth and unhurried.

For extremely high shots, open the clubface and lay it open, leaning the shaft away from the target to increase the club's effective loft.

The Lob. This is a high shot that stops quickly on the green. Open your stance and open the clubface. Swing the club back with your arms, letting the right wrist cock freely. Swinging down, dip your right shoulder so your weight falls to the right (back) side. Uncock the right wrist to snap the club into impact. Stay behind the ball, weight on the back side, and finish tall.

Punch Pitch. When the hole is well back on the green, take advantage of the wide-open putting surface. Rather than flying the ball all the way, hoping it stops before rolling off the back edge, hit a low shot that bounces once or twice, then checks up. Open your stance slightly, play the ball more toward your right (back) foot, hands angled ahead. Don't hit down and take a divot, but create extra backspin by swinging on a shallower plane, nipping the ball off the grass. Do this by turning away from the ball with the shoulders and arms, being careful not to take the club up with the hands. Coming down, drive your legs toward the target and turn your upper body through, keeping the clubhead on a level path through impact. Aim for the front of the green.

Knockdown Pitch. Similar to the punch, this shot won't stop as quickly on the green; it rolls a longer way. It's great hitting into the wind, because the ball stays low. Take a narrow, slightly open stance, aiming the clubface at the target. Set your hands ahead of the ball, most of your weight on the left (front) foot, the ball behind center. Choke down slightly to reduce the arc of the swing. Grip firmly, particularly with the left hand. Swing the arms, pushing the club straight back without consciously cocking the wrists. Swing as far back as you think necessary, but not higher than three-quarters; a big swing will send the ball too high in the air. If you need more distance, take a less lofted club and keep the swing short. Pull down and through with the left hand and arm; the "thunk" means you've made the proper descending blow. Finish with your arms and club pointing at the target. Even though the swing is abbreviated, the shot will travel farther than you think, because the club was delofted at impact.

Off Hardpan. Hitting from grass, it's easy to slip the clubface under the ball to lift the shot in the air. But there's no soft cushion with hardpan (sun-baked dirt), so you must hit down through impact. Play the ball from the middle of your stance. Make a half swing, taking the club back more slowly than usual. Start the downswing with the legs, driving them briskly toward the target. Keep your hands ahead of the clubhead and ball through impact; together with an aggressive swing, you'll make crisp contact. The ball will fly low and bounce a few times before checking up. Allow for roll when selecting the landing spot on the green.

Uphill Lies. As with any shot from a hilly lie, adjust your body so it is as level as possible to the ground. This means putting most of your weight on your uphill (front) side. Because it's hard to determine the middle of your stance when the feet aren't level, place the ball on line with the middle of your chest. Keep the swing simple: Use your arms and shoulders, swing the club back and through, and keep the wrists quiet. If your body is level, the club will catch the ball at the low point of its arc and produce a normal-trajectory pitch. The hill will have no influence on the swing until after impact, when it restricts your follow-through.

Downhill Lies. Again, set your body parallel to the slope. Play the ball back in your stance, again on line with the middle of your chest. Make an easy swing so you don't lose your balance. Because the ball is back in your stance, it's likely to fly to the right, so aim a little left to compensate.

PGA Tour player Mark Calcavecchia demonstrates the lob shot. Notice the cocking of the right wrist going back and the position of the body—behind the ball—coming down and through.

THE 3X4 METHOD

For golfers who can't practice enough to develop a feel for distance, Dave Pelz created the "3x4 Method," which combines backswings of different lengths with wedges of varying lofts to produce reliable, repeatable yardages.

The "3" refers to the position of the arms at the top of three backswings, expressed as if they were moving on the face of a clock. The shortest is the 7:30 swing, in which the hands go back only hip-high. In the 9:00 swing, the arms stop parallel to the ground. At 10:30, the hands go to shoulderheight.

The wrists must cock on every swing, even the very short 7:30 (which takes some practice). All three swings must accelerate through impact to a full finish.

By making a smooth, accelerating swing and stopping the backswing at these three points, you will produce consistent yardages. Furthermore, the 7:30 swing hits a shot that flies half the distance of the 10:30, while the 9:00 goes 75 percent as far. For example, if your normal 10:30 pitching wedge is 100 yards, with the same club the 7:30 swing will fly the ball 50 yards; the 9:00 swing will hit the shot 75 yards.

Once comfortable with the mechanics of the three backswings, carrying more wedges multiplies your control over a range of yardages. Pelz says that even average golfers should carry four wedges—the "4" in his method—each with a different loft. Hitting four wedges with the three swings creates 12 distinct yardages. Here are their lofts, with the names he has given each wedge:

- Distance wedge: 48–50 degrees of loft (similar to most standard pitching wedges).
- Mid wedge: 54 degrees (most standard sand wedges).
- Finesse wedges: 58–60 degrees (the "third" or "lob" wedges many companies make).
- Pop wedge: 64 degrees (the super-loft wedges a few companies make).

Here are typical distances created by the four wedges and three swings. Your distances may differ, but note that the 7:30 shot is half the distance of the 10:30 and the 9:00 is 75 percent; experiment to find the exact yardages for your game.

WEDGE	7:30	9:00	10:30
	BACKSWING POSITION		
Distance	50 yds	75 yds	100 yds
Mid	43	64	85
Finesse	35	53	70
Pop	28	42	55

Once you've determined your yardages for each wedge, write them down and tape the list to its shaft to help you choose the right club. It's legal to have this information on your club when you play.

When different combinations of wedge and swing produce similar yardages, use the one you find more comfortable. Pelz says golfers are most comfortable with the 9:00 swing, least with the 7:30.

Right: *Dave Pelz has devoted himself to the exclusive study of the short game since the mid 1970s.*

The approach shot in all its various forms is the most difficult and the most important part of the game of golf, and yet it is the stroke which the beginner, as a rule, practices least and attempts most erroneously.

H. J. Whigham

I pitch the ball whenever possible because there are no hazards in the air.

Byron Nelson

The great anxiety of the moderate player when making this stroke is to get the ball properly lofted, and in some obstinate cases it seems to take several seasons of experience to convince him completely that the club has been specially made for the purpose, and, if fairly used, is quite adequate.

Harry Vardon

In playing the mashie, a full swing should never be attempted. A swing with a half-shot will be found to carry just as far, and you will be much more accurate in direction.

Findlay S. Douglas

The common error is taking the club back too far and decelerating through impact, which is like a boxer pulling his punches. It causes all sorts of mishit and misdirected pitch shots.

Tom Watson

Pitching and chipping are two departments of the game where you are either great at them or just so-so.

Gene Sarazen

CHAPTER SEVEN

SAND PLAY

WALTER HAGEN SAID, "THE SAND SHOT OUGHT TO BE THE EASIEST SHOT IN GOLF. You don't even have to hit the ball." That is cold comfort to the legions of amateurs who regard sand play as the most difficult and irritating assignment in golf.

Unfortunately for them, sand is an intrinsic part of the game. The first courses traversed the "links land" separating the mainland from the water, where the soil was very sandy. This land also was favored by grazing sheep, who, legend has it, nibbled away the vegetation and nuzzled into little hillocks seeking protection from the elements. Animal burrows became enlarged, as did the holes dug by beachcombers searching for shells. These depressions were further worn away by the forces of nature, and became the bane of the shepherds and other early golfers trying to bang a rock or wooden ball toward a distant target.

The Old Course at St. Andrews, the game's original layout and the archetype against which all others are judged, has hundreds of bunkers: some large and with wonderfully descriptive names like Hell, Coffin, and the Beardies; others so small they can accommodate just "an angry man and his niblick." All were put there by nature. As man replaced Mother Nature in the course-architecture business, he followed her lead, placing bunkers around greens and along fairways to add challenge and strategic demands.

Hundreds of bunkers, of all sizes and shapes, dot the landscape of the Old Course at St. Andrews, Scotland.

The very early golfer, upon finding his ball in a bunker, had limited options for getting it out. He could use a wooden-headed niblick, probably his most lofted club, and make the same long, loose swing he made on every other shot, hoping to lift the ball up and away. Beginning in the late 1700s, if he carried a more durable iron-headed club, he might try blasting out. Period paintings show both clubs in play, although it often appears that the one selected was highly inappropriate for the shot at hand (which may account for the golfer's fear of sand over the centuries).

By the end of the 1800s, when irons were in wide use, the club of choice again was the niblick, but now a different weapon entirely. It was roughly equivalent in size and loft to a modern 9-iron, forged by blacksmiths or steam-powered mechanical hammers to have a big, heavy head and a flat, narrow sole. The name "niblick" comes from the Scottish for "short-nosed," which described the shape of the original rut iron, a small, round-headed club with a lot of loft, used for extrication from wheel ruts, hoof-prints, animal holes, and other devilish lies, natural or man-made. As the size of the clubhead grew, it retained its name, its loft, and its reputation for gaining freedom from tough spots. It was the original trouble club.

"We rarely look upon the niblick with any of that lingering affection which is constantly bestowed on all the other instruments that we possess. It revives only unpleasant memories," wrote the great English champion

Harry Vardon in *The Complete Golfer* (1905), one of the first and most influential instruction manuals.

In that book, Vardon described the sand shot of his day. The preferred stance was wide, as for a long-iron, but he acknowledged it wouldn't always be possible "inasmuch as it so frequently happens that this is governed by circumstances which are quite beyond the golfer's control." The swing would be more upright because the club was short, placing the golfer closer to the ball—"well over it," in Vardon's words—with the intended point of contact about two inches behind the ball.

"The club must hit the sand," instructed Vardon, as teachers do today, "and the sand must move the ball, but the iron blade . . . must hardly ever come into contact with the ball. Swing harder than ever on to the sand, with the knowledge that the swing will end there, for a follow-through is not desired and would in many cases be impossible."

With that forceful a swing, it is no surprise that Vardon said the shaft of the niblick must be as strong and stiff as possible, while the head must have plenty of loft and be very heavy: "It has rougher and heavier work to do than any other club, and more brute force is requisitioned in employing it."

The other great players—and authors—of the time said much the same thing. "Make no attempt to follow through, but let the club stop because of its own exhausted momentum after it has gone well down into the sand beneath the ball," wrote U.S. Amateur champion Jerome Travers in 1913.

"Swing, or rather lift, the niblick almost as you would a hammer,"

directed Findlay Douglas, U.S. Amateur champion of 1898. "Aim not to strike the ball, but the sand back of it. Think nothing about following through, but hit hard into the sand." There would be no follow-through because besides being big and heavy, the niblick they all advocated had the thin sole and sharp leading edge typical of other irons, so it dug into the sand and stayed there.

Besides agreeing on the club and the swing, the top teachers shared the same basic swing thought. "When the average player finds his ball in a bunker," wrote Bobby Jones, "his chief aim should be to get it out in one stroke." Getting out was Vardon's "golden rule" of sand play; to Travers it was "the most important thing to keep in mind."

Writing about two decades after Vardon, Jones varied the technique a bit. He still advised hitting sand instead of ball, but he laid the club slightly open, as golfers do today, so the face looked to the right of the tar-

The First International Foursome, painted by Allan Stewart in 1919, depicts a famous match played in 1682 over the Links of Leith. Note the golfer attempting to play from the sand with a club that seems uniquely suited to fail.

Along with his other qualities as golfer and gentleman, Bobby Jones was one of the first players to open the club-face in the sand, increasing the club's effective loft.

get (for right-handed golfers): "In this way, it is possible to hit harder with the knowledge that taking too little sand will be less likely to send the ball over the green." Opening the clubface also increased the club's effective loft and made it less likely to stick in the sand.

Vardon and his contemporaries didn't say much about regulating the distance of a sand shot because they were taking heavy blows. Jones added finesse to bunker play, controlling the length of the shot by changing the point of impact in the sand behind the ball—hitting closer to the ball for longer

shots, farther from the ball for shorter ones.

Freddie McLeod was a wee Scotsman who emigrated to the United States in 1903 and won the 1908 U.S. Open. In one of his books, Jones described McLeod's sand method but warned average players against it. Interestingly, it sounds a lot like the method used by Tour pros today: "Playing from a clean lie in sand near the green, Freddie lays his niblick well off [open] and takes a good, healthy swing. His club takes a mere feather of sand under the ball, so that the shot comes up with a terrific amount of spin; usually the ball drops past the hole and comes back toward it, often stopping very close indeed."

It's hard to believe McLeod could produce that kind of spin with the equipment available (Jones didn't say if the same technique worked from different kinds of sand). But since McLeod was such a small man (108 pounds, almost certainly history's lightest major-championship winner), he had to rely on his short game, which he worked on long and hard. He was famous for his prowess from the bunker, even continuing to use a niblick after the sand wedge became popular.

The sand game changed forever in the early 1930s with the invention of the sand wedge. In 1929, the L.A. Young Company had introduced the Walter Hagen Sand Wedge, which featured a wide sole and concave face. Clubs with concave faces were banned in 1931, but the broader sole lived on.

Most club designs are the product of evolution, but the modern sand wedge can be credited to a single man's radical notion. That man was Gene Sarazen, already a major-championship winner in 1931 when, while taking flying lessons, he noticed that at take off the pilot lowered, rather than raised, the plane's tail.

He began tinkering in his shop at home in Florida, soldering "gobs of lead" on the bottom of niblicks until he had one with "an exceptionally heavy, abrupt, wide curving flange. I was trying to make myself a club that would drive the ball up as I drove the clubhead down. . . . I was lowering the tail or sole of my niblick to produce a club whose face would come up from the sand as the sole made contact with the sand." More than simply wide, the sole of Sarazen's club was deep, actually hanging below the leading edge of the face. There was a bunker on the course behind Sarazen's house where he hit thousands of shots, returning to the shop to make adjustments. During his tinkering and practice, he also noticed that he had to change his technique, taking the club back more to the outside and flicking it down behind the ball, what he described as "not unlike the way you would swing an axe when chopping a tree." He finally settled on a club design and swing, and used them for the first time in public at the 1932 British Open at Prince's, on the southeastern coast of England. He won by five strokes while playing superbly from the bunkers. Shortly thereafter, the Wilson Sporting Goods Company, which had Sarazen under contract, introduced his wedge, called the R99. It was the answer to the average player's prayers.

"The Sarazen sand iron is one of Gene's pet ideas" was how Wilson's 1933 catalogue put it. "It's an entirely new development that is taking the fear out of traps for many players. Don't try to pick the ball clean—just hit down hard in back of it and immediately upon hitting the sand under the ball the club is forced upwards by its abrupt sole flange with the result that it gives a sharp upward lift to the ball, occasioning a much higher trajectory of the shot. The ball gets into the air fast to carry high bunkers and falls dead on the green." (Note that the ad says "don't try to pick the ball clean." None of the top players/authors favored such a method, but amateurs,

The first modern sand wedge was designed by Gene Sarazen, who unveiled his creation while winning the 1932 British Open.

unsuccessful at hammering, must have resorted to chipping out.)

As Sarazen found, the technique for wielding the new sand wedge had to change to take advantage of the broad, deep flange. Suddenly the club was supposed to bounce off the surface rather than digging in. But as Vardon, Jones, and the others advised, the club still had to hit the sand an inch or two behind the ball and not the ball itself. Most important, the new club promised to do what all the great players said was

essential—get the ball out of the sand and onto the green in a single shot, the closer to the hole the better.

With little modification, the sand wedge Sarazen designed is the sand club of choice today, although golfers should experiment with the pitching and lob wedges, as well as longer irons down to the 5 or 6, depending on the length and height requirements of the shot. Furthermore, Sarazen's modifications to the sand swing form the basis of the basic sand shot today.

PREVAILING WISDOM

Much of the work for the basic sand shot from a greenside bunker should be done at address. Set up properly and you can't help but make the right swing and produce the desired result.

Take an open stance. For right-handed golfers (lefties should reverse the following directions), that means aiming feet, knees, hips, and shoulders to the left of the target (and parallel to one another): For a standard sand shot of about 10 yards, start by turning your body from the 12 o'clock position—aiming directly at the target—to between 10 and 11 o'clock. Open the clubface, aiming it about 10 degrees (just inside 1 o'clock) to the right of the target: Don't simply turn your hands open, because the club will want to return to its original position at impact; stand outside the bunker, loosen your grip, turn the club, then regrip so that when the hands return, the clubface is open at impact.

An open stance ensures that the swing travels outside the target line going back, then across the ball (out-to-in) coming down. This puts cut-spin on the ball so it flies higher than normal and moves from left to right both in the air and after landing. (Compensating for the spin is one reason for aiming your body to the left at address.)

Don't exaggerate the out-to-in swing. That "promotes a too-upright back-swing and too deep a dig into the sand," says Ken Venturi. "You don't have to make an extra effort to do this, so just take the club back . . . along the normal path, or what feels like the normal path" as determined by your set-up.

To keep in balance, twist your feet into the sand, but not too much. If they are too deep, leg action will be restricted, so that you lose balance and flub the shot. Twisting in also will give you a sense of the sand's texture. (Feet—and experience—are all you can use. Touching the sand with your hand or grounding the clubhead before the shot is a two-stroke penalty.)

Suggestions for ball position run from the center of your stance to well forward, off the front big toe. Practice to learn what works best for you.

When settling in at address, don't look at the ball, but at a spot an inch or two behind it, for that's where you want the club to make contact. It is still true that proper technique demands hitting the sand, which pushes the ball out. The club should not hit the ball (unless you are playing a much longer sand shot from a fairway bunker).

Conventional wisdom is to hit consistently about two inches behind the ball, varying the length of the swing to control distance; this is usually the easiest method for most amateurs to

---

DIFFERENT STROKES

LOW HANDS

Great sand players have one key in common that is rarely noticed: low hands. Dropping the hands at address loosens the wrists, encouraging the "handsy" takeaway a sand shot requires. Lowering the hands at address to just above knee-height also raises the toe of the club in the air so the heel leads the way into the sand. With the toe out of the way, it's much easier for the club to slide through the sand, producing a higher shot with more spin and more control.

For the majority of sand shots, the club does not hit the ball but contacts the sand an inch or two behind the ball. The idea is to toss out a slice of sand, which pushes the ball out with it.

master, and reduces the likelihood of poor shots created by hitting too close or too far from the ball.

One way to keep your point of entry into the sand consistent is to imagine your ball sitting in the middle of a dollar bill lying on the sand. Make contact at one end of the dollar, trying to slice it off the surface of the bunker, with the club leaving the sand at the far end of the bill.

You have to learn for yourself where to hit the sand and how hard to swing, and nothing works like practice from a real bunker. Get in there with a bucket of balls, draw a line in the sand an inch behind the ball, and concentrate on hitting that line with your club. See how the shot reacts. Do the

same at two inches behind the ball, even three.

Keeping your tempo consistent, vary the length of your swing and see what effect that has. And try different clubs, especially the other wedges and 9-iron.

When the ball sits cleanly on top of the sand, make a shallower swing, so it has a U shape. This is a good image to keep in mind for longer bunker shots when you need a fuller swing. On shorter shots or when the ball is slightly buried, your swing should be steeper and be more of a V—up-and-down, almost knifing the ball out.

A final, but vital, point. As long as the ball isn't deeply buried or in some restricted spot, *always* make a full follow-through—at least as long on

Basic sand technique: Aim slightly left of the target and open the clubface. Stop the backswing short of parallel, then swing down and through, insuring acceleration by achieving a full finish.

DIFFERENT STROKES

BALL POSITION

Golfers who have trouble getting the ball up and out might try playing the ball farther forward, as advocated by short-game guru Dave Pelz. He teaches all his students, amateurs and pros, to play sand shots with the ball off the big toe of their front foot, just past the natural bottom of the swing's arc. This makes it easier to slide the club under so they don't have to "scoop" the ball into the air. (When the ball is in the middle of the stance, the club is still descending as it makes contact, which leads many players to subconsciously try helping the ball up and causing bladed shots that fly way too far.) Pelz also suggests opening the clubface 45 degrees to the right of the target—that is, to 2 o'clock.

For the basic sand shot, the club never hits the ball but contacts the sand behind it. The force of impact creates a wave of sand, which pushes the ball up and out. Accelerating through the sand is vital to a successful outcome.

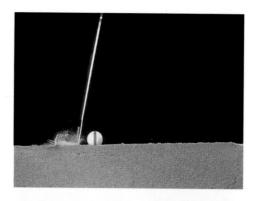

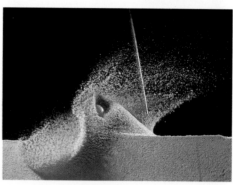

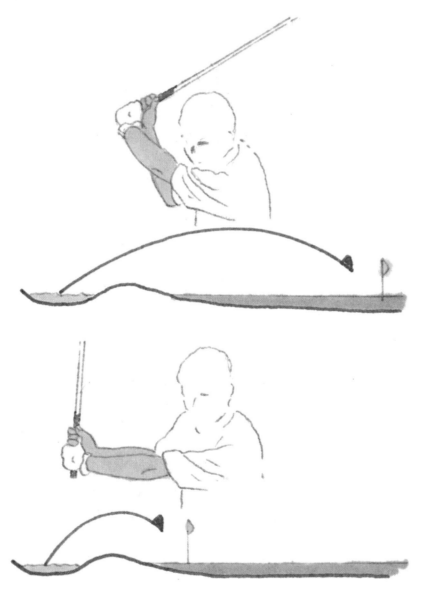

The standard way to vary distance is with the length of the backswing: Make a longer backswing for a longer shot, a shorter backswing for a shorter shot. Swing at the same tempo, and continue to a full follow-through.

the through-swing as the backswing, preferably all the way up over your left shoulder. Striving for a full follow-through ensures that you accelerate through impact, which is crucial to producing the clubhead speed and control necessary to get the ball out and headed in the right direction. Most flubbed sand shots are the result of a decelerating swing.

Another way to keep accelerating is never to let the clubhead pass your hands during the swing: Keep pulling with the hands so they lead the club down, into, and through the sand.

Sloping Lies

The bottoms of most bunkers are flat, but the ball doesn't always roll to the bottom. If it stays on the sides, you'll face a sloping lie—sidehill, uphill, or downhill. The secret to any sloping lie is to compensate in your set-up so you can play it as a normal shot relative to the incline.

From a sidehill lie, you are effectively nearer or farther from the ball, so you must change your stance and how you grip the club to make it feel and play like a flat shot.

When the ball is above your feet (and closer to you), choke down on the club so you don't hit the shot fat. Also stand a little taller, remembering to maintain your angles (hips, waist, knees) throughout the swing. From this lie, the natural action is to swing on a flatter plane, more around your body; counter that by consciously starting the club away to the outside, then picking it up on an upright plane.

When the ball is below your feet

DIFFERENT STROKES

VARYING DISTANCE

Better players might try moving their point of impact with the sand, as Bobby Jones suggested. Once you have that kind of control over the clubhead and your swing, try hitting closer to the ball for more distance, farther from the ball for less distance (especially on the very short bunker shot to a tight pin).

Another way to determine shot length is with your set-up: For shorter shots, make your stance and clubface more open, which also hits the ball higher; for longer shots, turn body and club closer to square, but realize that the ball will have a lower trajectory.

Ken Venturi says forget inches; there are too many types and textures of sand to allow a single distance to work for them all. Instead, Venturi says to imagine your ball sitting on a tee buried in the sand, then swing to "clip the ball off the tee."

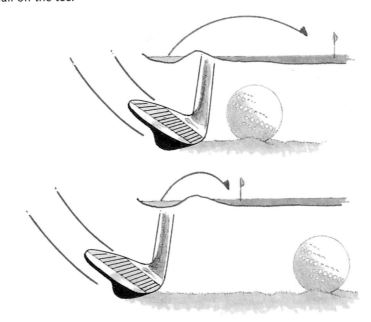

More accomplished players might try varying the length of the shot by altering the point of impact with the sand: Hit closer to the ball for longer shots, farther from the ball for shorter shots.

With the ball above the feet, stand taller and choke down on the club. Hold your angles through the swing.

With the ball below the feet, bend more at the hips and knees and hold on at the very end of the clubshaft.

From an uphill lie in the sand, your front foot will be higher than the back one. Try to maintain balance by angling your shoulders so they are parallel to the slope.

For the very difficult downhill bunker shot, the idea is the same as when uphill: Twist your back foot into the sand to keep in balance and set your shoulders parallel to the slope.

(farther from you), hold on at the end of the grip and deepen your hip and knee bend. To stay down through impact, drive your legs toward the target on the downswing. To keep the ball from sailing well to the right as it wants to do from this lie, take a slightly lighter grip so your hands turn over and close the clubface.

When you're trying to stand on an uphill lie in the sand, your main concern is maintaining balance. Your front foot will be higher than the back, and if the difference is significant, you might fall backward during the swing. That's okay, as long as you fall *after* the ball is on its way.

In *GOLF Magazine,* short-game expert Dave Pelz offered two methods for handling uphill sand shots, especially helpful if the ball also is plugged. When the slope isn't too great, position your upper body so your shoulders are parallel to the slope of the sand while your legs are perpendicular to it. (You'll know this is the right stance if you can maintain your balance.) Position the ball off the instep of your front foot, and because the slope increases the effective loft, take one club more than you usually would for a sand shot of this distance (e.g., a pitching wedge if you'd normally use a sand wedge). Open the clubface and swing through the sand to a full finish. The club will slide under the ball, which flies high and soft.

If the slope is steeper and you can't keep your shoulders parallel to the surface, stand as vertical as you can with the shoulders parallel to the horizon. Position the ball midway between your front foot and the center of your stance, or if your front foot is in an

One alternative from a steep, hilly lie is to stand vertically with your shoulders parallel to the horizon rather than the slope. Swing down hard, sticking the club in the sand close behind the ball. There will be no follow-through.

awkward position, play the ball three inches ahead of center. Using your normal club for the distance, make a full backswing, accelerate coming down, and stick the club into the sand with no follow-through. The key is hitting the sand just behind the ball. This is the slightly easier of the two shots, particularly on a buried lie, because you can make a big swing without losing your balance. But be sure to practice it first; slamming into the sand can hurt your hands and wrists, so start with shorter, easier swings.

The downhill lie in a bunker is one of the scariest shots in golf because the normal sequence is to take a big swing, which affects your balance so you straighten up during the downswing, then blading the ball and putting it into orbit. To guarantee good contact, start by thinking how this shot would look if you tilted the bunker back so your downhill lie was flat: It would be a regular sand shot over a high lip. Keep that image in mind as you set up with the clubface and your stance more open than normal, with grip pressure light. Twist your back foot securely into the sand to keep your balance; most of your weight naturally will be on your front foot because it is lower.

As with every other high shot, make the V-shaped swing: Pick the club straight up, then chop down into

the sand about an inch behind the ball. Don't let your right hand pass over the left, closing the clubface. This is another shot to practice before facing it on the course; then be satisfied simply getting the ball onto the green. Better golfers might try for the feeling of the club chasing the ball down the slope as the wrists release and straighten.

BURIED LIES

To escape from a buried lie, you have to knife the blade hard into the sand behind the ball, in effect punching it out and onto the green. This requires making an upright backswing and a sharp descending blow on the ball—the classic V swing.

Set up slightly open with most of your weight on your left side, the ball positioned in the middle of your stance, and your hands ahead of it. The clubface should be square or slightly closed. You might try using the pitching wedge since it has a sharper leading edge than most sand wedges, allowing it to dig more easily into the sand and get down below the bottom of the ball. On the backswing, pick the club up sharply with a quick wrist break. Coming down, swing harder than normal, with the hands leading the clubhead, and hit about an inch behind the ball. You probably won't get much of a follow-through, if any.

The ball will come out with little to no backspin, so it won't stop quickly on the green. Expect it to roll. And don't expect to stick the ball close to the hole; just getting out of the sand and onto the green is success.

The deeper the ball is buried, the

DIFFERENT STROKES

VARYING THE FOLLOW-THROUGH

Ken Venturi has a unique method for controlling the distance of sand shots. Always make the same-length backswing—halfway back, until the arms are parallel to the ground—while making a shorter follow-through for short shots, a longer follow-through for long shots.

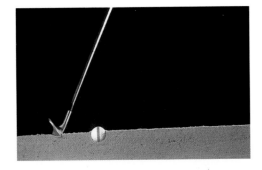

For a buried lie, once again the club does not hit the ball. But the downswing is steeper, creating a more vertical explosion of sand that pops the ball out. The ball comes out on a lower trajectory because the clubshaft was leaning forward at impact, decreasing effective loft.

FACE ANGLE

A key element of handling buried lies is the angle of the clubface, and you'll find different teachers/players offering all manner of advice. Raymond Floyd plays all his sand shots, regardless of the ball's lie, with an open face, turning it to square only if the ball is very buried and the shot is long. Amateurs also should try squaring and even closing the face when the ball is plugged; the more the club is closed, the more the leading edge is turned in so it can dig into the sand. If you have trouble extracting the ball when it's below the surface of the sand, try hooding the face and hitting hard, forgetting about producing any follow-through.

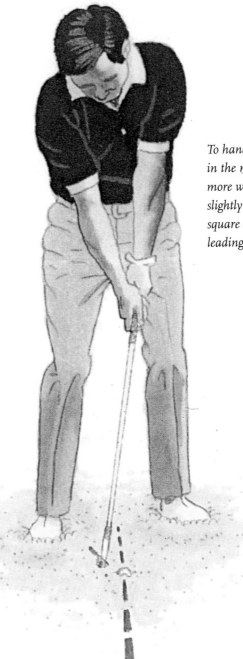

To handle a buried lie, put the ball in the middle of your stance, place more weight on the front foot, stand slightly open, and turn the clubface square or slightly closed so the leading edge digs into the sand.

Note the square clubface and steep, hard swing used by Jay Haas to get out of a buried lie.

more you square the club; and the more you square the club, the farther back in your stance you position the ball. Also choke down on your club to produce a more descending blow from a shorter swing arc. Closing the clubface and moving the ball back reduce backspin, so these shots hit the green and roll, sometimes a long way.

When the ball is totally buried, so you can just see the top of it, position it in the middle of your stance, and keep the clubface square to the target. The problem here is knowing how hard to swing, something only learned from experience.

A "fried egg" is the ball sitting in a little crater about halfway below the surface. With the ball just ahead of the center of the stance, make the same steep buried-lie swing, hitting the sand along the edge of the crater. Use this same technique when your ball is in a footprint or other depression in the sand.

OTHER SAND SHOTS

Chipping. This is the sand version of the bump-and-run, a great play when the ball is sitting up cleanly, there's no bunker lip, and the hole is well away from you (if the flag is close, play the normal explosion shot or putt). Position the ball off the big toe of your back foot and take one more club than you need (e.g., a 9-iron where you might ordinarily use an 8) since the ball-back position reduces effective loft. Choke down, angle your hands ahead of the ball, and take a narrow, open stance. Keep head and body still and make a firm-wristed stroke, the hands leading the club, hitting down into the back of the ball.

Putting. Again, you need a good lie and no bunker lip, but now the hole should be very close to the ball, when a chip or blast is a risky play. Position the ball a little forward in your stance so you meet it on the upswing. (If you played it back in your stance, contact would be made on the downswing, driving the ball into the sand.) Make a long, smooth, arms-and-shoulders stroke, the kind you would use for a long approach putt. You need this much action because sand is much slower than grass.

Under the Lip. When your ball finishes under the overhanging lip of a bunker, play it like an uphill shot, starting with your shoulders parallel to the slope. Then make these adjustments: Put more weight on your back foot for better balance; open the clubface wide for more height; and get your hands in line with or even slightly behind the ball at address. Then hit hard, making contact about two inches behind the ball. You won't get much follow-through, and the ball should pop almost straight up, land on the green, and roll a little.

Shots with Spin. Tour pros do it all the time: hit a sand shot that bounces near the hole, hops forward once or twice, then zips back toward the pin. It takes practice, but can be done.

You need a sand wedge with a moderate amount of bounce (see page 176). Open your stance and the clubface, and dig your feet in enough to stay stable. Instead of picking the club up quickly with the wrists, swing back on a shallow path and only hinge the wrists a little bit. On the downswing, hit half an

Play a "fried egg" lie as you would a buried lie, aiming to make contact with the sand on the back edge of the crater surrounding the ball.

THE ICE-CREAM SCOOP

South African teacher Phil Ritson calls his method of digging out of a buried lie the "Ice-Cream Scoop" shot, because by scooping under the ball while opening the face, the shot not only gets out of the bunker but has a little backspin on it for control.

Take a stance three inches narrower than normal to create a steeper swing. Play the ball well back in your stance, between its center and the heel of your back foot. Start with your hands ahead of the ball, the face of your sand wedge closed, and most of your weight on your front foot. Pick the club up with a quick wrist cock. Starting down, turn the hips back toward the target and pull down hard with your left (leading) arm.

Hit the sand an inch behind the ball, and as the club makes contact, push the left (front) elbow away from your body, what Ritson calls a "winging action"; the club will take a short, deep scoop of sand—like a scoop of ice cream—rather than a long, thin divot.

The clubface will rotate from closed to open, turning the flange under the buried ball, which should come out softly.

From a buried lie, teacher Phil Ritson makes an "ice-cream scoop" shot, digging into the sand about an inch behind the ball and then pushing the left elbow away from the body so the club takes a short, deep divot.

DIFFERENT STROKES

BOUNCE

The sand wedge was designed specifically to help extricate the ball from sand, but many golfers swing in such a way as to negate the club's design features.

On the bottom of the wedge is a rounded flange called "bounce." Upon contact with the sand, the club actually bounces back up because of this curved edge. Imagine bouncing a basketball off the surface of a firm bunker: The ball rebounds rather than burrows into the sand; if you bounce the ball on an angle, it will rebound on a corresponding angle.

Many players mistakenly try to scoop the ball from the sand, hoping to shovel out sand and ball. Instead, rely on the bouncing action for proper sand play. Swing the club down so it contacts the sand one to two inches behind the ball. The club will bounce, lifting sand and the ball and throwing them toward your target. Remember: Don't lift, bounce.

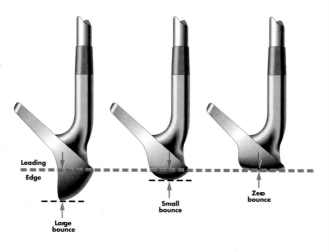

Different degrees of "bounce"—the metal that hangs below the leading edge of a wedge—have different purposes. Usually, more bounce is better for shoveling through softer sand; less bounce works better in hard sand.

inch behind the ball, taking a small sliver of sand; you want to take just enough sand to slide the leading edge under the ball, no more.

SAND TEXTURES

Hard Sand. When sand is hard, a club with a broad, deep flange will hit the surface and bounce off it—and probably into the belly of the ball, blading it low and hot instead of the soft, high flight you want. So either use a sand wedge with less than 10 degrees of bounce, or try your pitching wedge, which has a smaller sole and sharper leading edge. You may be able to handle harder-than-normal sand with one of these clubs and your standard sand technique.

For a larger margin of error from hard sand, widen your stance slightly more than normal for balance, and make a low, sweeping takeaway. Keep your swing U-shaped as you come

If the ball is sitting cleanly and the bunker lip is low, you can chip out. Play the ball back in your stance, choke down, angle the shaft slightly toward the target, and make your normal chipping stroke, as demonstrated by Don Pooley.

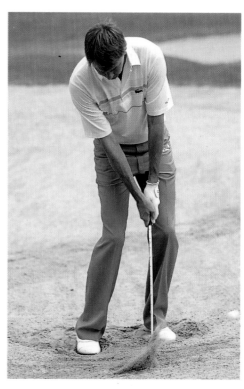

THE LONG AND SHORT OF IT

THE LONG BUNKER SHOT

Most players get overly aggressive, which results in their either jamming the blade into the sand or skulling the ball. But you don't have to swing that much harder for this shot than you do coming out of a greenside bunker. The secret: Swing on a very flat plane and take very little sand.

Take a wider stance. Play the ball ahead of the midway point in your stance and keep your head behind the ball.

In the backswing, allow wrists and forearms to roll freely away from the ball. Bring the club up to the three-quarter position.

Keep your head behind the ball through the downswing but drive your knees toward the target so you skim the club through the sand at impact and make a full follow-through.

You'll probably want to contact the sand about an inch behind the ball, but this will vary with the distance from the hole. For a longer shot, hit closer to the ball.

Seve Ballesteros

THE SHORT EXPLOSION

One shot from sand can spook even the best of players: the short explosion. The situation is paradoxical: The ball lies a few yards from the hole, yet it's hard to put close.

Because the ball has to move a short distance, even good golfers shy away from swinging as firmly as they should. Instead, they decelerate on the downswing and leave the ball in the bunker. Or they get anxious and catch the ball clean, launching it well past the target.

The key is to make a brisk swing without sending the ball too far. To do this, vary the club's point of entry into the sand: The farther behind the ball it hits, the more sand has to be moved and the shorter the shot. For example, you might want to take twice as much sand, so make contact three inches behind the ball instead of an inch and a half. Don't decelerate. Power the club into and through the sand to be sure of getting the ball out of the bunker.

Another key to the short sand shot is a steep swing: The more abruptly you pick the club up, the higher and shorter the ball will fly and the more quickly it will stop on the green.

GOLF Magazine

Seve Ballesteros's method for longer bunker shots calls for a wider stance with the ball just ahead of center. Keep your head behind the ball until impact. Make a flatter swing, driving your knees toward the target and hitting an inch behind the ball. Take a thin, shallow divot of sand.

GRAIN CHECK

Ever wonder why you rarely see the pros hit a bad sand shot? True, they have the skills, but they also almost never have a bad lie. For that they can thank the PGA Tour, which provides host courses with specifications for bunker preparation.

According to course superintendents, the PGA Tour has two commandments for bunkers: 1) The ball shall not plug, and 2) Players shall not get hurt. To prevent plugging, sand is thinned up the sides, especially the front face, so balls hit and roll down into the "collection area," otherwise known as the flat part at the bottom. The Tour insists the flat part have a three-inch base of sand, enough that a club can slide under the ball without hitting the hard subsurface, which could cause injury, particularly to the hands and wrists.

Tour sand is never fluffy because the grains must be of different sizes so they pack together well. In the weeks before the pros come to town, some ground crews spray the sand with water or special chemicals; others drive through the bunkers on a three-wheeled vehicle fitted with nubby tires that push the grains together.

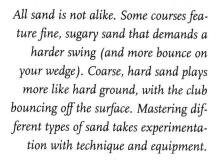

All sand is not alike. Some courses feature fine, sugary sand that demands a harder swing (and more bounce on your wedge). Coarse, hard sand plays more like hard ground, with the club bouncing off the surface. Mastering different types of sand takes experimentation with technique and equipment.

down, hitting about an inch behind the ball as you try to skim, rather than dig, it out.

If the sand is exceptionally hard—more like packed dirt—play the shot as you would off hardpan. Square the blade, position the ball back in your stance, set your hands ahead, and pick the ball cleanly off the surface.

Average Sand. From most bunkers, you'll be able to use your standard sand technique and a "standard" sand wedge, one with 10–14 degrees of bounce.

Soft Sand. When the bunker is especially fluffy, you have to guard against the club digging too deeply and going too far under the ball. The sand wedge from "sugar" should have a lot of bounce, more than 14 degrees, so it glides through rather than excavating.

Play your normal shot, but hit the sand a little closer to the ball, say one inch behind rather than the usual two. This way, if the club bounces too much off the sand, you won't blade the ball. Swing hard, trying to really move some sand; the big flange will see you through.

WIN WHEN WET

When sand is dry, it's easy to slide the clubhead under the ball so it comes out high and soft. Wet sand is heavy and hard, so the club wants to bounce rather than dig. For most golfers, achieving high flight is difficult: All efforts should be directed toward getting the ball up quickly with control.

But many good players like a damp, tightly packed surface of sand, a situation often found on Scottish courses. If

WORDS OF WISDOM

No bunker shot has ever scared me, and none ever will. The key to this bravado is practice. I've practiced and experimented from hundreds of lies with various swings, in effect creating a data bank in my memory that I can call on no matter what kind of sand shot I'm facing. Just as important, I've developed my imagination to the point that I'm confident I can think my way out of any bunker, no matter how tough the lie.

I think you get the message: There are no shortcuts; you must practice.

Gary Player

It is hard to judge the strength or thickness of the sand—a very important matter—because you are not allowed to touch the sand with your club. However, you can plant your feet firmly in the sand when addressing the ball, and after a little experience you will be able to estimate the strength of the sand by means of a pair of well-trained feet.

Jerome Travers

Except where strokes are vital, I'd much rather lay a ball dead from a bunker than hole it. In the latter case the gallery concludes it's luck. So do you. In the former case—great shot!

Bobby Jones

You must get yourself to the point where you can visualize the ball coming out of the bunker, hitting the green at the right spot, and rolling into the hole. At that point, you'll invariably hit the ball close.

Raymond Floyd

---

you have the control to make an aggressive swing while working the clubhead just right, "flicking" it under the ball and shaving a thin layer of sand, it's possible to put a lot of action on this shot so it checks up quickly on the green.

Set-Up: Open your stance, aiming your feet, knees, hips, and shoulders well left of the target.

Play the ball off your left heel, which will keep your head back through impact so you can slide the clubface under the ball for more height.

Use a sand wedge with less bounce, or a lob wedge (60 degrees or more) with minimal bounce, laying the clubface open so it points to the sky. Choking down about four inches creates a more upright swing plane so the club hits the sand with a scooping action.

DIFFERENT STROKES

UNDER THE LIP

Chi Chi Rodriguez is one of the most creative short-game players around, and that ingenuity extends into the sand, for which he has devised a few unusual methods. One of the wildest is his "knife" shot, for a buried lie under the lip of a bunker to a tight pin. Take your putter and turn it 90 degrees in your hands so the toe is pointing right behind the ball (a thin, blade-type putter works best). Stand open, as for a normal sand shot, put most of your weight on the front foot, then swing on a very steep upright plane, so the club is straight up at the halfway point (arms parallel to the ground). On the downswing, pull hard and stab the toe of the putter into the sand half an inch behind the ball, knifing it out.

Chi Chi Rodriguez demonstrates his unusual method of digging out a ball buried in an upslope under the lip. He turns his putter so the toe leads the way. Standing open, the swing plane is very steep; then the club comes down hard into the sand half an inch behind the ball.

Backswing: Keep your lower body quiet, feeling that just your arms and hands are swinging. Hinge your wrists as you swing back to the half-way point.

Downswing: Hold on tightly so the clubface stays open; if it closes, the ball will fly way left. Hit three inches behind the ball, rather than the usual two. Wet sand is hard and compact, so the club can't make as deep a cut. Hitting farther from the ball lessens the force of the blow, but you still want to strive for a follow-through, insuring acceleration on the downswing.

The wet sand technique of Gary Player, one of the best from bunkers. Set up open, with the ball off your front heel, the clubface wide open. Choking down the grip, swing back with the arms and hands. Hold tight coming down so the face stays open. Hit three inches behind the ball and make a full follow-through.

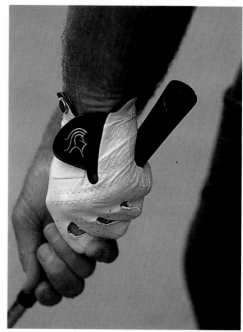

DIFFERENT STROKES

SIDESPIN SHOT

Greg Norman has a favorite long—40- to 50-foot—bunker shot that he hits with sidespin so it dances sideways, rather than backward, on the green.

Holding an 8-iron at the end of the grip, open both the clubface and your stance 45 degrees, and place the ball off your left (front) instep. Make a hard swing along the line of your body, hit 1 1/2 inches behind the ball, and take a shallow divot. The ball will come out low and hot, heading left of your target. It will hit well left of the flag, then shoot hard to the right with incredible sidespin action. Obviously you must play to a big green with the hole cut well right—and practice this shot before trying it on the course.

CHAPTER EIGHT

TROUBLE PLAY

GOLF'S INVENTORS, THE SCOTS, WERE A CALVINIST LOT WHO EMBRACED STERN punishment as the consequence of wayward behavior. Those who strayed from the straight and narrow paid a dear price. Indeed, if anything had the capacity to delight the game's dour-faced practitioners, surely it was the fact that, on their primitive courses, almost every shot was a trouble shot.

Why? Because the only greenkeepers were sheep. St. Andrews, the birthplace of golf, was the crudest of cradles, a stretch of raised beach full of humps and hummocks, whins and gorse. There was no such thing as a fairway, just a shaggy, craggy swath where even the most careful shot might settle in a mole heap, a rabbit scrape, or a clump of heather.

Indeed, golf was played for more than 400 years before anyone got around to mowing the grass, and even as late as 1911, after the Royal & Ancient Golf Club of St. Andrews had purchased its first power mower, a photo of the machine showed sheep grazing behind it on the 18th hole of the Old Course.

As the game expanded, its playgrounds moved inland, off the beach and onto the heaths and moors and meadows where trees, bushes, ponds, and streams joined the list of indigenous perils. As this happened, a debate raged in Scotland over whether these new pastoral courses could ever be regarded as

In the days when golf's only greenkeepers were sheep, every shot was a trouble shot.

true tests of golf, since they were so different from the classic coastal links.

A similar contrast arose among the first American courses. The St. Andrew's and Shinnecock Hills golf clubs, although both in New York State, presented distinctly different challenges—the former spread across an apple orchard in Westchester County and the latter set on a barren stretch of windblown eastern Long Island. When one of the St. Andrew's regulars, a Judge O'Brien, played Shinnecock for the first time, he declared with full confidence that it was "not a golf course at all, because it had no apple trees over which to loft and play."

Modern golf courses, like the TPC at Sawgrass in Florida, have brought a variety of new challenges to golfers.

Meanwhile, as the mower became more widely used, it assumed a major role not only in maintenance but also in the design and construction of courses. Before the twentieth century, the duty of the golf architect had been to make the best use of the land he was given. Now, he began to reconfigure the landscape, first with horse-drawn scoops and then with bulldozers. The result: trouble by design.

One school of architects fashioned penal courses with forced carries over water and other forbidden terrain while another school teased the player with strategic holes that invited him to bite off as much danger as he dared. Even on holes without hazards, the

Britain's Henry Cotton was a down-the-middle player who regarded scrambling as "poor-class stuff."

challenge increased as the earth-moving machines produced artificially banked, rolling fairways and greens perched on faux plateaus.

Since America led the way in the construction of these courses, one may safely argue that trouble play came into its own on U.S. soil. Whereas the Brits had taken a rather straightforward tee-to-green attitude toward the game—like their redcoat armies thumping purposefully forward across open turf—the plucky colonists brought a more unruly but imaginative style, smashing and slashing the ball through all sorts of terrain, then using Yankee ingenuity to return to the hole.

During the first half of this century, England's Henry Cotton and America's Walter Hagen were two of the best players on either side of the Atlantic, and each was the personification of his nation's attitude. Cotton, one of the game's most accurate ball-strikers, was also something of an aristocrat and admitted that he "grew up to think of scrambling as poor-class stuff." He built his reputation on an ability to keep his ball under the wind and inside the fescue. Hagen, on the other hand, attacked a golf course aggressively and confidently, never letting a difficult lie deter him from his appointed target. Muscling his ball from the rough, bending it around trees, and blasting it from bunkers, he showed the world a whole new brand of golf, where pars and even birdies could be produced from anywhere.

After Hagen, every great player recognized the importance of skillful trouble play, and some of the most charismatic champions—Arnold Palmer, Lee Trevino, Ben Crenshaw, and Seve Ballesteros—won tournaments and fans through the unrelenting inventiveness of their golf. Even the great Bobby Jones would look back on his career and make a confession: "I have always said that I won golf tournaments because I tried harder than anyone else and was willing to take more punishment than the others," said Jones. "More immodestly, I will now say that I think a large factor in my winning was a greater resourcefulness in coping with unusual situations and recovering from or retrieving mistakes."

In the modern era, golf course architects have become ever more inventive—some say gimmicky—with elaborately sculpted bunkers, island greens, and chocolate-drop mounds adding new challenges for the golfer. At the same time, cost-consciousness and a concern for the environment have combined to create low-maintenance courses with fewer acres of manicured fairway and large areas of unraked sand and native vegetation. Target golf has become today's game, with the tee shot played to a haven of fairway surrounded by danger.

No matter what design, however, America's courses offer trouble of every variety. In Vermont and Colorado it's the mountain slopes, in Hawaii the incessant wind. In the Southwest it's the desert, and just about everywhere it's tall trees and thick, lush rough. Golf's jails take many forms—and many prisoners—so the wise player comes to the first tee ready to play his best game but also ready to handle his worst.

Walter Hagen was the first of golf's magicians, a player who could make par—even birdie—from almost any situation.

PREVAILING WISDOM

THE ROUGH

Playing successfully from the rough is a two-part process. Step one is mental: Assess the situation and choose the appropriate shot. Step two is physical: Play the chosen shot with a combination of firmness and finesse. Simply stated, you must choose the right shot and then hit the right shot right.

Of course, that is the assignment for just about every golf situation. But deciding on the best shot to hit from the rough is more complicated than choosing a shot from the fairway. Since nine out of ten fairway lies are excellent, most players need consider only the distance from the green and whether or not there is any trouble to cross. Better players will note wind direction and pin placement.

In the rough, there is more to ponder. In addition to the considerations for a fairway shot, there is the delicate and important position of the ball. What sort of rough is it in—sparse, moderate, or thick? What about the height of the grass? Is it short, medium, or tall? Is the ball buried, perched atop the grass, or sitting somewhere in between? Is the grass just in front of the ball thick, and if so, is it growing toward the target or back toward the ball? Finally, how many yards of rough must you cross to reach the fairway? All of these questions, and occasionally one or two more, must be answered before you can make a competent and confident assessment.

Once you have made that appraisal and decided on the kind of shot you want to hit, the most important consideration is club selection. The choice is narrowed by the fact that, for most players, only eight or nine clubs may be used safely from the rough. According to Johnny Miller, the least lofted iron that can be played effectively from the rough is a 4-iron (and for the weekend player, a 5-iron might be the cutoff), while a 4-wood should be the limit of ambition with the fairway woods. Unless you are possessed of unusually strong limbs and a powerful, downward-hitting swing, you will not be able to extricate the ball from heavy grass with a low-lofted club.

Besides, a long iron or wood is rarely necessary, since a ball struck properly from a nest in light or moderate rough will usually jump out faster, fly a bit lower, and bounce and roll farther than a fairway shot hit with the same club. This is the "flyer" effect. The extra flight and distance occur because blades of the long grass come between the clubface and ball, reducing the ability to impart backspin. The result is a virtually spinless shot, like baseball's knuckleball.

Figure on one club less, and sometimes two, when playing from a flyer lie. Where a 5-iron would be the club of choice from the fairway, take a 6, perhaps a 7, when the ball is sitting well (neither perched nor plugged) in light or moderate rough. However, since this shot is spinless, it is more difficult to control in both distance and direction. Do not expect to be able to play an intentional fade or draw from a flyer lie—or any lie in the rough—and

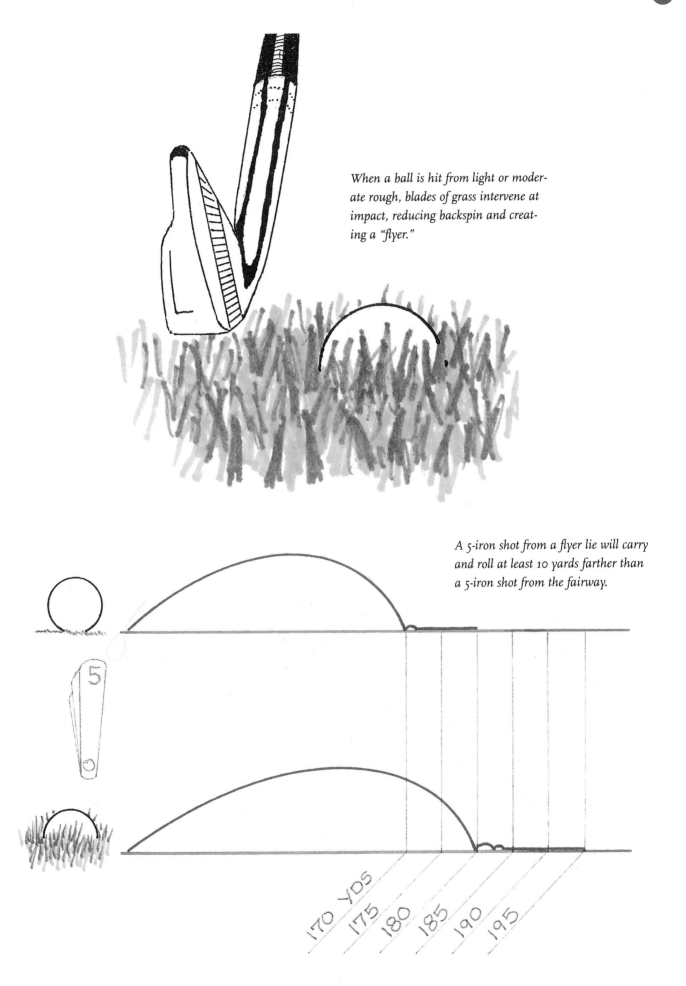

When a ball is hit from light or moderate rough, blades of grass intervene at impact, reducing backspin and creating a "flyer."

A 5-iron shot from a flyer lie will carry and roll at least 10 yards farther than a 5-iron shot from the fairway.

170 YDS 175 180 185 190 195

SPECIAL CONDITIONS

Reading a lie in the rough is a subtle art that takes a bit of experience, but a couple of rules always apply. When you have a flyer lie and the rough is coated with dew, expect even more height and flight than usual. But extremely wet grass will slow down your club and thus require a slightly harder swing. At the other end of the scale—extremely dry rough—even a ball that appears to be sitting down in the grass will be relatively easy to extricate.

Pay attention also to the direction in which the grass is growing. When it is growing toward your target, escape is much easier—indeed, a flyer becomes a superflyer. When it grows against the shot, however, you will need some extra power to get the ball up and flying: Sometimes wedging the ball to safety is the only alternative.

Finally, be aware that the Bermuda grass rough found in most southern climes is more tangly and grasping than northern grasses. In two inches of bentgrass or ryegrass you may be able to play a 200-yard shot, but from the same height of Bermuda, the best tactic often is damage control—just get it back into the fairway.

To minimize the flyer effect, set up with the ball farther back in your stance than usual, and maintain a firm grip.

do not expect the ball to bite when it hits the green. That is why Greg Norman's advice is to "aim for the center of the widest opening to the green, and then plan to land the ball short of it."

No matter what club you select, the shot should be played a bit differently than a shot from the fairway. The changes take place at address, where the ball should be positioned an inch or so farther back in the stance—this will promote a more downward blow, which will minimize interference from the grass. As a general rule, the worse the lie, the farther back your ball position should be.

Make no changes in alignment or grip except to hold onto the club a bit more tightly than you would for a fairway shot. The firm grip is needed because the thick grass has a tendency to wrap around the hosel of the club and close the face.

The swing for a shot from rough requires little or no alteration in technique, although a firm and accelerating hit is important to get the ball up and out of its nest. "Down and through" is the best swing thought.

Jack Nicklaus recommends two variations on this method, depending on the objective of the shot. When he wants maximum distance, he closes his clubface a bit at address and hits a sort of power punch shot that jumps out low and bounces and rolls endlessly. When he needs to make the ball land as softly as possible, he moves the ball an inch or so forward in his stance, opens the clubface a bit, and plays a lob type of shot, with plenty of wrist release through the ball. Just bear in mind that this shot becomes a little easier if you have the brute strength and steeply vertical swing of a Jack Nicklaus.

HEAVY ROUGH

When the ball is buried in the thickest of lies, more drastic measures are needed. Here, the primary objective is a clean escape, and the first need is to select a club that will insure a return to the short grass—usually meaning some variety of wedge. To protect against the clubface-closing effect of the grass, open the face of the wedge a few degrees. That way, when the grass grabs it, the club will close to a square position.

As more insurance, stand a bit closer to the ball than you normally would and position the ball even farther back in your stance—for a wedge shot, this means a ball position near your right toe. Since it is a short shot, you should also open your stance slightly. All of these tweaks will help you produce the steeply up-and-down swing needed to extricate the ball.

During the swing, keep most of the weight on your left side and pull downward firmly through the ball, hanging on tight as you move through impact.

PERCHED LIE

The opposite of the buried lie—a ball perched high atop the rough—can seem like a good break but actually calls for a great deal of care. Pop flies and even whiffs can be the result if the lie is not handled correctly.

In contrast to all other lies in the

To escape from the deepest rough, play the ball back even farther in your stance, and pull down sharply with a wedge.

DIFFERENT STROKES
ADVANTAGE SLICERS
Certain players are more capable than others from the rough. In general, tall players have an advantage, since taller people tend to have more upright swings that allow them to hit down and through the turf, whereas shorter players, with flatter swings, tend to snag the club in the grass. And, surprising as it may be, those who slash at the ball with a slice will not suffer—and occasionally have a slight edge—in the rough, again because of the chopping, cross-cutting swing. Also, since the rough strips the ball of all spin, the shot will not stray right as it normally does.

The danger with a perched lie is hitting under the ball. Guard against that by setting up with the left shoulder a bit higher than usual, and be sure not to sole the club.

When the ball is in light clover, sweep it out with a long, low takeaway and a good extension through impact.

rough, this one must be struck with a shallow, driving impact, not unlike a tee shot. The first rule is to address the ball with your clubhead at the same height as the ball, whether it is an inch or a foot above ground. (Your club will tend to return at impact to the position from which it began at address.) This means gripping down the shaft of your club of choice—and that choice might be any of the 14 clubs in the bag, from the driver to the putter. Also, stand to the ball with your left (front) shoulder higher than your right.

The one swing necessity is to take the club back long and low. This will set up the same type of return to the ball, with the shallow, picking impact that is needed. During the swing, think about keeping that left shoulder high. If you can do that, you will keep the swing shallow and never hit under a perched ball.

BAD LIES

Clover: One of golf's unluckiest lies is clover, four-leaved or otherwise. When your ball settles into this mushy weed, expect the plant's soft stems and leaves to get between the clubface and ball at impact, producing the flyer effect. To counteract the extra roll, take one club less than normal. Clover, unless it is deep, is not difficult to get through because it is so soft. Take your normal stance and grip, then make a long, low takeaway while delaying your wrist cock. A shallow, sweeping arc with good extension through the ball should give you a close to normal shot.

Sandy Rough: In certain areas of the country—notably the sandhills of North Carolina and the Pine Barrens of New Jersey—you will encounter these lies. In such situations, the first

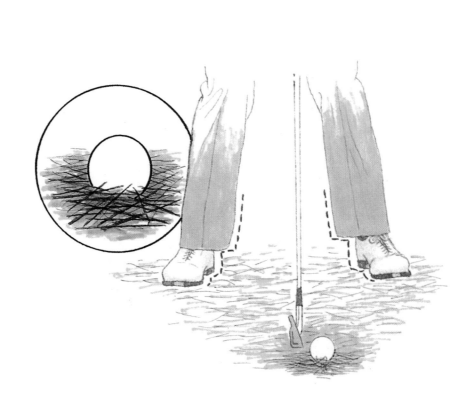

thing to do is determine the type of sand. If it is soft, use the same technique you would use from a fairway bunker. If it is firm, take a slightly wider than normal stance, align yourself to the target, and increase your grip pressure to insure that the club does not twist in your hands. The object is to hit down crisply on the ball with a three-quarter swing. If you hit this shot properly, it will come out with a lot of backspin, so take one club more than usual—a 6-iron instead of a 7—and expect very little roll.

Pine Needles: Unstable is the word when your ball rolls onto a bed of pine needles. Exercise extreme caution when preparing to play this one. Playing off pine needles can be like playing "Pick-Up-Sticks," and if you set off a chain reaction that causes the ball to move, you lose—it's a one-

stroke penalty. For this reason, do not ground your club at address. However, be sure to grip down a proportionate amount to insure that you do not hit under the ball. Square your stance and body to the target, and carefully assume solid footing. (Since pine needles are slippery, a slightly wider than normal stance is best.) On the backswing, make a wide arc with minimal wrist cock. This firm-wristed swing is essential to sweep the ball cleanly off the needles.

Leaves: When the ball is resting on top of, or buried in, a bed of leaves, caution is again the key. Although you may and should remove any loose impediments, you must be careful to do so without moving the ball. Treat this lie as if it were a fairway bunker— do not ground the club. Take a slightly open stance, with your weight favoring

From firm, sandy rough, the best alternative often is to punch the ball out with a three-quarter swing that hits down crisply on the ball.

On pine needles, be careful not to set off a chain reaction that will move the ball. Take a wider stance, and do not ground your club.

When the ball sits among leaves, be sure your footing is solid, keep your swing short and with minimal wrist action, and hit downward to minimize contact with the leaves.

A ball in a divot usually requires a punch shot. Play the ball back in your stance, take one club more than usual, and drive the club downward at the ball, as if you were trying to enlarge the divot.

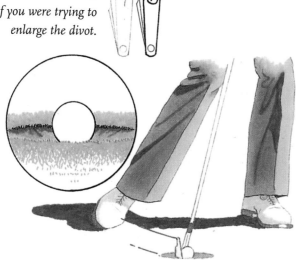

the left side and the ball slightly behind the left heel. Be sure your footing is solid before you swing. The idea is to hit the ball before the leaves with a descending blow. Some instructors suggest looking at the front of the ball to avoid hitting a fat shot. Control is critical, so keep the backswing to three-quarter length or less, and keep the wrists firm throughout. A punch shot often is the best way out.

Divot Hole: One of the most frustrating experiences in golf is to hit a fine drive down the middle of the fairway, only to discover that your ball has rolled into a divot. Golfers have had to deal with this bad luck ever since the first Scotsmen found the first rabbit scrapes.

To minimize the divot's effect, take a less-lofted club than you would from a good lie, and play the ball back in your stance. This will insure that you come down on top of the ball without the club touching any part of the divot. Your backswing should be steeply upward. Make a full turn to generate maximum clubhead speed. On the downswing, slam the clubhead hard into the back of the ball. Imagine driving the ball straight into the ground in an effort to make the divot hole even deeper. Expect the ball to come out low, with less carry but more roll.

A ball sitting at the front of a divot usually is not too dire a situation, but if it touches any of the other divot walls, strange things can happen. Greg Norman says that when he has a ball sitting at the back of a divot, he intentionally tries to skull it—hitting directly into the exposed middle of the ball rather than trying to chop down on it.

When the ball hugs the outside of the divot, he expects the toe of the club to get snagged in the turf, thus opening the clubface and causing a pushed shot, so he aims a bit left. When the ball is up against the divot's near side, the heel tends to grab, so he aims a bit right.

Hardpan: The shot from hardpan, such as a dirt road or any other bare, sun-baked ground, is similar to the divot shot in that your club must strike the ball first. If you hit the ground first, the club will bounce up, skulling or topping the shot. Play a pinching sort of punch shot; take a square stance with the ball farther back than normal, so your hands are well forward of the ball.

If you are also standing on hardpan, be sure your footing is solid and you have good balance—you may have to widen the stance a bit to be sure. (A couple of quick practice swings will tell you.) Your backswing should be as rock-steady as your stance—once again a stiff-wristed, three-quarter move. Be firm and deliberate on the way to the ball, letting your hands and wrists lead through impact and out toward the target. This shot will fly lower than any other, so take that into account in your club selection.

Fairway Bunkers: When your ball finds its way into a fairway bunker, take one club longer than from a fairway lie. But be careful about hitting anything less lofted than a 4-iron unless you have an excellent lie and virtually no bunker lip to clear. Grind your feet into the sand for good footing and grip down an inch on the club to allow for your newly lowered stance.

From hardpan, the key, once again, is to trap the ball against the turf with an abbreviated, punching swing. To achieve firm footing, you may have to widen your stance a bit.

Fairway bunkers require a controlled, sweeping impact. Grind your feet in well, shorten up on your grip a bit, play the ball about a ball-width forward in your stance, and sweep the club into the back of the ball.

THE DISTANCE EXPLOSION

When your ball is in a less than ideal lie in a fairway bunker—anywhere from sitting down a bit to half buried in the sand—try a variation on the greenside bunker shot. Take plenty of club—for instance, if you would normally hit a 7-iron from the fairway, take a 5—assume an open stance, and then try to play the same pick-it-clean shot you would from a good lie. The result will be a sandy, fading 5-iron shot that will travel about the same distance as a 7-iron from the fairway.

Don't try to play out of water unless at least some part of the ball—preferably at least half—is above the surface. Use a pitching wedge and play an explosion shot, as you would from a greenside bunker.

As with the divot and hardpan shots, the object is to hit the ball first, but this time you do not want to hit down on the ball but to sweep it off the sand. The best way to do this is to position the ball perhaps a ball-width forward of its usual spot in your stance and then make a controlled swing of the arms and shoulders, using very little lower-body movement. Keep your eye on the back of the ball and visualize the club sweeping laterally into that spot.

Water: Bobby Jones once said that "the difference between a sand bunker and water is the difference between a car crash and an airplane crash. You have a chance of recovering from a car crash."

Of course, even Jones would have conceded that in rare cases people have survived airplane crashes, and the same is true in golf—on occasion, you can recover from a ball sitting in water. The key is knowing not so much how as when to play the recovery shot, the water blast.

In general, if at least half the ball protrudes above the water line, the shot is playable. Stronger players can go after a ball that is more than half submerged, but no one should attempt to extricate a ball entirely under water. Unlike sand play, the weapon of choice is not a sand wedge, because the thick flange on that club will cause it to bounce off the top of the water. Instead, use a pitching wedge, which will slice through the surface and under the ball.

Proper balance is particularly important on this shot, and in most cases that means keeping the majority of weight on the left foot (which is also apt to be the dry foot). The shot is hit similarly to a sand explosion, with an early wrist break and a sharp downward chop to the ball. Keep your eye on a spot two inches in back of the ball and then hit down on that spot. The only other key is to swing with plenty of force and to be sure to finish—if you leave the clubhead in the water, the ball will stay there as well.

TRICK SHOTS

The Left-Handed Shot: Chapter 4 describes the specialty shots—fade, draw, high, and low—needed to negotiate around trees and other obstacles. But occasionally the situation is so dire that more drastic measures are required. The most widely recognized of these is the left-handed shot.

When the ball lies so close to an object that a right-handed swing is impossible, the lefty shot can serve you well. If you have a plain blade putter, equally hittable from either side, this should be your club of choice. Otherwise, you have two options: 1) Take a short iron such as an 8-iron and turn it so that the toe of the clubface is soled on the ground; or 2) Take a long iron such as a 3-iron and flip it around so that you can hit the ball with the back of the club. The design of your clubs will tell you which of these options offers the best chance of success, but method one is, generally speaking, better for short shots, method two for the longer ones.

Reverse the positions of your hands on the grip—for right-handers, this means gripping the club with the left hand below the right—and then keep things simple. Try a few practice

For a left-handed shot, turn an 8-iron so the toe is on the ground. Reverse your hand positions, increase your knee flex, and keep the swing short and smooth.

DIFFERENT STROKES

THE ONLY TIME YOU MAY HIT A MOVING BALL

If a ball in the water begins to move, the Rules of Golf permit you to swing at it. You may not, however, delay hitting the ball in order to let it drift to a more advantageous position.

When the situation calls for a one-handed shot, position the ball about five inches directly to the right of your right foot, choke down on a 9-iron or wedge, and make a straight-up, straight-down chop on to the ball.

swings, then make an abbreviated swing at the ball—no more than halfway back on the backswing. Try to keep the right arm extended, swing slowly and easily, and keep your head and body down to the ball—the most frequent error on the lefty shot is a whiff.

The One-Handed Chop: From the same sort of situation, a worthy alternative is the one-handed chop. Played with only the right hand, it is relatively easy to execute and provides plenty of distance. Stand with your back to the target and position the ball so it is about five inches directly to the right of your right foot. Taking a 9-iron or wedge, square the club to your intended target (this will mean turning it several degrees counterclockwise before you take your grip) and choke down to the middle of the grip. Then make a straight up-and-down chop onto the ball; for chips and shorter shots, you should stiff-arm the shot; for longer shots, cock the wrist and take a full swing.

PLAYING FROM HILLS

Hilly lies come in four basic varieties—uphill, downhill, sidehill with the ball above the feet, and sidehill with the ball below the feet. Each situation calls for a different adjustment in technique.

Uphill: For beginning golfers, an uphill lie often is easier than a level lie, since loft is built into the slope. The ball will tend to fly higher—and shorter—than normal; for this reason, the first advice

DIFFERENT STROKES

REMEMBER ALTITUDE

As a course's elevation increases, the air becomes thinner and shots travel farther. The general rule is that for every 1,000 feet above sea level, the ball will fly 2 percent farther. This is why, when the PGA Tour plays The Sprint International, 5,000 feet up in the Colorado Rockies, the players have little trouble negotiating the layout's 7,559 yards; at sea level the course would play at approximately 6,800 yards. When playing at a much higher or lower altitude, add or subtract the appropriate percentage before choosing a club.

is to take one club longer than you would from a level lie. If the hill is really steep, move up two clubs—instead of a 7-iron, hit a 5.

When playing from an upslope, your left side is higher than your right at address. To counteract this awkward stance, put some extra flex in your left knee, lean into the slope a bit, and try to get your hips parallel with the incline of the hill. This will create a more normal address position, which will facilitate solid contact with the ball. The other pre-swing adjustment relates to ball position. From an uphill lie, play the ball an inch or so forward of its normal position in your stance.

Keep the swing controlled—a bit shorter and slower than normal—to guard against falling down the slope on the backswing. A predominantly arm-and-shoulder motion should take the club down the slope. This will insure that you bring it back up the slope and into the ball on the forward swing.

This situation tends to inhibit lower-body movement, with the result that the hands roll through impact more quickly than usual, creating a draw or hook. For this reason, you should always aim a few yards to the right of your target when playing from an uphill lie.

Downhill: The downhill lie presents the exact opposite of the uphill situation. Loft will be relatively difficult to impart—the ball will fly lower and "hotter" than usual—so it is wise to take one club less than you would from a level lie, a 6-iron instead of a 5. Because of the nature of the lie, however, the clubface will be delofted, so

you will lose little or no distance, especially if your target is well below you.

As with the uphill shot, the most important principle is to get your hips parallel to the slope. Once again, this is done by putting extra flex in the uphill knee (this time it is the right knee for right-handers). A couple of practice swings will tell you that you need to play the ball an inch or so in back of its usual position in your stance. For most people this will be about midway between the feet.

For an uphill shot, lean into the hill, putting some extra flex in your left knee and getting your hips parallel to the slope. Play the ball an inch forward, and in the takeaway let the club follow the downward slope.

When hitting downhill, put some extra flex in your right knee, play the ball at midstance, and use an arm-and-shoulder takeaway to move the clubhead up the slope.

This set-up will leave you with most of your weight on your right side, and it should stay that way throughout the swing—otherwise you could lose your balance and stumble off the ball. Make the clubhead follow the slope of the hill upward to a three-quarter-length backswing. The correct forward swing is a controlled down-and-through movement. (Nicklaus says to feel as if you are "chasing" the ball with the clubhead well beyond impact.)

There will be a tendency to fall forward ahead of the ball, with the result that pushed and faded shots are almost unavoidable, so compensate by aiming well to the left of your intended target. And if you do fall forward, there is no shame. Indeed, Bobby Jones recommended that on the steepest downward slopes "the player must take a step or two in the direction of the slope in order to maintain his balance."

Ball Above the Feet: The first thing to do when you have a sidehill lie with the ball above the feet is sole your club behind the ball so that the bottom of the club lies flush with the sidehill slope. If you take your address with the club in this position, you will find that you are standing relatively far from the ball, and yet your hands are closer to the ball than normal. Thus, the first compensation you must make is to grip down a couple of inches on the club. When you grip down, your hands will be farther from your body than on any other shot, and you will be set up for a rather flat, around-the-body swing, one that tends to produce pulls, draws, and hooks—all shots that go to the left. Prepare for this either by aiming yourself well to the right or by opening the clubface a bit. (If opening the face, take at least one more club to offset the higher trajectory.)

Set your weight toward your toes and make a smooth, compact swing. Maintaining your balance is the key to solid impact.

Ball Below the Feet: With a sidehill lie with the ball below the feet, the challenge is to keep the body down through impact while also keeping the club from opening. Increase the bend in your knees to produce a "sitting" posture. This will move more weight onto the heels. On a severe slope, stand a bit closer to the ball and bend more from the hips to reach the ball. The ball will tend to fade or slice, so compensate by aiming to the left of your target. If the situation dictates that you hit a straight shot from this lie, close the clubface a bit and move the ball back in your stance an inch or two—and expect a lower trajectory.

As with all hilly lies, the swing should be "quiet," a compact movement made mostly with the arms and upper body, not the legs. It is particularly important with this lie to keep the head still to guard against a shank.

WIND AND WEATHER

While golfers know wind will affect nearly every one of their shots, they usually underestimate its effect. In *Search for the Perfect Swing,* authors Alastair Cochran and John Stobbs measured the effect of headwinds and tailwinds and found that a drive into a 30-mph wind will travel more than 100 yards shorter than the same drive

When the ball is above your feet, grip down on the club, shade your weight toward your toes, aim right, and keep the swing compact.

From a sidehill lie with the ball below the feet, put extra bend in both knees so there is more weight on your heels. Aim left of your target, and, once again, keep the swing short and controlled.

with a 30-mph tailwind. The study also found that, into a 30-mph headwind, the shot will hook or slice five times more than it will downwind. Here is the wind's effect on a distance for shots with a driver.

WIND SPEED (IN MPH)	CARRY (IN YARDS)	TOTAL DISTANCE (IN YARDS)
30, headwind	158	162
15, headwind	187	208
no wind	200	232
15, tailwind	209	255
30, tailwind	223	268

The Tour players, who cope with breezes every day, have a few tricks for gauging the wind. On any hole with a pond, Tom Watson looks to the water for guidance: The upwind side of the lake will be calm while the downwind side will be choppy. On wooded courses, Curtis Strange looks at the tops of the trees both behind the tee and in the landing area. Tom Kite looks at the flags on adjacent holes for additional input, because mounds or trees near the green he is playing may conceal the true wind speed and direction.

On a downhill shot, the wind's effect increases because the ball is in the air longer. Conversely, the wind's effect is diminished in an uphill situation. And on any windy day it is wise to plan on additional roll, as the wind quickly dries out fairways and greens.

Four points of advice apply to any shot in the wind: 1) Play for square club-to-ball contact; 2) Widen the stance to provide a more stable base; 3) Make a slightly shorter, more compact swing; and 4) Swing with a smooth

tempo—do not let the wind make you rush the shot.

Tailwinds: When playing with a tail-wind, tee the ball a little higher than usual to add some trajectory. (With a light tailwind, this will add distance; with a strong tailwind, it will help you get your usual distance, as strong gusts tend to knock the ball down.) Focus on making a full backswing turn and swinging through into a full, high finish. Consider hitting your tee shots with a 3-wood, as its higher trajectory and added backspin will help the shot travel farther and straighter than the same shot with a driver.

Headwinds: Into a headwind, tee the ball a bit lower than normal to encourage hitting the ball low on the clubface. From the fairway, move the ball back, but no more than an inch from its usual set-up position. Both of these

Three U.S. Open champions have three different tricks for gauging the wind. Opposite above: *Tom Watson checks the surface of water hazards.* Opposite below: *Tom Kite watches the flags.* Above: *Curtis Strange looks to the treetops.*

DIFFERENT STROKES

JACK DISAGREES

Jack Nicklaus advocates a different strategy when playing in tailwinds and headwinds. Into a tailwind, he tries to play the lowest shot possible in order to minimize the wind's effect on his ball. Into a headwind, he tees his ball at normal height, reasoning that this enhances his ability to pull all the clubface onto the back of the ball. Also, he points out that teeing the ball low encourages a more downward blow, which adds backswing and makes the ball soar upwards, the one thing you definitely do not want.

Four keys to remember in any kind of wind: 1) Play for square club-to-ball contact; 2) Widen your stance; 3) Shorten your swing; 4) Swing smoothly.

In a tailwind, consider hitting a 3-wood instead of a driver. Tee it high and make a full backswing.

tactics will help produce a lower trajectory, a necessity when playing into a headwind. As extra insurance, Greg Norman advocates a wider stance for lower shots, saying that it lowers his center of gravity for a flatter, more forward-driving swing.

Take plenty of club so you do not try to overpower the ball in order to reach the target. Into a strong breeze, this may mean as much as a 4-iron or more instead of an 8. The idea is to "swing with ease into the breeze," to take enough club that you do not have to swing as hard as usual. By easing up on the swing you will impart less backspin, which helps the ball bore through the wind with less resistance.

In a stiff headwind, minimize your weight shift to the right during the backswing. A big weight shift can make it difficult to move back to the left with the wind pushing against the body on the forward swing. Finish with your hands lower than normal to promote more of a punch-type shot.

Crosswinds: When hitting in a crosswind, the better player, who can curve the ball in either direction, should work the ball against the wind to cancel the breeze's effect, creating a more-or-less straight shot that lands softly. Players who are not able to hook or slice on command must take their chances, letting the wind maneuver the ball for them.

There are two strategies when playing tee shots in a crosswind. If you're confident and want to get every inch of distance out of your drive, tee the ball as near as possible to the side the wind is coming from and maximize the downwind effect of the breeze. (The difficulty with this strategy is that the ball will land moving at an angle and will continue rolling in that direction. If the ground is hard, even a well-played shot can end up in the rough.) A safer ploy is to tee on the side that opposes the wind—the right side of the tee in left-to-right wind, for example—and hit against the breeze, letting it blow your ball back toward the center of the fairway, while accepting a reduction in yardage.

If you are a habitual slicer or hooker, you can mix the above methods to match the curve of your shots. Play for a straight shot if your ball will be curving into the wind, or let it take a long ride on the wind if the breeze and your shot pattern move in the same direction.

Rain: Into every golfer's life a little rain must fall. Wetness is by far the worst of nature's pranks, and it demands extra concentration. The first and most important adjustment is mental: Accept the fact that you will lose distance. Slippery grips and wet fairways mean less-than-optimum impact and little roll. You also will have to swing with less force and greater control.

The overall advice for playing in the rain is the same as for doing anything else in the rain: Keep as dry as possible. Use your umbrella not only as a shield from the rain but as a place to hang a dry towel that will keep your hands and equipment dry. On extremely wet days, carry an extra glove or two, preferably of the water-resistant variety. Some teachers recommend wrapping a handkerchief around the club to promote a secure hold as you swing. A chamois—the

Widen your stance and tee the ball low when hitting into a headwind. These adjustments will help you hit a low, boring shot.

For maximum distance in a crosswind, tee the ball on the side of the tee that the wind is coming from, then hit down that side and let the wind blow the ball diagonally forward. For maximum accuracy, tee the ball on the opposite side and hit diagonally against a crossing wind, letting the breeze blow the ball into the center of the fairway.

There is only one important key when playing in the rain—stay dry. Use your umbrella not only for cover but to keep a towel dry and handy.

WORDS OF WISDOM

To be really expert at recovering from any kind of trouble, a player must possess a certain amount of club control. Many of the shots made from such places are not golf shots at all, but are acts of club manipulation possibly never tried before. The player who can handle his tools and has a spark of inspiration can often do wonders.

Bobby Jones

The keenest delight in golf is given to those who, finding themselves in trouble, refuse to be depressed, and, with some recovery, snatch from their opponents what seemed for them certain victory.

Robert Hunter

Amateur golf is a game of trouble shots and one-putt pars. It follows therefore that good scrambling is the amateur's fastest, most direct route to better golf.

George Peper

Golf is the game that evolved over humps, hollows, sand craters, ridges, dikes, and clumps of heather and gorse. These features made up a game that is a trial of luck and ingenuity. How dull to have no obstacles to dodge or need no "escape" shots in one's repertoire.

Peter Thomson

cloth used to dry cars—also can be a big help in drying grips on a wet day, and such cloths now are produced and sold especially for golf. A good rain suit should be in the bag as well as a rain hat and, of course, waterproof shoes.

On days of hard, constant rain when a tournament or other commitment forces you to keep on hitting, stay under the umbrella as much as possible, and keep your clubs under either a bag cover or a towel. Before playing a shot, follow this routine: Position the bag under the umbrella and select your club. Re-cover the clubs and dry both the grip and face of the club you have selected. Dry off your hands and then grip the club while you are still under the umbrella. Then, with a minimum of delay, leave the umbrella, address your shot, hit it, and get back under cover.

As far as technique is concerned, control is the key. Widen your stance for firm footing, take at least one club more than normal, and swing well within yourself, with a firm grip on the club and a minimum of leg action. The ideal impact is a picking motion that minimizes the chance of a fat shot. Whenever possible, choose a wood over an iron—the smooth, wide sole of the wood makes it much less likely to dig into the wet ground. Your ultimate objective is to keep the ball in play; because if there's one thing worse than trouble on the golf course, it's wet trouble.

Cold: The tactics are much the same in cold weather. Keep as warm as possible without sacrificing freedom of movement—several layers of light clothing are better than wearing a parka. Above all, keep your hands warm—use mittens, a hand warmer, keep them in your pockets or under your arms—but keep them warm. You will lose distance, so adopt the more-club-and-less-force strategy. Also, before taking any swings, allow plenty of time to loosen up your muscles.

A good way to get extra distance on a cold day is to play a draw, which will give you plenty of bounce and roll. Also, assuming the ground is hard, expect a bit of extra distance no matter what kind of shot you hit—another reason to keep the swing under control.

Studies have shown that a golf ball loses between 5 and 10 percent of its distance in cold conditions. However, it takes several hours for a ball to become cold, so if you keep the balls in a warm place the night before your round, there will be little or no effect.

Heat: In extremely hot weather, the best advice is, of course, to keep as cool as possible. Do not hit too many balls before playing; dress in lightweight, light-colored clothing, and always wear a hat. Use a towel to keep your hands dry, and carry an extra glove as well. For protection against dehydration, drink water at every opportunity. Finally, be aware that in hot weather your muscles will be loose and elastic, the ball will be warm and resilient, and the fairways likely will be dry and hard. That means you will not have to swing hard to hit long. This may be the one time when, if you are undecided between two clubs for an approach shot, you should go with the shorter stick.

Tour pros, such as 1996 British Open champion Tom Lehman, know that the best way to stay warm and fluid is to dress in several light layers, rather than one bulky garment.

CHAPTER NINE

PUTTING

PUTTING WOULD APPEAR TO BE THE EASIEST ACTION IN GOLF. THE STROKE IS SHORT (relative to the full swing), the ball doesn't have to get into the air, and the terrain being traversed is the best tended on the course. Yet putting is the bane of golfers at all skill levels.

According to Dave Pelz, a former NASA scientist who has spent the last 20 years studying the short game, putting accounts for 43 percent of the modern player's score. Think about that: Nearly half the shots made by pros and amateurs are putts! That statistic is even more amazing when one realizes that in the game's early days, putting was little more than an afterthought.

Perhaps the first golfers were swinging their shepherd's crooks and tree limbs in an attempt to knock stones into a rabbit burrow. Certainly by the time golf societies were forming along the eastern coast of Scotland, players were aiming at a crudely cut hole of indeterminate size. The first of the original 13 rules of golf, adopted in 1744 by the Honourable Company of Edinburgh Golfers, reads, "You must tee your ball within a club length of the hole." That means the area around the hole would have been marred and compacted by footprints as golfers walked about preparing to hit their next drive. Some historians suggest the hole provided the sand on which the ball was teed.

The large double greens on the Old Course at St. Andrews actually serve two holes each—one going out, one coming in (the white flag is for hole 5, the red for 13).

The earliest greens were nothing more than extensions of the fairway, possibly patches of land where the grass had been "mown" by grazing sheep and goats. Sometimes the land suggested a spot for hole placement, such as in a hollow or atop a plateau. Similarly, the positioning of hazards around the hole was entirely natural. (Deliberate siting of hazards around greens came later as a way to protect a course's integrity once equipment and course conditioning improved.)

Writing in *A History of Golf,* Robert Browning (the golf historian, not the poet) said, "The modern idea of the putt as a shot in which the ball is rolled into the tin is not entirely applicable, because greens in the early days were not specially tended and prepared, and a purely rolling shot could not always be trusted to roll straight."

In the early 1800s, cups were small flower pots, set in holes cut by dinner knives. It is believed that the first cup-cutting tool was used in 1849 at Royal Aberdeen. Holes were first lined with a metal cup, Browning's "tin," about 1874 at Crail, to keep the hole from collapsing. Despite these advances, it wasn't until 1891 that the Royal and Ancient Golf Club of St. Andrews standardized the size of the hole at 4.25 inches. The rationale for this dimension is lost to history, but logic suggests that holes were cut just wide

enough for the ball to fit in next to the flagstick.

The poor condition of greens affected the golfer's choice of weapons. Well into the nineteenth century, players carried two kinds of putters. The driving putter was for low approach shots over open terrain. Green putters were for use closer to the hole, but they had more loft than modern putters to compensate for the shagginess of the greens. (This remained true for many years. Said Charlie Price of Bobby Jones's putter "Calamity Jane," it "seemed to have the loft of a one-iron. But then I realized all the chickweed and poa annua and other agronomical garbage Bob had to putt over in his

day. Some loft was a necessity.") The heads of early putters were long and thin, made of soft wood that wouldn't damage the light, feather-stuffed balls. After harder gutta-percha balls came into use in 1848, clubs became shorter and thicker, looking like the half-moon mallet-head putters of today.

The first great advocate of putting was Willie Park Jr., of Musselburgh, Scotland, son of the first winner of the British Open. In 1880, at age 16, Willie Jr. was a golf professional and green-keeper; he won the 1887 and 1889 British Opens. According to Harry Vardon, Park struck the ball off the toe of the putter, bringing it in from the right side of the hole. More important

Bernhard Langer shows the agony of a wayward stroke. This missed putt of only a few feet cost the Europeans the Ryder Cup in 1991.

Putting on the first hole of the Old Course at St. Andrews, Scotland, in 1798. Note the long-nosed putter, open stance, and less-than-perfect putting surface. Also note the clubhouse of the Royal and Ancient (back left), which still stands today, and the nongolfers out for a stroll—with dogs (back right).

than his method was his diligence, sometimes spending all day on the practice green. He wrote a book titled *The Art of Putting* (one of the first single-topic instruction manuals) and uttered one of the game's most famous quotes: "The man who can putt is a match for anyone."

Park became a noted designer both of courses (including England's Sunningdale) and equipment. He used a putter he built—named "Old Pawky"—that was notable for its gooseneck: The hosel was bent, so the head was offset slightly behind the shaft. This meant the hands led the face into impact, producing crisper contact. In 1894, Park patented the Wry Necked Putter, which featured the gooseneck hosel and a

longer, thinner, blade-shaped head made of steel; within a few years, the most popular putters were metal blades. To this day, most putters have an offset hosel.

In the old days as in ours, there was no single technique for putting. Horace Hutchinson, writing in the highly influential *Badminton Library* in 1895, said that "the stroke is made almost exclusively with the wrists."

Two years later, H. J. Whigham's *How to Play Golf* counseled, "Do not putt entirely with the wrists. The arms and even the shoulders should enter into the stroke."

In 1913, U.S. Amateur champion Jerome Travers, one of the first great American putters, wrote, "the wrists and arms should work in unison. The true putting stroke is best described as a pendulum movement in which neither the wrists nor arms predominate."

The same breadth of advice could be found for the grip, stance, alignment, and other subsections of technique. Yet for the most part, putting was done the way Harry Vardon demonstrated in his *The Complete Golfer,* published in 1905. Vardon is bent way over, his back almost parallel to the ground. The putter is very short so his hands are knee-high and holding on with nearly the same grip he applied to the full swing. His stance is wide open, with the left (front) foot pulled way back off the line. About the only similarity to modern technique is the position of his head and eyes directly over the ball.

Besides providing fodder for post-round conversations, the wealth of instruction meant that putting was becoming an increasingly important part of the game. Some of the credit goes to great players like Vardon, the short-game genius Walter Hagen, and great putters like Travers, Bobby Jones, and Walter Travis (who won the 1904 British Open using a center-shafted putter, which was outlawed by the R&A in 1910, a prohibition that lasted 40 years). These men not only talked about putting's significance, they proved it by winning tournaments rolling the ball.

They were able to do so because greens improved after the turn of the century. More care was given to maintenance, particularly watering. Noted golfer and analyst Henry Cotton said that the golden age of putting began in

"The Old Man," American Walter Travis, caused a sensation in 1904 by winning the British Amateur with his center-shafted "Schenectady" putter (shown here). This style of putter was then outlawed by the Royal and Ancient Golf Club for 40 years.

Above: *In putting as in every other facet of the game, Bobby Jones was the ideal. His long, loose stroke is best described in one word: natural.*

Opposite, above: *Throughout his career, Bobby Jones used but one putter, which he called "Calamity Jane." It carried quite a bit of loft, necessary to handle the scruffy greens common in his day.*

Opposite, below: *Bobby Locke, who won all over the world in the 1940s and 1950s, set up in a closed stance and tried to hook the ball—curving it from right to left—into the hole.*

the 1920s, when players "on the gradually improving putting surfaces, could regularly rely on getting by with brilliant putting (when the rest of their game was below first-class average) . . . golfers with inferior long games began to win events through skillful performances on and around the greens. How could this happen? I believe it was because competition and analysis showed more clearly the supreme value of good putting."

The methods of the great putters varied, proving this to be the most idiosyncratic motion in golf. According to Bernard Darwin, Travis was the first to use the reverse-overlap grip, still the most popular today: "To see him putt was a liberal education in smoothness and rhythm."

Hagen was all movement, starting from a wide stance and placing the ball well forward in his stance to give it top spin; as a result, his putts were rarely short. He also was famous for his confidence, which improved with every tough putt he routinely holed. Darwin said, "It would hardly be possible to name a better putter day in and day out."

Jones, who may have been taught putting by Travis (and, indeed, used the reverse-overlap grip), was known for a long "sweep" through the ball and the same smoothness demonstrated in his full swing. In *Golf Secrets of the Masters*, Tom Scott and Geoffrey Cousins sum up Jones's putting, and the rest of his game: "The stroke was, to him, of the greatest importance, and was best done naturally and without fuss."

There have been many other great putters through the years, from the tall

George Archer (who nearly doubled over his six-foot-five-inch frame by bending at the hips and knees) to the tiny Jerry Barber. Lloyd Mangrum, Dave Stockton, and Nancy Lopez make most lists of the greats, as does South African Bobby Locke, who studied the line for what seemed an eternity, set up in a closed stance with the ball well forward—trying for topspin like Hagen—then "hooked" it into the hole like Willie Park.

Paul Runyan, known as "Little Poison," won the PGA Championship twice in the 1930s. He was famous for putting with his palms facing out so the Vs formed by the thumb and forefinger of each hand pointed at their respective shoulder. Then he made an arm-and-shoulder stroke, with little wrist action, and kept the putterhead moving on a straight line directly at the target.

Another 1930s phenomenon was Leo Diegel, who, despite 20 wins in the United States, battled nerves throughout his career. For a few years, he conquered the greens by spreading his feet far apart and bending way over at the waist so his chin nearly touched the top of his putter. He stuck his elbows straight out to the sides, then rocked his shoulders back and forth. The method became known as "diegeling."

More recently, Billy Casper locks his knees straight and uses a very wristy stroke. Jack Nicklaus crouches over, takes an open stance, and sets his eyes behind the ball, yet manages to make more than his share of heart-stopping putts long and short. Arnold Palmer, a great putter early in his career, knocks his knees together,

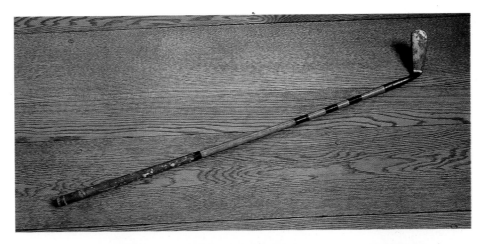

squats down, and tries willing the ball into the hole. And possibly the best putter of the last 20 years, Ben Crenshaw, makes a long, loose, unbelievably natural arm-and-shoulder stroke; his magician's touch has tamed the toughest greens in the world, those at Augusta National. (Similar in method to Crenshaw are the two best left-handed putters of this or any day, senior Bob Charles and youngster Phil Mickelson; both have had tremendous success with flowing, and fearless, strokes.)

As befits an action with so many variations in technique, there have been an infinite number of designs for the putting weapon. Jones's "Calamity Jane" was a hickory-shafted blade putter, long and low like Park's "Old Pawky." After Jones retired from competitive golf in 1930, Jane was mass-produced and a best-seller for many years (despite Charlie Price's comment that "it looks and feels like something you'd find in a box of Cracker Jacks"). In 1946, John Reuter unveiled the elegantly curved Bull's Eye, which is still very popular. The years have seen many versions of the mallet-head, a throwback to the putters designed for the first gutta-percha ball.

There's been every other manner of clubhead as well. Some have had moving parts (later deemed illegal), some with loft and some without (and even "negative loft," to impart topspin), with the shaft entering at the toe, round like a sausage, long like a croquet mallet. It is tempting to say every possible design has been attempted, but new ones are released almost daily.

In the 1960s, Karsten Solheim, an engineer, garage-tinkerer, and frustrated

Opposite: *Paul Runyan, "Little Poison,"*
won two PGA Championships in the 1930s,
relying on magical putting to defeat much
stronger, longer-hitting opponents.

Above: *Leo Diegel developed his own method*
of putting, adopting a wide stance, bending
over sharply at the waist, and sticking his
elbows straight out to the sides. This practice
became known as "diegeling."

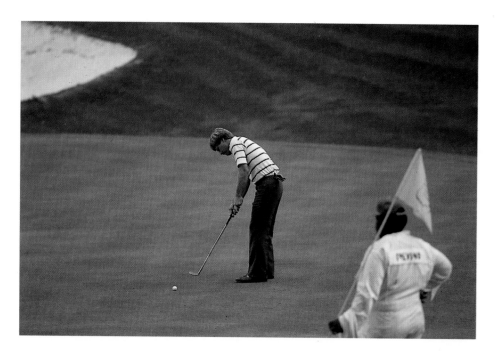

A long, syrupy stroke earned Ben Crenshaw acclaim as one of the greatest putters of his day. He twice conquered the treacherous greens of Augusta National, winning The Masters in 1984 and 1995.

Left to right, the evolution of putter design: Early putters were long, low, and made of wood. Literally thousands of designs have been introduced over the years. The most common type today is heavily weighted at the heel and toe to resist twisting at impact and transmit full power to the ball no matter where it contacts the face.

golfer, designed a putter with the weight that's usually concentrated behind the sweetspot moved to the heel and toe, which seemed to lick the problem of the face twisting at impact. He threw a few in his car and tried getting them into pro shops and the hands of Tour pros. When Julius Boros won the 1967 Phoenix Open with one of Solheim's "Ping" putters—named for the sound it made at impact—the revolution began; heel-toe designs are far and away the most popular today.

Nicklaus won the 1986 Masters using a heel-toe weighted putter roughly twice the size of most other such models. Palmer experimented with thousands of putters, particularly later when his will stopped working. Yet Crenshaw stuck with "Gentle Ben," a simple blade putter—the classic Wilson 8802—that would have looked as at home in 1935 as it did winning The Masters in 1995.

In the late 1980s, when former stars earned the chance to play again on the Senior Tour, they looked for help recovering lost putting prowess

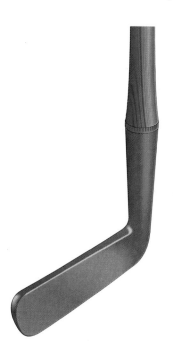

Arnold Palmer keeps his lower body quiet by knocking his knees together and squatting over the ball.

and battling the "yips," an involuntary spastic stabbing at the ball that afflicts many older golfers. Charlie Owens stuck an extra-long shaft in an old head and created a 50-inch putter (standard length is 35 inches). The top of the grip is anchored to the chest with the left hand; the right is placed about 12 inches down the grip, where it controls the action, creating a pure pendulum stroke. The long putter had a flurry of success, then lost favor. Only a few, like Scotland's Sam Torrance, who rests his chin on the top of the grip, continue to use this extra-long crutch.

Amateur golfer/engineer Karsten Solheim designed a putter with the weight concentrated in the heel and toe. As a result, the face did not twist at impact and energy was not lost when the ball was hit off-center. His putters launched a revolution that also led to the development of game-improvement woods and irons.

PREVAILING WISDOM

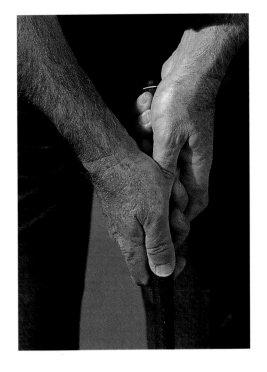

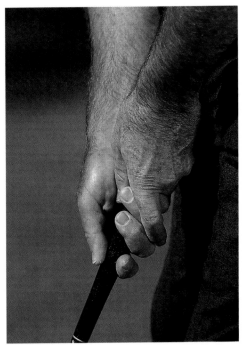

The reverse-overlap is the most common putting grip, preferred because it makes the two hands work as a single unit. The left forefinger overlaps the last few fingers of the right hand.

THE GRIP

As much as any action in the game, good putting depends on a good grip. How you hold the club determines the path of the stroke and the angle of the clubface at impact. Because the stroke is short and the target small, it's critical that you keep the club on line so the ball stays on line.

There is no ideal way to hold the putter, but all good grips share a few fundamentals. First, the palms are parallel to each other and parallel to the face of the club; as the palms go, so goes the putterface. Second, the thumbs lie straight down the top of the shaft, keeping the putterhead from wavering and encouraging an on-line stroke. Third, a good grip places the palms down the sides of the shaft, the fingers wrapping around it: This way the fingers regulate feel while the palms provide power.

The most common grip is the reverse-overlap, so called because the left forefinger, which usually intertwines or hides under the right pinkie during the full swing, emerges and overlaps the last few fingers of the right hand. The reverse-overlap makes the two hands work as a single unit while letting the fingers have feel. As Ken Venturi said, the reverse-overlap "is the simplest to learn and repeat and has the fewest moving parts to go wrong."

Some golfers extend the right forefinger down the side of the shaft for more stability and control. Craig Stadler points his right forefinger "so it acts as a guide for the direction of the putterface." (He calls this his "old man method," because it is used by many older golfers searching for consistency. Others have referred to it as the "over-40 finger.")

Often overlooked is wrist position.

WHAT TO LOOK FOR IN A PUTTER

Factors to consider when buying a putter, from Dave Pelz.

THE THREE NECESSITIES

1) The length and shaft angle (lie) must complement your physique and posture in the following ways:
• Length: Long enough to allow practice without back pain.
• Length: Short enough to avoid getting hung up in rain gear and other clothing.
• Length and Lie: You must be able to position your eyes directly above the putting line and your hands directly under your shoulders.

2) Compensation for your impact errors. Check your impact pattern by sticking impact tape on your putterface and stroking 30 putts.

If you mishit toward the toe, use a center-shafted putter.

If you mishit toward the heel, use a heel-shafted putter.

3) The combination of head shape and alignment aids (lines, arrows, etc.) should help you aim the clubface properly.

THREE IMPORTANT CONSIDERATIONS

1) The weight of the clubhead should be appropriate for your touch. Find the lightest putter you can and putt with it, taping dimes to the back or bottom until you learn which headweight gives you the best touch.

2) Grip size and shape.

Small enough to promote control (a solid connection between your arms and the shaft).

Large enough to keep hands and fingers from interfering and overlapping too much.

Contoured to situate your hands in the same position every time. Grips with flat areas, corners, and edges help.

3) Combination of moment of inertia (head-twisting at impact) and balance (weight distribution) should promote the feeling of a smooth swing and stroke. This usually means choosing between a putter with a lot of feel and little forgiveness on off-center hits, and a more forgiving putter that, because of heel-toe weighting, provides less feel.

MINOR CONSIDERATIONS

1) A putter that returns to the same position when soled allows easy, repeatable gripping and set-up without affecting aim.

2) Appearance. It's nice if you like its looks, but realize that ugly putters can work, too.

3) Solid feel and sound at impact promote confidence.

TOTALLY IRRELEVANT CONSIDERATIONS

1) Price.
2) Use on pro tours.
3) Opinions and recommendations of friends and other golfers based on their experience.

Wrists should be arched, riding high, so when seen from behind, the putter shaft is a straight-line extension of the arms. Along with a reverse-overlap grip, this position keeps the wrists quiet—they won't hinge and unhinge during the stroke, which produces unwanted power and putterface rotation.

How tightly should you squeeze the putter grip? H. J. Whigham's advice of 100 years ago is still appropriate: "You must not hold your club as in a vise, nor must you allow either hand to dominate the other. The grip should be even with both hands—just tight enough to obviate any turning of the [club]head, and not so tight as to stop the circulation or freeze the muscles."

ADDRESS

Set your eyes directly over the ball, or if you must, slightly behind the ball but still over the target line. (This also means your eyes are over the clubhead at address.) To check eye position, stand over your ball: Hold another ball against the bridge of your nose, then release it; the dropped ball should hit the one on the ground or else hit just behind it but still on your target line.

If you set up with your eyes inside the target line, the tendency is to make an inside-to-inside stroke; some golfers like that (more below), but for others it leads to off-line putts, usually finishing right of the hole. Setting your eyes outside the line leads to an outside-to-outside stroke, which no one advocates, and putts missed to the left.

Once in position, don't lift your head to take a final look at the hole. Turn your head, and turn it back so

SEEING IS BELIEVING

Putting allows golfers to get away with wide deviation from the norm. That certainly is true of the grip. But Tour players who are successful with a strange hold have worked long and hard to make it work.

Corey Pavin positions his hands more under the club, thumbs to the outside. This grip takes the wrists out and creates an arms-only stroke.

Bernhard Langer clamps the top of the shaft to the inside of his left forearm with his right hand. This prevents the left wrist from breaking down during the stroke and helps Langer fight the yips.

Mark Wiebe splits his hands, which lets the lower (right) hand dominate.

Paul Azinger gets his hands working together by intertwining them in several spots. It also quiets the wrists.

For a few months of 1995 and 1996, Mike Hulbert putted with only his right hand on the grip (the left rested against his side). He said it kept his head and body still. What began as a practice drill worked on the course.

Mike Hulbert began putting with only the right hand on the club as a way to keep his head and body still in practice. The results were so good that he actually putted this way on Tour for a few months.

Putting is the most tolerant part of the game, allowing for wide variation from the accepted norms. Nowhere is this more true than the grip. Among current Tour pros using unusual grips are, left to right, Corey Pavin (thumbs to the outside), Paul Azinger (numerous overlaps and intertwines), Dave Barr (all 10 fingers on the grip), and Craig Stadler (right forefinger down the shaft).

your eyes return to their original spot.

And a word about the head. Billy Casper's "one basic fundamental to putting" is that it must remain still throughout the stroke. If your head moves, chances are the body is moving, too. And you can't make a solid stroke and hit the ball solidly in the center of the clubhead if the body doesn't remain still. (One way to keep the head still all the way through the stroke is to listen, rather than look, for the ball to fall into the hole.)

Stand with your feet, knees, hips, and shoulders parallel to the target line.

This is the easiest way to be sure of swinging the putter on that line. Jack Nicklaus sets up slightly open, which he says gives him a better view of the line and a little more room for the arms to swing through unimpeded by the body; he has grooved his stroke so it travels on the target line. (Closed-stance putting has been rare since Bobby Locke in the 1950s; it demands too much manipulation to produce square impact and not hit your front foot.)

Bend slightly at the knees and hips, with your arms hanging comfortably. At address, your hands should be

Right: To encourage a straight stroke, your eyes should be directly over the ball at address. To check your position, hold a second ball against the bridge of your nose and let go: It should hit the first ball or just slightly behind it on the target line.

Opposite: The typical Jack Nicklaus putting crouch: Stance slightly open, well bent over at the waist, hands close to the body. He putts this way because he feels it gives him a better look down the target line.

under the shoulders, the clubhead under the eyes. (Keep these parameters in mind when buying a putter: Get one that lets you comfortably reach this position.) Your arms should be almost straight, but neither tense nor locked at the elbows.

Stance width is largely a personal choice, as long as the feet are far enough apart to form a stable base. Start with the feet shoulder-width apart. Widening the stance might make you feel steadier (it often is suggested for windy days) because it lowers your body's center of gravity. A narrower stance makes you stand taller. Comfort and feel are your principal objectives.

The final ingredient of a good set-up is ball position. Ideally, club meets ball at the low point of the stroke (the bottom of the swing arc), which is almost always beneath your sternum in the middle of the stance; start by positioning the ball there.

However, if you stand open and put

DIFFERENT STROKES

LEFT HAND LOW

Also called "cross-handed," this method reverses the common placement of the hands on the grip so the left hand is below the right. Recent proponents include Fred Couples, Nick Faldo, and Tom Kite, all of whom had been hitting putts off-line as a result of a wristy stroke. "I originally thought it would fight the problem of my left wrist 'breaking up,'" said Kite. "It does that and more. My left-hand-low posture also squared my alignment and clubface and eliminated the cause of my left-wrist problems, which were required to compensate for my too-far-left alignment."

Said Couples, "It eliminates my tendency to stand open and aim left."

This method is not new with today's Tour stars. Bruce Lietzke made his "Case for the Cross-Handed Grip" in *GOLF Magazine* in 1982. Lietzke noted he could accelerate through the ball without worrying about left-wrist breakdown. And, "the grip helps you keep your shoulders square for more accuracy."

Fred Couples demonstrates left-hand-low, or "cross-handed" putting, in which the normal position of the hands is reversed. Many golfers, pro and amateur, have tried this grip as a way to eliminate wristiness during the stroke.

more weight on your back foot, the low point will have moved back, about off the right heel. If you lean well forward, set the ball off the left heel.

If your eyes are over the ball and you still tend to push putts (hitting them to the right), you probably are making contact before reaching the low point; move the ball forward in your stance. If you pull putts (to the left), you're meeting the ball past its low point; move the ball back in your stance.

THE STROKE

Envision your arms and shoulders forming a triangle. To make the putting stroke, keep the triangle intact (the wrists don't hinge) and swing it away from the ball, then back toward the ball, accelerating through impact. The clubhead stays just above the grass, lifting slightly on the backstroke and again in the follow-through. But the sole should not brush the ground; the center of the face—the sweetspot—should strike the equator of the ball.

On all but the longest putts, the putterhead will stay above the target line for almost the entire stroke; only when you have a long putt will the putter come slightly inside at the top of the backstroke and again at the finish as a result of the shoulders turning around the spine. This "straight-back, straight-through" stroke is easy for most golfers to learn because it requires limited practice time and doesn't require much feel.

Another way to perform this stroke is to think of the back of your left hand swinging along the target line, always remaining perpendicular to it.

FIND THE SWEETSPOT

Whether or not your putter already has a mark on the topline, locate your putter's true sweetspot and mark it for yourself. Factory-made marks are often wrong and being off even a fraction of an inch leads to missed putts.

Hold the putter grip between two fingers: Do *not* hold it vertically, but angle it as if you were putting, with the sole parallel to the ground. Tap the face with a metallic point, such as the end of a key. Keep tapping until you feel the spot that makes the head swing straight back and forth without face rotation or wobble, and minimum vibration. That's the sweetspot. Make a mark on the topline (scratch a line with a file and fill it with paint) directly above the sweetspot so you can see it when addressing the ball.

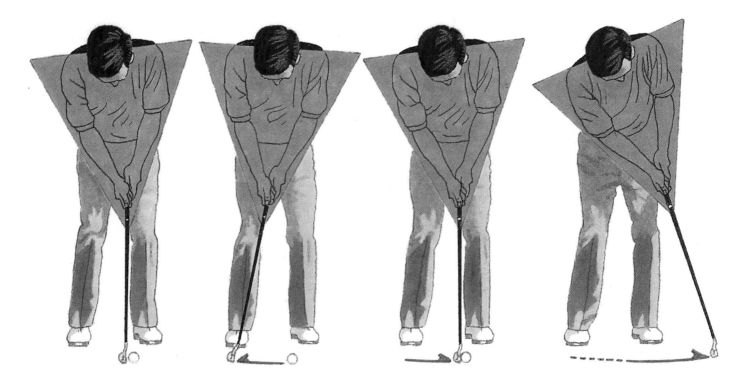

Keeping the triangle formed by the arms and shoulders intact, swing the putter away from the ball, then back through the ball, being sure to accelerate through impact. Keep the head and body still throughout the stroke.

DIFFERENT STROKES

CROQUET-STYLE

In the early 1960s, Tour pro Bob Duden advocated putting "croquet-style," one foot on each side of the target line and the body facing the hole. He contended it was easier to keep the blade square to the line, easier to set the body to the ball and the hole, and, thanks to the first two reasons, produced more solid contact.

Duden putted fairly well this way, but it probably won him more funny looks than money. Nobody thought much about it until the 1966 PGA Championship, when Sam Snead followed a yipped double-hit on a single putting stroke by going croquet-style on the next green. It was a successful cure for the 54-year-old Snead until the method was outlawed by golf's ruling bodies. So he varied the method slightly, moving his right foot until it was next to his left: His body still faced the hole, but both feet were on the same side of the line. Furthermore, he separated his hands more than a foot on the shaft—the left hand holding the top of the putter steady while the right swung the club back and forth, like a pendulum, along the line.

Snead's yips vanished because putting "sidesaddle" uses the big muscles of his arms, back, and shoulders, while eliminating the smaller, twitchier muscles in the hands and wrists. Both sidesaddle and croquet-style keep the putterhead on line, so contact is square. Snead also said his method forced him to accelerate through the ball naturally. He used it to win a number of senior events.

When Sam Snead saw his putting prowess fade in his 50s, he went "croquet-style," facing the hole with his feet on either side of the ball and wielding the putter like a croquet mallet. Snead said this method eliminated use of the less reliable small muscles of the hands and wrists.

Another great putter, Morris Hatalsky employs a classic stroke. His head and body are still, the stroke is long and flowing, and he accelerates through impact.

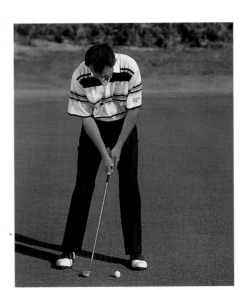

A MULTITUDE OF MOTIONS

Putting allows for individuality, which for most golfers means a slightly different grip or opening the stance just a hair. But there have been quite a few putting iconoclasts over the years. Here are a few of the more interesting.

George Low was a Tour pro in the late 1940s and early 1950s, but his real fame came as a teacher of putting. He honed a stroke that was virtually unbeatable; he got so good, he could win matches stroking the ball with his foot.

Low's method took liberties with many accepted maxims of putting. He altered the grip so the club was held mostly in the fingers, with the right thumb and forefinger positioned as if firing a gun; he shortened the right thumb so the pad under the thumbnail—the most sensitive part of the hand—rested on the top of the grip.

He insisted on standing stock-still, eyes directly over the ball, weight "concentrated" on the left heel, in a square or slightly open stance. The stroke was inside-square-inside, with a little wrist action, then hitting slightly down on the ball to give it overspin for truer roll: "It has been shown to my satisfaction that a ball can be made to roll immediately upon impact without skid or slide, if it is struck above its center, which is the case with my downbeat stroke. The top half of the putter face must strike the ball just above its equator to make this work. . . . " He also preached making a very slow, deliberate takeaway and an evenly paced stroke.

Low wrote a book on putting and was widely sought out, particularly by other pros. He traveled from tournament to tournament, hanging around the putting green and imparting his wisdom for a fee. He was jokingly referred to as "America's Guest," relying on others to pay his way.

The most successful Japanese golfer of all time is Isao Aoki, who has had great success with a putting technique that violates nearly every rule. Addressing the ball off the heel of his putter, he bends his wrists so his hands are low and the toe of the club is off the ground. (This requires a putter with a rounded sole. Aoki also adds lead tape to the heel of the club to move the sweetspot in that direction.) Without moving his arms, he putts by hinging and unhinging his wrists, rapping the ball, then stopping the putterhead with little or no follow-through. Hubert Green once noted, "Aoki may look funny, but his figures don't look funny on the scorecard."

Another funny-looking technique is "The Perfect Putting Method," first promulgated by Englishman Paul Trevillion in the early 1970s. A high-handicapper, he studied putting for two years and developed a style that closely resembles Sam Snead's sidesaddle stroke, but with the body positioned as it is when putting normally. Bending way over, he splits his hands about a foot apart on the shaft, with the right (bottom) hand less than a foot above the clubhead and the right forefinger extended. Holding the top of the club with the left hand, which is anchored against the right forearm, he swings back and through with his right arm, making a pendulum stroke straight along the target line. Trevillion claims his method is all but foolproof from inside four feet, saying it made him the world's greatest putter. (He once made 1,000 consecutive four-footers.) In 1996, to coincide with the release of a videotape and special dual-grip putter, he challenged the world's best golfers to a million-dollar putting match; he got no takers.

Finally, in the 1930s, Mark G. Harris, a Chicago businessman, moved to Los Angeles for his health and, in his 60s, took up golf. He honed an unusual short game that was documented in film and, at the time, widely lauded for its success.

Harris thought the putting stroke was the basic motion in golf and every other swing a larger version of it. His putting grip was the Vardon overlap, and the stroke a miniature version of the swing, employing some body turn, plus arm, hand, and wrist motion. He actually released the clubhead, turning it over slightly through impact.

In the long term, Harris had little influence on putting instruction, but it is interesting to note how far afield his thinking—and that of these other innovators—traveled.

The other common putting stroke is inside-square-inside. Watch Ben Crenshaw and you'll see he swings the putter on an arc around his body—inside the line going back, square at impact, back to the inside on the through-stroke. Some instructors prefer this method because the putter traces the same path (albeit in smaller form) as a full swing; also, the shoulders rotate around the spine, keeping the putterhead close to the ground so it sweeps through impact. But most also note that Crenshaw is blessed with tremendous feel, which is necessary to assure solid contact time after time when using this method.

Clubhead acceleration is vital for good putting. One way to be sure your stroke keeps moving is to regulate the length of your putts by the length of your backswing: The longer the putt, the longer your backswing. But don't make it so long that you suddenly realize it's too much, forcing you to decelerate coming into the ball. As with every other shot in golf, if the clubhead is slowing as it approaches the ball, contact will not be crisp and the results will be erratic. You are better off making a slightly shorter backswing and a longer follow-through.

Hand in hand with the length of the putting stroke is tempo. No matter how long the putt, your stroke should have a consistent rhythm. This means your stroke takes the same amount of time whether it's a five-footer or a 25-footer. Find a comfortable tempo with a metronome, then use it to practice your stroke for putts of all lengths.

Harry Vardon was a firm believer in "never up, never in," saying, "the hole

DIFFERENT STROKES

THE PRO SIDE

When average golfers miss a breaking putt, it usually isn't on the "pro side," or high side, of the cup. Facing a big breaker, most amateurs don't allow for enough curve, so the ball rolls by on the low, or "amateur" side and never has a chance to go in. A big break requires a harder hit, and that's not easy when worrying about knocking the ball four or five feet past. Also, putting off sidehills tends to open or close the clubface with the direction of the hill, making unwanted pushes and pulls common.

One way to avoid the amateur side is to adjust your stance for big sidehill putts. On putts that break right to left, stay above the cup by closing your stance; for left to right, open your stance. Another precaution is to play the ball off the toe of the putter for the right-to-left putt, off the heel for left-to-right. By hitting the ball out at the ends, you keep the putterhead from twisting with the hill at impact. But you won't be hitting the ball on the sweetspot, so swing a little harder to get it to the hole.

Some tricks for handling breaking putts from the pros. Seve Ballesteros, a true short-game genius, claims to have an unorthodox approach to breaking putts. No matter which way the putt breaks, he takes an open stance and swings the putter on an out-to-in path, making contact on the toe of the putter to deaden the hit. Since hitting off the toe imparts left-to-right "cut" spin, he starts the ball slightly inside the line running to his target spot; the spin takes it up to that spot, then it drifts back to the hole.

Cary Middlecoff used to suggest playing a left-to-right breaker farther forward in the stance, off the big toe of the front foot, while standing a little closer to the ball. He reversed the instructions for a right-to-left breaking putt: Position the ball closer to the middle of the stance and stand farther away. Chi Chi Rodriguez offers much the same advice, although he doesn't move the body, just the ball, for breaking putts.

will never come to you." He advised playing for the back of the hole, hitting the ball firmly to be sure of getting it there. Of course, in Vardon's day greens weren't manicured but often mangled, and a firmer stroke made sense. At the other end of the scale is Harvey Penick, who hated "never up, never in" and recommended that all putts die in the hole. His imagery is unforgettable: "I like to see a putt slip into the hole like a mouse." Jack Nicklaus wants the ball to drop over the front lip, but he thinks "never up, never in" just the same. He wants the putt to "die at the hole—not before it ever gets there!"

There is no right or wrong, but whichever you prefer—dying in or banging in—try to be consistent.

READING THE GREEN

Because a putt rolls to the hole, the lay of the land it traverses has a huge impact on its progress. You must study each green and analyze how numerous factors will affect the ball's motion.

There is no such thing as a flat green. Putting surfaces are constructed with slopes so water can run off them. Therefore, you will rarely encounter a perfectly flat putt unless you are just a few feet from the hole. That means you must know how to handle uphill, downhill, and sidehill putts.

You must develop a green-reading routine that lets you quickly look over the line of your putt to determine what slopes are present. Actually begin looking before you reach the green, as you walk up the fairway: Look for the overall slope of the land around the green, as that's usually the way the green will slope, too. Once on the green, while other players are lining up and stroking their putts, you should read yours from the ball to the hole, the hole back to the ball, and at least one side, looking for the most pronounced slope. Learn to do this quickly, and not only to maintain pace of play: The longer you look, the more likely you are to see more or different slope from what really is there.

Uphill Putts: Once you've determined that the putt runs uphill, resolve to hit

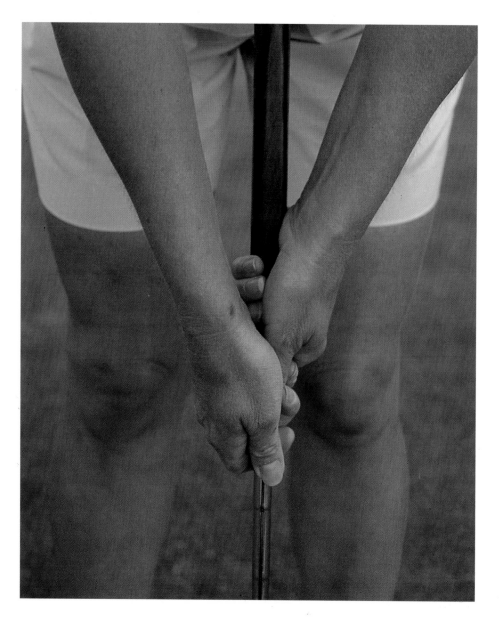

One way to handle fast, downhill putts is to grip well down the club, almost to the metal of the shaft, and make a normal stroke. Choking down shortens the club, reducing the energy imparted to the ball at impact.

it solidly so it gets to the hole. Putting uphill, the back of the cup is slightly higher than the front. This "backstop" allows you to charge the hole instead of trying to die the ball over the edge.

Charging the cup also means you don't have to worry as much about pace and break (sideslope); simply aim for the back of the cup and be aggressive. If you miss, the hill should keep the ball from running too far past the hole.

The steeper the slope, the harder you must strike the ball. Solid contact is crucial, since any distance lost by hitting away from the sweetspot or with poor putter path will be magnified by the slope. A common fault when trying to putt aggressively is moving your head and body forward during the forward stroke. This sway increases the chances of missing the sweetspot. Keep your body steady on uphill putts.

Downhill Putts: On a downhiller, the back of the cup is lower than the front, so there's no backstop to save you. Your stroke must be more conservative. Too quick a putt can jump right over the hole.

Aim for the front lip of the cup and try to roll the ball with just enough speed for it to topple in. Guard against making a nervous jab that causes the ball to jump and race down the hill. The slope will magnify your mistakes.

One way to take speed off a quick downhill putt is to hit the ball off the toe of the putter. Striking it away from the sweetspot produces a "dead" impact, preventing the ball from coming off hot and speeding down the hill.

Another way to deal with slick downhillers is to choke down the grip,

---

STIMPMETER

Green speed is measured with a device called a Stimpmeter, a 36-inch aluminum bar with a V-shaped groove down the middle and a notch six inches from one end. It was invented in the late 1940s by Edward Stimpson, a leading amateur player. He was looking for a way to ensure that a green rolled uniformly, and that all greens on a course were the same speed. The Stimpmeter is placed on a flat area of the green, a ball resting in the notch; the notched end is raised slowly until the ball rolls down the groove and onto the green (about a 20-degree angle). The length of the roll, measured in feet, becomes the Stimpmeter rating.

---

even onto the shaft itself, and make your normal stroke. "Shortening" the putter reduces energy transfer the same way choking down shortens a full-swing shot. Hit the ball off the sweetspot so the face remains square.

Sidehill Putts: Uphill and downhill slopes are easy to see and relatively easy to read. Bigger problems come when you have to judge "break," the sidehill slopes that are very common to greens.

There are numerous ways to play break. Some golfers try to ignore it completely, hitting putts extra hard to reduce the influence of any sideslope; they usually hit too hard for the distance, and unless it squarely hits the back of the hole, the ball races well past. (This method makes more sense on short putts, when hitting the ball slightly harder than normal reduces break but still gives the ball a good chance of going in.)

To play break, start the ball to the side of the hole and let the sidehill steer it back. Identify a spot to aim at, then set up to hit a straight putt at that spot. A common mistake golfers make is looking at the target spot but think-

THE AMAZING TRUTH

In April 1995, *GOLF Magazine* ran a groundbreaking instructional article, "The Amazing Truth About Putting." After years of research and working with both pros and amateurs, Dave Pelz has determined that golfers incorrectly read—and stroke—breaking putts. Pelz's statistics show that about 85 percent of all missed putts fall on the low side, below the hole. By comparing where golfers aim with where they *think* they aim, he determined that golfers underread by a factor of four! That means when a putt really breaks four feet, golfers read only one foot of break.

But that's not the end of it. Although golfers see only 25 percent of the break, they make subconscious adjustments to start the putt higher than they think. Without realizing it, they aim their putters at a spot higher up the slope—about 65 percent of the way—then manipulate their strokes to steer the ball to about 85 percent. So everything is bad—the read, the alignment, the stroke, and the result.

These numbers prove true for pros as well as amateurs, although PGA, LPGA, and European Tour golfers see slightly more of the "real" break, aim a little higher, and steer it almost to 100 percent. But most of the time they still miss.

Pelz blames human nature: We golfers see only what we want to see. We don't think we can make a big-breaking putt, so we convince ourselves it is straighter, therefore easier to handle. Then our subconscious attempts to supply the necessary corrections.

There is another downside. Because golfers steer all their breaking putts (to one side or another, and to different degrees depending on the read), they are unable to make a simple, straight stroke. That means even the short, straight putts are at risk since golfers haven't grooved a straight path and flush, sweetspot contact.

Pelz has two suggestions: 1) Learn to make a straight stroke (using string or other practice aids), and 2) play more break than what you see. Until you start to miss on the high side, indicating you've read too much break, double whatever break you think is there. If you see a six-inch left-to-right break, play it as a foot. Eventually your brain will learn to recognize the real break, and, along with a straight stroke, you'll handle breakers properly.

A final note: As part of Pelz's research, he showed that golfers who plumb-bob are no more likely to see the real break than golfers who don't. They, too, see only 25 percent of the break, proving to Pelz that plumb-bobbing is a waste of time and trouble.

According to Pelz, nearly all golfers drastically underread the break of a putt, then make subconscious manipulations to start the ball closer to the correct line. He says the true break is often as much as four times greater than what they "see."

ing about the hole; their body subconsciously alters the stroke, steering the ball toward the hole, inevitably causing it to miss.

PLUMB-BOBBING

One way many golfers, particularly pros, read slope is by plumb-bobbing. They stand or squat behind the ball, dangling their putter at arm's length, squinting as they look down the shaft at the ball and the hole. Plumb-bobbing helps them see how the ground slopes under their feet (it does not indicate slope around the cup, so it won't pick up double-break). They claim plumb-bobbing helps when break is hard to detect.

To plumb-bob, stand directly behind the ball so the cup, ball, and one eye are aligned. Set your body so your eyes are parallel to the sideslope you're on; stand with your knees, hips, and shoulders also parallel. Spread your feet shoulder-width apart, stand comfortably, and face the target. Flex your knees and let your body tilt naturally with the slope. (Some golfers squat to plumb-bob, but that makes it more difficult to set the eyes parallel to the ground.)

Hold the putter grip lightly between the thumb and forefinger, suspending it at arm's length in front of you: The putter must hang freely for an accurate reading. (Point the toe either at or directly away from you so the weighting doesn't make it list to one side or the other. Some putters won't hang straight from every angle; check that yours does.) Sighting with your open eye, position the putter so the

One of the most controversial ways to read a green is "plumb-bobbing," holding the putter close to the eyes and sighting down the shaft to determine the break. Some players swear by it, others consider it worthless.

DON'T PUTT LIKE THE PROS

In 1977, Ben Crenshaw authored an article for GOLF Magazine titled "Don't Putt Like Me." He offered ten reasons amateurs should putt aggressively rather than copy the more careful attitude Tour players have when playing for big money.

1) Pros putt for birdies, amateurs for pars. "I'm able to hit most greens in regulation and thereby have the luxury of two-putting for par, sometimes even for birdie. So I can afford to be cautious." Amateurs, who don't hit most greens, usually have one chance to make par. They should be more aggressive, regardless of a putt's length.

2) Pros play medal, amateurs play match. "In my case, because it normally takes about 275 strokes to win a tournament, I have comparatively little to gain by rushing the hole on a long putt. My own goal is to avoid three-putting. In match play, sinking a long putt often means winning a hole."

3) Pros play on faster greens. "Consequently, the pros are forced to putt very cautiously."

4) Pros play more often. "I can usually judge the effects of slope, grain, moisture, surrounding terrain, and other factors, and come up with an accurate reading on the break of a putt." Amateurs, he says, who have less experience, should hit the ball harder while playing less break.

5) Bold is best on short putts. "This will increase both your confidence and competence on two- and three-footers."

6) Comebackers are easy to sink. "Because when you hit your first putt boldly you can watch the way the ball reacts as it passes the cup." Therefore, you know how to handle the short one coming back.

7) A firm stroke is a good stroke. "If you become a bold putter you will always hit the ball firmly, with an accelerating motion through impact, and will give the ball a good roll."

8) The psychological factor. "Chronic shortness can undermine even the most confident putting strokes." Missing long is not as destructive because you know that at least you got it to the hole.

9) Boldness lets you be your own coach. "If you get the ball to the cup every time, you can begin to see a pattern in your putting." Learn from your mistakes and work on stroke or alignment cures until you fix the fault.

10) Always up, more in. "There are four ways to miss a putt—right, left, long, and short. If you always reach the hole you eliminate one of those four ways."

lowest point of the shaft covers the ball. Without moving your head, look up at the cup: If it appears to the right of the shaft, the ground slopes left to right; if it is to the left, the ground slopes right to left. If the cup is directly in line with the shaft, the ground is level.

Plumb-bobbing will show you the direction of the break, not the amount. However, if the hole is just to the side of the shaft, the amount of break is less than if the hole is well to the side. But generally, plumb-bobbing is only useful as a rough estimate of break, and only the break where you are standing—not all the way to the hole.

If you plumb-bob, make it just one part of your green-reading routine, not all of it. Only practice—stroking lots of putts—will teach you to feel how and how much slope will influence the roll of a putt.

GRASS AND GRAIN

The greens on most American courses are bent or Bermuda grass. Bent generally is found in the North, since it cannot tolerate constant hot weather. In the South, Bermuda is more common.

Bentgrass has softer, finer blades than Bermuda; bent even feels softer to walk on. Bent blades grow closer together, creating more of a "carpet" than Bermuda. These qualities mean a putt rolls truer on bentgrass, whereas a ball rolling on Bermuda will be more susceptible to its sparser growing pattern and spikier blades.

Both bent and Bermuda have grain, the general direction of the grass's growth, but because Bermuda blades are longer and tougher, its grain is stronger and will have greater effect on a putt. Rolling into grain, the ball will slow down—quickly on Bermuda, not as much so on bent. Rolling with the grain, Bermuda putts will be faster than normal and faster than with-grain putts on bent.

Cross-grain also influences a putt: If the grain is growing in the same direction as the slope, the break will be exaggerated; conversely, if the break goes against the grain, any contour will be reduced and the ball will hold a slightly straighter line. In both cross-grain cases, the effects will be greater on Bermuda grass than bent. (When putting cross-grain, you'll probably aim the ball a little higher. Notice that means you're also putting slightly more into the grain, which kills some of the power and increases the cross-grain's effect. So stroke cross-grain putts more firmly and play a little more break.)

Reading grain is not difficult. Stand behind the ball and look down the line of your putt. (Checking for cross-grain, stand on the high side and look toward the hole.) If the grass between you and the hole appears shiny, you're putting with the grain. If the grass has a dull appearance, you're putting against the grain. Raymond Floyd suggests looking at spike marks left by previous players to see how the grass has been pulled up; that will tell you which way the blades are growing.

Some other grain tendencies to consider: Grass usually grows toward the sea, toward the setting sun, and away from mountains (water drains off the mountain and continues across the green in the same direction).

Another factor to consider is green speed. Improved maintenance tech-

DIFFERENT STROKES

RAP IT

A number of notable professionals—Gary Player, Chi Chi Rodriguez, Paul Azinger, and others—make a rap stroke. They take the putter back a short way, then rap or "pop" it into the ball, completely eliminating the follow-through. Some golfers go to the rap on short putts when they want to be sure to hit it firm and hold the line. It's hard to judge the amount of rap necessary on longer putts, so this method demands a lot of practice. It also goes against the theory that all putting strokes have the same tempo.

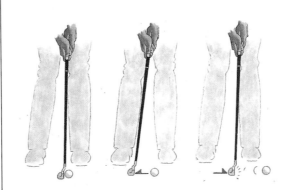

When making a "pop" or "rap" stroke, the putterhead is drawn back a short distance, then quickly brought forward, popping the ball forward. There is little or no follow-through after impact.

DIFFERENT STROKES

THE CHIPUTT

If long putting is a problem, try Dave Pelz's "Chiputt," which is like chipping with your putter.

Hold your putter with your chipping grip. Stand tall with your feet together, stance slightly open, as you do when chipping. Play the ball about centered between the heels. Make a long, smooth swing of the arms and shoulders, with the hands leading the clubhead into the ball. Don't be afraid to release your knees a bit, letting your lower body turn just enough to give the stroke some rhythm.

Another Pelz suggestion of interest no matter how you handle long putts: Don't waste too much time reading a long putt; see the line, then focus on hitting the ball the right distance.

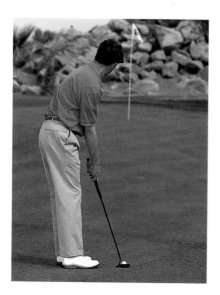

Facing a long putt, the "chiputt" may be easier to control than an extra-long stroke. Play the ball back in a very narrow stance and angle the putter shaft slightly toward the hole. Hit the putt with a descending blow, like a chip. The ball will roll a long way with minimal effort.

niques and stronger strains of grass (which can withstand being cut very short) have increased green speeds over the years. While it's unlikely you'll play many courses cut to the speeds favored by the pros, you still have to know, in general terms, if a course's greens are fast or slow. Someone in the pro shop probably can tell you; ask if the practice green's speed is indicative of what's on the course. You may have to practice stroking the ball harder or easier to compensate for greens slower or faster than what you are used to.

A few other general rules about green speed. A green surrounded by overhanging trees probably will be slow because the sunlight is blocked. Raised or exposed greens tend to be fast because moisture drains quickly, especially when helped by the wind; similarly, bowl-shaped greens hold water and are slower. Greens usually are slower later in the day because the grass doesn't stop growing.

Don't neglect weather conditions when sizing up a putt. Wet greens are slow, and the wetter they get, the slower the ball rolls. Even a light coating of morning dew will make the ball glide on a thin layer of water, slowing the ball and reducing the influence of grain (while allowing you to be more aggressive). Dry greens become hard and fast; watch out for greens so dried and baked that grass almost disappears, producing unpredictable roll. Fast greens usually mean more pronounced breaks.

On windy days, you must create and maintain a stable stance. Place your feet at least shoulder-width apart (wider if necessary), flex your knees, and bend from the hips. Think about what the wind will do to the ball. If the wind and grain are going in the direction of your roll, expect the putt to be straighter and faster. If the wind and grain are against your putt, it will break more than usual, especially as the ball loses momentum near the hole. If wind and grain run with the break, eliminate the low side of the hole from your mind; the high side is the only part likely to let the ball fall in. Wind and grain going against the break straighten the roll, so play for less curve.

THE YIPS

Every golfer lives in fear of the yips, even if he isn't quite sure what they are. He'll know them when he gets them.

The yips usually are described as an involuntary twitching of the muscles in the hands and wrists, resulting in a spasmodic stroke that sends the ball way past the hole. Some people say they were too tense to take the putter back when it suddenly sprang to life on its own, jerking back and through, with no hope of control. Ray Floyd says, "The yips are simply a case of bad strokes, usually on short putts," and like many others, he thinks the problem is mental rather than physical. Nonetheless, the yips are very real: Just ask Ben Hogan, Bernhard Langer, Sam Snead (who is credited with coining the term), Arnold Palmer, Tom Watson, and countless other golfers who have been afflicted at one time or another.

There is no surefire cure for the yips. But there are numerous suggestions. Floyd, who says he gets them from time to time, concentrates on

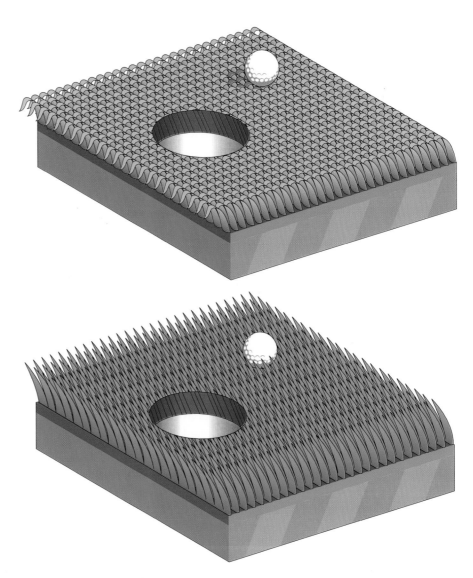

Different grasses affect a putt's success. Bentgrass (above), found in the northern United States, has soft, fine blades and allows for smooth, true roll. Bermuda grass (below), found in southern states, has longer, coarser blades, so the ball does not roll as smoothly. Bermuda also has more pronounced grain—the direction the grass grows—which means putts rolling into the grain need to be hit harder than normal while putts rolling downgrain do not need to be hit as hard.

DIFFERENT STROKES

USE THE WRISTS

You usually want to use the same basic technique on long putts that you do on short—a straight-back, straight-through stroke controlled by the shoulders and arms. However, long putting calls for a little more feel to handle the distance. So you might allow a little more play in your wrists as you change direction from backstroke to forward-stroke, and also at and past impact. Wrist action allows you to hit the ball farther with less effort, so you can better feel your way to the hole. This is also true if you usually make an inside-square-inside stroke.

PROFESSOR PUTT

Playing on a golf scholarship at Indiana University, Dave Pelz regularly competed against a young Jack Nicklaus, and regularly lost. As a scientist with the space program in the 1970s, Pelz worried about launching projectiles much larger than golf balls. Since leaving NASA, he has spent the last 20 years bringing scientific methods to the study of the short game, with particular attention to putting. Labeled "Professor Putt," many of his findings have changed the way golfers think about this part of the game. A number of his contributions to the science of putting are explained elsewhere in this chapter. Here are some other notable observations:

1) How well should you putt? Most amateurs have unrealistic expectations for their putting. According to Pelz's research, Tour pros make at most 55 percent from six feet; 30 percent from 10 feet; and 16 percent from 20 feet. Amateurs' numbers are far worse. So don't get too excited about missing putts, particularly long ones. Be realistic about what is possible.

2) Greens have hazards, too. The average green is a minefield of ball marks, spike marks, and foot prints, all of which can knock a ball off-line. If you make a good stroke and the putt misses, shrug it off. It's not your fault.

3) The "lumpy doughnut." The average foursome leaves 500 footprints on a green, some an eighth of an inch deep, each taking up to 2½ hours to heal. These prints are everywhere—except within one foot of the hole. Golfers are careful not to step that close to the cup, which means the area closest to the hole is pristine and slightly raised. This is the "lumpy doughnut": The ball actually has to run up a little ramp the last six inches to the hole, precisely where a putt is rolling its slowest (which explains why some putts hang on the lip or curl away at the last moment). To conquer the doughnut, see number four.

4) The 17-inch Rule. After rolling thousands of balls at different speeds, Pelz determined that your putt should be traveling fast enough so that if the hole were covered, the ball would roll 17 inches past. This speed gives the ball its best chance of holding its line through the lumpy doughnut and other green hazards while not traveling fast enough to cause too many lip-outs. The 17-inch rule works on all types of grass as well as on uphill, downhill, and sidehill putts (but, obviously, is not necessary on very short putts).

5) The Big Three. These three factors have the greatest influence on putting success.

PUTTER PATH. At impact, the putter should be traveling straight down the target line. If it hits the ball at an angle, either inside or outside the line, 20 percent of the degree of deviation is transmitted to the roll: On a 20-foot putt, striking the ball with the putter moving 10 degrees off-line results in missing by eight inches.

FACE ANGLE. The face must be square to the target at impact. If not, 90 percent of the deviation is imparted to the putt. On a 20-footer, if the face is open 10 degrees, the putt will miss by three feet.

IMPACT POINT. Every putter has a perfect impact point, called the "sweetspot." Miss it by a quarter of an inch and 95 percent of the error is put on the ball. That's enough to make you miss everything over eight feet. Hitting well out at the toe or heel hurts your chances even more.

Golfers are careful not to step within a few inches of the hole, which means the area around the cup is slightly raised. Pelz calls this "the lumpy doughnut": It means the putt runs up a little ramp the last six inches at the end, often causing a rolling ball to curl off-line.

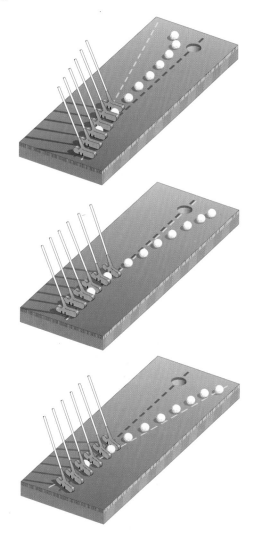

Pelz measured the impact of three mistakes on the likelihood of making a putt. A mistake in putter path—when the putter isn't traveling directly down the target line—imparts 20 percent of the degree of deviation. A mistake in face angle—the putter face is not square to the target at impact—has a 90 percent effect. A mistake in impact point has the greatest effect, transmitting 95 percent of the error when the putter's sweetspot is missed by as little as a quarter of an inch.

keeping the head and eyes still. He also notes that some players putt while looking at the hole instead of the ball; he cites Johnny Miller, who won the 1987 AT&T Pebble Beach National Pro-Am that way. (A corollary is to look at the bottom of the grip rather than the ball. Both methods force you to focus on something other than the ball and clubhead.)

Other possibilities: Change your grip, changing your feel for the putter so your muscles work differently. Squeeze the club as tightly as possible: Tom Watson does this on full shots when he wants to increase blood flow to the hands for more feel. Close your eyes, which stops you from being "ball-bound." Practice one-handed; if you stand tall, bend over; if you putt stiff-wristed, get a little flippy; change the putter you're using. In fact, any remedy can work if it takes your mind off the problem and past disasters.

LONG PUTTING

Putting from 30 or more feet away, your strategy, and method, must change. From this long a distance, you don't have a realistic chance of holing the putt. But unless you are careful, you have a very good chance of finishing so far from the hole that your next putt is no sure thing. The cardinal rule of long, or lag, putting is to avoid the three-putt.

The prospect of three-putting usually causes a player to tense up mentally and physically. The hands, wrists, and forearms get tight as you try to control the putterhead, so you produce a poor swing path and a jerky or decelerating stroke.

Learn to relax and let the putterhead go. Take a deep breath, exhale, then release the club so it swings freely. Concentrate on feeling the weight of the clubhead: Let it coast to a stop on the backswing, then swing it forward at the same speed you swung it back (tempo is still crucial). Don't control the putter, but let it swing. You'll find that your instincts have a better sense for distance and direction than you do. (You may even find your lower body helping out, adding a little leg action on really long putts.)

Because you're making a bigger stroke on a long putt, mistakes will be magnified. If you mishit a 10-footer, it will come up two feet short; mishit a 50-footer and it stops 10 feet short of the target. So it's imperative that you keep your body and head still to ensure that the clubface returns to the ball squarely.

The hardest thing about rolling a long putt close is getting the distance right. Most people gauge a putt's dis-

---

KNEEKNOCKERS

They're the three-foot comeback putts left after a long lag. Or the short putt on the last hole to shoot your best-ever score. Or the little putt to tie or win a match. Whatever the situation, the short distance suddenly looks much longer and it seems every part of you is shaking. How can you make a good, smooth stroke?

1) Keep your head and body still. Don't stand so tense that nothing moves, but think about holding your head and body in place as the arms make the stroke.

2) Putterface square. Keep your grip light so your stroke, and the club path, remain natural. Squeezing the grip stops any natural rotation of the putterhead, which usually means the face is open at impact, sending the ball to the right.

3) Putterhead on the line. Take the club back straight and consciously stroke it down the line in the follow-through. It may help to exaggerate the length of the follow-through slightly.

4) Hit it! Get the ball to the hole. Hitting a little harder is better than not hard enough, which has no chance of going in.

After graduating to the Senior Tour, Orville Moody was one of many pros to adopt a long putter. Almost all its advocates say separating the hands and anchoring the top hand against the chest promoted a smoother, yip-free stroke.

tance by how hard they have to hit it. You can ease some of the pressure on the length of the stroke by picking an intermediate target—a spot on your intended line about 10 feet in front of the ball—and calculate at what speed the ball should be rolling when it reaches that spot so it loses momentum near the cup. Imagine what would be too fast, too slow, and just right. Stroke the ball toward the spot at the speed you've picked. (If the long putt is a breaker, pick the break point, where you think the ball will begin to curve.)

Another way to reduce pressure on the stroke is to take your practice strokes, pick your intermediate target, get set properly, then close your eyes and let your instincts take over. This is an especially useful practice drill, but some golfers do this on the course as well.

What is a good lag putt? Most golfers are happy to leave the ball within three feet of the hole. Thinking about a much bigger target—that's a six-foot-wide circle—also eases the pressure, so don't be surprised if you begin making some long ones just by not trying to.

HOW TO USE A LONG PUTTER

Grip: To hold a long putter, split your hands 12 to 16 inches (nearly all of them have two separate grips, one for each hand), and turn the left hand upside down. The right hand is positioned farther down the club for more leverage and club control. Wrap the left (top) hand about the end of the grip firmly, but not so tightly as to inhibit a free swing. Anchor the left hand against your chest: Start with it against the sternum; move it slightly forward and see if the results improve. Placement of the right hand is a personal choice, high or low. Either wrap the hand around the grip or slide the shaft between the right forefinger and middle finger like a claw. Either way, don't squeeze too tightly.

Stance and Alignment: Posture is determined by the length of the shaft. You want to stand almost upright; pick the shaft length that lets you stand tall. Bend only slightly at the waist and knees. Feet are just inside shoulder-width, weight distributed evenly between them.

Set your feet perfectly square to the target line. You may find it hard to putt with square hips and shoulders, so open them slightly to give the right hand and shaft the freedom to swing.

Place the ball on-line with the left (top) hand so contact is made at the bottom of the swing arc. Eyes are over the target line, just as in normal putting.

Stroke: The right arm and shoulder swing the putter back. Let it move naturally, first along the target line, then slightly inside. Unlike normal putting, don't try to keep the putterhead low; it can't be done with the top hand anchored to the chest. The clubhead will swing up both on the backswing and follow-through.

Make a smooth transition from backstroke to downstroke. The right hand doesn't push going down, only working to keep the head on-line and provide a little push through impact to keep the clubhead accelerating. Be careful not to "pop" the ball, especially on short putts. Practice to keep the downstroke smooth.

Head and body must remain still throughout the putt.

WORDS OF WISDOM

My experience shows conclusively that the really good putter is largely born, not made, and is inherently endowed with a good eye and tactile delicacy of grip which are denied the ordinary run of mortals.

Walter Travis

The key to good putting is comfort and confidence.
Billy Casper

Every sort of instrument, from a respectable wooden putter to a croquet mallet or a billiard cue, has been used, and used successfully, on the putting green. No style or position is left untried, no muscle unturned which may help the ball to its much coveted resting place. Some grip the shaft at the top, some at the bottom; some stand severely erect in the attitude of command, some crouch low over the recalcitrant gutta percha, that they may the better coax or control its movements. . . . Every way is right which fulfills the purpose in view, and each individual is convinced that his style is the best.

H. J. Whigham

Most golfing strokes, it used to be said, could be cultivated, but putting was an inspiration.

Joyce Wethered

I love putting because no element of golf is so tolerant of personal methods and idiosyncrasies.

Bob Charles

The chief reaction among amateurs to poor putting, it seems to me, is exasperation, combined with a sort of vague hope that, by some kind of mini-miracle, it will all have gotten better by the next time they play.

Jack Nicklaus

Great putting can make up for a lot of sins.
Tiger Woods

CHAPTER TEN

STRATEGY

IT'S A SAFE GUESS THAT THE STRATEGIC ELEMENT OF GOLF BEGAN ONLY MOMENTS after the birth of the game itself. Let us presume that the first golfer was a shepherd striking a small stone with his crook. We can envision his progress as a three-part education: First, he learned how to hit the stone; next, he learned how to hit it powerfully; and finally, he learned how to hit it cleverly. It was with that third discovery—when the shepherd graduated from mere stone-beater to a planner and player of shots—that golf strategy was born.

Since then, strategy has evolved in direct response to two other parts of the game—course design and improvements in equipment.

"Architecture," says Tom Doak in *The Anatomy of a Golf Course,* "was an integral part of golf on the earliest Scottish links. The greens were located on the best patches of turf, but since there were no formalized fairways, it was up to the players to 'design' the best route to the hole while avoiding the natural hazards."

Allan Robertson, the St. Andrews ballmaker who is generally agreed to be the game's first professional, may also have been the first bona fide course architect. He was responsible for numerous improvements to the Old Course, the most important of which came in 1848 when he cut down hundreds of gorse bushes, thereby widening the fairways from 40 yards to nearly 100 yards.

When Allan Robertson widened the fairways of the Old Course, strategic shot planning became important for St. Andrews golfers.

Suddenly, the menacing bunkers that until then had to be dealt with head-on could be avoided by tacking to the sides. Negotiating the terrain became as important as striking the ball, and from that point forward architects and golfers have played a relentless game of attack-and-defend.

The influence of equipment has been equally forceful, and one cannot help but assume that it dates to the very beginning. After all, that first shepherd-golfer surely had a special incentive in avoiding the gorse and deep grass: Round stones of the proper size were difficult to come by.

With each development in the game, new strategic considerations arose. As the feather ball gave way to the more resilient, faster-spinning gutta-percha, and then the Haskell, shots flew not only farther but higher and wider. The dreaded slice was born,

but at the same time golfers learned how to spin the ball intentionally to avoid trouble and better attack the hole. Golf evolved from a land campaign into an aerial assault, and the architects responded with raised greens, water hazards, and out of bounds.

And so it has continued. Armed with an ever-larger arsenal of weapons and shots—but confronted by ever-toughening places to play—all serious golfers have become full-time tacticians, picking their spots and choosing their shots to fit the flow of the terrain and the tenor of the match.

As the ball evolved from the feathery (top left) to the livelier gutty (top right) and Haskell (below), golfers learned to impart spin that enabled them to maneuver their shots from tee to green.

PREVAILING WISDOM

YOUR FIRST MATCH IS WITH YOURSELF

The dictionary defines strategy as "a careful plan or method for achieving an end." For most golfers on most days, that end is either a low score or victory in a match. Whichever the goal, the strategic plan begins the same way—with an honest self-appraisal.

Before a golfer can beat an opponent or conquer a course, he needs to win the battle with himself. Tom Watson, one of the game's canniest competitors, devoted an entire book to golf strategy, and it began with these words: "Playing strategic golf is a matter of negotiating with yourself. You have to negotiate how much risk you are going to take and whether the potential reward is worth it."

That negotiation, if it is to be successful, must be done in good faith—you must be honest with yourself. At some point in your development as a golfer, you must make a brutally frank appraisal of your strengths and weaknesses. It is there that wise golf strategy begins.

Admitting one's limitations is the toughest part. Every normal human being wants to play the hero shot—we

are all wishful thinkers—and each of us, at one time or another, pulls it off. These fleeting triumphs may bring us joy and win the odd hole or match, but over the long haul they do us nothing but damage, as in future situations we try unsuccessfully to duplicate our low-percentage gamble. Ultimately, we are all victims of our best shots.

So the first advice is from Shakespeare: "To thine own self be true." Be honest with yourself about the quality of your play. The best way to do this is to write a one-paragraph description of your game. It might go something like this:

I am not Tiger Woods and I never will be. Most of my scores are between 85 and 90. I drive the ball about 230 yards with a fade that sometimes becomes a slice, so the longest par fours are out of my reach. My iron game is inconsistent so I miss more greens than I hit, but I get up and down about a third of the time because I've always been a good putter. Still, until I decide to spend lots of time and money on lessons and practice, I'll never get my handicap much lower than 13.

Greg Norman does an analysis similar to this at the end of every season, rat-

Good strategy is based on an honest self-appraisal. For most golfers, the goal is not par but "personal par," based on 18 realistic, reachable target scores.

HOLE	1	2	3	4	5	6	7	8	9	OUT
Championship Yardage	390	405	235	565	500	430	160	330	395	3410
Regular Yardage	370	375	190	515	485	380	145	320	375	3155
Men's Par	4 5	4	3	5 6	5	4 5	3	4	4 5	36 40
Men's Handicap	⑬	⑫	⑭	⑧	⑨	④	⑱	⑯	⑦	

ing each area of his game from one to ten and then developing an improvement plan for the next season.

Depressing as this type of self-appraisal may seem at first, it is the fastest way to a well-adjusted and street-smart approach to the game. Once you've made an honest assessment of your strengths and weaknesses, you'll be able to fit your game to the course and match situations you encounter—you'll know when to play within your limitations and when to get aggressive.

COURSE MANAGEMENT

Course management is actually the wrong term: It's your game that must be managed throughout 18 holes. Assuming you play most of your golf on one course (GOLF Magazine surveys have shown that the great majority of golfers play nearly 90 percent of their rounds on a "home" course), you should establish your personal par, a target score based on your handicap or average score that offers you a realistic goal. For a 15-handicap player, personal par is not 72, it's about 83.

Once you establish an 18-hole target, break it down and set personal pars for each of the holes. Don't pay attention to the course's ranking of the holes; consider each hole's difficulty to you based on your ability to move your ball from each tee to each green. For instance, if you're a powerful but inaccurate hitter, you probably will want to give yourself a par on the long, open par five; but by the same token, you may want to play for a bogey on the short, tight par four. If you have a natural fade, you may not need to give up a shot at the 420-yard dogleg right, but you may want to cut yourself some slack at the 350-yard dogleg left.

Once you have a personal par for each hole, your mission is to pick each hole apart, shot by shot, and set your plan of attack. In his book *Go for Broke,* Arnold Palmer devoted an entire chapter to "Conquering the Course." In it he said, "An amateur rarely appreciates how useful it is simply to take a long, studied look at the course, to understand how best to use his skills on it and against it."

A personal plan of attack on a course is relatively simple to establish but endlessly difficult to fulfill. As Bobby Jones said, "It is nothing new or original to say that golf is played one stroke at a time, but it took me many years to realize it."

And yet, Jones would have admitted that he rarely played a golf shot without having his next shot in mind. Another Bobby Jones, golf architect Robert Trent Jones, Jr., observes in his book *Golf by Design,* that "like pool, golf is primarily a game of position. The professional pool player never takes one shot at a time. He organizes a series of shots in his mind in order to sink all of the balls on the table. The key is to get a good 'leave,' or an ideal position for the next shot."

The way to do that on a golf hole is to think backward: Play each hole mentally from back to front. Start at the green, and ask yourself how you'd like your ball to make its approach. If, for instance, a huge, deep bunker guards the right front of the green, then the best approach usually will be

Golf is like pool in that the goal of each shot is to set up an easy assignment for the next shot.

from the left side of the fairway, so that the ball does not have to fly across sand. That means you'll want to play your tee shot to the left side of the fairway (assuming there's no dire trouble to dissuade you). This in turn will mean that you'll want to tee your drive at the extreme right side of the teeing area and aim at a target to the left-center of the fairway (just as a bowler approaches from the right side of the lane to knock down the 7 pin).

The other major consideration in managing your course is distance. Before a Tour pro sets foot on any golf course, he and his caddie know the exact distance of every shot he is likely to face. Every serious amateur player is armed with the same knowledge of his home course.

Mapping out one's course takes only a couple of hours. Measuring from landmarks such as prominent trees, bunkers, and sprinkler heads that are close to where your tee shot usually finishes, pace off the yardages to the front, middle, and back of the green, so that you'll know the distance no matter where the pin is placed. You'll find that on some greens the difference between a front and back pin is much bigger than it is on others (sometimes it's as much as two or three clubs longer for the back pin).

Before you do any pacing, however, be sure to measure the length of your pace—it may be longer (but likely will be shorter) than 36 inches—then adjust your stride accordingly. On par-three holes, pace off the yardage from the very back of the tee; then it's a simple matter of subtracting from that figure when the tees are placed forward.

Of course, knowing the distances

DIFFERENT STROKES

WATSON AND MILLER DIFFER ON DOGLEGS

Tom Watson advocates an aggressive strategy on dogleg holes. On a left-to-right dogleg, for instance, he advocates moving to the left side of the tee and driving down the right side of the fairway, thus reducing the bend of the hole. (Faders of the ball can accomplish much the same by teeing on the right side and letting their shots drift back.)

Johnny Miller is more conservative. He suggests never trying to cut a dogleg, either with a straight shot, as Watson suggests, or with a fade or draw. Miller prefers a straight shot down the middle as the percentage play. If, on a left-to-right dogleg, it fades, then great; if it draws a little, you'll just have a slightly longer shot. By contrast, trying to cut the dogleg with a fade leaves less margin for error—a fade that becomes a slice will usually mean big trouble.

Each hole should be played backward in the mind. If the pin is on the left, the best approach is from the right; that usually means the drive should be played from the left side of the tee.

The Old Course at St. Andrews is a good example of the design theory of safe and dangerous routes. On most holes, a tee shot to the left side will be safe, but will leave a difficult approach. A more daring shot, down the right side, will be rewarded with a good look at the flag.

you face on your home course is of little value unless you also know the distance you hit each club in your bag. The pros know their precise yardage with every club. Most amateurs, because they strike the ball inconsistently, will never have such exact knowledge, but every smart player knows at least the average distance he hits his clubs.

It's a matter of pacing off your shots. Ideally, you should do this during a quiet time on your course or practice area. Hit a dozen or so balls with each club and pace off the distances. Discount any severe mishits, and average the distance of the others, being sure to subtract the distance the ball bounces and rolls—you don't want the total distance of your shots, you want the carry (in-air) distance. Once

you have all your distances, memorize them or tape them to the shafts of your clubs (it's legal).

From the Tee. Every well-designed hole offers a safe route and a risky route. The safe route allows you to give hazards and other trouble a wide berth. However, this route usually leaves a longer second shot and a less inviting entry to the green. By taking the risky route you may flirt with trouble, but if your gamble pays off you'll be rewarded with a prime position from which to attack the green.

Most of the holes at the Old Course at St. Andrews play this way. From virtually every tee, the safe but longer route is to the left side, where a parallel fairway offers the haven of open ground—but from that side, the shot

View each fairway as a two-lane highway, then mentally eliminate one side as you plan and play the shot.

to the green must invariably cross a bunker or other obstacle that inhibits one's ability to get close to the hole. Drive down the right side and bunkers and out of bounds await, but if the tee shot is successful, the second shot will have a good look at the flag.

Arnold Palmer never met a risky route he didn't like, but he was well aware of the temptation. "It's a little like walking up to a fenced-in pasture," he said in *Go for Broke.*" You can always go down to the gate in the fence and go through it easily. But it may be a long way around, and you're tempted simply to go through the fence, despite the height, the barbed wire, and the muddy ditch that runs in front of it."

Teaching professional Jim McLean advocates viewing a fairway as a two-lane highway, then mentally eliminat-

ing one of those sides, depending on your ball flight and the set-up of the hole. For instance, if you hit a draw or hook, you should forget about the right side of the fairway and plan every tee shot to finish on the left side of the fairway. In that case, you want to tee your ball at the far left side of the teeing area, aim right, and give yourself plenty of room to let the ball drift back to the left. (If you fade or slice, you should do the opposite—eliminate the left side of the fairway, tee on the right side of the tee box, and let the ball drift back to the right side of the fairway.)

Even if you hit a straight ball, the smart strategy is to hit straight away from trouble. Testing done by teaching professional Chuck Cook has shown that more penalty shots are incurred as a result of a poor starting direction

You are allowed to tee your ball anywhere between the two markers and up to two club-lengths behind them.

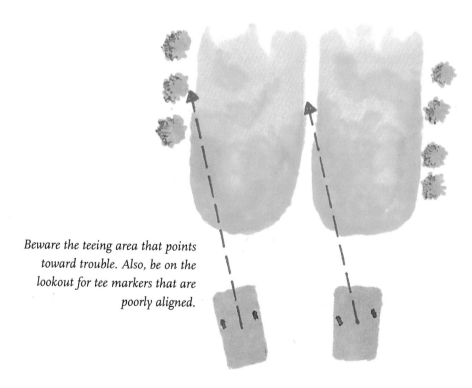

Beware the teeing area that points toward trouble. Also, be on the lookout for tee markers that are poorly aligned.

than from a curving shot, by a ratio of 12:1. The clear advice is to tee your ball on the side of the tee where most of the drive-zone trouble is and aim your shot to the opposite side of the fairway. (You can even stand outside the markers as long as your ball is teed between them.)

Since the tee shot is the one shot where you may give yourself a perfect lie, you should never fail to take full advantage of it. In addition to being able to tee the ball anywhere between the two markers, you have the benefit of going back as much as two club-lengths, an option that can be particularly useful on par-three holes.

A couple of warnings. Watch out for a misaligned tee. Sometimes it's a matter of poor greenkeeping, other times the architect just wanted to fool you—whatever the reason, occasionally a teeing area will be pointed well away from the center of the fairway. Just as often, the green crew will position the two tee markers so that they point at something other than Position A. Be sure to aim your drive where *you* want it to go, not where the tee wants you to go. Also be careful of teeing areas that are uneven. It's not uncommon to have a slightly uphill, downhill, or sidehill lie on a tee. Don't tee in such a spot unless you think it's to your advantage. For instance, if you want to hit a draw, you might help yourself by teeing up in a sidehill lie with the ball slightly above your feet—this promotes the slightly flatter swing that produces a draw.

Your final strategic consideration on the tee relates to distance and club selection. A driver is not always the best choice, even when you want to maximize your power. Studies of thousands of golfers have proved that unless you can generate at least 85 miles per hour of clubhead speed (in other words, unless your average drive is about 240 yards), you will actually carry the ball farther with a 3-wood than with a driver. Thus, particularly on a wet golf course where there is little or no roll, a 3-wood might serve you better.

Besides, virtually every course has a hole or two designed to give even medium-length hitters pause. On such occasions, ask yourself: Will my Sunday punch take me clear through the dogleg and into trouble? Will it put me on a downhill/sidehill lie from which I won't be able to make a good swing? Will it leave me the dreaded half-wedge instead of a full shot that's easier to control? If the answer to any of these questions is "yes," tee off with something other than your driver.

Into the Green. When planning approach shots, it helps once again to do a bit of mental geometry: Think of each green divided into quadrants. Then ask yourself which quadrant is easiest for you to hit (Palmer calls this the "ball position," as opposed to the pin position). If the flagstick is in the same quadrant, you should be aggressive with your shot—go for the pin. If it isn't, exercise some discretion.

Johnny Miller likes to view approach-shot situations in terms of red, yellow, and green lights. If there's nothing to stop him from gunning for the flag, he calls it a green light. If there are a couple of factors going against him, he deems it a yellow light and tries to play to the fat part of the

Studies have proven that the wisest strategy is to aim directly away from trouble rather than trying to hit a shot that starts at the trouble and bends back to the fairway.

DIFFERENT STROKES

JACK RANKS HIS WORST FEARS

Jack Nicklaus long ago established a ranking of the potential pain levels of golf's principal hazards, and he uses this ranking to evaluate the risk–reward of every shot he plays. His ranking, in descending order, is: out of bounds, lost ball, unplayable lie, water, woods, severe rough, deep or high-lipped bunker, severely angled lie, shallow bunker, light rough, slightly angled lie.

Even when swinging his very best, Nicklaus will never attempt a shot where a slight miscue could cost him an out-of-bounds or lost-ball penalty.

When planning approach shots, think of the green divided into quadrants. If the pin is positioned in the quadrant you can hit most easily, then you can be aggressive with your shot. If not, you should be more cautious.

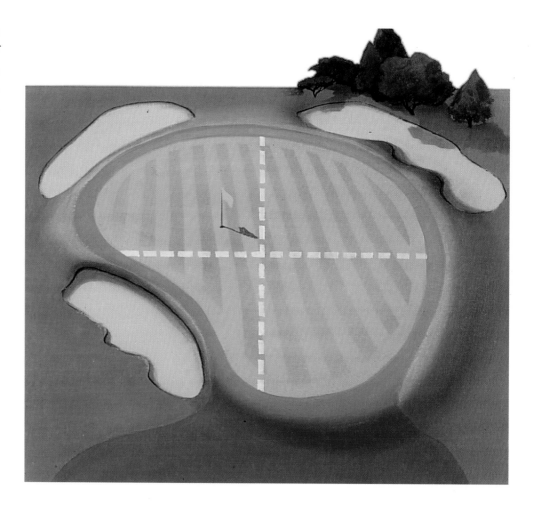

green. And if the combination of lie, pin position, trouble around the green, and his situation in the tournament or match suggests extreme caution, Miller sees the red light and lays up short of the green.

Architects love to deceive golfers by designing greens with pin positions that lure them into overly aggressive shots. The pros call these "sucker" pins since only a sucker would go for them. For instance, a pin that is dead center and in the middle depth of a green may appear to be there for the taking, but if the green is shaped like an hourglass front to back with two bunkers pinching at its middle, then that dead-center pin is for suckers only.

Teaching professional David Lee was among the first to observe that the diametric center of a green is not always the best place to hit your ball. Instead, he advocates playing for what he calls the "optimum center," usually at one side or the other, where there is more putting surface and less threat from sand or water.

Knowing your yardages is of course an invaluable help on approach shots, but yardage is only the beginning of strategic club and shot selection. You need to consider more subtle factors as well. In general, you should take a shorter club than the distance dictates when any of the following conditions exists:

- You're playing downhill.
- You're playing downwind.
- Your ball will land on a hard, dry surface.
- The worst trouble is beyond your target.

- You're playing an intentional draw or hook.
- You have a flyer lie.
- You're excited and your adrenaline is pumping.

Conversely, you should take a longer club than the yardage suggests when:

- You're playing uphill.
- You're playing into the wind.
- You're playing in cold weather.
- You're playing to a wet or otherwise soft surface.
- You're hitting from a fairway bunker or hardpan.
- The worst trouble is short of your target.
- You're playing an intentional fade or slice.

Par-Three Strategy. On a par-three hole, you need to make only one good shot to virtually guarantee par. Yet one bad shot can kill you. Thus, when you're standing on the tee of a par three, careful planning is of the utmost importance.

The first advice is always to use a tee. Some pros, including Laura Davies and Lee Trevino, have been known to pinch up a piece of turf with their club and play from that, but a standard tee offers the same advantage with much less risk.

Invariably, the teeing area will be scarred with dozens of divots, and you should of course avoid these, although Johnny Miller suggests teeing up just in back of a divot that points directly at the target, using it as an alignment aid, and Greg Norman has been known to tee his ball at the forward end of a divot when he wants to be sure of getting his club under the ball for a high, soft shot.

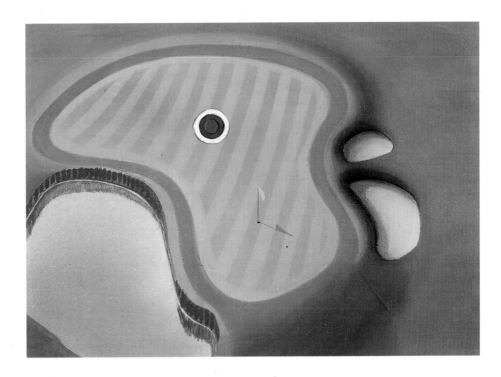

In general, most of the trouble on par-three holes is right before your eyes, in front of the green, where it can best intimidate you. For that reason—and because most amateur golfers tend to underclub—the best strategy is to take plenty of club.

In general, short par-three holes (160 yards or less) tend to have small, well-guarded greens. The wise tactic on such holes is to avoid the worst trouble and play for the fat part of the green, since any shot that finds the putting surface will leave a reasonable chance for a two-putt par. Conversely, longer par-three holes (200 yards and over) tend to be less fiercely defended and have large greens, so the general strategy is to gun for the flag under the theory that the penalty for a slight miss will not be severe, whereas a cautious tee shot might leave an enormous first putt.

On the very longest par threes, there is no shame in laying up short of the green. With a shorter, more lofted club, most amateurs will hit a more solid and straighter shot, leaving a

Be alert for "sucker pins" like this one, and play instead for the fat part of the green.

Here are examples of what Johnny Miller calls red-, yellow-, and green-light situations. If Player A wants to go for the flag, he must come out of the rough, over the bunker, and make his ball stop quickly on the green—a tall assignment. There also is a chance he will overshoot the green and go into the water, so this is a red-light situation. Player B has a good lie in the fairway, but he still has the bunker to contend with—a yellow light. Player C is in the fairway with the ideal angle to the flag—he has the green light to attack the pin.

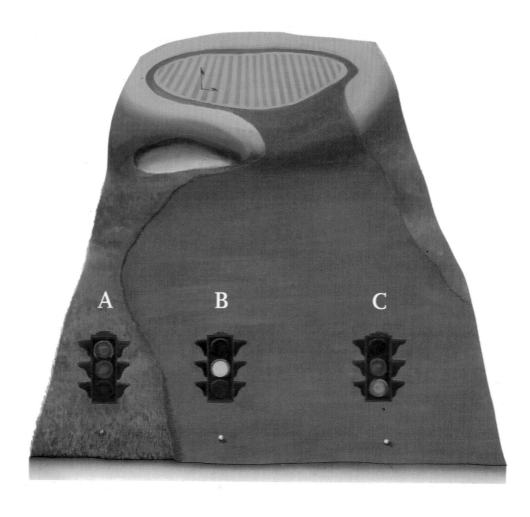

Club selection is much more than distance, as these two equal-length par-three holes show. A tee shot to the hole on the left may call for a 3-, 4-, or 5-iron, while the one on the right may be reached with a 5-, 6-, or 7-iron.

simple pitch or chip to the pin. This strategy may not yield many birdies, but it's very effective at eliminating double bogeys and worse. When Billy Casper won the 1959 U.S. Open at Winged Foot, he laid up four days in a row at the 216-yard third hole, and made four straight pars.

Par-Four Strategy. Just as with par-three holes, the strategy for par fours can change with the length of the hole. Short par fours—although sometimes driveable—are usually packed with danger and demand control of both direction and distance. A long iron or lofted wood often is the wise club selection from the tee, rather than the driver. Your goal should be to find the fairway and leave an approach shot

that gives you the ideal angle to the flag at a distance that gives you comfort and confidence. Tom Watson says the only exception to this strategy would be when he's playing downwind to an inviting target area or when the match-play situation dictates taking the risk.

On narrow holes, where you're asked to hit your tee shot through a chute of trees, or between water on one side and sand on the other, it's again a good idea to consider hitting a fairway wood or iron instead of the driver. Chances are you'll have more confidence in the shorter club, and thus have a better likelihood of threading the needle. You may have to hit a 5-iron instead of a 7-iron into the green, but that's a small price to pay when

you consider the peril you might find with an errant driver. Jack Nicklaus won his first British Open by using this strategy to avoid the thick rough and menacing bunkers of Muirfield. In 56 opportunities on the par-four and par-five holes, Nicklaus used his driver only 17 times.

For many amateurs, a long par four is like a par five—and it should be played that way. If you need a 3-wood to reach the green with your second shot, you'll usually do better by laying up short of the green with a middle iron, then pitching to the pin. Indeed, the wisest players will often tee off with an iron, lay up with another iron, then wedge on. This strategy—playing three safe shots rather than two risky ones—prevails more often than not.

Left: *Johnny Miller suggests using an old divot mark as an alignment aid on par-three holes.*

Right: *When Greg Norman wants a high, floating shot, he sometimes will tee the ball at the forward edge of a divot hole, to insure getting his club under the ball.*

No matter how many shots you take, you should continue plotting as you walk the hole. Much has been written about Nicklaus's legendary concentration, but Jack admits he allows his focus to drift in and out. As he walks off the tee, he allows himself time for daydreaming and casual conversation, but as he reaches his ball and begins planning his next shot, the focus returns, and it tightens to a peak at address and during the swing.

Greg Norman does the same thing. "At a point about 40 yards short of the ball I begin to analyze the situation that's facing me," he says. "I look at the tops of the trees to check the wind, I look at the pitch and roll of the green area to get an initial feel for the way the ball will roll, and I look at the peo-

The key to Jack Nicklaus's legendary concentration is his ability to drop in and out of focus during the play of a hole, sharpening his concentration as he approaches his ball.

ple around the green to get depth perception. By the time I get to my ball, I'm fully focused on the shot."

Par-Five Strategy. Bobby Jones was not a fan of par fives. The trouble with most of them, he said, was "you don't start playing golf until the third shot." That's one reason the par fives at Jones's Augusta National Golf Club offer so much excitement each year in The Masters—they're all reachable to the long-hitting pros.

Jones's feelings notwithstanding, par-five holes pose unwarranted difficulties for many players. After all, chop the normal par five into three equal parts and you have shots averaging about 175 yards—shorter than the two shots on most par fours. Yet, as Arnold Palmer points out, "the overall length of the hole seems to intimidate the average player, with the result that he swings too hard on both the drive and the second shot." This explains in part why the scorecard at many courses shows the number-one handicap hole to be a par five.

Despite the length of the hole, the strategy for the tee shot on a par five is not to get more distance than on a par four but to get the ball safely into the fairway. If you can succeed in that, you probably will save at least one shot. The same sort of care should be taken with the second shot, where the temptation of most players is to swing for the fences . . . and the result is a topped shot. The fact is, in many cases the last thing you want on your second shot to a par five is maximum distance. On many fives a water hazard, cross bunker, or other peril taunting the golfer crosses the fairway at about the

450-yard point. In such cases, if you aren't sure you can carry the trouble and reach the green with your average shot, lay up and leave yourself an uncomplicated third shot to the hole.

Getting close, even if you're in the middle of the fairway, often leaves a half-wedge, one of the most awkward shots in the game. A proper lay-up, on the other hand, will leave you a distance you can handle easily and give you the ideal angle from which to attack the flag. In this way, a lay-up is a more aggressive play than it seems. Besides, since the greens on par fives usually are small and well protected, most players should defer their aggressiveness until the third shot.

MATCH-PLAY STRATEGY

While virtually every tournament on the professional Tours is conducted at stroke play, the game that most amateurs play throughout the world is match play—a hole-by-hole confrontation where victory goes to the player (or two-man team) winning the greater number of holes.

Since match play is a head-to-head battle, its strategy is more complex than that for stroke play. In addition to managing your game and contending with the course, you must stay constantly in tune with the match; on each hole you must know and understand your opponent's situation as clearly as you do your own, then plot your moves accordingly.

With each set of opponents and each hole, a new confrontation unfolds, calling for a unique response. Gene-

One way to take the intimidation out of a par five is to envision it as three medium-length shots.

DIFFERENT STROKES

WHO TEES OFF FIRST?

Three strategies prevail on the question of batting order in team play.

Strategy one is to establish a comfortable order on the first tee and stick with it for all 18 holes. If one player is impatient and likes to step up and hit, he should lead off. If one player likes the pressure of hitting last, then he should.

Strategy two calls for the shorter, straighter hitter to put a ball in the fairway, allowing the long hitter to let out the shaft.

Strategy three advocates constant juggling, fitting the batting order to the demands of the hole. On each tee the player with the better chance of handling the problems of the hole plays first—the accurate player leads on a tight hole, the better iron player leads on the par threes. The theory is that a successful shot on his part will take pressure off his partner, who will then be better able to make a good shot as well.

England's John Ball was a match-play master, winner of a record eight British Amateur Championships.

ralized advice is therefore dangerous. Still, through centuries of match play at all levels, certain tactics have gained virtually universal acceptance.

TACTIC 1:
Play the Course, Not Your Opponent

The game's first supreme match player was John Ball, a taciturn Englishman who won eight British Amateur Championships between 1888 and 1912. Ball was blessed with steel nerves and a smooth-flowing swing that never varied—two undeniable assets for match play—but he claimed his secret was that he played "against par." Said Bernard Darwin, "It was his business to go faultlessly down the middle and let the other man make the mistakes, and the more intense the crisis, the more closely he stuck to business."

In one competition, Ball's opponent hit into a bunker on a par-five hole. "He's in a bunker," said one of the gallery members. "You didn't see, did you?"

"No," answered Ball. "Why should I? It's my business to get a five."

Bobby Jones had similar success playing against "Old Man Par, a patient soul who never makes a birdie." That game plan was sound enough to win one British Amateur and five U.S. Amateurs.

Of course, as with all match-play advice, there are exceptions. If the match is tied with one hole to go and your opponent has stuck his approach six feet from the flag, you have no choice but to go for a birdie yourself. If, on the contrary, your opponent hits his approach into a pond fronting the green, discretion will be the better part of valor.

Fundamentally, however, it's best to consider the golf course your chief adversary. In the words of Bernard Darwin, "We must to some extent watch our enemy, but we must not let what he has done influence us too easily."

TACTIC 2:

Know Your Game—and Play It

Unless you are a five-handicap player or better, do not take literally the notion of playing against par. Play instead against your personal par (see above), a scorecard that you have a reasonable chance of beating.

Sadly, many players try to bring a course to its knees. Match play seems to induce a euphoria that makes the 18-handicapper think he will perform like Jack Nicklaus. (The brutal truth is, on most days he won't even play to his 18.) You should stem this urge to pull off the spectacular shot. In the words of the nineteenth-century golfer/philosopher Horace Hutchinson, "You must root this futile vanity out of your golfing system as you would the plague."

Assuming you have established a plan of attack for the course you're playing—a plan that fits your game—stick to it. Such a plan will force you to recognize your strengths and weaknesses. If your plan calls for a 4-wood on a lengthy par 3, you won't stubbornly take a 3-iron, no matter what club your partner may select.

A final but important aspect of playing your game is to maintain your usual pace of play—don't let an exceedingly slow or fast player get you out of rhythm. This can be difficult advice to heed if you're a fast player

Horace Hutchinson was among the first to relate match-play strategy to the vagaries of the golf mind.

Above: *Jerome Travers won four U.S. Amateur Championships, all of them at match play.*

Opposite: *"Old Muffin Face," Bobby Locke, was a feisty competitor who never showed his inner feelings on the course.*

being held up by a slower player, but if you keep yourself busy and use the extra time to plan your shots, you can overcome the situation.

TACTIC 3:
Put on Your Poker Face

You will have some good holes and some bad holes, and so will your opponent—this is the essence of match play. The key is to maintain your composure. Don't get too elated when you go ahead or too dejected when you lose ground.

"Absolute idiots play steadiest," said W. G. Simpson over a century ago in *The Art of Golf.* "An uphill game does not make them press, nor victory within their grasp render them careless."

Jerome Travers won four U.S. Amateur Championships in part because he knew that "in the game of golf confidence is a great helper. Let a player lose it and he is marked for slaughter. On the other hand, an attack of overconfidence is apt to be fully as disastrous. Overconfidence and carelessness are teammates."

South Africa's Bobby Locke, as

tough a competitor as ever strode the fairways, maintained an absolutely stolid demeanor. "I try to avoid all extremes," he said. "I have been called many things when I am playing, because my expression never changes—'poker face,' 'muffin face,' etc., but that is due to a determination never to convey to my opponent what my inner feelings are."

Hutchinson wrote, "Of a noted professional we have heard it said, 'he is a dour player.' The phrase is excellent. The characteristic Scotch adjective most aptly describes the quality of dogged purpose which is most useful in the old Scotch game." It was also Hutchinson's view that "the best competitive golfers are the distrustful and timorous kind, who are always expecting something terrible to happen— pessimistic fellows who are quite certain when they come upon the green that the ball farthest from the hole is theirs. This kind of player never takes anything for granted and cannot be lulled into complacency by a successful run over a few holes."

One more reason to keep an even keel: You'll be better prepared for the inevitable surprise from your adversary. According to W. G. Simpson, "a secret disbelief in the enemy's play is very useful. This contempt must, however, be largely seasoned with respect."

TACTIC 4:
Try Hard from the Start

The natural tendency is to be a bit lackadaisical about the first few holes of a match. "There's a lot of golf left" is the standard rationalization for a poor start. Some players even cling to the

DIFFERENT STROKES

DON'T BE FOOLED ON THE GREEN

Most instructors advise watching your opponent's putts to get an idea of the speed and break of a green, but putting guru Dave Pelz cautions against such a practice.

"It's unlikely that you have the same type of stroke—and therefore putt the ball with exactly the same force—as your opponent," he says. "On top of this, there is the difference between the two putters to consider. The ball jumps off the face of some putters much more quickly than others. Unless you're aware of these specific differences, you shouldn't expect to learn much from your opponent's putts."

Above: Nine holes down with 12 holes to play, Bobby Cruickshank came back to beat Al Watrous in the 1932 PGA Championship.

Opposite: In 1996, Tiger Woods came from five holes down to win his third consecutive U.S. Amateur title.

perverse belief that a victory at hole number one is a bad omen.

But the first hole is just as important as the last—in fact, a fast start puts immediate pressure on one's opponent. The wise player thus gets straight to business, with a minimum of socializing on the early holes. In the cautionary words of Hutchinson, "Applying oneself fully to one's work is impossible while discussing politics, the crops, weather, and the grouse."

TACTIC 5:
Don't Give Up When You're Down

Golf history is full of stories of players who came back from seemingly impossible deficits. The most astounding may be the match between Al Watrous and Bobby Cruickshank in the 1932 PGA Championship. Nine holes down with 12 to play, Cruickshank fought his way back and won in sudden death. More recently, Tiger Woods capped his amateur career in 1996 by coming from five holes down in the final match to win his third consecutive U.S. Amateur.

Never say never, either in the course of a match or the play of a hole. Let's say Player A puts his approach to a par four on the green 30 feet away, and then Player B knocks his ball into a pond in front of the green. Too often, this is where B concedes the hole, in his mind if not aloud. The fact is, he still has a chance. By taking a drop, pitching close, and holing the putt he'll make a 5, forcing Player A to two-putt for victory or three-putt and halve. In singles match play, many holes are won with a bogey.

Furthermore, once you show your-self to be a quitter, your opponent will be encouraged—and the opposite is also true. As Darwin observed, "There is nothing more wearing to a leader who is playing well than the knowledge that his enemy is refusing to crack. If by hanging on we can drive that knowledge into him, we may make him crack instead and that crack will be a bad one when it comes."

Bobby Jones had this tremendous ability to withstand early adversity and then turn the tide of a match, knowing that as he began to gain ground his opponent would crumble. Darwin, again, said it best: "Some golfers are very brave men, but there is no golfer in the world who has not, at least once in his life, felt limp and terror-stricken when a winning lead began suddenly and horribly to diminish."

TACTIC 6:
Don't Let Up When You're Ahead

It's human nature to ease up a bit when you hold what seems to be a comfortable lead. But the Watrous/Cruickshank match is ample proof of the danger of complacency. As Jerry Travers said, "Never prematurely announce the funeral of your opponent."

Says Simpson, "With five up, play greedily for more—play a five-yard putt as if match depended on it. With five up, express, as is polite, regret at laying a stymie, but rejoice in your heart."

Bobby Locke never was accused of being one of golf's nice guys, but he rarely finished last. He was proud of his "killer instinct," a quality that he said British professionals lacked. In *Bobby Locke on Golf,* he observed that the Brits "have the golf and they have

DIFFERENT STROKES

HIT FIRST OR SECOND?

In a tight match situation, is it better to be hitting first or second? Two of modern golf's most successful players hold differing views.

Curtis Strange takes the majority view. "I like nothing better than to tee off first and put the ball in the fairway, then step back and let my opponent make the next move. The same goes for approach shots and even putting. On the green I like the security of being first in, putting pressure on the other guy to match me."

Tom Watson says, "I'd rather hit second in match play, no matter what my opponent does. I want all the information possible at my disposal."

It's worth noting that each player's strategy is fitted to his strong suit—Strange is a very straight driver but not long, while Watson, though not as accurate as Strange, has always been one of the longest hitters in the game.

Straight-hitting Curtis Strange prefers to hit first and put the pressure on, while longer-hitting Tom Watson likes to wait and see his opponent's shot.

the ability, they have everything except the will to tell themselves, 'I'm going to beat this fellow over the head and keep on beating him until his skull cracks.' " Assuming Locke was correct, it explains why, between 1933 and 1985, Great Britain and Ireland won the Ryder Cup only once.

It is this Lockean willingness to beat an opponent until his skull cracks that marks the toughest match players. As Hutchinson says, "It is an un-Christian counsel, but the mood for success in golf matches is a silent hatred—temporary only, be it observed—of your opponent."

TACTIC 7:
Watch the Course

Since the golf course is your first opponent, you should make a point of knowing what sort of condition it's in. Some practice putting before the round will help you with the speed of the greens. If your match is part of a tournament, you may get a sheet that shows the pin positions—if not, as you walk through the holes of the match you should pay attention to flag positions on the upcoming holes. Most important, watch the way your ball and your opponent's ball behave on landing—this will give you an idea of the hardness of the fairways and greens, a factor that affects club selection both off the tee and into the green.

Jack Nicklaus claims he won the 1959 U.S. Amateur because he paid close attention to the course. By the last hole of the 36-hole final between Nicklaus and Charlie Coe at The Broadmoor Golf Club in Colorado, the course had become hard and dry. Coe, hitting first, played an 8-iron approach

Keep your eye open for pin positions on upcoming holes.

On the final hole of the 1959 U.S. Amateur, Jack Nicklaus watched Charlie Coe's approach shot bounce through the dry, hard green, then adjusted his own shot to allow it to bounce to the hole.

that landed near the flag but bounded well over the green. Observing this, Nicklaus punched a low 9-iron that ran along the ground and stopped within eight feet of the hole. He then sank the putt for a 1-up victory.

TACTIC 8:
Watch Your Opponent

It should go without saying that you pay close attention to your opponent. Says Curtis Strange, "In match play I want to be fully aware of what my opponent is up to at all times, because it can influence whether I play a particular shot aggressively or cautiously."

Beyond this, you can learn things about the golf course, as Nicklaus did by watching his opponent's ball. On a par three, if your opponent hits first, you can judge your own club from the club he selects. (Although the Rules prohibit you from asking what club he hit, it's perfectly legal to take a peek in his bag and see which club is missing.) This assumes, of course, that you know your own strength relative to your opponent's—what is a 5-iron for him could be a 6-iron or a 4-iron for you. Around the green in particular it pays to watch how a ball runs, as you can often observe the effects of grain, slope, and wetness.

If you aren't familiar with your opponent's strengths and weaknesses, by watching him closely you may learn something early in the match that could help you later on. Let's say he hits into a couple of greenside bunkers and plays poor recoveries, then later in the match he hits into another bunker while you're just outside him, facing a ticklish downhill chip. Armed with the knowledge

that your opponent is shaky from the sand, you can play a conservative chip shot—get the ball on the green and settle for a six-foot uphill putt for par rather than risk a delicate little flop shot that might stay in the fringe.

The final reason for watching your opponent is to note any change in his mannerisms or pace of play. Sam Snead was one of the best at sizing up opponents. In his book *The Lessons I've Learned,* he says: "One of the best ways to judge when the pressure is getting to your opponent is by watching his routine. Everyone has a pace of play and a routine that he follows, but when the noose starts to tighten, he falls out of his pace and routine. Instead of taking two practice swings, he may take three. He may hesitate over club selection. If he smokes, he may chain-smoke to try to calm his nerves. When you sense this, it's time to pour it on and turn up the pressure."

TACTIC 9:
Keep It in Play

According to Curtis Strange, "the best way to put pressure on an opponent is to keep the ball in play." In most matches, accuracy is much more important than distance. Even when you are outhit from the tee, you have an opportunity to be the first one on the green, thus putting the pressure back on your opponent.

Although scramblers and magicians in the tradition of Walter Hagen and Seve Ballesteros can unnerve their opponents, the inexorable assault of a fairways-and-greens grinder like Strange is far more fearsome, as the pressure is unrelenting.

"Drive for show" has little meaning unless part of the show is accuracy. Indeed, if ever you should divert from your game plan in a match, it is to err on the side of caution from the tee—take a 3-wood occasionally rather than a driver—and wait for your opponent to make the big mistake.

TACTIC 10:
When in Trouble, Be Patient

Every golfer must fight the urge to follow a bad shot with a spectacular recovery, or a bad hole with a spectacular hole. Spectacular play succeeds only in making the player foul up and lose the hole. In most instances, the smart move is to get safely and surely back in play, and then resume the attack.

Horace Hutchinson wrote, "Perhaps the most fatal beam of all that can float over your mental vision is the vision of a past hole badly played which you are filled with some insane notion of 'making up for.' The idea of 'making up' by present extra exertions for past deficiencies is one of the most deadly and besetting delusions that is prone to affect the golfing mind. Its results are inevitably ruinous."

A century later, Curtis Strange used slightly less flowery language to say much the same thing: "Don't bet the farm until you're sure you have to."

One situation where patience is particularly vital is on the tee after you've hit a drive out-of-bounds. At this point, most golfers hastily tee up a second ball despite the fact that, strictly speaking, it is their opponent's turn to hit. The wise move is to back off and allow the opponent to play (after all, he too may hit into trouble), allow your-

You can learn a lot about the surface of a green by watching the behavior of your opponent's ball on chips and pitches.

DIFFERENT STROKES

IN BETWEEN CLUBS—SUIT YOURSELF

For decades, the advice to the player in between clubs on an approach was to take the longer club and swing smoothly. In recent years, however, this has given way to a more personalized approach that calls for the player to go with his psychological makeup. For instance, if you're an aggressive, hard-swinging type in the mold of Greg Norman or Tom Watson, take the shorter club and hit it hard. But if you're a milder, more placid individual like Ben Crenshaw or Scott Simpson, you'll be better off taking an unhurried pass with the longer club.

In this situation, A and B are playing against C and D. All four players lie two on a par four. Although A is away, the smart strategy is for B to putt out first. If he makes it, A can't improve, but A and B have put the pressure on C and D—one of them has to make a 15-foot putt: If B misses, he still makes the par and A gets a chance for an all-or-nothing birdie out of the bunker before C and D get a chance to try for their birdies. If, on the other hand, A shoots first and puts his ball on the green inside C and D, then A and B allow C and D two cracks at a birdie before B has the opportunity to sink his. If either C or D makes the birdie, B's putt will seem a mile long.

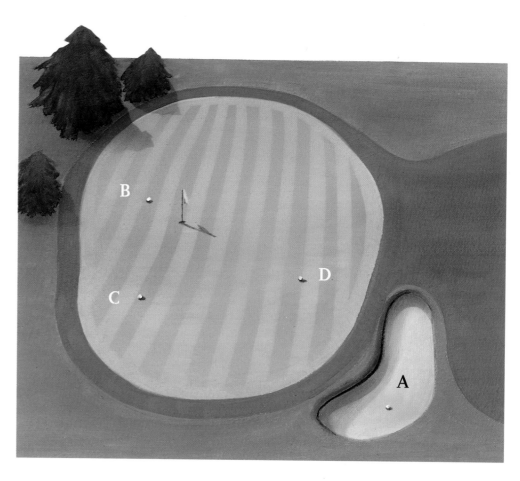

self some time to cool off, and then tee up a second ball.

Most battles on the golf course are won not by the transcendent brilliance of the victor but by the mistakes of the vanquished. Be patient and eventually your opponent will win you the match.

Four-Ball Strategy. In four-ball match play, the competition is between two teams of two players each. Holes are decided by matching the "better ball" scores, the lower of the two scores made by each pair of players.

Most of the advice for singles match play holds true for four-ball matches as well, with the caveat that, with two chances on each hole, you should play a bit more aggressively—take a few more chances—than you would in a singles match. Think birdies, because in four-ball match

play, holes are seldom won with pars.

Assuming the match is something more competitive than your regular weekend game, you should give some thought to the choice of your partner. Ideally, you want someone whose game fits well with your own; if you are a long but occasionally erratic hitter, you'll do best with someone who may not be as powerful but keeps the ball in play. Even more important, pick a partner who is compatible with you psychologically, someone whose company you enjoy and who shares your overall attitude toward the game.

One of the most important aspects of four-ball strategy is determining which member should hit at any given time. In team play, the farther player from the hole is not compelled to hit first—he has the option of letting his partner precede him. Most golfers know to take advantage of this option on the green, letting Player A tap in a two-footer for par so Player B can gun a 20-footer for birdie.

However, few teams extend the option to the fairway, where it can be just as effective. As an example, consider the 15th hole at the Augusta National Golf Club, a reachable par five with a pond that stretches in front of the green. Let's say Player A has hit a long drive and has a chance of getting home in two, while his partner Player B has laid up short, as have their opponents. Even though A is away, the smart strategy is to allow B to pitch his ball onto the green; if B gets close, then A can go for the heroic shot over the pond; if B chunks his ball into the water, A will know to lay up.

Seldom do you want to concede your opponents a lengthy putt, but on one occasion it's the best tactic. Let's say your opponent, Player A, faces a four-foot putt for par and his partner Player B has a seven-footer for birdie and is putting on exactly the same line as Player A. If they're wise, A and B will opt to have A putt first and get the safe par (while also showing B the line of the putt), then let B go for the birdie. Your strategy is to preempt that opportunity by conceding Player A his par putt, so that A must pick up his ball and will be unable to give B a view of the speed and break.

Foursomes Strategy. Foursomes is a format played only occasionally in America (most notably among the pros in the biennial Ryder Cup and Presidents Cup matches), but it's frequently used in Great Britain. Basically, it's an alternate-shot format:

Player A drives, his partner Player B hits the second shot, Player A hits the third, Player B the fourth, etc. Each member of the team hits first on half the holes, one of them taking the odd-numbered holes, the other the even.

This is the most pressure-filled team format, since your partner depends directly on your play—if you hit a ball into a bunker, it is your partner who must step in there and blast it out. For this reason, the overall strategy tends to be more cautious than in singles or four-ball play. The key is to keep each other out of trouble.

Still, you should also take every opportunity to play to each other's strengths. This begins with the decision of how to split the drives between the odd- and even-numbered holes. If your partner is a better iron player than you and all the par threes fall on even-numbered holes, then you should hit on the odds, he on the evens. If you play a reliable draw off the tee and most of the odd-numbered holes dogleg from right to left, you should tee off on those holes.

The same type of thinking should apply when planning your progress from tee to green. For example, if you know your partner is a good sand player, you can go ahead and gun your second shot for the green of that sand-surrounded par five. If, however, you have more confidence in your partner's wedge game than in his sand play, you might want to lay up and hope that he'll pitch close enough for you to make the birdie putt.

Gamesmanship. Gamesmanship is the dark side of strategy—it's not illegal, but it can border on unsportsmanlike.

Lee Trevino is a consummate games-man, who says the key is to plant a seed of doubt in your opponent's mind.

Still, in most instances the "victim" is not harmed unless he allows himself to be.

Some of the game's greatest players, from Walter Hagen to Lee Trevino, have been effective gamesmen. Trevino claims that gamesmanship "is nothing more than the power of suggestion. The minute you plant the tiniest seed of doubt or fear in your opponent's mind, you might as well figure the trophy is yours."

A prime planting ground is the tee of a par-three hole. Back in the 1940s, Dutch Harrison was well feared for his ability to hoodwink players by selecting a 5-iron and then putting a soft hit on it so that it landed pin high, then watching his pigeon hit the same 5-iron well over the green. Less skillful gamesmen will hit their usual 5-iron and comment, ostensibly to themselves or their caddies, "Man, I killed

that thing," hoping their opponents will take the bait and overswing or hit too much club.

In his book *Shark Attack,* Greg Norman admits to using gamesmanship. "Sometimes on the tee of an extremely long hole, if I'm hitting second, I'll take out a one-iron and lean on it as my opponent gets ready to play his shot. Occasionally I can actually see him thinking, 'This hole is 470 yards and Norman's teeing off with a 1-iron—my God, he must be even longer than I thought.' If I can get those types of thoughts going through my opponent's mind, he might do anything. Then when my turn comes, I put the iron back and take out my driver.

"I do the opposite, too. On a tight hole where I know everyone's debating about club selection, I'll quickly take out my driver and waggle it for everyone to see. The other guys then may make the mistake of selecting too much club for the shot. After they hit, I'll put the driver, which I had no intention of hitting, back in the bag and select a more intelligent club."

The best players know how to use their intimidating presence, and none better than Tom Watson, who in his heyday was well known for standing near his opponents as they played their approach shots. Typically, Watson would take up a position a few feet from his competitor's ball and stand there, arms folded, facing the player—out of sight but not out of mind.

One of the slyest forms of gamesmanship is the compliment. "Wow, you're driving the ball great—you haven't missed a fairway all day," is a comment that invariably elicits an errant tee shot. Others that work: "This hole fits your game perfectly," and "There's no one better at that shot than you."

The best way to get to a habitually fast player is to slow down the pace of the match by taking extra time over your shots—as long as this doesn't put you off your own pace. Walter Hagen was a theatrical master at this gambit, often changing his mind and club selection several times and seeming at a total loss as to how to play a shot, when in fact he was completely confident. When at last he did bring the shot off perfectly, the effect on his opponent was doubly unsettling.

In a 1978 article for *GOLF Magazine* titled "How to Psych Out Your Opponent," Trevino admitted to a fondness for gamesmanship on the greens. "If you putt first and should happen to put a weak stroke on it and end up way short, shake your head in

WORDS OF WISDOM

A golf course is a field of manoeuvre and action, employing, as it were, the military and engineering side of the game. It opens up a series of tactical and strategical opportunities, the implications of which it would be well for every golfer to grasp. . . . It is important to emphasize the necessity for the golfer to use his head as much as his hands; or in other words, to make his mental agility match his physical ability.

H. N. Wethered and Tom Simpson

The first golfers must have been seafaring folk, loving strenuous battles with nature; and whether facing the hazard of the oceans with boat and sail or the hazard of the sand dune with ball and stick, they were thrilled with the hope of victory, and not cowed and depressed with the fear of failure and its penalties. They did not look upon the ocean or upon the land, with their various degrees of hazard and their unequal penalties, for lack of skill and for failure, as places of torment but as wonderful fields for glorious achievements.

Robert Hunter

I say this without any reservation whatsoever: It is impossible to outplay an opponent you can't outthink.

Lawson Little

Knowing what to do and when to do it is the necessary complement to mechanical skill that maintains a few men at the head of the procession, with many others clutching closely, but vainly, for their coattails.

Bobby Jones

The little ball is tricky and eccentric. Consequently, it behooves you to keep on playing golf with all the skill at your command until your man is actually beaten.

Jerome Travers

The difference between the effect of boxing and the effect of golf on the human system is that golf hurts more and the pain is more enduring, for it is psychological.

Henry Leach

The perfect partner, without letting you know it, looks upon himself as the backbone of the game, on you as the flesh which may err. He plods on whilst you miss—plods on still when you are brilliant. If you are efficient, he lauds you; if variable, he says nothing; if hopeless, he smiles and says "It can't be helped." To him you are the chances of the game.

W. G. Simpson

utter disbelief and say something like 'This is the slowest damn green I've ever been on!' Chances are, your opponent will send his putt into the bunker on the other side of the green."

Interestingly, Norman relates an incident from the 1986 U.S. Open when Trevino used that very tactic on him. "At the 10th hole one day, each of us had a tricky downhill birdie putt. Trevino hit first, and when his putt finished a foot or so past the hole he said to his caddie (for my benefit), 'Herman, that is the fastest putt I've seen all year long.' It worked—I left my approach putt five feet short and then missed the next one. Lee parred the hole and I bogeyed."

It is with the last stroke of the hole, the inside-the-leather putt, that gamesmanship reaches its subtle epitome. One theory is to concede only the putts that result from an opponent's failure to reach the hole with his approach putt—a way of reinforcing a stroke that has no chance of holing the ball.

Walter Hagen's policy was to concede short putts for halves in the early stages of a match, but never to concede a putt for victory and never in the closing stages of a match.

Jack Nicklaus, although best known for the putt he conceded to Tony Jacklin that enabled Great Britain and Ireland to tie for the 1969 Ryder Cup, was actually more calculating than that gesture suggests. The Golden Bear had a standard practice of making his opponent hole out short putts on the first few holes of a match, just to get an idea of his opponent's nerves. If the fellow tended to wish the ball in, Nicklaus continued to concede nothing; otherwise, he conceded the shorties during the middle holes before returning to a hole-everything policy for the closing stretch. You don't become the greatest champion golfer in history without knowing something about gamesmanship.

On the tee, Greg Norman often waggles a decoy club to goad his opponent into an unwise club selection. Once his opponent plays, Norman puts the decoy back in the bag and pulls out the club he had always intended to use.

Jack Nicklaus is famous for the putt he conceded to Tony Jacklin in the 1969 Ryder Cup, but the Golden Bear is generally more stingy than that gesture would make him appear.

On the early holes, Nicklaus keeps an eye on his opponent's short-putting nerves, then concedes putts on the middle holes before returning to a hole-everything policy for the closing stretch.

CHAPTER ELEVEN

THE MENTAL CHALLENGE

As long as golf has been played for pride or prizes, its champions have been well aware of the impact good thinking has on good scoring. Bobby Jones and Walter Hagen both commented that proper handling of the game's mental hazards accounted for up to 75 percent of their success. While assigning exact quantitative values to the game's physical and mental aspects is impossible, every experienced golfer has come to the realization that controlling the flight of the ball means first controlling his or her thoughts. Yet, it was not until the mid-1970s that golf psychology began attracting widespread interest similar to that showered upon the swing theories touted by more traditional instructors.

This trend should come as no surprise. If any sport is fraught with mental challenges, it is golf. Certainly, no other sport has gone to as much trouble and expense to create an environment of fear and intimidation.

The very first book about golf discussed many of the factors today's sport psychologists focus on in their research. *The Golfer's Manual*, written by H. B. Farnie in 1857, noted that "the great stumbling block in the way of all players, veterans and recruits, is excitement," that "indecision should be overcome

Even golf's greatest stars fought mental demons. Years after the fact, Sam Snead admitted that his triple bogey on the last hole of the 1939 U.S. Open at Philadelphia Country Club, shown above, was the result of "bad thinking." Snead needed only a par five on the hole to win the championship.

At the 1966 U.S. Open at The Olympic Club, Arnold Palmer held a seven-stroke lead with nine holes to play before the wheels fell off and he closed with a four-over-par 39 to Billy Casper's 32. Palmer, unable to regroup, lost the playoff to Casper the next day.

boldly and promptly by the player," and that the golfer "must have confidence in himself." Today, sport psychologists would say that Farnie was talking about anxiety to score well, positive mental imagery, and the development of a positive attitude.

The Mystery of Golf, written by Arnold Haultain in 1908, was the first book entirely devoted to exploring the influence of the mind on the game. Little is known about Haultain except that he was a Canadian who took up golf shortly before writing his opus, and that he wrote authoritatively on a wide variety of topics ranging from religion to romance. He concluded his thesis by saying that the golfer "wages a warfare against self . . . it is not a wrestle with Bogey; it is not a struggle with your mortal foe; it is a physiological, psychological, and moral fight with yourself; it is a test of mastery over self; and the ultimate and irreducible element of the game is to determine which of the players is the more worthy combatant."

Jerome Travers, four-time United States Amateur champion, included a chapter on psychology in *Travers' Golf Book* (1913). He noted that "the golfer who keeps perfectly cool, holds his temper no matter what happens, plays with thoughtful deliberation and carefully studies his opponent, will have a decided advantage over an adversary who gets nervous, loses his temper because of bad luck or a bad shot, plays hastily and devotes but little thought to his shots and to the temperament of the man he is playing."

By the 1920s, a half-dozen books and at least a handful of magazine articles were devoted to the mental side of the game. Two of the most forward-thinking ideas came from Seymour Dunn and Eddie Loos.

Dunn, a Scottish professional, dwelled extensively on the role of the mind in his 1922 book, *Golf Fundamentals.* Dunn explained that "too many golfers . . . do not look attentively at a certain point or direction of play. How can you expect your eyes to register impressively on your mind the exact thing to be done if you do not look attentively?" Three-quarters of a century later, his words reflect the targeting fundamentals being preached by sport psychologists.

Loos, referring to the space between the ears in his 1924 *American Golfer* article, "The Eight-Inch Golf Course,"

Doug Sanders is one of at least five golfers (along with Ed Sneed, Hubert Green, Sam Snead, and Scott Hoch) to lose majors by missing short putts on the last hole. At the 1970 British Open at St. Andrews, Sanders lipped out a two-and-a-half-footer that would have earned him the claret jug; he lost in a playoff to Jack Nicklaus.

said that creating a routine for each shot helped create reliable results. This was the first known mention of a preshot routine. Today, a preshot routine is an essential part of every good player's game.

Less than a decade later, Joyce Wethered, the extraordinary English-woman who won four British Amateur championships, first discussed "visualizing the shot" in an article she wrote for the September 1931 issue of *The American Golfer*. Wethered said: "The mind must be as free as possible from technical worries and able to concentrate upon visualizing what has to be done. . . . The first-class player, when in full practice, is certain of what he is trying to do. He knows where his ball is to pitch, what it will do when it lands, and how it will find its way to the hole side. He sees it all, and his power over the club makes the result inevitable. But should he waver and be undecided, the ball will answer the mental vacillation to which he has yielded."

Yet Wethered's insight fell on deaf ears: Amateur golfers did not take to visualizing their shots until decades later, after Ben Hogan and Jack Nicklaus credited visualization as a key element of their extraordinary successes.

The rest of the early mental movement also found little support from the general golf population. Instead of gaining momentum, the push for more information and research on golf psychology dwindled after the United States came out of the Great Depression, and remained dormant for nearly three decades.

It was not until 1962, when psychologist Dr. Peter Cranford published

The Winning Touch in Golf, that an entire book was filled with practical advice for improving a golfer's mental technique. Until then, books and articles written about golf's mental challenges merely sensitized players to the game's many mental hazards; they offered no solutions on how to avoid them. Cranford, a low-handicap golfer, compiled trial-and-error experiments for more than 25 years before presenting his findings in nearly 50 short chapters including, "To Think or Not to Think"; "Taking Off the Pressure"; and "How to Gain Confidence." By today's standards, most of Cranford's advice is basic common sense, such as: "Never play a careless shot"; "Create pressure situations while practicing so that you'll be prepared for the pressure of an actual match"; and "Give up the feeling that you are 'entitled' to become upset." But at this time, nobody had put all of these thoughts together in one place.

Unfortunately for Cranford, *The Winning Touch* received little attention, and the vast majority of golfers continued to believe that the only way to lower their scores was to take more lessons and pound more balls. Soon after Cranford's instructions were published, the social turbulence and experimental counterculture of the 1960s heightened Americans' search for mind expansion and an understanding of the psyche. This chaotic time created the incubator for much of the mental research and science that has become the current body of golf psychology.

America's social unrest was peaking when golf's premier metaphysical manuscript appeared with the 1972 publication of Michael Murphy's *Golf in the Kingdom.* The tale is a parable employing the game as spiritual discipline. The story is told as a fictitious trip by Murphy to Scotland and his accidental meeting with Shivas Irons, a local golf pro whose search for "true gravity, the deeper lines o' force, the

Fear and intimidation come in many forms. Opposite, from the top: At Royal Birkdale in Southport, England, it's the long rough; at Sahalee Country Club in Redmond, Washington, it's the towering trees; at famed Cypress Point in Pebble Beach, California, it's forced carries over water. Above: At PGA West's Stadium Course in La Quinta, Calif., it's deep bunkers.

Ben Hogan tried to achieve complete mental isolation on the golf course, rarely uttering a word to his fellow competitors. Hogan also was one of the first players to use visualization as a key element of his preshot routine.

The Shivas Irons Society, started by Michael Murphy as a nonprofit organization, explores the game's many mysteries. At a recent society tournament, classical music was played on a tee to soothe participants' mental states. Did it help? One player made a hole-in-one.

deeper structure of the universe" collides with a naive Murphy's view of life and golf. In an amazing 24-hour whirlwind of personal discovery, Murphy begins to delve inside the game's many complex emotional and psychological layers. *Golf in the Kingdom* makes a convincing case that the control all golfers seek for their own games is deeply rooted inside the mind's ability to create the desired shots by natural intuition, if only the golfer stays out of his own way by not trying so hard to force the desired result.

No one since Haultain had probed so deeply and exposed so many parts of golf's enigma as Murphy. A native Californian, Murphy studied philosophy at Stanford University and in India before starting the Esalen Institute in 1962. Esalen is a psychological and spiritual laboratory located near Pebble Beach that studies life's metaphysical boundaries. (Murphy also founded the Shivas Irons Society, a nonprofit organization that furthers the pleasure of golf and explores its many mysteries. It is open to all who share an admiration for the qualities of mind, body, and spirit exemplified by *Golf in the Kingdom*'s Scottish golf pro.)

While *Golf in the Kingdom* touched a nerve—identifying the many emotions golfers have on the course and the unending search for personal control to maximize enjoyment and proficiency of the game—it did not offer practical solutions. What was needed next was not simply a recognition of the mind's immense role in playing golf, but instruction in how to best use it to overcome the game's fear factors.

Michael Murphy wrote golf's premier metaphysical manuscript, *Golf in the Kingdom*. The fictional story makes the case that the mind has the ability to create good shots by intuition alone.

No golfer has personified confidence and concentration under extreme pressure like Jack Nicklaus. And nobody hit more great shots to finish victorious.

By the mid-1960s, Jack Nicklaus had become the game's finest practitioner, in part due to his high confidence level and amazing ability to focus under pressure. At that time, few touring pros and even fewer amateurs were seeking ways to raise their mental capabilities on the course. By the end of the decade, the game's psychological barriers were being mapped out by dozens of researchers and, for the first time, practical advice was flowing from many directions. This growing body of research identified an array of mental skills needed by athletes in general, and golfers in particular, to perform at—or near—their peak ability level.

As the 1970s drew to a close, mental performance enhancement was receiving vastly increased space on bookshelves and in national magazines. The sports psychology boom was on. Like the wagon trains heading West in search of gold, golf's mental gurus were scrambling to stake their claims. Among those making the biggest splashes were Dr. Gary Wiren, a highly respected swing instructor, who wrote *The New Golf Mind* in 1978 with a psychology professor, Dr. Richard Coop. It was the first golf-specific book to espouse the "two-sided brain" approach since adopted by many sport psychologists. By then, researchers had learned that the brain is split down the middle, with each side handling separate functions; as Wiren and Coop referred to them, the left side is the "Analyzer," the right side the "Integrator."

Just as a golfer uses both arms to swing, he needs both sides of his brain. But many golfers play almost exclusively with one hemisphere or the other, which leads to poor decision-making. The Analyzer half is the rational and critical thinker, handling computation and problem-solving. The Integrator specializes in creative endeavors, emotions, and feelings; it is intuitive rather than analytical, overseeing visualization and execution. For example, when putting, the Analyzer evaluates the green for slope, grass length, and grain; then the Integrator converts that information into a feel for speed and direction.

According to Wiren and Coop, the crucial moment in the Analyzer/Integrator partnership occurs immediately prior to making the swing, when the Analyzer is put on standby and the Integrator takes over. Making this happen is a swing cue that allows the mind to focus on the feeling of the intended swing. Much of the book deals with creating useful cues, as well as learning how to identify mental mistakes and track them back to the responsible part of the brain.

Three years later, W. Timothy Gallwey, author of the best-selling *The Inner Game of Tennis,* wrote a three-part series in *GOLF Magazine* on "The Inner Game of Golf." Gallwey also promoted a two-sided approach to the mental side, but instead of brain hemispheres he emphasized the opposition of two selves: Self One, the verbalizing boss who sets out to instruct, criticize, and otherwise intimidate Self Two, the body. Self Two is perfectly capable of swinging the club, provided Self One doesn't interfere. But Self One does interfere—frequently. Gallwey devised a series of concentration techniques to occupy Self One, leaving Self Two free

Dr. Richard Coop was the first psychologist to develop the "two-sided" brain approach to managing the mental portion of the game. Coop and collaborator Dr. Gary Wiren offered golfers new ways to identify mental miscues and useful tricks for avoiding them.

Meditation, mantras, and group therapy are all part of Sweden's government-sponsored golf training program. One of the program's first graduates, Annika Sorenstam, has already established herself as one of the world's finest golfers, winning back-to-back U.S. Women's Opens in 1995 and 1996.

to swing unimpeded. One of Gallwey's favorites is called "Back-Hit": The student concentrates on feeling the clubhead during the swing, saying "Back" to himself when the club reaches the top of the backswing, then "Hit" at the instant of impact. The virtue of this method lies in its simplicity and its effectiveness in liberating Self Two.

Also in 1981, Dr. Bob Rotella's *Mind Mastery for Winning Golf*, co-authored by Linda K. Bunker, focused on goal-setting and tension reduction and offered pencil-and-paper motivational assessment tests. Rotella believes golfers trying to cultivate their maximum mental potential on the golf

course must first identify, and then change, their deficient motivational tendencies. The results of the book's numerous self-tests identify the attitudes and behaviors that have positive and negative effects on the reader's game.

Charles "Chuck" Hogan (no relation to Ben), a former golf professional and cofounder of Sports Enhancement Associates, believes mental difficulties stem from the golfer's use of words like hope, try, concentration, positive, and negative, which inhibit the body from performing correctly. "These are just dumb labels that don't mean anything," says Hogan. "We want to replace them with feelings, ideas, sensorial stuff." Hogan encourages the development of images that free the mind to relax, letting the golfer trust his ability to hit the proper shot. A popular putting image is two rows of worms, one on each side of the ball's intended path. For a greenside sand shot he suggests imagining a parachute attached to the ball as it lands softly on the green. Or see the glowing rocket afterburner propelling the ball down the fairway. Sound corny? Tour winners including Peter Jacobsen and Mike Reid swear by Hogan's images.

Hogan is convinced that with the proper mental coaching, in the near future at least a handful of professionals will compile a stroke average of 68 or better for an entire season. To put this in perspective, no one has ever averaged under 69, and only a handful have ever gone an entire season taking fewer than 70 strokes per round. Still, most sport psychologists agree with Hogan's assessment that as mental barriers fall, so will traditionally untouchable scoring barriers.

Many more obscure methods—from acupuncture to Zen—have been proposed for achieving a heightened state of mental ability and stability on the course. Before you dismiss these as silly, consider that former U.S. Open champion Payne Stewart swears by acupuncture. Another U.S. Open champion, Scott Simpson, credits his religious studies with reducing tension (see Different Strokes, page 291).

As golf psychologists take some of the spotlight from traditional swing instructors, Tour professionals—who are always looking for an edge—increasingly solicit advice from these

mentalists. Today, at least half the golfers on the major professional tours see a sport psychologist on a regular basis. Some of the most popular mentalists, including Dr. Deborah Graham, Dr. Fran Pirozzolo, Hogan, Coop, and Rotella, spend hours on the phone each day discussing mental strategies with their clients.

Even with the increasing emphasis by Tour pros on improving mental skills, most amateurs still consider this part of the game a low priority. But for the game's future stars, mental training is a staple. Nearly all of the NCAA Division I men's and women's golf teams have a sport psychologist

Chuck Hogan, a former golf professional, encourages the development of images that free the mind from swing mechanics while helping to visualize success.

Tiger Woods's father, Earl, began training his son in early childhood to handle mental distractions on the golf course. A psychologist, Dr. Jay Brunza, caddied for Tiger when he won his three U.S. Junior and the first two of his three U.S. Amateur championships.

on retainer or on loan from the school's psychology department for team members' use.

Overseas, Sweden's government-sponsored national women's golf team is pushing the envelope of New Age golf psychology. In one drill they practice with a potato chip between their teeth, trying not to crush it during the swing (too much tension translates into a tightened jaw and a broken chip). This creates an awareness of tension, which signals the golfer to begin relaxation techniques.

The Swedes also play a game called "No Judgment Golf," in which they are not allowed to react, positively or negatively, to a shot. The purpose, says team psychologist Kjell Enhager, author of *Quantum Golf,* is to stay focused on the shot at hand, ignoring the previous one and those hit by opponents.

Meditation, mantras, and group therapy sessions also are part of the Swedish game plan, as is the slogan "Vision 54," which players say is their ultimate goal: Hit every green in regulation and one putt every hole to shoot 54. Among the graduates of the program are Helen Alfredsson and two-time U.S. Open champion Annika Sorenstam; many promising prospects are well on their way to following in their footsteps.

Despite the insights offered by today's mentalists, the leaps in performance envisioned by Chuck Hogan and Vision 54 have yet to materialize. Still, competition continues to intensify on all the pro tours, thanks, in part, to improving mental abilities. We are just now seeing the emergence of golfers who have been reared with state-of-the-art schooling in handling the game's psychological warfare.

Perhaps the first cradle-to-king mental giant will be Tiger Woods. Since he was in diapers, Woods has been trained by his father, Earl, a former Green Beret, and mental coaches including Dr. Jay Brunza in the proper techniques for developing and maintaining concentration and controlling stress.

When Tiger was a first-grader and already a golfing prodigy, his father was installing heavy-duty psychological armor for future battles. Earl would jingle change in his pocket as Tiger was lining up a putt or tear open the Velcro on his glove just as the boy hit an approach. Sometimes he'd remind Tiger about the out of bounds running down the left side as the youngster was teeing up his ball. No matter what distraction the father could create, the son had to learn to concentrate through it.

"I wanted to make sure," said Earl, "he'd never run into anybody who was tougher mentally than he was." So far Tiger hasn't. Before reaching his 21st birthday, Woods had six national championships on his résumé, an unparalleled record. Will he continue his early pace and become modern golf psychology's first perfectly programmed champion? That question won't be answered for another 20 years, but if Woods's early results are indicative of what today's psychological techniques can accomplish, Pete Dye and Co. will need to add more hazards and a new set of back tees.

PREVAILING WISDOM

Focusing on a specific target fills the mind with nonmechanical thoughts and creates a greater margin for error.

Dr. Bob Rotella, a sport psychologist at the University of Virginia and consultant to dozens of Tour golfers, succinctly explains the necessary mental edge as the maximization of the four C's: Confidence, Concentration, Composure, and Commitment. To increase the four C's and cultivate better shotmaking through better thought-making, golf's current crop of mental gurus build their advice around a half-dozen practical guidelines:

- Stay in the present.
- Choose a specific target.
- Use the identical routine to prepare for each shot.
- Create a visual picture or mental feeling of success before swinging.
- Stay within your basic personality type.
- Stay focused without becoming overly excited.

Stay in the Present. Concentration is the ability to focus upon the task at hand: In golf, this means the next shot to be played. During the 30- to 45-second period before hitting a shot, the golfer must practice both "broad" and "narrow focus." Broad focus is the ability to gather information on the big picture—wind, lie, slope, hazards, the opponent's situation, the leaderboard, and any other outside influences that may affect the shot. Narrow focus is honing in as tightly as possible on the chosen target while blocking out unnecessary thoughts and distractions.

Golfers who cannot switch from no focus (walking down the fairway chatting) to broad focus (analyzing) and then to narrow focus (targeting) will find they are still conversing while the wind changes direction, or thinking about the out of bounds left as they start their backswing. In either case, their chances for hitting a poor shot are significantly increased.

Dr. Richard Coop, professor of Educational Psychology at the University of North Carolina and a popular sport psychologist on Tour, calls these varying stages of concentration "disciplined" and "flow." Disciplined concentration is the first stage, when all factors influencing the shot are calculated and the preshot routine is executed. Flow concentration is the state created by the preshot routine, in which the golfer simply lets the swing happen without conscious interference.

The biggest stumbling block to focused concentration is the enormous amount of time between shots. If a typical golfer takes 90 shots per round and spends an average of 30 seconds preparing for and hitting each one, focusing takes no more than 45 minutes during the round. The other three-plus hours are spent thinking about how much he would like to win the match or how he made triple bogey on the hole the last time he played it or whether or not he locked his car. It is this huge amount of down-time that makes golf a unique mental exercise among sports. The golfer's ability to refocus his concentration over and over during the round is essential to playing well.

DIFFERENT STROKES

UNCONVENTIONAL METHODS FOR IMPROVING MENTAL SKILLS

Golfers on the professional tours know good thinking can be the difference between winning tournaments and missing cuts. Not surprisingly, their search for a physical or psychological edge has led many down varied paths of enlightenment. Yoga, martial-arts breathing techniques, Zen, hypnosis, acupuncture, religion, music therapy, positive self-talk, negative self-talk—you name it, golfers have tried it.

Payne Stewart won the 1989 PGA Championship and the 1991 U.S. Open with needles stuck in his ears, saying acupuncture helped him relax on the course and stay focused. Stewart's acupuncturist inserts three to seven needles in each ear based upon the reading from a machine that reveals his patient's current mental state. "He can tell me from those results how I've been feeling," says Stewart, who has used the treatment since his amateur days, "and he's always right."

Scott Simpson, Tom Lehman, Bernhard Langer, and Betsy King use religion to relieve tension and keep a healthy perspective on what is important in their lives. "I've found a lot of helpful things in the Bible," says Simpson, who prays regularly for mental strength. "It's easy to dwell on the negative, to think you're a jerk when you hit a bad shot. . . . That's the key to my belief. After a bad shot, I'm mentally prepared to go ahead and hit a good one."

Gary Player has long been a staunch supporter of positive self-talk, the conversation a person wages inside his head. Self-talk is a way of keeping in touch with yourself, triggering pictures and feelings stored in the Unconscious. Early in Player's career he would stand in front of a mirror each morning and repeat: "I am the greatest golfer in the world. I am the greatest golfer in the world." His self-talk supported and built the self-image that he wanted to achieve.

Hubert Green and Johnny Miller have used negative self-talk to keep them from becoming too excited. Green would walk into a press conference and tell the assembled media that he "wasn't playing well enough to carry Jack Nicklaus's clubs." Miller was known to tell reporters that he wasn't expecting to win even when he had the lead going into the final round. "Emotions in golf are like a tachometer," says Miller. "You must keep your emotions under the red line or else you'll blow up." Miller, who played with more natural emotion than Player, knew he had to downplay any situation to keep from getting overexcited, while Player had to psyche himself up to approach his personal "red line."

Richard Zokol walked the PGA Tour's fairways in 1982, his rookie season, listening to music and baseball on a portable radio to keep him relaxed and get his mind off his game until it was time to play his next shot.

One of the most aggressive quests for mental help began in 1983. With his Tour career going nowhere, Denis Watson read a book on Zen and the martial arts, then studied breathing and looked into something called "Neuro-Linguistic Programming." He began to control his allergies psychosomatically. Watson also read *The Psychic Side of Sport* by Michael Murphy to learn the mind's role in other sports. Watson's career took off the next season. He won three events and finished second on the PGA Tour money list. Unfortunately, soon after his rise to the top, Watson suffered a debilitating wrist injury from which his game never fully recovered, proving there are still some things even good thinking cannot overcome.

Payne Stewart has used acupuncture—including needles in his ears—to help him relax, stay focused on the course, and win two major championships.

CHARACTERISTICS OF
MENTALLY TOUGH COMPETITORS

Dr. James Loehr is CEO of LGE Sports Science, Inc., and one of the world's best-known sport psychologists. He has authored 11 books about his research with hundreds of well-known athletes in dozens of sports, including golf. After more than 30 years of study, Loehr has dissected the mental characteristics of champion athletes, male and female, old and young:

SELF-MOTIVATED AND SELF-DIRECTED. He doesn't need to be pushed or forced from the outside. His direction comes from within. He's involved because he wants to be, because it's his thing, not somebody else's.

POSITIVE BUT REALISTIC. He's not a complainer, a criticizer, or a faultfinder. He's a builder, not a destroyer. His trademark is a blend of realism and optimism. His eye is always fixed on success, on what can happen, and on what is possible—not on their opposites.

IN CONTROL OF HIS EMOTIONS. Every competitor understands the unfortunate performance consequences of poor emotional control. Bad refereeing, stupid mistakes, obnoxious opponents, poor playing conditions, etc., represent powerful triggers of negative emotion. Anger, frustration, and fear must be controlled, or they most certainly will control you. The tough competitor has tamed the lion inside.

CALM AND RELAXED UNDER FIRE. He doesn't avoid pressure; he's challenged by it. He's at his best when the pressure is on and the odds are against him. Being put to the test is not a threat, but another opportunity to explore the outer limits of his potential.

HIGHLY ENERGETIC AND READY FOR ACTION. He is capable of getting himself pumped up and energized for playing his best, no matter how he feels or how bad or meaningless the situation. He is his own igniter and can, in spite of fatigue, overcome personal problems or bad luck.

DETERMINED. His sheer force of will to succeed in what he has started is beyond the comprehension of those who do not share the same vision. He is relentless in his pursuit of his goals. Setbacks are taken in stride as he inches his way further forward.

MENTALLY ALERT AND FOCUSED. He is capable of long and intensive periods of total concentration. He is capable of tuning in what's important and tuning out what is not, whether there is no pressure or great pressure.

DOGGEDLY SELF-CONFIDENT. He displays a nearly unshatterable sense of confidence and belief in himself and in his ability to perform well. He rarely falls victim to his own or others' self-defeating thoughts and ideas. As a consequence, he is not easily intimidated.

FULLY RESPONSIBLE. He takes full responsibility for his own actions. There are no excuses. He either did or he didn't. Ultimately, everything begins and ends with him, and he is comfortable with that. He is fully aware that his destiny as an athlete is in his own hands.

Choose a Specific Target. As in all target sports, picking a specific target is crucial to creating precision and focusing the mind on the shot. An archer doesn't aim for the entire target, he aims for the bull's-eye. In golf, the narrower the focus, the less chance there is to be distracted and the better one's chance of putting the ball safely in play. For example, instead of aiming at the entire fairway when hitting a drive, aim for the left half and play for a fade; instead of aiming at the entire green, focus on a large tree trunk behind the center of the green.

Focusing on a specific target fills the mind with nonmechanical thoughts and helps avoid what many instructors call "paralysis by analysis," a common affliction whereby the brain tries consciously to control so many specifics of the swing that its signals to the muscles become muddled. The result is almost always a poor shot.

Use the Identical Routine to Prepare for Each Shot. "A sound preshot routine is the rod and staff of the golfer under pressure, a comfort in times of affliction and challenge," explains Rotella. It is the routine that prepares the mind and body to execute, and, when the pressure is on, creates a positive diversion from distractions.

Tour professionals understand the critical importance of a consistent preshot routine to discipline mind and body to control static elements such as aim and alignment. While no one can completely control all the variables of his swing once it is in motion, one can control every variable before starting the backswing.

The following elements are found

in the preshot routines of nearly every professional golfer: A trigger, isolation, computation of outside factors, a specific target, and physical and mental calm.

The trigger may be adjusting the glove, the act of pulling a club out of the bag, or tugging on a shirtsleeve. It doesn't matter what the trigger is as long as it signals the mind and body to begin concentrating on the upcoming shot. Those Tour players with the most effective routines say that once they make their trigger move, they feel enclosed in their own little room or as if a thick curtain comes down separating them from their surroundings.

Once isolated and tuned in to the situation, they assess the outside factors affecting the shot and choose the club and shot shape that provide the best opportunity for hitting the target. Many players also pick out an intermediate target on their intended line of play. Curtis Strange chooses a spot 12 inches in front of his ball directly on his intended target line; he continually checks to make sure he is aligned with that spot as he prepares to swing. At this point the golfer may make a rehearsal swing or just an extended waggle to increase his feel for the shot he wants to execute.

Finally, just before starting the swing, many pros visualize the ball fly-

Dr. Bob Rotella (left) is one of the better-known mental gurus working with professional golfers. Rotella boils down the mental side to four Cs: Confidence, Concentration, Composure, and Commitment. Here he consults with Tour pro Brad Faxon.

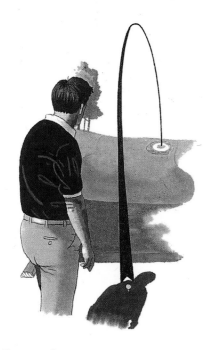

Once you have a target in mind, try to generate a mental picture or feeling for the shot you want to produce.

Good concentration means focusing solely on the shot at hand. Thinking about the tee shot on the next hole while still waiting to putt out will destroy present concentration.

ing through the air with the chosen shot shape (left-to-right or right-to-left) and trajectory (high or low), then landing and stopping near their target.

By now the golfer has surveyed the situation and acknowledged all significant factors, chosen a club, chosen a target, and visualized the shot he wants to play. His mind is calm and concentrating on where he wants the ball to go.

Now it's time to take a last look at the target, look at the ball, and begin the swing. "Further delay," explains Rotella, "can only be an opportunity for unwanted thoughts and distractions to disturb your concentration and pollute that pure and unconscious reaction."

There are three important caveats to making a preshot routine effective: 1) It should be as simple as possible—having as few steps as possible and taking no more than 30 seconds to complete; 2) It must be learned, rehearsed, and consistently duplicated during practice for it to be automatic and effective on the course; 3) A routine works as long as it does not become a ritual. A routine is a set of actions performed at a high level of conscious awareness. In contrast, a ritual is a set of repetitive actions that may be done with little purpose and at a low level of awareness. It is the difference between having a purpose and simply going through the motions.

Create a Visual Picture or Mental Feeling of Success Before Swinging. Jack Nicklaus claims he's never hit a shot, even in practice, without first seeing a picture and rehearsing it in his mind.

"I see the ball where I want it to finish, nice white and sitting up high on the bright green grass. Then the scene quickly changes and I see the ball going there; its path, trajectory, and shape, even its behavior on landing. Then there's sort of a fadeout and the next scene shows me making the kind of swing that will turn the previous images into reality," says Nicklaus in *Golf My Way*. While Nicklaus "goes to the movies" before hitting each shot, Dr. Rotella notes that fewer than half of all professionals actually visualize the ball flying through the air before they swing.

But most professionals do call up images of some type to help improve their focus. Some "see" the ball finishing near the target, others picture the swing they want or another pro's swing and tempo. Images may include a swing path line etched on the ground or the clubhead traveling from inside the target line and striking the ball on the rear-inside quadrant. Any image that ties the target to the swing is useful.

If you have trouble visualizing the shot before hitting it, visualize success. In his 1960 book *Psycho-Cybernetics*, Dr. Maxwell Maltz described this as "creative imagination," which Tour pros Dave Stockton and Scott Simpson have credited with unleashing their full potential on the course. Before starting their swings, Maltz, a medical doctor, suggested that athletes picture how they would act and feel after succeeding. Filling the mind with the positive sensations keeps it from calling up any negative thoughts.

According to Stockton, who read the book just before winning the 1970 PGA Championship, he walked as tall

Very few golfers can focus on the game for the entire time they are on the course. Lee Trevino chats with the gallery between shots to keep his mind fresh.

Dr. Deborah Graham uses a personality-profile test to indicate how individuals, such as Tour pro Lee Janzen, think on the course. The results help Graham focus players' practice time on improving areas where they could better sharpen their shot planning and execution.

as he could and tried to feel as if he had made every putt before hitting it. Stockton said he never worried about what might go wrong, and, despite a few bad holes in the final round, never experienced indecision coming down the final stretch.

Maltz said "self-concept"—your feelings about yourself—is developed, not genetic, so a person's self-image can be changed for better or worse. What Stockton did at the 1970 PGA— and many pros do every time they play—is create the self-prophecy of success by thinking good thoughts. Even if these thoughts aren't true— "I'm the best putter in this tournament"—repeating them and reinforcing them with constructive instruction

and practice is likely to turn them into reality.

Stay Within Your Basic Personality Type. If Jack Nicklaus had tried joking with the gallery the way Lee Trevino does, he'd probably be back in Columbus, Ohio, managing his father's drugstore. If Fuzzy Zoeller had tried to emulate Ben Hogan's cold, aloof style during tournaments, you probably never would have heard of him, either. Great competitors learn to use their natural personalities to help them prepare for the next shot.

Dr. Deborah Graham, a psychologist based in Boerne, Texas, believes strongly in improving golfers' mental performance by first understanding their personality strengths and weaknesses. Graham offers advice based on the results of a personality-profile test that gives her a strong indication of a player's general traits and how they will affect thinking on the golf course. Coupled with left brain–right brain analysis (right-brained people tend to be more creative, emotional, imaginative, and unpredictable; left-brainers are practical, logical, organized, and more focused), Graham determines which side rules the golfer, using the results to develop the skills they lack. For example, a right-brained golfer may need to become more logical— getting precise yardages and managing his game on the course. A left-brained player may need to stress visualization while downplaying practice.

Other sport psychologists and swing instructors use similar tests, sorting the golfer's dominant personality traits into general categories. Peter Kostis, swing guru to many Tour

Craig Stadler is the poster boy for Expressive golfers.

professionals, slots his students' on-course attitudes into four general types: 1) Analyticals, who are technically oriented and serious; 2) Drivers, self-controlled and determined; 3) Amiables, agreeable and ingratiating; 4) Expressives, outgoing and emotional. Left-brained athletes tend to fall into Driver and Analytical personality types, while right-brained athletes tend to be identified as Amiable or Expressive.

Chuck Hogan, in conjunction with Dr. Michael O'Connor, a behavioral scientist, has sorted golf personalities into 15 distinct types. Each one, Hogan explains, requires a different management style to maximize performance on the course.

No matter how you identify an individual, these psychologists all agree that no one personality is better or worse as long as the golfer adapts his game and practice habits to keep his dominant traits from taking complete control or squelching other traits needed for peak performance. For example, Craig Stadler, who has been identified as a right-brainer with Expressive tendencies, is right to vent his frustration rather than suppress it. Keeping his emotions inside would increase his tension to a dangerous level, causing him to misplay shots. By letting off steam with the occasional club toss, Stadler lowers his tension level between shots.

The Amiable, right-brained (non-analytical) Ben Crenshaw was slumping in the early 1990s when he decided to analyze his swing's technical parts. He began soliciting swing advice from any and all quarters. His slump deepened. A couple of years went by

Ben Crenshaw is an Amiable personality.

Tom Kite's personality drives him to work extremely hard to reach perfection.

before he stopped listening and concentrated on the swing feelings he had been taught as a junior; his game soon returned to top form, culminating in his second Masters victory, in 1995. Conversely, a Driver personality with left-brained tendencies—e.g., Tom Kite and Tom Watson—won't feel comfortable with a swing change unless he completely understands it.

Stay Focused Without Becoming Overly Excited. Studies of athletes have found that different sports require different levels of physical excitement to create the ideal performance state. Dr. Fran Pirozzolo, a professor in the Department of Neurology at the Baylor College of Medicine in Houston, explains that strength sports such as football and weight lifting require a high degree of excitement to improve performance levels. Reactive activities, such as playing defense in basketball, also require high excitement. But target sports such as shooting, archery, and golf can handle only a moderate degree of excitement. Pirozzolo and other psychologists describe the golfer's ideal performance state as "somewhere between anger and despair," the middle region of emotional extremes.

But arousal usually increases as interest in the situation or competitive pressure increases. Many times, a golfer becomes so caught up in the moment that he doesn't realize his adrenaline level is rapidly increasing while his ability to analyze and perform is rapidly deteriorating.

Arousal also has a pronounced effect on breathing, heart rate, and muscle tension. If a golfer finds himself too aroused, he should slow his breathing and shake his arms or lightly stretch to reduce muscle tension. If a golfer is underaroused, he should try breathing faster and walking more quickly between shots to get his heart rate up.

Golf requires a moderate degree of excitement, described as "somewhere between anger and despair." Walking briskly from shot to shot should provide the proper amount of physical arousal for most golfers.

WORDS OF WISDOM

We can, if we wish, pretend to enjoy the shots which frighten us. We can positively make ourselves look forward to playing as many of them as possible. Instead of fearing them we can stimulate an interest in them. A delicate pitch over a bunker can be converted by a little judicious mental effort into a delightful adventure.

Joyce Wethered

Most golfers prepare for disaster. A good golfer prepares for success.

Bob Toski

When you miss a shot, never think of what you did wrong. Come up to the next shot thinking of what you must do right.

Tommy Armour

Good players aren't worried about what anybody else thinks of them.

Dr. Bob Rotella

Everyone has his own choking level, a level at which he fails to play his normal golf. As you get more experienced, your choking level rises.

Johnny Miller

In the game of golf, confidence is a great helper. Let a player lose it and he is marked for slaughter.

Jerome Travers

The trouble with the purely rational, technique-oriented approach is that it has made people focus compulsively and exclusively on score and performance, and they have often lost the whole deeper joy of the game.

Michael Murphy

CHAPTER TWELVE

PRACTICE

WHO CAN DENY THAT THE GREATEST PLEASURE IN GOLF COMES FROM IMPROVEMENT, and that improvement comes only from faithful practice? But, as instructor Dave Pelz notes, practice doesn't make perfect; only *perfect practice* makes perfect.

Watch the bustle of activity on the range at a professional tournament and it's hard to believe that practice is a relatively new strategy for improving one's golf swing. Since the game's origin hundreds of years ago, every player has tried to find a better way to hit the ball from point A to point B. However, evidence suggests that the notion of actually working on one's swing to improve it did not exist until the early twentieth century.

The high replacement cost of a lost or damaged feathery or gutta-percha ball discouraged early golfers from keeping a shag bag. The financial constraints began disappearing with the advent of the much less expensive rubber-core ball in 1898. In 1913, the burgeoning Pinehurst Resort and Country Club in North Carolina built the first known practice range in the United States. Complete with a tee, fairway, and bunker, the site was soon dubbed "Maniac Hill."

A few years later, British author Bernard Darwin, commenting on the early movement in the United States to serious practice, said, "American golfers have carried practicing to a point that we have not reached and have not hith-

America's first practice range was built in 1913 at Pinehurst Resort and Country Club in Pinehurst, North Carolina. The site was soon dubbed "Maniac Hill."

erto approved. All, or nearly all, our teachers have advised us to 'end with a good one'; in other words, to stop practicing as soon as we have hit on the something that we wanted. They point out that we cannot hit better than well, that we have only in us a certain number of good shots, that we shall waste them and grow stale and tired. The Americans, on the other hand, say that the moment when the practicer has found the secret is precisely the moment for him to go on and on and nail the secret to the counter.

"It is instructive to watch the American professionals on the morning of a match. Each takes a multitude of balls, sends his caddie out into the deep field and snows him under with balls hit from various distances and with various clubs. A Briton, having hit two or three good ones, would stop,

but the American goes on. He wants to make himself as much of a machine as possible, and this daily routine is, he thinks, the best way to do it. Judging by the results, I suppose he must be right."

Perhaps by British standards Americans were more keen on practice, but in the early days of the PGA Tour, most pros spent more time driving to events and playing cards in the hotel lobby than they did honing their swings. Since most courses did not have a practice range, the pros who did practice kept a bag of balls in their car trunk and hit them into a park or field away from the tournament site. There were no tractor-mounted pickers slithering around to scoop up the expended balls; instead, caddies stood in the landing area and retrieved the balls one by one.

Byron Nelson was the first great champion to be considered a serious practicer by his peers, but he backed off from long sessions after the mid 1930s, when he began winning. Even in his swing-grooving heyday, Nelson never practiced as much as Ben Hogan. After World War II, the shy pro from Fort Worth made ball-beating fashionable. Hogan had been around the Tour for nearly a decade, but he had never won; most of the other pros thought he was wasting his time practicing all day. The belief among good players was that to improve you had to play a lot and learn from the players who were better than you. Hogan turned that theory upside down with his dedication to high-volume practice.

Every day he was not playing, Hogan would be on the range from 10 A.M. until noon, then return after lunch for at least three more hours. During these sessions he was known to hit an entire bag of balls with each club in his bag. Most nights Hogan took his wedge, putter, and some balls back to his hotel room, where he putted across the floor and chipped into chairs, oblivious to his neighbors' complaining about the noise. To this day, Hogan's extraordinary practice habits are as much a part of his legend as his victories.

Hogan was a classic case of maximizing feedback to increase learning. As British physicist Alastair Cochran and writer John Stobbs noted in their groundbreaking 1968 scientific study of the game, *Search for the Perfect Swing,* one of the essential requirements for learning is knowing the results of our efforts. The more complete that knowledge, the more

Ben Hogan single-handedly changed golfers' views of practice by hitting an entire shag bag with every club every day he wasn't playing a competitive round. Until he began beating everyone, most professionals spent more time on their post-round card games than on honing their swings.

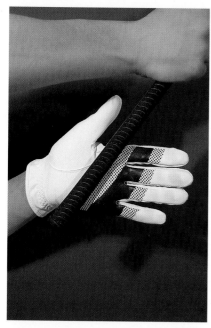

progress can be made. This is called "feedback," since the results of all attempts are fed back to the brain and used to correct later attempts.

Only through many correct repetitions can a sound golf swing be learned and remembered. Cochran compares it to remembering a phone number: If a number is read out of the directory, it is remembered only long enough to dial it immediately; if the dialer is distracted and does not make the call right away, he most likely will have to recheck the listing. But if the number is dialed regularly, it will come to mind whenever needed. (And if an often-used number is changed and no longer used, it will soon disappear from memory.)

The same is true in golf. Even after learning the swing, it is imperative to play and practice regularly to keep the swing fresh in the memory (which is separate from needing to keep the appropriate muscles in shape).

Cochran also explains that the golfer is not striving to "groove one unique swing to be repeated time after time. The very nature of a golf course, with variations in slopes, lies, grasses,

wind, and hazards demands constant alterations to the basic swing. Even when playing from the same exact spot, no golfer can make exactly the same swing two shots in a row.

"Rather, the goal is to learn a series of alternative swings whereby the golfer can produce the unique swing that best matches the conditions present and results in acceptable, although not in every case perfect, shots."

Developing a swing that effectively adjusts to different conditions requires overlearning the fundamentals, then letting the subconscious react appropriately to the situation and target. Overlearning is habit formation and thus requires repetition. Lots and lots and lots of repetition. Medical science and behavioral psychology say that to make a new habit permanent, the muscles and the Creative Subconscious— the part of the mind that performs an operation without thinking about it— must practice the correct motion for at least 21 separate sessions spaced over no less than 21 days.

The bad news is that most golfers do not put in this many practice sessions during an entire season. A study by the PGA of America found that 47 percent of high handicappers *never* practice. The good news is that if a fundamentally correct swing is practiced often enough to become a habit, it will become as difficult to perform incorrectly as it once was to perform correctly.

It is generally agreed among instructors that swing changes will take hold faster when they are practiced without watching the resulting ball flight. In his book *How to Win the Three Games of Golf*, Hank Johnson explains the learning process as golf swing, golf shot, and golf score. Johnson says that the swing is best learned away from the course, in front of a mirror. The correct positions are drilled and checked until they become comfortable. Next, the new mechanics are put into practice by hitting and evaluating shots on the driving range, which builds target awareness and develops a sense of the trajectory and distance for various clubs. Only then should the swing be taken to the course.

Johnson says the trick to making the transition from mechanics to shotmaking is to step away from the pile of range balls whenever mechanical thoughts reappear. Go to the back of the practice tee—or back to the mirror—and practice mechanics without hitting shots; only once the mechanics become comfortable again should you go back to hitting shots. On the course, think solely about scoring by implementing the different shots that have been practiced; the only thoughts allowed are about nonmechanical concerns such as tempo, strategy, lie, and weather.

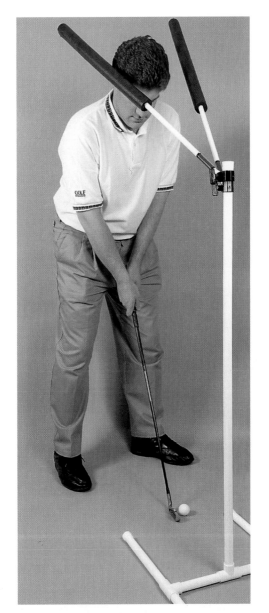

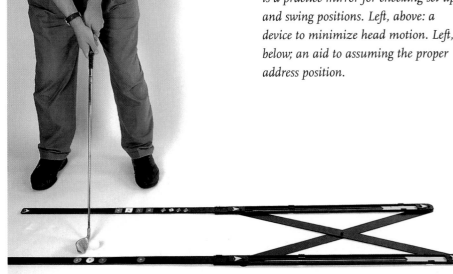

Hundreds of practice training aids are currently available. Ranging from simple to complex, they also vary in value from extremely helpful to nearly worthless. The gadgets shown on the opposite page, from the top, include a light beam that checks putterface alignment; a glove with reminder markings for a proper grip; an alignment aid for the stance and upper body. Opposite right is a practice mirror for checking set-up and swing positions. Left, above: a device to minimize head motion. Left, below; an aid to assuming the proper address position.

Top: *Indoor practice facilities, such at this one in Norwalk, Connecticut, are on the rise as golfers in cool climes extend the season to work on their games year-round.*

Middle: *At the forefront of computerized teaching is Dr. Ralph Mann at the Grand Cypress Academy of Golf in Orlando. He has spent more than a decade creating a model swing from data of more than 50 Tour professionals. At the Academy, amateurs can compare their swings to the computer model.*

Bottom: *Even in midtown Manhattan, golfers can keep their swings tuned. The four-story Chelsea Piers driving range was built in 1994 on a pier stretching into the Hudson River. Tee times on a hitting bay must be reserved during busy periods.*

A growing industry wants to help golfers practice more efficiently and effectively. Hundreds of inventors are marketing thousands of learning aids, from the elegantly simple to the absurdly complicated. Noted instructor Gary Wiren runs "Golf Around the World," a clearinghouse for more than 150 different practice products. Teaching gurus David Leadbetter and Dave Pelz have leveraged their popularity into catalogues of branded practice aids. Former PGA Tour player-turned-teacher Wally Armstrong sold hundreds of thousands of videotapes demonstrating how to take household items—brooms, tools, hula hoops, footballs, and more—and turn them into effective practice devices.

Another sign of the progress of practice are the 2,000 stand-alone driving ranges in the United States, which include indoor facilities in old warehouses and under inflated domes. Modern golf learning centers featuring full-length practice holes, multiple practice greens, perfect turf, and computerized video facilities have proven enormously successful since coming on-line in the early 1980s. The Hills of Lakeway in Austin, Texas; The Sea Island Learning Center in Sea Island, Georgia; and the Grand Cypress Academy of Golf in Orlando, Florida, are among the finest examples of these full-service practice palaces.

Meanwhile, most established courses have improved and expanded their ranges. It is not uncommon to find short-game practice areas complete with sand traps, bunkered target greens, and soft-cover practice balls. Muirfield Village Golf Club in Dublin, Ohio, and World Woods in Brooksville,

Florida, have built circular ranges that allow golfers to practice from any direction into any wind condition they choose.

Thanks to the growing number of acceptable practice facilities, there is no excuse for not practicing. But it is how, not where, one practices that is the real secret to improving.

DIFFERENT STROKES

PRACTICE FROM GOOD LIES OR BAD?

Most teachers recommend that beginners only practice from flat, perfect lies. In fact, some suggest the novice learning the fundamentals hit all shots from a tee. "When you are working on your basic swing, you won't get the right feedback [from a bad lie]," explains instructor Carl Lohren. "You will not be sure you have made a good swing, because you will instinctively respond to the lie and make swing adjustments to get the ball out of it." Even Jack Nicklaus says he always looks for a perfectly flat practice area with firm, dry, close-cut turf.

As a player becomes more proficient, he needs to become familiar with every situation he may see on the course. So set aside a portion of each session—perhaps one-fourth—to work on shots from various slopes and lies. Gary Player says better golfers should hit out of bad lies and from slopes to keep practice from becoming boring.

Player also says there is one exception to the good lie rule for beginners. "Practicing out of rough will improve any golfer," he explains. "Hitting from rough teaches you how to hit through the ball. Practicing in the rough forces you to stay down on the shot and strengthens your golf muscles."

PREVAILING WISDOM

Here is a 12-step program based upon research on how people learn, the prevailing recommendations of respected instructors, and the training habits of successful touring professionals. It will transform basic ball-beating into perfect practice.

1) Practice the percentages. According to most instructors, practice time should be allotted in relation to how the game is played. Full swings account for 35 to 40 percent of total strokes in most golfers' rounds, while the other 60 to 65 percent of shots are partial swings or putts. This means that two of every three hours of practice time should be devoted to the short game—shots within 100 yards of the hole. As a general rule, short-game practice should be divided one-third for putts, one-third for pitches, and one-third for chips and sand shots.

For full-swing practice, allot time proportionately to the actual number of shots you will hit with each club during a typical round. This means approximately 40 percent of full-swing practice time goes to hitting drives and full wedges.

2) Schedule frequent, short sessions. As previously mentioned, it takes at least 21 sessions over 21 days to make or break a habit. Short, frequent sessions have been proven more successful in habit formation than an equal amount of time spent in one or two long sessions.

A good time to schedule some of these sessions is right after a round. Most Tour pros go to the range immediately after a round, so they can address problems that cropped up that day and identify a course of action while the mistakes are fresh in their minds. After a good round, many pros hit a bag of balls to further ingrain the successful swing.

Personality and attention span play

a role in planning a practice schedule. Ben Crenshaw and Bruce Lietzke have little patience for practice and lose interest after a dozen or so swings; their games would crumble if they started hitting the 300-plus balls of Vijay Singh's daily routine. Meanwhile, Tom Kite and Lee Trevino are as focused after their fourth bucket as they are on their first swing of the day.

Jack Nicklaus, who—along with Ben Hogan and Gary Player—is among the most focused practicers ever, determines the length of his practice sessions by starting with a specific goal. Once he achieves it, he stops. "I learned long ago that there is a limit to the number of shots you can hit effectively before losing your concentration," he says. "I have to believe that some of the guys who virtually live on the practice tee on Tour often weaken their games by letting their practice become pointless through sheer monotony or fatigue."

Take a cue from Nicklaus and don't practice when fatigue, boredom, or weather conditions, such as strong winds or very cold temperatures, inhibit a normal swing. Also, it is better to curtail a practice session if your shots are becoming worse rather than better.

3) Warm up before hitting. Loose, warm muscles respond faster and with less chance for strain. A Tour pro never hits shots until completing a simple stretching routine. Nicklaus starts by taking a few full swings with a loose, wristy motion that puts some feel into his hands and loosens his wrists and forearms. Then he holds a club behind

Tom Kite has hit as many practice balls as anyone during his 25 years on Tour. But his Hoganesque regimen won't work for all golfers.

THE PREROUND WARM-UP

Practicing and warming up are often confused. Practice is where you learn to play; warm-up is where you prepare to play. Don't make the mistake of turning a preround warm-up into a swing-rebuilding session that leaves you demoralized and tired.

All professionals begin their warm-up with a few light stretches to loosen their muscles, particularly in their backs. Once stretched, Jack Nicklaus suggests starting out with the easiest-to-hit clubs, the wedges. As you work through the bag, pick the club in which you have the most confidence. If you like the 4-iron better than the 3, hit a few 4-irons and leave the 3 in the bag. By swinging your favorite clubs, you're less likely to start tinkering with your swing and more likely to build confidence.

Curtis Strange's preround warm-up mirrors that of many Tour professionals and includes 40 to 50 full shots using the same clubs and the same number of balls with each before every round. Strange's full-swing warm-up includes:

CLUB	NUMBER OF BALLS
PW	10–12
7-Iron	7–8
5-Iron	7–8
3-Iron	7–8
4-Wood	2–3
3-Wood	2–3
Driver	5–7

Strange wants to make sure that when he gets to the first tee he feels as if he's already played a few holes. Some professionals end their warm-up by hitting the clubs and the shot shapes they will probably need on the first couple of holes.

Tom Kite, who uses a full-shot warm-up very similar to Strange's, hits the first two or three shots with each club focusing on his preshot routine and tempo. When he reaches the final two or three shots with each club, he tries to hit specific shots such as a low punch or a hook. This way, Kite gets his mind off mechanics and onto shotmaking, which he will have to do on the course.

If there is a short-game practice area available, Strange recommends hitting pitches and chips while concentrating on smooth rhythm and solid contact.

On the practice green, instructor John Elliott recommends first rolling some long putts from a spot in the middle of the green to various points along the fringe; this sharpens distance control and fine-tunes the stroke to the green speed on that particular day without worrying about direction. That is followed by 10-foot putts from all sides of a hole to get a feel for breaks in the green. Finally, stroke three-footers from all around the hole. Finish by knocking in at least six in a row to build confidence before heading to the first tee.

The entire warm-up, from stretching to walking to the first tee, should not last more than 30 to 40 minutes.

his back with his arms extended, and rotates his body back and forth from above the hips to loosen the muscles in his upper back and shoulders. Finally, with a club across the middle of his back, he hooks his elbows over it and rotates from the hips up to stretch the lower back. The entire routine takes less than a minute, and Nicklaus believes it is one reason he has played for so long with so few injuries.

Another popular routine is swinging two clubs at once. Hold them with a baseball grip and slowly swing back and forth. Let their weight loosen the back, shoulders, legs, and arms.

When you do make your first swings of the day, start with the shorter, more lofted clubs. Shorter shafts and higher lofts reduce the vibration and shock at impact, because clubhead speeds are slower and a large portion of the impact energy is deflected upward. Starting with these clubs puts less strain on the body and helps the muscles finish loosening up before taking on the more jarring impact of the long irons and woods. The more lofted clubs also are easier to hit solidly, letting you build some confidence before moving on to those less forgiving.

4) Hit to a target. Simply hitting balls is exercise. Hitting balls to a target is practice. On the course, everything relates to a target. And practicing to a target lets you check aim and alignment, the most critical of all swing fundamentals.

Hank Johnson notes that the temptation on the practice range is to hit the same shot over and over, using the same club. But this is not what hap-

PUTTING PRACTICE

There is no one best way to practice putting. Good practice is personalized practice. Bill Rogers, 1981 British Open champion, used to gear his putting practice around short putts. "From three feet and in I begin to feel as though I'm never going to miss," said Rogers, "and hearing and seeing the ball go into the hole repeatedly builds my confidence."

Bobby Locke, universally known as one of the finest putters ever, believed that the putting stroke was a miniature golf swing and that the stroke needed the same rhythm as that used with any other club. Therefore, Locke concentrated on long-putt practice from 30 to 50 feet to develop this miniature swing and get the putterhead moving at the correct rhythm.

Tom Weiskopf divides his practice between long and short putts. "I practice from 20 to 40 feet to develop a feel for distance and the ability to lag the ball around the hole. This minimizes three-putting," he says. "I also practice from three to six feet, because if I miss a green, I'll probably face a putt of this length after my chip or pitch. To me the very long putts and the very short ones are the most important to practice."

Bruce Lietzke practices putting with an object such as a tee or another club placed a few inches behind the head of the putter at address. This abbreviates the backstroke, which promotes acceleration and crisp contact with the ball.

Gary Player recommends putting to a tee stuck into the practice green—rather than a hole—to develop confidence. After practicing to such a small target, the hole will look like a bushel basket, an image that has to inspire confidence.

Another confidence-building drill is suggested by Bobby Clampett, who surrounds the hole with six balls, each one foot from the hole. After holing all six, move the balls two feet away: after sinking them, continue moving out in one-foot increments. Seeing the balls fall in repeatedly builds confidence, and the pressure of having to make the last few putts of each cycle is good preparation for those testing short putts on the course.

Dave Stockton, who putted his way to two PGA Championships, practices the majority of his strokes from no more than 12 feet from the hole. He uses only two balls and constantly changes the putt he's hitting. "I'll hit a 12-footer with a right-to-left break, then a three-footer going the other way," Stockton explains. "I'm trying to groove a stroke based on feel, not repetition. Practicing this way is more like actual putting, where no two putts are ever the same."

Nicklaus, the greatest pressure putter ever, also says his practice routine helps develop feel rather than repetition. Once he achieves a consistent rhythm, striking the ball solidly and rolling it well, he stops, reasoning that any further practice would only deteriorate what he has already found.

Dave Stockton strokes most of his practice putts from within 12 feet of the hole, continuously varying their length and break.

GAMES FOR PAINLESS PRACTICE

If you think about it, the only important distinction between play and practice is a psychological one, specifically, a penalty/reward aspect. On the course, you reap the benefits of a good shot and suffer after a bad one. But on the practice tee, neither of those sensations is particularly strong. When nothing is at stake, sessions "on the rock pile" can be pretty boring. That's why every serious practicer should play games. By competing—either against yourself or others—you can put the pressure into practice and feel the penalty or reward after every swing. Here are 10 competitive games recommended by Tom Watson:

1) MATCH SHOTS WITH A FRIEND. One of the most enjoyable practice games is competing against another golfer, shot for shot. Try to find someone whose ability is about equal to yours, then pick targets on the practice range and set up your own contest. The loser pays for the range balls.

2) BE A TRICK-SHOT ARTIST. After working through the bag, try hitting the unconventional shots—hooks, slices, high and low shots. Practicing these shots helps develop a better feel for how the golf swing can be changed to produce different ball flights. Call the shot-shape before hitting each shot.

3) PLAY YOUR COURSE FROM THE PRACTICE TEE. Hit the same shots in the same succession that you would if you were actually playing holes 1 through 18. There's no better way to sharpen the shots you use most often.

4) CHIP TO A CIRCLE OF TEES. Create a competitive element in chipping practice by placing a circle of tees in a three-foot radius around the hole. See how many chips in a row you can put into the circle, then try to top your personal best.

5) CHIPPING CONTESTS. Probably the most common is to play a nine- or 18-hole match in which the chip that finishes closest to the hole wins. Compete either against a friend or against yourself with two balls.

6) "THIS ONE'S FOR THE OPEN." In putting practice, it is particularly important to create some kind of pressure. Tell yourself the next putt you are going to hit will win the U.S. Open. The more internal pressure you create in practice, the better you will handle real pressure on the course.

7) MAKE 30 IN A ROW. When practicing two- and three-foot putts, try to sink 30 in a row. You may be out there all night, but it's extremely good training for both your stroke and your nerves, especially when you get to the last five.

8) PLAY 18 HOLES WITH SIX CLUBS. If you want to learn what shotmaking is all about, take your 3-wood, 4-iron, 6-iron, 8-iron, pitching wedge, and putter and play an entire round.

9) HIT THE GREEN TWO WAYS. If you're alone and the course isn't busy, try hitting a couple of different shots from each position. On drives and long approaches, try hitting an intentional hook or slice; on shorter approaches, try to punch and cut the ball to the hole.

10) PLAY AN IMAGINARY MATCH. Once again, if the course isn't crowded or it's late in the day, play two balls for 18 holes and have an imaginary match. You'll get 36 holes of practice out of an 18-hole walk.

Practice producing various shots with the same club to improve shotmaking skills and to get a feel for the effect of different swings.

Left: *One way to improve confidence and nerves is by not leaving the practice green until you have holed 30 short putts in a row.*

Right: *Chipping to a circle of tees provides a constant target and creates a competitive element whether against a friend or your "personal best."*

pens on the course. Johnson suggests alternating clubs and targets. This keeps the mind sharp and is a more realistic rehearsal for actual play.

For a psychological boost on the course, spend part of each session hitting to a smaller-than-normal target. For example, putting to a coin or tee or trying to land drives within the width of a tree at the far end of the practice range will make the targets on the course look bigger, and easier to hit.

Better players should watch and try to replicate the trajectory of shots with each club. Ben Hogan found that if his shots had consistent trajectory from swing to swing, he was striking the ball properly. He believed that if he had control of trajectory, accuracy would follow.

Tour professionals continually check their body and clubface alignment to their target by asking their caddies for feedback or by building a practice station—one club on the ground parallel to the target line a few inches outside the ball, another club perpendicular to the target line slightly inside the left heel. This simple setup offers immediate awareness of ball position, clubface aim, and body alignment relative to the target.

5) *Isolate one desired outcome.* "Understanding the essentials of a correct swing is valuable, but one cannot expect to think consciously of them while actually playing a stroke," noted 1931 U.S. Amateur champion Helen Hicks. "If the player is to profit from such understanding, he or she can do so only by practicing one or two of them at a time."

Nicklaus has pointed out that

another of his keys to effective practice is to focus on one goal at a time. To avoid distraction and too many swing thoughts, think only about the one change being implemented. If a new problem crops up, make a mental note and return to it later, *after* corrections to the original problem have been made.

6) *Practice with a preshot routine.* On the course, a preshot routine helps focus the mind and relax the body only if it is done automatically during play. For this to happen, the routine must be learned and rehearsed during practice. Many golfers hit shot after shot on the range without thinking about a preshot routine. David Leadbetter contends that if a golfer is hitting more than 30 to 40 shots per hour on the practice tee, he most likely is not including a preshot routine.

Gary Player recommends placing practice balls two or three steps behind you so that you must step back after each shot. This becomes a strong reminder to reset for the next shot by initiating the routine from its beginning. A preshot routine also should be carried out before every practice putt.

7) *Use drills to ingrain swing changes.* Studies have shown that athletes learn fastest once they have felt a correct motion (kinesthetic learning), rather than being told how (verbal) or seeing a demonstration (visual). Verbal cues are inexact because of the game's inexact teaching vocabulary, and demonstrations don't necessarily translate into the correct motion.

A good drill done correctly will isolate and cure a specific problem by letting the golfer feel for himself the cor-

A tale of two extremes. Bruce Lietzke (above) is well known for an almost nonexistent practice schedule. He prefers to take summers off and coach his son's Little League team. Vicki Goetze (opposite) has been rolling hundreds of putts a day since she began winning junior tournaments as a five-year-old. The practice has paid off as Goetze, now on the LPGA Tour, is considered to have one of the finest short games on any Tour.

rect position or motion. After a suitable number of repetitions, the neuromuscular response will be reprogrammed to incorporate the drilled motion. While it would be impossible to include every one, a sampling of popular drills matched to the swing problems they help correct can be found in Chapter 5, Faults and Cures.

8) Sharpen competitiveness. Play in challenge matches, arrange games with another player, or set personal goals during solo practice such as chipping 10 balls in a row within five feet of the hole (see Tom Watson's "Games for Painless Practice" on page 312). Anything that makes practice resemble the pressure felt on the course will create more comfort and confidence during a real match. So play practice games with a friend, making the loser pay for the range balls or after-practice drinks.

On the range, set targets for each club. For example, with a 7-iron, try landing at least half of the shots within 10 yards of the 150-yard flag. The goal should be difficult to achieve, but attainable for the golfer's skills.

Gary Player used targets to become one of the best bunker players in history. Every day, he practiced until he holed five shots. No matter how long it took, he stayed until the fifth ball rolled in.

9) Keep a diary. Ben Hogan and Patty Berg were among the first professionals to keep a diary of their practice sessions. A log book helps you understand and remember what was learned in each session, and can help recapture forgotten keys or feelings that will put a swing back on track weeks, months, even years later. A video camera also can be used to record drills and swing thoughts and can include an instructor's comments and demonstrations.

10) *Measure each club's carry distance.* Few amateurs know the true distance they carry the ball with each club. But every professional does. Amateurs usually remember their best shot with a club and incorrectly believe every subsequent shot will fly that far. Use a practice session to hit a dozen shots with each club and pace off the distances; compute the average and use it as your on-course distance standard. Recheck these distances at least twice each season, more often if you're working on swing changes or playing new equipment.

11) *Improve shotmaking with on-course practice.* The logical bridge between the driving range and the scorecard is practice on the golf course. Only on the course can a player learn and ingrain the subtle alterations that must be made to the basic swing to handle the infinite permutations in lies, shot selection, and weather conditions. Instructor Jim McLean suggests going out on the course alone in the evening or whenever the course is uncrowded and hitting two or three balls on each hole. Emphasize hitting shots from as many different situations as possible, including fairway bunkers, thick rough, unusual pitches and chips, double-breaking putts, and any other shots that can't be learned on the range.

Improve shotmaking skills by hit-

DIFFERENT STROKES

PRACTICE INTO THE WIND

Practicing in windy conditions can be beneficial or harmful, depending upon the direction the wind is blowing. If you have a choice, it is more desirable to practice hitting into the wind or into a right-to-left wind. Hitting into the wind magnifies all errors, a definite benefit when practicing, as it demands maximum concentration and control. A right-to-left wind encourages an inside path on the downswing, a plus for most golfers.

Less desirable is downwind practice, which masks errors by straightening out poor shots. Least desirable is hitting across a left-to-right breeze, which blows the shot off-line to the right: Your body instinctively compensates by swinging outside the target line on the downswing and starting the ball left of the target, ingraining slice-producing habits.

ting three different clubs to the hole from the same spot; hit two drives on each hole—one fade and one draw; play the course hitting an iron off every tee. The variations are limitless, but all of them will help sharpen the skills needed to score better.

Another McLean favorite is to play a one-man scramble, hitting two or three balls and playing the best one. This gives a good idea of a golfer's potential. Or play a "worst ball" scramble to pinpoint weaknesses.

DIFFERENT STROKES

LEARN AND PRACTICE BEHAVIORALLY

Practice is critical to building confidence on the course. But scientists who study human behavior believe golf is taught—and practiced—backward, especially when it comes to beginners. Traditionally, a golfer's first experience with the game is being handed a 5-iron and a bucket of balls and told to make full swings. Little wonder that National Golf Foundation statistics show that for every two new golfers who attempt the game, one will leave owing to frustration and lack of improvement.

Evidence suggests that beginning golfers should learn and practice behaviorally: From the simplest skill to the hardest, starting with the one-foot putt and working back from the hole. By proceeding in this fashion, golfers achieve immediate success and the game becomes a series of logical steps.

Richard O'Brien and Tom Simek, psychologists who have worked with athletes in a variety of sports, measured groups of golfers who learned and practiced in the traditional manner (full swings first) versus groups who learned and practiced behaviorally (putting first). The behavioral group outperformed traditional learners by an average of 17 strokes in their first 18-hole round and reported playing with less tension and greater confidence. Two-thirds of the behavioral learners broke 100 for the first 18 holes they ever played.

The rules of practicing behaviorally are simple: Start at Step 1 and do not proceed to Step 2 until Step 1 is mastered. In D. Swing Meyer's *The Method*, a behavioral-learning study guide for golf, the mastery chain for putting contains 10 steps, from holing eight consecutive one-foot putts to rolling eight consecutive 30-foot putts within 24 inches of the hole. Only after successfully completing all 10 putting steps does the golfer move on to the seven chipping and pitching steps, then to the five approach shot steps, and finally to the driver.

12) Reinforce mechanics and feel away from the course. There are many ways to improve one's swing without going to the course or range: Chipping and pitching around the yard; hitting plastic balls; hitting into a net. Seve Ballesteros became one of the world's finest bunker players by hitting thousands of shots on the beach near his home.

Swing in front of a mirror to identify proper positions and their corresponding feelings. Swinging a weighted club strengthens the golf muscles and builds stamina. Putting on a carpet, gripping and regripping a club, or simply waggling a club indoors can improve your touch and set-up. The legendary teacher Ernest Jones recommended practicing hitting into a net instead of on a range because it is easier to focus on the swing's movements and feelings when you're not worrying about where the ball goes.

SIX MUST-HAVE PRACTICE AIDS

Since the 1920s, the U.S. Patent Office has been receiving design applications for items supposed to help golfers build a better swing. Today, hundreds of products are specifically manufactured as training aids, while dozens of household products can be used to monitor and improve a golfer's swing. Here are half a dozen of the most popular training aids that are inexpensive and readily available at any hardware store or golf shop.

Carpenter's chalk/waterbase paint. Carpenter's chalk is a favorite among good players for checking the path of a putting stroke. A six-foot chalk line is applied to a flat section of the green and putts rolled along the line. If the putter deviates from a straight-back-and-through motion, the line will make it obvious. Waterbase paint, like that used to mark hazards on the golf course, can be used to draw alignment or path lines. Hitting balls off a paint line drawn perpendicular to the target line also can identify where the club is contacting the ground in relation to the ball.

Club shafts. A shaft angled into the ground a few yards in front of the ball makes for a perfect intermediate target and helps identify the ball's starting direction. Shafts also can be placed vertically in the ground a couple of inches outside the legs at address to identify a sway. Shafts laid on the ground parallel and perpendicular to the target line check alignment and ball position.

Wood two-by-fours. Practice putting with a "trough" consisting of two two-by-fours side by side on the practice green. There should be enough room between them for the putter head plus five-eighths of an inch outside the heel and toe. Keeping the putterhead between the boards develops a stroke controlled by the arms and shoulders that never wavers from the target line and keeps the club low throughout the stroke. In full-swing practice, a two-by-four placed parallel to the target line an inch outside the ball can be very effective in curing the slicer's out-to-in swing path: Try to swing without hitting the board.

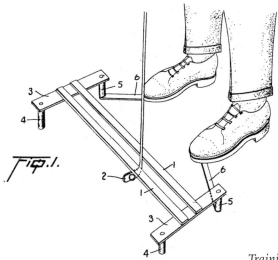

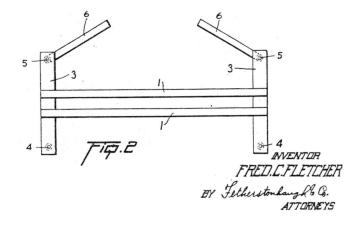

Training aids are certainly not a new phenomenon, as these patent drawings from the 1920s and 1930s attest.

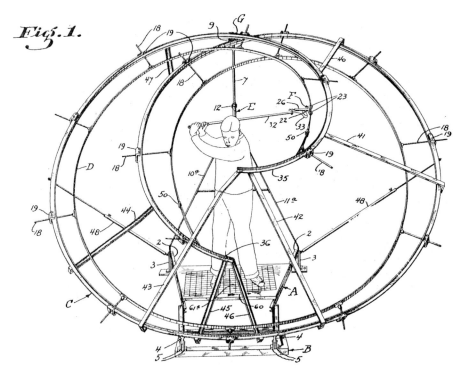

WORDS
OF WISDOM

The two things that motivate me most are closely allied. They are failure and a desire for self-improvement.

Jack Nicklaus

The more I practice, the luckier I get.
Gary Player

If I miss one day's practice I know it; if I miss two days' practice the spectators know it, and if I miss three days the world knows it.

Ben Hogan

Practice must be interesting, even absorbing, if it is to be of any use.
Bobby Jones

You can learn more about the game on the practice area than anywhere else, and the higher your goal, the more time you must spend there.

Arnold Palmer

There's really only one thing that can make you a better putter: Practice. Only after hitting thousands and thousands of putts will you begin to develop feel. And feel is what makes a good putter.

George Archer

If you are really committed to being as good as you can be at golf, then understand that there is no finish line.

Hank Johnson

Head covers. A head cover placed under each arm keeps the arms "connected" to the torso during the swing, which improves timing and helps create the proper sequence of motions. During the swing, don't let the head cover fall. Swinging to avoid a strategically placed head cover also can be effective in correcting a faulty clubhead path. Place it along the target line two inches outside the ball to correct an out-to-in swing path; two inches inside the ball is a good cure for a swing path that approaches impact from too far inside the target line; placed one foot behind the ball, it promotes a more descending blow with the irons.

Full-body mirror. A golfer's perception is often much different from reality. Practicing in front of a mirror provides instant feedback that allows the golfer to match the correct position to its corresponding feeling. Some courses have mirrors at the end of their practice tee for use by anyone hitting balls.

Weighted club. An old wooden driver with the head bored out and filled with something heavy will do the same job as commercial versions that weigh around 35 ounces. Swinging a weighted club 25 or more times each day will strengthen and stretch the golf muscles. Sam Snead swung a heavy club 100 times daily throughout his career.

WHAT IS A GOOD SHOT?

Practice can help you improve your weaknesses, but you need to know which parts of your game are better or worse than the norm. You can use research by Dave Pelz, *GOLF Magazine*'s Short Game and Technical Consultant, to see how your shots stack up against those of other golfers in your handicap group, or against Tour professionals. Pelz measured golfers from Jack Nicklaus to beginners to determine the level of efficiency with each club at various skill levels.

Pelz found that the average wood or iron shot hit by a Tour pro finishes within a 6 percent range of the target, while a good shot finishes within 4 percent. For example, a good 5-iron, hit 175 yards, finishes within 7 yards—short, long, left, or right—of the target (175 yards x 4% = 7 yards).

Amateurs have much greater differences in proficiency, depending upon the club being hit. For example, 10–15 handicappers hit their average short-iron shots with a 9 percent margin of error; medium irons, 10 percent; long irons, 11 percent; fairway woods, 10 percent; and the driver, 12 percent.

To find your game's strengths and weaknesses, pace off the distances your shots finish from the target and compare the results to the accompanying chart. Become a stronger player by practicing the clubs that are producing the weakest results.

GAUGING YOUR GAME

CLUB	TOUR PLAYER *	**	***	0–9 HANDICAP			10–15 HANDICAP			16–25 HANDICAP			26-PLUS HANDICAP		
PW	120	7	5	110	7	6	100	9	6	90	14	8	80	20	12
9-Iron	130	8	5	120	7	6	110	10	7	100	15	9	90	23	14
8-Iron	140	8	6	130	8	7	120	11	7	110	17	10	100	25	15
7-Iron	150	9	6	140	10	8	130	13	9	120	19	12	110	30	18
6-Iron	160	10	6	150	11	8	140	14	10	130	21	13	120	33	19
5-Iron	175	11	7	160	11	9	150	15	11	140	22	14	130	36	21
4-Iron	185	11	7	170	13	10	160	18	12	150	27	17	140	49	25
3-Iron	195	12	8	180	14	11	170	19	13	160	29	18	150	53	27
2-Iron	210	13	8	190	14	11	180	20	14	170	31	19	160	56	29
4-Wood	220	13	9	210	15	13	195	20	14	180	29	18	170	47	27
3-Wood	235	14	9	225	21	15	210	21	15	195	31	20	180	50	29
Driver	255	15	10	240	19	16	220	27	18	210	38	25	190	71	34

* Average distance player is expected to hit club

** Distance average of all attempts finishes from target, in yards

*** Distance good shot finishes from target, in yards

APPENDICES

GLOSSARY

TIMELINE

THE 100 BEST GOLF TEACHERS

BIBLIOGRAPHY

INDEX

GLOSSARY

Note: Words that appear in *italic type* also have independent entries.

A

Ace: *n.* A shot played from the tee ending up in the hole. Also called a hole-in-one. *v.* To play such a shot.

Acceleration: *n.* The increasing change in velocity of the hands, arms, and clubhead, from the beginning of the down-swing through impact.

Address: *n.* The position taken by a player in preparation for playing a shot. *v.* To take a stance over the ball and ground one's club.

Advice: *n.* Counsel given to a player relating to the game of golf, which could affect how a shot is played or what club is used.

Aggregate: *adj.* Describing a stroke or score made over two or more rounds of golf, or by two players playing as partners. An aggregate score.

Aim line: See *target line.*

Air shot: *n.* A stroke that misses the ball entirely. Also called an "air ball" or *whiff.*

Albatross: *n.* A score of three strokes under par on a hole. Also called a *double eagle.*

Alignment: *n.* The arrangement of the shoulders, hips, feet, and clubface in relation to the target line. Used to aim shots in a particular direction.

All square: *adj.* Even or tied in *match play.*

Alternate-shot: *n.* A variation of the game in which two part-ners take turns playing strokes until the ball is in the hole. This format is used in international team competitions such as the Ryder, Walker, and Solheim Cups, as well as in many smaller tournaments.

Angle of approach (or attack): *n.* The angle at which the club-head approaches the ball.

Approach: *n.* A shot played to the putting green, usually rela-tively short in length. *v.* To aim or play a shot onto the putting green.

Apron: *n.* The narrow area of grass surrounding a putting green, cut shorter than the fairway but not as short as the green. Also called the *fringe.*

Arc: *n.* The route of the clubhead during the swing.

Architecture: *n.* The theory and practice of golf course design; the nature and design characteristics of a particular course or architect.

Attack: *v.* To play a hole or course aggressively.

Attend: *v.* To hold and remove the flagstick as a partner or opponent putts from a long distance. Also "tend."

Automatics: *n.* An extra *Nassau* bet that goes into effect when-ever a player is a set number of holes or points behind an opponent.

Away: *adj.* Describing a ball lying farthest from the hole, and therefore the one to be played next.

Axis: *n.* An imaginary straight line through the center of the body, around which it should rotate during the swing.

B

Back nine: *n.* The final nine holes of an eighteen-hole golf course. Also referred to as the back side.

Backspin: *n.* The reverse spin imparted to the ball at impact by the grooves of the club, causing it to fly on a relatively upward trajectory, stop quickly upon landing, and sometimes roll backward.

Backswing: *n.* The initial part of the swing, when the club, hands, arms, and body move away from the ball and rotate back over the head.

Back tees: *n.* The teeing ground located the farthest distance from the hole, usually used by better players. Also called *tiger tees* and "championship tees."

Baffing spoon: *n.* A wooden club, no longer in production, that was the shortest, most lofted of the set; considered equal to the modern wedge.

Baffy: *n.* A small-headed, steeply lofted wooden club no longer in production; equivalent to the modern 4- or 5-wood.

Bail out: *v.* To deliberately play away from a hazard or other trou-ble. *n.* and *adj.* Referring to, or the shot played away, from trouble.

Balance: *n.* Address position at which equilibrium is obtained; can also apply to a well-positioned follow-through.

Ball at rest: *n.* A situation in which the ball is not moving and is not being influenced by the actions of a player.

Ball deemed to move: *n.* A ball that has left its position and comes to rest in another place.

Ball flight laws: *n.* The physical relationships between clubhead path and angle that influence the golf ball's flight, identical for every golfer and for every swing.

Ball in play: *n.* A ball that has been struck by a player and stays within the bounds of the golf course. It stays in play until holed or replaced in accordance with the Rules.

Banana ball: *n.* A shot that curves enormously from left to right for a right-hander (see *slice*).

Bank shot: *n.* A shot played from close to the green with a steep bank in front of the player, so the ball hits the face of the bank and pops up into the air, landing softly on the green.

Barranca: *n.* A typically rocky or heavily wooded deep ravine, sometimes played as a hazard.

Baseball grip: *n.* A grip characterized by having all ten fingers on the club; also called the "ten-finger grip."

Beach: *n.* Common name for any sand hazard. *v.* To land a ball in a sand hazard.

Behavioral practice: *n.* The process of learning the game in a series of steps, from the simplest skill to the hardest.

Behind the ball: *n.* The body position at address and during the swing in which the head and torso are to the right of an imaginary line drawn vertically from the ball.

Bend: *v.* To cause a shot to curve using sidespin imparted at impact.

Bentgrass: *n.* A durable, resilient grass with very fine blades able to withstand harsh temperatures; used on northern golf courses.

Bermuda grass: *n.* A coarse grass that can withstand oppressive heat; used on southern golf courses.

Best-ball (better-ball): *n.* A match in which the lowest single score of a foursome on each hole counts as the score for the entire team on that hole. Called "better-ball" when referring to a team of two players.

Birdie: *n.* A score of one under par on a hole.

Bird's nest: *n.* A lie in which the ball is deeply cupped in grass.

Bisque: *n.* In match play, a handicap stroke that may be taken at any hole chosen by the player who is receiving it.

Bite: *n.* The *backspin* applied to a ball at impact that causes it to stop dead on the green or spin back toward the player. *v.* To land the ball on the green with backspin.

Blade: *n.* The hitting part of an iron clubhead, not including the *hosel*. Also, a type of putter having an iron head similar in shape to standard numbered irons. *v.* To hit the ball across its equator with the bottom edge of an iron club, resulting in a low shot that tends to fly too far. Also called a *thin* or *skull* shot.

Blast: *v.* To play a forceful shot from a sand bunker, hitting behind the ball and displacing a large amount of sand; to play an *explosion shot.*

Blind: *adj.* Hidden from the player by a large hill, tree, or other obstruction. A blind shot is one in which the player cannot see the target.

Block: *v.* To prevent or delay rotation of the arms, body, wrists, or club during the swing, resulting in a shot that starts and remains to the right of the target.

Bluegrass: *n.* A cool-weather grass with moderate-size blades that can thrive in a variety of climates. Most commonly found in Kentucky.

Body coil: *n.* The full turn away from the ball made by the hips and shoulders; the source of power in the golf swing.

Bogey: *n.* A score of one over par on a hole.

Bold: *adj.* Refers to a shot played too strongly and going past the intended target. Also, a bravely played shot, such as an approach to a well-guarded pin position.

Boring: *adj.* Refers to a low shot that holds its course through a wind.

Borrow: *n.* The amount of compensation taken on a green required to putt across a slope. *v.* In putting, to aim to one side or the other of the direct line to the hole in order to account for the slope of the green.

Bounce: *n.* The rounded flange attached to the sole of the sand wedge designed to prevent the club from digging into the sand, thus allowing the ball to be lofted toward the target.

Brassie: *n.* A wooden club with a brass sole plate and a bit more loft than a driver. Considered equal to the modern 2-wood.

Break: *v.* The cocking of one's wrists during the backswing. *n.* The curved line on which a ball travels because of the slope or grain of the green (see *borrow*).

Broad focus: *n.* The ability to gather information on the big picture, such as wind, lie, slope, hazards, and any other information that may affect the shot.

Bump-and-run: *n.* A shot around the green intended to hit into a bank or slope and then roll forward toward the hole.

Bunker: *n.* A sandpit, often edged with embankments, defined as a hazard and forming an obstacle to both drives and approach shots.

Bunt: *v.* To hit an intentional short shot.

Buried lie: *n.* When part or all of a ball lies below the surface of soft turf or sand.

Burn: *n.* A Scottish term for a creek or stream.

Buzzard: *n.* A score of two strokes over par on a hole, also known as a *double bogey.*

C

Caddie: *n.* A person who carries a golfer's clubs during a round, giving advice and otherwise assisting the player. *v.* To work as a caddie.

Calamity Jane: *n.* The name Bobby Jones gave to his favorite wooden-shafted putter.

Cap: *n.* The top end of a club's grip and shaft.

Carry: *n.* The distance the ball travels in the air. *v.* To play over a hazard or other obstacle.

Cast: *v.* To release the cocked wrists prematurely on the forward swing, causing the clubhead to arrive at the ball ahead of the hands and arms. Same as "hitting from the top."

Casual water: *n.* Any temporary accumulation of water on a course that is not part of a defined water hazard. A player may lift his ball from casual water without penalty.

Center of gravity: *n.* The point in the body, somewhere in the pelvic area, where the torso, legs, and hips all balance.

Center of rotation: *n.* The axis around which the body winds and unwinds, usually thought of as the spine.

Center-shafted: *adj.* A type of putter in which the shaft joins the head some distance in from the heel. A common example is the Bull's Eye putter.

Centrifugal force: *n.* The action in a rotating body that moves mass away from the center; it is felt in the downswing as the clubhead is pulled outward and downward in a circular path.

Centripetal force: *n.* The force that moves mass toward the center of a rotating body.

Charge: *v.* To roll a putt toward the hole with a bold and powerful stroke.

Chicken wing: *n.* A fault in the downward swing in which the left arm folds or collapses at the elbow and points away from the body.

Chili dip: *n.* A mishit of this type. *v.* To mishit a chip shot by hitting the ground before the ball, resulting in a weak, lofted shot that travels only a short distance.

Chip: *n.* A short, low-trajectory approach shot, usually hit near the green, that rolls farther than it flies. Also called a chip shot. *v.* To play a chip shot onto the green.

Chip-in: *n.* A chip shot that goes into the hole. *v.* To hole out a chip shot.

Chip-and-run: *n.* A chip shot that rolls a great deal upon hitting the ground.

Chipper: *n.* A club designed only for chip shots.

Choke: *v.* To collapse under a great deal of pressure, so the muscles are incapable of performing to their greatest ability.

Choke down: *v.* To shorten the effective length of a club by gripping down the shaft.

Chop: *v.* To hit down on a ball with an axe-like motion to impart extra spin.

Chunk: *v.* Similar to a *chili dip*, the process of taking a large piece of turf before hitting the ball, resulting in a mishit that does not travel very far. *n.* A mishit of this type.

Clearing the left side: *v.* Turning the hips to the left of the target during the downswing so the arms may follow in sequence.

Cleek: *n.* **1.** The name given to a wooden (or metal) club with narrow rails on the bottom of the clubhead, used to hit out of the rough. It generally has the loft of a 4- or 5-wood. 2. Old name for a 4-iron.

Closed clubface: *n.* When the toe of the club leads the heel, causing the clubface to point to the left of the target line. This can occur at any point during the swing.

Closed stance: *n.* The positioning of the feet whereby the back foot is farther from the target line than the front.

Closed-to-open: *adj.* Describing the clubhead when the player closes the clubface during the backswing, then opens it during the downswing.

Clubface: *n.* The grooved surface of the club that makes contact with the ball.

Clubface alignment: *n.* The direction in which the clubhead is aimed at address relative to the target line.

Clubhead: *n.* The hitting portion of the club, attached to the end of the shaft, which also contains most of the weight of the club.

Clubhead angle: *n.* The direction in which the clubface points at impact; it influences the direction the ball will curve during flight.

Clubhead path: *n.* The path traveled by the clubhead during the swing, relative to the target line.

Clubhead speed: *n.* The force with which the club swings through the ball, measured in miles per hour.

Club length: *n.* The length of the club from grip to head.

Club shaft: *n.* The long, thin part of the club connecting the grip and the clubhead. Also *shaft*.

Cocked wrists: *n.* The position in which the wrists are flexed, or hinged, during the backswing.

Coil: *n.* The circular windup of the body during the backswing, creating a source of power in the swing.

Collar: *n.* See *apron*.

Comeback putt: *n.* The follow-up putt after the previous putt has rolled past the hole.

Come off the ball: *v.* To lift the body prematurely during the swing.

Come over the top: *v.* To steepen the plane or arc of the swing during the downswing and throw the clubhead outside the target line prior to impact.

Compression: *n.* The degree of resilience a golf ball has when struck by a clubface.

Concede: *v.* In match play, to grant one's opponent a putt, hole, or match that has not been completed.

Connection: *n.* Maintaining the various body parts in the appropriate relationship to one another during the swing.

Controlled shot: *n.* A stroke made with less than full power.

Course rating: *n.* The measure of the difficulty of a course relative to other courses, evaluated by the United States Golf Association. It is expressed in strokes and fractions of strokes, and based upon the ability of a *scratch golfer*.

Crack: *adj.* Referring to a first-class or champion-caliber player. *v.* 1. To suffer a sudden collapse of good play, as in *choke*. 2. To hit a good drive.

Croquet-style: *adj.* A putting stance in which the player straddles the target line and faces the hole, swinging the putter like a croquet mallet.

Cross bunker: *n.* A generally elongated bunker that runs across the fairway at a right angle to the player's line of flight.

Cross-handed: *adj.* A putting grip in which a right-handed golfer places the left hand on the putter below the right. Also referred to as "left hand low."

Crossing the line: *v.* Manipulating the clubhead so it comes from outside the target line to the inside during the downswing, resulting in a shot that flies left to right.

Crosswind: *n.* Breeze blowing from one side to the other across a golf hole, perpendicular to a player's line of flight.

Cup: *n.* The hole.

Cuppy lie: *n.* When the ball rests in a cuplike depression, frequently on bare ground between two tufts of grass.

Cut: *n.* A score that eliminates a percentage of the field from a tournament. *v.* To make the ball move from left to right (for right-handed golfers).

Cut shot: *n.* A high, soft shot that moves from left to right and does not have much roll upon hitting the ground.

Cutspin: *n.* The clockwise rotation of the ball (for right-handed golfers) that causes it to fly in left to right.

D

Dance floor: *n.* The putting green. See *Green*.

Dead: *adj.* 1. Describes a ball that lands so close to the hole there is no doubt it will be holed with the next stroke. 2. Describes a shot that hits the green and stops immediately, with no roll. 3. Describes a position from which it is impossible to escape.

Dead wrists: *n.* When the wrists remain firm, without cocking or releasing through the swing.

Deceleration: *n.* Slowing the speed of the clubhead through the ball, usually resulting in a weak mishit.

Delayed hit: *n.* Retaining the wrist cock until the last possible moment in the downswing, just before impact. Also "late hit."

Divot: *n.* A piece of turf displaced by the clubhead during the swing.

Dogleg: *n.* A hole or fairway characterized by a sharp turn in either direction, as in a dogleg-left or dogleg-right hole.

Dormie: *adj.* In match play, a situation where a player or team is as many holes ahead as there are left to play. The opposing player or team must win every hole to tie the match.

Double bogey: *n.* A score of two over par on a hole.

Double eagle: *n.* A score of three under par on a hole. Also called an *albatross*.

Downhiller: *n.* A downhill shot or putt.

Downhill lie: *n.* When a player's back foot is higher than his front foot at address, causing him to make compensations to hit a good shot.

Downswing: *n.* The movement of taking the club from the top of the swing down to the point of impact with the ball.

Drag: *v.* An aerodynamic force that resists the forward movement of an object, affecting clubhead speed and ball flight.

Drain: *v.* To sink a putt.

Draw: *n.* A controlled shot that flies slightly right to left for a right-handed player. *v.* To deliberately play such a shot.

Drawspin: *n.* The counterclockwise rotation of the ball, which causes it to fly right to left for a right-hander.

Drills: *n.* Exercises and movements designed to ingrain swing changes in a golfer's body and mind.

Drive: *n.* The first shot on a hole, played from the tee. *v.* 1. To hit the opening shot. 2. To hit the ball with maximum power.

Driver: *n.* The No. 1 wood, usually the longest, longest hitting, and, except for the putter, least lofted club in the bag.

Driving iron: *n.* Old name for a 1-iron, the iron club with the least amount of loft, designed for maximum distance.

Driving range: *n.* An area for hitting practice shots.

Drive the green: *v.* To reach the green in a single stroke on a par-four or par-five hole.

Drop: *v.* To put a ball back in play after it has been lost or retrieved from an unplayable lie. *n.* An instance of a ball being dropped.

Dub: *n.* 1. A poorly played shot, usually one that dribbles along the ground. 2. A player who hits a high number of such shots. *v.* To hit such a shot.

Duck hook: *n.* A violent hook (right-to-left) shot that normally travels low and hits the ground quickly.

Duff: *v.* To mishit a shot by hitting the ground before the ball.

Duffer: *n.* A bad golfer.

E

Eagle: *n.* A score of two under par on a hole.

Early hit: *n.* Premature release of the wrists on the downswing, causing deceleration at impact.

Effective loft: *n.* The actual loft of the clubface when it strikes the ball. Owing to the design of the clubhead and the player's technique, this may be different from the built-in loft of the club.

Embedded ball: *n.* When a portion of the ball is below the surface of the ground.

Explode: *v.* To escape from a sand bunker with a shot that displaces a large amount of sand along with the ball. Also called a *blast*.

Explosion shot: *n.* A shot in which the ball is exploded from the sand.

Extension: *n.* The straightened position of the left arm at impact and the right arm in the follow-through. May also apply to arm position at the top of the swing.

F

Face: *n.* 1. The grooved hitting surface of the clubhead. Also called the *clubface*. 2. The front wall of a sand bunker.

Fade: *n.* A controlled shot that flies left to right for a right-handed golfer. *v.* To deliberately play such a shot.

Fadespin: *n.* The rotation of the ball that causes it to fly left to right.

Fairway: *n.* The closely cropped grass that lies between the tee and the green and between the rough.

Fairway wood: *n.* Any of the wooden- or metal-headed clubs that have more loft than the driver.

Fan: *v.* To make a stroke that misses the ball completely. Also called a *whiff*.

Fanning the face: *v.* An exaggerated rolling of the clubface into an open position during the takeaway.

Fat: *adj.* 1. Describing a shot in which the clubhead strikes the ground before the ball, taking a large divot, so the ball does not travel as far as intended. 2. Referring to the widest, safest, and easiest-to-hit part of the green.

Feather: *v.* To hit a high, soft-landing shot that usually fades a little and stops quickly upon landing.

Fescue: *n.* A cool-weather grass commonly found near salt water; it is standard on *links* courses.

First cut: *n.* The strip of rough closest to the fairway.

Flagstick: *n.* A tall, narrow stick placed in the hole, indicating its location on the green.

Flange: *n.* The additional surface area protruding from the bottom of a clubhead that prevents it from digging too deeply into the sand or ground.

Flash trap: *n.* A small, shallow sand bunker.

Flat swing: *n.* A swing that moves the club on a more horizontal plane, more around the body.

Flex: *n.* The amount of flexibility or bend in a shaft.

Flyer: *n.* A shot, usually struck from long grass, that flies much farther than normal owing to a lack of spin.

Flyer lie: *n.* Any lie where the grass is certain to get between the club and the ball at impact, and tending to produce a flyer.

Flight: *n.* 1. A division of players in a tournament based on their ability. 2. The ball's path in the air.

Flip wedge: *n.* A short, less-than-full wedge shot with a high trajectory meant to stop quickly on the green. Also called a *flop shot*.

Floater: *n.* 1. A shot struck from deep grass that comes out slowly and travels shorter than normal. Opposite of a *flyer*. 2. A variety of golf ball, rarely used, that floats in water.

Flop shot: *n.* A soft, high shot usually played to the green with an outside-to-in swing path. Useful when pitching over a bunker or other hazard. See *flip wedge*.

Flub: *v.* To mishit a shot badly. *n.* A poor shot, usually caused by hitting the ground before the ball.

Fluffy lie: *n.* A lie in which the ball is sitting up on light blades of grass with room for the club to get under the ball.

Fly: *v.* To hit the ball too far.

Follow-through: *n.* The continuation of the swing after the ball has been struck.

Forecaddie: *n.* A person employed to go ahead of a group of players and mark the positions of any balls in play.

Forward press: *n.* A movement of the hands and arms toward the target that can assist the player in starting the backswing smoothly.

Forward swing: *n.* The motion of the arms, hands, and club toward the target and through the ball after the backswing is completed. Also *downswing.*

Four-ball: *n.* A match in which two partners match their better score on a hole against the better score of another team.

Foursome: *n.* 1. A match in which two partners alternately hit the same ball *(alternate shot),* playing against another team doing the same. 2. A group of four players playing together.

Free drop: *n.* A *drop* without penalty.

Fried egg: *n.* A lie in which the ball is partially buried in the sand, sitting in its own hole. Also *plugged lie.*

Fringe: *n.* The short grass just off the putting green. Also *apron.*

Frog hair: *n.* Same as *apron or fringe.*

Front nine: *n.* The first nine holes of an 18-hole golf course. Also the "front side."

Full swing: *n.* The longest swing you can make.

G

Gap wedge: *n.* A wedge with loft somewhere between that of a pitching wedge and sand wedge.

Gimme: *n.* A very short putt, often conceded by an opponent in match play.

G.I.R.: *n. Greens in regulation.*

Gorse: *n.* A thick, prickly shrub usually found on *links* courses (especially in Great Britain) and apt to swallow errant golf shots.

Go to school: *v.* To learn about the speed and break of a putt by observing someone else's putt.

Grain: *n.* The direction in which the blades of grass on a putting green grow, which can affect the speed and direction of putts.

Green: *n.* 1. The area of closely cropped grass where the hole is situated; the putting surface. Also *putting green* 2. The entire golf course.

Greenie: *n.* Bet won by the player whose tee shot on a par-three hole finishes closest to the pin.

Greens in regulation: *n.* A statistic, expressed as a percentage, that measures how often a player hits his approach shot onto the green in two strokes less than whatever is par for the hole.

Greenkeeper: *n.* The employee responsible for the maintenance of the course. Also called "golf course superintendent."

Grip: *n.* 1. The part of the shaft, covered with leather or other tacky material, that the player holds while swinging. 2. A player's way of holding the club. *v.* To hold a club in a specified manner.

Groove: *n.* 1. A narrow scoring line cut into the clubface that imparts spin on the ball. 2. A consistent succession of good swings. *v.* To practice a swing and develop consistency.

Gross: *adj.* Describing a score made before the deduction of handicap strokes.

Ground: *v.* To touch the clubhead to the ground behind the ball at address.

Ground under repair: *n.* An area of a course undergoing maintenance work and designated as such, from which a player may receive a *free drop.*

H

Hack: *v.* 1. To hit the ball violently and imperfectly, especially from heavy rough or a bad lie. 2. To play poor golf.

Hacker: *n.* An unskilled golfer, also *duffer.*

Half: *n.* In match play, a tie score on a hole.

Half-shot: *n.* A shot made with approximately 50 percent of a full swing and meant to fly about half the normal distance.

Halve: *v.* In match play, to play a hole in the same number of net strokes as an opponent.

Ham-and-egg: *v.* To play well with a partner, so both golfers contribute to the team's success.

Handicap: *n.* The number of strokes a player is able to deduct from his gross score. It is based on past performance and the difficulty of the course, designed to adjust his scoring ability to that of a scratch golfer. *v.* To assign a handicap to a player.

Handicap differential: *n.* The difference between a player's gross score and the course rating.

Handicap index: *n.* The measure of one's golf ability, it is the number that determines a player's handicap on a given course.

Hanging lie: *n.* When the ball rests on a downhill slope.

Hardpan: *n.* Very firm turf, often without grass.

Hazard: *n.* A sand bunker or any defined water obstacle on a course from which a *free drop* is not allowed.

Head: *n.* See *clubhead.*

Headwind: *n.* A breeze blowing into a player's face, causing the ball to travel a shorter distance than normal.

Heel: *n.* The end of the clubhead nearest to the player at address, usually where the shaft enters. *v.* To hit the ball with this end of the club.

High side: *n.* That area of the green above the hole, especially when the cup is on a slope. Also called the *pro side.*

Hit: *v.* To play a stroke or shot.

Hitting area: *n.* Part of the swing from where the club is parallel to the ground on the downswing to just after impact.

Hog's back: *n.* A large ridge running across a green or fairway.

Hole: *n.* **1.** The round receptacle in the putting green, 4.25 inches in diameter and up to 4 inches in depth. Also called the *cup.* **2.** The nine or 18 distinct units on a course, each extending from a tee to corresponding green. *v.* To get the ball in the hole, also to "hole out."

Hole-high: *adj.* Referring to a shot that finishes even with the hole.

Hole-in-one: *n.* A tee shot that finishes in the hole; a hole played in one stroke. Also *ace.*

Homeward nine: *n.* The back nine of a golf course.

Honor: *n.* The privilege of hitting first off the tee, awarded to the player who had the lowest score on the previous hole.

Hood: *v.* To tilt the clubface forward by leaning the grip toward the target, reducing the club's *effective loft.*

Hook: *n.* A shot that moves from left to right for a right-handed player. *v.* To hit a shot of this nature.

Hookspin: *n.* The counterclockwise rotation of the ball that causes a hook.

Horizontal: *adj.* and *n.* The desired position at the top of the swing, with the clubshaft parallel to the ground. Also *parallel.*

Horizontal axis: *n.* An imaginary line, parallel to the ground, running through the center of the ball. Hitting below this line will lift the ball into the air; striking above it will cause a *topped* shot. Also called the "ball's equator."

Hosel: *n.* The hollow part of the clubhead extending up from the heel where the shaft attaches.

Hustler: *n.* A golfer who purposefully maintains (or claims to maintain) a handicap higher than his true skill level so he can easily defeat other golfers. Also *sandbagger.*

I

Impact: *n.* The moment the club strikes the ball.

Impediment: *n.* Loose debris that may be moved from around a ball as long as it is not in a hazard. Also *loose impediments.*

Improve your lie: *v.* To move the ball illegally or affect the area around it so the next shot is easier.

Inside: *adj.* Nearer to the hole than another player's ball.

Inside-to-in: *adj.* Describes a swing path in which the clubhead approaches the ball from inside the *target line*, makes contact, then returns inside the *target line* on the follow-through.

Inside-to-out: *adj.* Describes a swing path in which the clubhead approaches the ball from inside the *target line*, makes contact, then swings outside the line.

Intended line of flight: *n.* An imaginary line drawn through the ball and extending to the intended target. Also called the *target line.*

Interlocking grip: *n.* For a right-handed player, a way of placing the hands on the club with the right pinky meshing with the index finger of the left hand.

In-the-leather: *adj.* Describing a putt that is closer to the hole than the length of the putter's grip or the distance from the putterhead to the bottom of the grip.

Intermediate target: *n.* A leaf, divot, or other object or mark just in front of the ball and directly between it and the target, used as an alignment aid.

Iron: *n.* Any of numerous clubs with an iron clubhead and available in a variety of lofts.

J

Jail: *n.* A spot from which it is almost impossible to play a safe shot.

K

Kick: *n.* An unpredictable bounce taken by the ball after it lands.

Kikuyu: *n.* A fast-growing grass, common in California and other mild climates, with thick, wiry blades that can wrap around the clubhead, causing errant shots.

Kinesiology: *n.* The scientific study of human movement and the motions of tools and equipment used in sporting activities.

Kinetic energy: *n.* The energy associated with the speed of an object. Increasing clubhead velocity produces more kinetic energy and thus more distance.

Knee-knocker: *n.* A short putt, in the two- to four-foot range, that causes a golfer mental and physical anxiety.

Knockdown: *n.* A deliberately low, boring shot that holds its line into the wind. Sometimes used to escape from or avoid a tree or other trouble. Also a *punch.*

L

Lag: *n.* A long putt hit with the intention of stopping the ball close to the hole and leaving an easy second putt.

Lateral hazard: *n.* A water hazard running approximately parallel to the line of play and defined by red stakes.

Lateral shift: *n.* The movement during the forward swing in which the body's weight is transferred from the back foot to the front.

Launch angle: *n.* The angle at which the ball comes off the clubface immediately after impact.

Lay off: *v.* To point the club to the left of the target at the top of the swing.

Layout: *n.* A golf course, especially when considered in terms of architectural style and routing of the holes.

Lay up: *v.* To deliberately hit a shot short of a green or hazard to avoid trouble and leave a manageable approach shot. *n.* A shot of this nature.

Leak: *v.* To fade undesirably to the right, for a right-handed player, as a shot does while flying toward the target.

Leg drive: *v.* The movement of the legs toward the target during the downswing.

Lie: *n.* 1. The position of the ball on the ground after it has come to rest. 2. The angle at which the clubhead is attached to the shaft, measured between the shaft and the ground when the club is soled. *v.* 1. To be at rest in a certain position or situation on the course. 2. To have played a specified number of strokes.

Lift, clean, and place: *v.* To pick up the ball when playing in extremely wet conditions, clean the mud off, and replace it without penalty. *n.* The Rule that goes into effect when the ball can easily become embedded in the course of normal play.

Line: *n.* The intended or correct path of a shot or putt.

Line of flight: *n.* The direction in which the shot actually travels.

Line up: *v.* To study the line of a shot; to take aim.

Links: *n.* A seaside course laid out along a body of water, usually the ocean. Often used to refer to any golf course.

Linksland: *n.* The seaside terrain typical of British courses.

Lip: *n.* The edge or rim of the cup.

Lip out: *v.* To hit a putt that circles the edge of the cup but does not fall in.

Lob: *v.* To deliberately play a high, soft-landing pitch shot, usually over a sand bunker or other hazard. *n.* A high, soft-landing shot.

Local knowledge: *n.* The tricks of playing a course that regular patrons know.

Local rules: *n.* A set of rules, particular to a certain course or tournament, established to handle situations unique to that venue.

Loft: *n.* The measurement of the degree to which a clubface is set back from vertical. *v.* To play a high-trajectory shot.

Long game: *n.* Those parts of the game in which distance is required—driving, fairway woods, and long irons—and usually demanding a full swing.

Long irons: *n.* Iron clubs without much loft, used when distance is required; the 1-, 2-, 3-, and 4-irons.

Loop: *n.* 1. A round of golf. 2. A swing quirk in which the player takes the clubhead back on one line, then reroutes it with a circular motion near the top. *v.* To carry a player's bag; to *caddie*.

Loose impediments: *n.* Objects that are not fixed or growing on the course, and thus may be moved from near a ball without penalty (except when in a hazard). Also *impediments*.

Low finish: *n.* A follow-through that stops, deliberately or otherwise, shorter than normal, as for a *punch*.

Low side: *n.* Part of the green below the hole, especially when the hole is cut on a slope. Opposite of *high side*.

M

Mallet putter: *n.* A putter with a semicircular head.

Marker: *n.* 1. An object on the tee that indicates the forward boundary of the teeing ground. Also called a "tee marker." 2. A coin or small object placed behind a ball to indicate its location on the green. Also "ball marker." 3. In stroke play, someone appointed to keep another player's score, particularly in an odd-numbered field when the player would be teeing off alone.

Mashie: *n.* An iron club, no longer in use, used for medium-length shots to the green. Considered equal to a 5-iron.

Mashie-iron: *n.* An iron club, no longer in use, used for driving and full shots to the green. Considered equal to a 3- or 4-iron.

Mashie-niblick: *n.* An iron club, no longer in use, having a loft between that of a mashie and a niblick. Considered equal to a 7-iron.

Match of cards: *n.* A way to break ties in which scorecards are compared, with the lower score on a particular hole winning the match.

Match play: *n.* The original form of golf competition, where the winner is the player or team that wins the most individual holes. The match does not necessarily extend to 18 holes, e.g., if a player is four holes up with three to play, he wins the match, 4 & 3.

Mechanics: *n.* The techniques a player uses during a golf swing.

Medal: *n.* A prize awarded to the player who scores the lowest in a stroke-play tournament. *v.* To score the lowest in a stroke-play qualifying tournament.

Medalist: *n.* The person who scores the lowest in a stroke-play qualifying tournament for a match-play championship.

Medal play: *n.* Competition in which the winner is the player who scores the lowest number of strokes over a designated number of rounds. Also *stroke play.*

Middle irons: *n.* The iron clubs used for intermediate distances, generally the 5-, 6-, and 7-irons. Also called "mid-irons."

Mid-iron: *n.* Old term for a 2-iron.

Mid-mashie: *n.* Old term for a 3-iron.

Misclub: *v.* To play the wrong club for a certain situation or shot.

Mishit: *v.* To hit a shot poorly; to make bad contact with the ball.

Misread: *v.* To read a green incorrectly and play the putt on the wrong line.

Muff: *v.* To mishit a shot badly.

Mulligan: *n.* A second attempt at the same shot, usually off the first tee. Sometimes permitted in a casual round but never in competition.

N

Narrow focus: *n.* Mentally honing in as tightly as possible on the target while blocking out unnecessary thoughts and distractions.

Nassau: *n.* A three-part bet in which a point or wager is awarded for winning the front nine, the back nine, and the overall 18.

Net: *adj.* A player's gross score minus any handicap strokes.

Neutral grip: *n.* A way of gripping the club so the hands will return to the same position at impact, usually parallel to the clubface.

Niblick: *n.* A very lofted iron club, no longer in use. Considered equal to a 9-iron.

O

Obstruction: *n.* Anything artificial, whether erected, placed, or left on the course, except for markers defining course boundaries and cart paths.

Offset: *adj.* Describing a club with a bent neck or hosel so the clubhead is set slightly behind the line of the shaft, designed to give the player an extra split-second to square the clubface at impact.

One-piece takeaway: *n.* The desired motion for the early portion of the backswing, with the arms, hands, and wrists moving away from the ball together.

One-shotter: *n.* A par-three hole.

One-up: *adj.* In match play, describing a player or team that has won one more hole than his opponent.

Open: *v.* 1. To turn the toe of the clubface slightly out from the target line. 2. To align one's body so it is aiming to the left of the target for right-handers. *n.* A tournament open to amateurs and professionals.

Open clubface: *n.* One in which the heel of the club leads the toe through impact, causing the clubface to point to the right of the *target line.*

Open stance: *n.* For right-handed players, when the left foot is farther back from the *target line* than the right foot.

Open-to-closed: *adj.* The rolling of the clubface open during the backswing, then closed during the downswing.

Out of bounds: *n.* Outside the boundary of the golf course; a ball which lands here cannot be played and must be rehit with a penalty stroke. Also referred to as "O.B."

Outside agency: *n.* Any object not part of a match that stops, deflects, or moves a ball while in play.

Outside-to-in: *adj.* Describing a swing path in which the clubface approaches the ball from outside the *target line,* makes contact, then swings inside the line.

Overclub: *v.* To hit with a club that produces too much distance for the situation.

Overlapping grip: *n.* The most popular grip for right-handed players, it involves placing the little finger of the right hand in the space between the index and middle fingers of the left hand. Also *Vardon grip.*

Overspin: *n.* The forward rotation of a ball in motion. Also *topspin.*

Overswing: *v.* To swing too hard, usually resulting in a mishit.

Over-the-top: *adj.* Referring to a swing that starts on an outside-to-in path as soon as the downward movement begins.

P

Pace: *n.* 1. The speed of the green. 2. The rate at which a putt is rolling. 3. The rate of movement in a swing or stroke. *v.* To measure the distance of a shot by walking from the ball to the target.

Par: *n.* 1. The theoretical number of strokes it should take a scratch golfer to complete a hole. 2. The standard of good performance. *v.* To make a score of par on a hole.

Parallel: *adj. and n.* The desired position at the top of the swing, with the clubshaft parallel to the ground. Also *horizontal.*

Path: *n.* The directional arc on which the club is swung.

Penalty stroke: *n.* A stroke added to a player's score for a violation of a Rule or as punishment for hitting into a water hazard, unplayable lie, or out of bounds. Also a "penalty shot."

Pendulum stroke: *n.* The desired motion in putting in which the big muscles of the shoulders and back move together, so the arms rock around a fixed point (the spine).

Piccolo grip: *n.* A very loose hold on the club, especially at the top of the backswing.

Pick up: *v.* To swing the club away from the ball with a sharp cock of the wrists, rather than a one-piece takeaway, resulting in the club lifting prematurely.

Pin: *n.* The pole that marks the position of the hole on the green. Also *flagstick*.

Pin-high: *adj.* Referring to a ball that comes to rest level with the pin. Also *hole-high*.

Pinehurst: *n.* A game in which partners play each other's drive, then select one ball with which to finish the hole.

Pin placement: *n.* The positioning of the hole on the green on a given day or occasion.

Pitch: *n.* A short shot with a steep trajectory, typically with backspin, that flies in the air farther than it rolls after landing. *v.* To play a pitch shot.

Pitch-and-run: *n.* An approach shot consisting of a low, short pitch shot that lands on the green, then rolls a long way. *v.* To play a pitch-and-run shot.

Pitching niblick: *n.* Old term for a pitching wedge.

Pitching wedge: *n.* A high-lofted iron club used primarily for *pitch* shots to the greens.

Pivot: *n.* Rotation of the shoulders, torso, and shoulders during the swing. *v.* To rotate the body in this manner.

Plane: *n.* An imaginary flat surface that describes the path and angle of a swinging club. Also *swing plane*.

Play club: *n.* Old term for the driver.

Playing partner: *n.* A golfer playing in a partnership or on the same team as another.

Playoff: *n.* A tiebreaker in which the players continue play after the regulation number of holes. *v.* To decide a tie by playing extra holes.

Play through: *v.* To pass through golfers playing ahead, giving faster players the chance to continue at a quick pace.

Plugged lie: *n.* A ball that is partially buried beneath the surface. Also "embedded lie."

Plumb-bob: *v.* The act of lining up a putt by sighting along the shaft of a putter hanging vertically in front of the face.

Poa Annua: *n.* A weedlike grass found on many courses in the cooler spring months before dying out in the summer heat.

Point of contact: *n.* The spot on the clubface that strikes the center of the ball.

Pop: *v.* To play a short shot, hitting under the ball so it rises quickly. *n.* A shot of this type.

Pot bunker: *n.* A small, deep sand trap, often invisible from the tee.

Power: *n.* The amount of force with which a golf ball is struck.

Practice aids: *n.* Devices—videos, swing trainers, special clubs, etc.—designed to make practice more worthwhile and productive.

Practice tee/green: *n.* Areas of a golf course devoted to practice.

Preferred lie: *n.* The spot to which a ball is moved, when the Rules allow. Part of *winter rules*.

Preshot routine: *n.* A physical and mental routine done before hitting a shot, to promote consistency.

Press: *n.* An additional bet made during the course of a match. *v.* To try too hard in playing a stroke or shot.

Pro-am: *n.* Competition in which professionals and amateurs team together.

Pronation: *n.* Inward rotation of the wrist; at address, toward the target with the right hand, away from the target with the left for right-handed golfers.

Pro side: *n.* On a sloped green, the side above the hole. Also *high side*.

Provisional ball: *n.* A ball played when there is the possibility that the original shot may be lost or out of play.

Pull: *v.* For right-handed players, to play a shot that starts left of the *target line* and flies straight left. *n.* A shot of this type.

Pull-hook: *n.* For right-handed players, a shot that starts left of the *target line*, then hooks farther left.

Pull-slice: *n.* For right-handed players, a shot that starts left of the *target line*, then slices to the right.

Punch: *n.* A hard, low-flying shot often hit with a good deal of backspin; same as a *knockdown*. *v.* To play a shot of this type.

Punchbowl: *n.* A putting green that sits in a hollow.

Push: *v.* For right-handed players, to play a shot that starts right of the *target line* and flies straight right. *n.* A shot of this type.

Push-hook: *n.* For right-handed players, a shot that starts right of the *target line*, then hooks left.

Push-slice: *n.* For right-handed players, a shot that starts right of the *target line,* then slices farther right.

Putt: *v.* To stroke a ball toward the hole on a putting green. *n.* A shot hit on the putting green, designed to get the ball into the hole.

Putter: *n.* 1. A club designed for putting. 2. Someone who putts.

Putting green: *n.* 1. Any putting surface. 2. A *practice green.*

Putt out: *v.* To stroke the ball into the hole.

Q

Quail-high: *adj.* Describing a shot hit on a low, flat trajectory (after the way quails fly).

Quarter-shot: *n.* A shot hit with approximately 25 percent of normal power.

Quit: *v.* To give up on a shot while hitting it; to decelerate through impact of a shot.

R

Radius: *n.* The distance between the center of the swing arc and the hands.

Range: *n.* The *driving range or practice tee.*

Rap: *v.* **1.** To hit a putt firmly. 2. To stroke the putt with a long backstroke and short follow-through. Also a "pop" or "pop stroke."

Read: *v.* 1. To determine the direction and speed necessary to stroke a putt. 2. To survey the slope of the putting green. Also referred to as "reading the green." *n.* The direction or line of a putt.

Recover: *v.* To play back to the fairway or other safe spot from rough, a hazard, or other undesirable position.

Recovery shot: *n.* The shot played when trying to *recover.*

Release: *v.* To uncock the wrists and rotate the forearms in the downswing so as to square the clubface and create power. *n.* The uncocking of the wrists and rotating of the arms on the downswing.

Relief: *n.* When a player is allowed to lift and drop the ball without penalty.

Reverse-C: *adj.* Describes the position in which the back and legs are arched backward at the finish of the swing.

Reverse overlap: *n.* For right-handed players, a putting grip in which the little finger of the right hand overlaps the index finger of the left hand.

Reverse pivot: *n.* A motion in which the body's weight stays on the front side during the backswing, then shifts backward

to the back side on the downswing; the opposite of the weight shift in a good swing. Also "reverse weight shift."

Rhythm: *n.* The *tempo* of a golf swing.

Roll over: *v.* To rotate the wrists and arms during the swing.

Rough: *n.* Long grass, usually found along the edges of the fairway.

Round robin: *n.* A tournament in which every player or team plays one match against every other player or team.

Rub of the green: *n.* 1. A ball in motion stopped or deflected by an outside agency. 2. Any misfortune, such as a bad bounce or other unintended result.

Run-up: *n.* A low, running shot onto the green. *v.* To play this shot.

Ryegrass: *n.,* A cool-season grass that dies in intense heat; similar to *Poa Annua.* Often used to overseed Bermuda grass fairways in winter to provide a healthier-looking surface.

S

Sandbagger: *n.* A golfer who lies about his playing ability in order to gain an advantage, particularly when betting.

Sand trap: *n.* A *bunker;* also referred to as a *trap.*

Sand wedge: *n.* An iron club with a lot of loft, used for explosion shots from bunkers and short approach shots around the green.

Sandy: *n.* A par on a hole after being in a *bunker.*

Save: *v.* To recover after a misplayed shot. *n.* A well-played recovery shot.

Sclaff: *v.* To hit the ground unintentionally before the ball, resulting in a mishit. *n.* A mishit shot of this type.

Scoop: *v.* To attempt to lift the ball by dipping the club through impact.

Scotch foursome: *n.* An *alternate-shot* match in which partners take turns hitting the same ball.

Scramble: *v.* To play erratic golf, yet still be able to score well by playing good *recovery shots. n.* A team format in which each player hits his drive, the best one is chosen, each player hits the next shot from that point, the best of those is chosen, and so on until the ball is holed.

Scrambler: *n.* A player who plays erratically, yet still scores well.

Scratch: *adj.* Refers to a player with a zero *handicap.*

Scratch golfer: *n.* A player whose *handicap* is zero; one who receives no handicap strokes.

Scuff: *v.* To mishit the ball so as to damage its cover slightly. *n.* A slight damage mark on the cover of the ball.

Second cut: *n.* Second level of rough, longer than the *first cut.*

Set: *n.* A complete collection of golf clubs. *v.* To place the clubhead behind the ball at address.

Set-up: *v.* To position oneself to hit the ball. Also called *address.* *n.* A golfer's position when he is about to swing the club.

Shaft: *n.* The long, thin part of the club connecting the clubhead to the grip.

Shallow: *adj.* Refers to a flat *swing plane or angle of attack.*

Shank: *v.* To hit the ball with the *hosel* of the club, causing it to fly dramatically right and short. *n.* A shot of this type.

Shape: *v.* To move the ball deliberately from one direction to the other while in flight; purposely to hit a *fade* or *draw.*

Short game: *n.* Shots played on and around the green; pitching, chipping, the sand game, and putting.

Short irons: *n.* The shorter hitting, higher lofted clubs. Generally the 8-iron, 9-iron, and any wedges.

Shot: *n.* 1. A stroke that results in the movement of the ball. 2. A particular type of stroke.

Shotmaker: *n.* A player who can consistently move the ball in a variety of different ways.

Shotmaking: *n.* The art of playing a range of different shots.

Shut: *adj.* Describing the clubface when it is tilted forward relative to the line of play. Also *hooded.* *v.* To manipulate the clubface in this manner.

Side: *n.* 1. In match play, one of the two teams or players competing. 2. The front or back half of the course.

Sidehill: *adj.* Situated on the side of a hill, especially a putt that breaks over the hill on its way to the hole.

Sidespin: *n.* The way the ball spins when the clubhead is moving in a direction other than the way the clubface is pointing. It causes a ball to *fade/slice* or *draw/hook.*

Single: *n.* A match between two players.

Sink: *v.* To hole out a putt.

Skins: *n.* A betting game in which the lowest score on a hole wins the wager for that hole; if any players tie, the bet carries over to the next hole.

Skull: *v.* To hit the ball above its equator with the leading edge of the club; to *top* the ball. *n.* A shot of this type.

Sky: *v.* To hit the ball extremely high. *n.* A shot of this type.

Slice: *v.* For right-handed players, to hit the ball sharply from left to right. *n.* A shot of this type.

Slicer: *n.* One who habitually slices the ball.

Slope: *n.* 1. The tilt in a green. 2. A measurement of the difficulty of a golf course, used to compute a player's *handicap* for that course.

Smother: *v.* To hit down on the ball with a closed clubface so it runs along the ground, usually with *hookspin.* *n.* A shot of this type.

Smother hook: *n.* A violent hook that falls quickly to the ground, caused by a closed clubface at impact.

Snake: *n.* A very long putt, usually one that breaks several times.

Snap-hook: *v.* To hit the ball with a severe, fast *hook.* *n.* A shot of this type.

Snipe: *n.* A *snap hook or smother hook.*

Socket: *n.* The *hosel* of an iron clubhead; where the shaft joins the clubhead.

Sole: *n.* The bottom of a clubhead. *v.* To set the club on the ground at address.

Spade-mashie: *n.* A deep-faced mashie, no longer in use, generally considered to be equal to a 6-iron.

Splash: *v.* To explode the ball from a sand *bunker* or deep *rough.* *n.* A shot of this type.

Spoon: *n.* An old term, somewhat still in use, for a fairway wood; generally considered equal to a 3-wood.

Spot putting: *n.* The act of aiming a putt toward a mark or discoloration in the green or some other intermediate target.

Square: *v.* To tie a match. *adj.* 1. Referring to the position of the body's stance when parallel to the *target line.* 2. Referring to the position of the clubface when perpendicular to the *target line.*

Stab: *v.* To hit a putt halfheartedly. *n.* A shot of this type.

Stableford: *n.* A way to keep score in which points, rather than the number of strokes, are given for the result of a hole.

Stance: *n.* The position of the feet at *address.*

Steer: *v.* An exaggerated attempt to control the direction of a shot by manipulating the body or club.

Stick: *n.* 1. The *flagstick.* 2. Slang for a golf club. *v.* To play a shot that finishes close to the hole.

Stiff: *adj.* Referring to a shot that finishes very close to the hole.

Stimpmeter: *n.* A device used to measure the speed of a green.

Stroke: *n.* 1. A player's attempt to hit the ball. 2. A shot or shots added to a player's score when penalized. *v.* To strike the ball with a fluid and rhythmic motion, especially a putt.

Stroke hole: *n.* Hole at which a player either receives or gives a shot, depending on *handicap.*

Stroke play: *n.* Competition in which the total number of strokes in a round or rounds determines the winner.

Strong grip: *n.* A grip on the club in which the hands begin rotated away from the target at address so they will close the clubhead through impact.

Summer rules: *n.* The ordinary playing of golf by the stipulated Rules, playing the ball as it lies.

Supination: *n.* Outward rotation of the wrist; at address, away from the target with the right hand, toward the target with the left (for right-handed golfers); the natural rotation of the wrists through the swing.

Sway: *v.* To move the weight to the back side on the backswing. *n.* An excessive *weight shift*.

Sweet spot: *n.* That point of the clubface where the club does not torque when striking a golf ball.

Swing: *v.* To move the body and the club for the purpose of hitting the ball. *n.* The movement of body and club to strike the ball.

Swing arc: *n.* The path traced by the clubhead during its complete motion.

Swing center: *n.* The point around which the swing rotates, located roughly between the base of the neck and the top of the spine.

Swing plane: *n.* The *plane*.

T

Tailwind: *n.* A breeze that blows in the same direction as the shot, helping it fly farther.

Takeaway: *n.* The first twelve to eighteen inches of the backswing.

Tap-in: *v.* To hole a very short putt. *n.* A very short putt; a *gimme*.

Target line: *n.* The imaginary line running from the ball to the target.

Tee: *n.* 1. A small wooden peg on which a ball is placed in preparation to being hit from the *teeing ground*. 2. The area from which tee shots are played. *v.* To place the ball on a tee.

Tee box: *n.* *Teeing ground.*

Teeing ground: *n.* The beginning of a hole, defined as an area the width of the tee *markers* and two club-lengths deep.

Tee off: *v.* To play a tee shot.

Tempo: *n.* The rhythm of a golf swing.

Texas wedge: *n.* A shot played with a putter from off the green.

Thin: *adj.* Referring to a shot hit above the equator of the ball with the leading edge of the club, causing the ball to fly low and usually far. *v.* To hit a shot in this manner.

Three-quarter shot: *n.* A shot made with approximately 75 percent of a full swing.

Three-putt: *v.* To take three putts to get the ball in the hole from on the green. *n.* A situation in which a player takes three putts to hole out.

Through the green: *n.* The entire course except the *teeing grounds* and *greens*.

Tiger tees: *n.* The tees farthest away from the hole; the *back tees* or "championship tees."

Tight: *adj.* 1. Referring to a fairway or hole that is very narrow, usually lined on both sides by trees or hazards. 2. Referring to a lie when the ball is very close to the ground, with little grass beneath it.

Timing: *n.* The pace and movement in a swing; also, the way in which the muscles coordinate to produce a good golf swing.

Toe: *n.* The end of the clubhead farthest from the shaft. *v.* To hit a shot with the toe of the clubhead.

Toed shot: *n.* A shot hit off the toe of the clubhead.

Top: *v.* To hit the ball above its equator with the leading edge of the clubface, so it runs low along the ground rather than getting in the air. *n.* A shot hit in this manner.

Top of the swing: *n.* The position of the body and club at the completion of the backswing.

Topspin: *n.* Forward rotation of a ball in motion. Also *overspin*.

Torque: *n.* Twisting of the shaft and clubface at impact.

Trajectory: *n.* The height and direction of the ball's path in the air.

Transition: *n.* The change in direction from backswing to downswing.

Trap: *n.* *Sand trap or bunker.*

Triple bogey: *n.* A score of three over par on a hole.

Trouble: *n.* Rough, hazards, trees, or other obstacles on a course.

Trouble shot: *n.* A recovery stroke made from or near an obstacle on the course.

Turn: *n.* 1. The halfway point in an 18-hole round of golf. 2. The motion of rotating away from the ball on the backswing. *v.* To rotate away from the ball on the backswing.

U

Uncock: *v.* To allow the wrists to straighten during the forward swing.

Underclub: *v.* To select a club that does not provide enough distance for the required shot.

Unplayable lie: *n.* The position of a ball at rest that makes it too difficult to attempt a stroke.

Uphill lie: When a player's front foot is higher than his back foot at address, causing him to make compensations to hit a good shot.

Up and down: *n.* Playing the ball from off the green into the hole in two shots.

Upright: *adj.* 1. Referring to a very steep swing path.

Upswing: *n.* The backswing; the portion of the swing from address to the top of the swing.

V

Vs: *n.* The V-shapes formed by the thumb and forefinger of each hand when gripping the club.

Vardon grip: *n. See overlapping grip.*

Visualization: *n.* Forming a mental picture of the correct swing or shot needed as a way better to prepare to make it happen.

W

Waggle: *v.* To move the clubhead and wrists in a flexing motion before swinging; used to relieve tension as part of a *preshot routine. n.* Any movement in this manner.

Water hazard: *n.* A defined body of water on a course.

Weak grip: *n.* A grip on the club in which the hands begin rotated toward the target at address so they will keep the clubhead from closing through impact.

Wedge: *n.* A *pitching wedge, sand wedge,* or other high lofted club primarily used for short shots around the green. *v.* To play a shot using a wedge.

Weight distribution: *n.* The division of body weight between each side of the body at *address.*

Weight shift: *n.* The movement of body weight during the swing, preferably to the back side on the backswing and to the front side on the downswing.

Whiff: *v.* To miss the ball completely with a swing. *n.* A shot that misses the ball completely; "air ball."

Whins: *n.* Another name for *gorse.*

Wind cheater: *n.* A low, driving shot that remains relatively unaffected by the wind.

Winter rules: *n.* Rules in force when the course is in bad condition; allows a player to improve lies on the fairway.

Wormburner: *n.* A mishit shot that travels very low to the ground.

Wrist cock: *n.* The hinging of the wrists during the swing.

Y

Yardage rating: *n.* The evaluation of a course's difficulty based on its distance.

Yips: *n.* Extreme nervousness over short putts that causes a player to miss the hole badly.

Z

Zoysia: *n.* A warm-climate grass with coarse blades that can handle extreme temperature change.

—COMPILED BY GREG MIDLAND

TIMELINE

Fifteenth century—Golf, or a game very similar, is played over land now known as the Old Course, at St. Andrews, Scotland.

1744—The original 13 Rules of golf adopted by the Honourable Company of Edinburgh Golfers.

1754—The St. Andrews Society of Golfers is formed. In time, it is renamed the Royal and Ancient Golf Club of St. Andrews (or the R&A).

Early 1800s—Cups are small flowerpots, set in holes cut by dinner knives.

1848—Allan Robertson widens the fairways at the Old Course at St. Andrews, enabling players to tack around bunkers instead of having to loft over them. For the first time, strategic shot planning becomes vital.

1849—The first cup-cutting tool is used, at Royal Aberdeen Golf Club.

1857—H. B. Farnie pens *The Golfer's Manual*, the first known book to include golf instruction.

c. 1874—Holes are lined with metal (tin), at Crail Golf Club, Scotland.

c. 1875—Separate teeing areas, well away from previous hole, come into use.

1887 and 1889—Willie Park, Jr., wins the British Open.

1890—Publication of *Golf: The Badminton Library*, by Harold Hutchinson, offering interesting insights into the St. Andrews swing and other techniques employed by the early Scottish golfers.

1891—Royal and Ancient Golf Club of St. Andrews standardizes size of the hole at 4.25 inches.

1894—The United States Golf Association (USGA) is formed.

1894—Willie Park, Jr., receives a patent for the Wry Necked Putter, featuring a goose-necked hosel.

1896—Harry Vardon wins the first of six British Open titles, using an upright swing.

1897—H. J. Whigham writes *How to Play Golf*, the first instruction book published in the United States.

1904—American Walter Travis wins the British Amateur using a center-shafted putter.

1905—Publication of *The Complete Golfer*, by Harry Vardon.

1908—Arnold Haultain publishes *The Mystery of Golf*, the first work entirely devoted to the philosophy and psychology of golf.

1910—R&A outlaws use of center-shafted putters in its competition; ban lasts 40 years.

1913—Pinehurst Resort and Country Club in North Carolina builds the first practice range in the United States. Soon dubbed "Maniac Hill," it contained a practice tee, fairway, and bunker.

1916—PGA of America, an association for club professionals and teachers, is founded.

1919—*Picture Analysis of Golf Strokes*, by two-time PGA champion Jim Barnes, is the first book to use high-speed sequence photography of the swing.

1920—*The Art of Putting*, by Willie Park, Jr., is published.

1923—Ernest Jones sets up the first indoor golf school, in New York City.

1924—Eddie Loos publishes "The Eight-Inch Golf Course" In *The American Golfer*, containing the first written mention of a preshot routine.

1930—Robert Tyre Jones, Jr., wins all four majors of his time—U.S. and British Amateurs and Opens—then retires from competitive play. Replicas of his "Calamity Jane" putter are offered in mass-produced quantities.

1931—Gene Sarazen, tinkering with niblicks and solder, creates the first "sand wedge" with a large, deep flange hanging under the club's sole.

1931—Joyce Wethered makes the first-known mention of "visualizing the shot" in the September issue of *The American Golfer*.

1932—Alex Morrison launches his left-side-dominance theory in his instruction book, *A New Way to Better Golf*.

1937—Byron Nelson wins his first Masters, using the modern upright swing and clubs with steel shafts.

1938—The USGA limits the number of clubs that may be used during a round to 14.

1940s—Ben Hogan single-handedly makes ball-beating fashionable.

Late 1940s—The Stimpmeter, for measuring green speed, is invented by Edward Stimpson.

1946—John Reuter's "Bull's Eye" putter is first manufactured.

1946—Percy Boomer presents the "Connection" swing theory in *On Learning Golf*.

1949—The Ladies Professional Golf Association (LPGA) is formed.

1951—*Golf Digest* magazine begins publication.

1953—In *How To Play Your Best Golf All The Time,* Tommy Armour recommends golfers control the swing with their right side.

1957—Ben Hogan's *Five Lessons: The Modern Fundamentals of Golf* is published. One of its highlights is the visual image of a pane of glass representing the swing plane.

1959—*GOLF Magazine* begins publication.

1960—After driving the green of the first hole, a 350-yard par four, in the final round, Arnold Palmer fires a 65 to win the U.S. Open.

1962—Dr. Peter Cranford's *The Winning Touch in Golf* is published. It is the first golf book to address the "how to" practical application of psychological principles while practicing and playing.

1967—Julius Boros wins the Phoenix Open using a heel-toe-weighted Ping putter designed by Karsten Solheim.

1968—The PGA Tour splits off from the PGA of America, becoming a separate, self-governing body.

1968—Englishmen Alastair Cochran and John Stobbs publish their ground-breaking study of the game, *Search for the Perfect Swing.* It is the most comprehensive scientific study ever produced on golf.

1969—Homer Kelley's *The Golfing Machine,* the most technical instruction book ever assembled, is published.

1970—The first graphite shaft is commercially available.

1971—The first national column devoted exclusively to the mental aspects of golf appears in *Golf Digest.* Written by Dr. Michael Morley, it appeared regularly until 1974.

1972—Michael Murphy publishes *Golf in the Kingdom,* the quintessential exploration of golf's inseparable, and sometimes magical, melding of mind, body, and spirit.

1972—*Practical Golf* by John Jacobs brings cause and effect golf instruction to the masses.

1973—*Laws, Principles, and Preferences* by Dr. Gary Wiren is published. Wiren takes the Ball Flight Laws and builds a complex model of principles that must be adhered to within the swing's framework to create the ideal impact conditions.

1974—Jack Nicklaus helps create an entire generation of steep swing planes with the publication of *Golf My Way.*

1975—Dave Pelz quits his job as an engineer for NASA's Goddard Flight Center and begins manufacturing putters and conducting research on Tour pros' putting and short games.

1978—Dr. Gary Wiren and Dr. Richard Coop publish *The New Golf Mind,* the first book to discuss the individual roles of the brain's hemispheres in planning and executing good golf shots.

1980–The Senior PGA Tour begins, with two events and total prize money of $250,000.

1981—Academy of Golf at The Hills of Lakeway, near Austin, Texas, opens. It is the first practice facility designed and built specifically for practicing every facet of the game. Full-scale holes, multiple practice greens, indoor classrooms, and extensive video capabilities are all included.

1981—*The Inner Game of Golf* by W. Timothy Gallwey lands in bookstores on the heels of his best-selling *The Inner Game of Tennis.*

1981—The Stadium Course at the TPC at Sawgrass opens, featuring vast waste areas, pot bunkers, oceans of water, and other hazards that put a premium on "target golf."

1982—Tom Watson chips in at the 17th hole of the final round of the U.S. Open at Pebble Beach to win the tournament.

1984—Representatives of the USGA and R&A reorganize The Rules of Golf to aid in compliance and interpretation.

1985—Nick Faldo begins taking lessons from David Leadbetter.

1987—Larry Mize chips in from 140 feet off Augusta National's 11th green, the second hole of a playoff with Greg Norman, to win The Masters.

1987—Nick Faldo wins his first major, the British Open.

1991—Long-hitting John Daly, who'd begun the week as an alternate, wins the PGA Championship.

1991—Oversized, metal-headed woods become available to the public for the first time.

1996—Tiger Woods wins his third consecutive men's U.S. Amateur title, then turns professional and wins two of the first eight official PGA Tour events he enters.

1997—*GOLF Magazine* establishes a Hall of Fame for golf instructors, the first time teaching professionals have been so honored.

THE 100 BEST TEACHERS

It took a year of canvassing, conferring, and considering, but that means we can say without reservation that every teacher on *GOLF Magazine's* list of America's 100 Best Golf Instructors, compiled in 1996, has demonstrated extraordinary swing knowledge, dedication to helping his or her students, and the communication skills necessary to make the game's complexities understandable to all.

Are there other exceptional teachers among the tens of thousands of instructors working our nation's lesson tees? You bet. But we believe this list of 100 truly finds the best of the best.

Why are we so sure? Because we received unprecedented support from the teaching community as we scoured the country for worthy nominees. All 41 PGA of America sections and all six LPGA Teaching and Club Professional sections helped identify their region's finest. We also asked numerous Tour pros, golf industry veterans, and the 50 Best Teachers from our original 1991 list to supply the names of the instructors they most respect.

More than 400 top teachers were nominated. All filled out a detailed questionnaire about their theories and other personal teaching data. We narrowed the field by scrutinizing each teacher's experience, knowledge, professional reputation, successes, innovative techniques, and industry awards.

The very best are listed below: Biographies detail their teaching philosophy, career highlights, and lesson rates (as of 1996)—in case you'd like to book a lesson or two from at least one of these terrific teachers.

RICK ACTON, Sahalee CC, Redmond, Wash. PGA Senior Tour player with balanced four-pronged approach to teaching: full swing, short game, course management, and mental preparation. Lessons: $35 per half-hour for members, $60 for nonmembers.

MIKE ADAMS, PGA National Academy of Golf, Palm Beach Gardens, Fla. Creative instructor who builds swings around individual's body type and strength limitations. Sought out by numerous Tour pros. Booked months in advance. Lessons: $125 per hour.

MIKE AUSTIN, Studio City, Cal. Student of kinesiology (the study of human movement). Teaching based upon physics and human physiology. Has given more than 200,000 lessons during 67-year career. Produced video titled *Mental Imagery.* Lessons: $100 per hour.

JIMMY BALLARD, Key Largo, Fla. "Connection" theory has made Ballard a long-time guru to more than 100 Tour pros, including Curtis Strange and Hal Sutton. Wrote *How to Perfect Your Golf Swing.* Lessons: $250 per hour.

PEGGY KIRK BELL, Pine Needles Resort, Southern Pines, N.C. This LPGA charter member offers "women only" schools. Focuses on developing good balance and proper sequence of motion. Authored two videos, including *Women's Golf.* Lessons: $50 per hour.

MIKE BENDER, Timacuan G. & CC, Lake Mary, Fla. Up-and-comer quickly making a name with pros. Believes efficiency of motion is key to improvement; focuses on reducing excess swing compensations. Lessons: $70 per hour.

PAUL BERTHOLY, Foxfire Village, N.C. Sixty-four-year teaching career has included nearly a quarter-million lessons. Teaches six key positions in the swing. Has students swing a heavy pipe to groove proper feel. Author of many books and magazine articles. Lessons: $250 per hour.

CRAIG L. BUNKER, Scottsdale, Ariz. Does most of his teaching as instructor at John Jacobs' Golf Schools. Looks closely at impact factors to diagnose swing corrections. Enjoys working with all skill levels. Lessons: $120 per hour.

KENT A. CAYCE, Hudson National GC, Croton-on-Hudson, N.Y. Strong proponent of videotaping lessons. Works with many juniors. More than 90 of his students have earned scholarships during a 26-year teaching career. Bill Glasson and Brian Claar among his pupils. Lessons: $100 per hour.

CHUCK COOK, Barton Creek Lakeside CC, Spicewood, Tex. All-around instructor with 22 years' experience. Has worked extensively with Payne Stewart, Tom Kite, and Corey Pavin. Lessons: $125 per hour.

HARRY "LIGHTHORSE" COOPER, Westchester CC, Rye, N.Y. Played against and learned from Bobby Jones and Ben Hogan. A wealth of knowledge at 91 years young. Teaches five half-days per week. Lessons: $75 per hour for members, $80 for nonmembers.

WILLIAM A. DAVIS, The Jupiter Hills Club, Tequesta, Fla. Emphasizes playing lessons and "scoring shots" within 50 yards of the hole. Also stresses course management and emotional skills. Lessons: $100 per hour for members, $150 for nonmembers.

MANUEL DE LA TORRE, Milwaukee CC, Milwaukee, Wis. Follows tenets of 1930s instructor Ernest Jones, who taught that the clubhead swings the hands, not the other way around. Lessons: $40 per hour. Teaches only members during peak summer season.

BEN DOYLE, The GC at Quail Lodge, Carmel, Cal. Long-time disciple of Homer Kelley and highly mechanical *The Golfing Machine,* uses geometry and physics to explain the swing. Good for analytical students. Lessons: $60 per hour.

JOHN ELLIOTT JR., CC of Ocala, Ocala, Fla. Excellent communicator who eschews overly mechanical approaches. Focuses on improving preswing and short-game skills. Works with LPGA winner Julie Piers. Long-time Golf Digest Schools instructor. Lessons: $110 per hour.

DICK FARLEY, Shawnee-on-Delaware, Pa. Operates Swing's the Thing Golf Schools with partner Rick McCord. Wrote *Six Days to Better Golf* and produced videos based on the schools. Lessons: $100 per hour.

JIM FLICK, Desert Mountain GC, Scottsdale, Ariz. Headliner at Nicklaus/Flick Golf Schools. Extremely creative, with many innovative drills to help students groove a sound swing. Coaches Tour pros including Jack Nicklaus and Tom Lehman. Lessons: Fee varies as to program.

BILL FORREST, TPC of Scottsdale, Scottsdale, Ariz. Busy teacher, logging average of 100 lessons a week. Very active with juniors. Instructs Tom Purtzer and Per-Ulrik Johansson. Lessons: $100 per hour.

JANE K. FROST, Holly Ridge GC, Sandwich, Mass. LPGA's 1994 National Teacher of the Year operates own golf schools. Focuses on creating perfect grip and posture and on the short game. Lessons: $100 for 45 minutes.

SHELBY FUTCH, Scottsdale, Ariz. Specializes in full swing. Focuses on isolating one or two key fundamental corrections for each student. Owner of John Jacobs' Golf Schools operating at 28 locations. Lessons: Corporate schools at $3,000 per day. No hourly rate.

JOHN GEERTSEN JR., Pebble Beach, Cal. Studied under his father, who taught Johnny Miller. Swing theory based on creating maximum leverage and centrifugal force during the swing. Students have included Miller and Mike Reid. Lessons: $100 per hour.

JIM GERBER, Fort Wayne, Ind. Starts with realistic goals, then creates straightforward plan to achieve them. Lessons: $100 per hour.

JOHN GERRING, Bloomfield Hills CC, Bloomfield Hills, Mich. Stresses learning to hit the ball right-to-left, the first key to becoming a good golfer. Larry Nelson among former students. Does not use video. Lessons: $70 per hour.

DAVID GLENZ, Crystal Springs GC, Hamburg, N.J. Five-time New Jersey PGA Teacher of the Year. Co-author of *10 Fundamentals of the Modern Golf Swing.* Teaches many Tour professionals. One of the top club-pro players in the country. Lessons: $125 per hour.

RICK GRAYSON, Bill and Payne Stewart GC, Springfield, Mo. Believes most swing problems can be fixed by improving the set-up. Junior program has sent 25 golfers to college on scholarships. Lessons: $35 for 50 minutes.

FRED GRIFFIN, Grand Cypress Academy of Golf, Orlando, Fla. All-around instructor uses biomechanics and unique computer system to compare pupil's swing to model compiled from Tour pros' movements. Lessons: $120 per hour.

MARTIN HALL, Palm City, Fla. Teaches all facets of the game; especially gifted short-game instructor. Uses many teaching aids to help students feel proper swing motion. Also instructs at Nicklaus/Flick Golf Schools. Lessons: $100 per hour.

BRUCE D. HAMILTON, Spanish Hills GC, Camerillo, Cal. Best known as Corey Pavin's swing coach. Tries to make the student feel comfortable during lessons and makes sure student understands personal swing motion. Lessons: $75 per hour.

BOB HAMRICH, Beachwood, Ohio. Has written numerous magazine articles during his 46-year career. Prefers playing lessons to help students improve their scoring ability. Special interest in teaching blind and handicapped golfers. Lessons: $80 per hour.

HANK HANEY, Hank Haney Golf Ranch, McKinney, Tex. PGA's 1993 National Teacher of the Year. Emphasizes swinging the golf club on the correct plane. Sought after by dozens of Tour pros, including long-time student Mark O'Meara. Lessons: $220 per hour.

DEREK HARDY, Pelican Hill GC, Santa Ana, Cal. Stresses positive preswing thoughts and simple swing keys. Works with many LPGA players such as Helen Alfredsson and Liselotte Neumann. Lessons: $75 per hour.

JIM HARDY, Houston, Tex. Limited teaching schedule because of other golf-related businesses. Teaching focuses on getting club on the proper plane throughout the swing. Has helped Peter Jacobsen and Dave Stockton, among other Tour pros. Lessons: $150 per hour.

BILL HARMON, The Vintage Club, Indian Wells, Cal. First of four sons of 1948 Masters champion and world-class teacher Claude Harmon, Sr., to make this list. A big proponent of playing lessons. Consulted regularly by Jay Haas. Lessons: $80 per hour.

CLAUDE "BUTCH" HARMON JR., Las Vegas, Nev. Credited by Greg Norman for raising his game to next level. Now works regularly with Tiger Woods. Lessons: $100 per hour for members, $200 for nonmembers.

CRAIG W. HARMON, Oak Hill CC, Rochester, N.Y. Teaches full-swing and short-game secrets learned from his father. Jeff Sluman's instructor. Lessons: $100 per hour for members, $60 per hour each, in groups of four, for nonmembers.

DICK HARMON, River Oaks CC, Houston, Tex. Another Harmon son who shares his father's classic stories and shot-making skills. Named PGA section teacher of the year three times. Lessons: $70 per hour for members, $150 for nonmembers (must be sponsored by member).

MICHAEL P. HEBRON, Smithtown Landing CC, Smithtown, N.Y. Well known among fellow club professionals. Wrote *See and*

Feel the Inside Move the Outside. PGA's 1991 National Teacher of the Year. Lessons: $125 per hour.

GREGOR JAMIESON, Lake Nona Club, Orlando, Fla. Son of Bob Jamieson, pro at Turnberry in Scotland. Emphasizes preswing principles and creating a swing that stays in balance. Also teaches in Germany. Lessons: $100 per hour.

DARRELL KESTNER, Deepdale G.C., Manhasset, N.Y. One of the finest club-pro players in the country and a busy teacher. Highly respected by his peers in metropolitan New York. Lessons: $100 per hour for members, $200 for nonmembers.

PETER KOSTIS, Scottsdale, Ariz. Teaches with Gary McCord at Kostis/McCord Learning Center at Grayhawk GC in Scottsdale when not doubling as announcer for CBS/USA golf telecasts. Known for book *The Inside Path to Better Golf*. Lessons: $250 per hour.

JACK KUYKENDALL, Kuykendall Golf, Naples, Fla. A physicist by education, believes in an ideal mechanical golf stroke and says he has found it. Technique similar to swing of world-renowned ball-striker Moe Norman also minimizes back strain. Lessons: $200 per hour.

MIKE LABAUVE, Kierland GC, Scottsdale, Ariz. A favorite with better players and juniors. Builds lessons around proper swing plane and set-up. Golf Digest Schools instructor. Lessons: $125 per hour.

SANDY LABAUVE, Kierland GC, Scottsdale, Ariz. Teaches many women and junior girls. Founded LPGA's Junior Girls Golf Club, now in 47 cities worldwide. Daughter of Jack Lumpkin. Lessons: $80 per hour.

DAVID LEADBETTER, David Leadbetter Golf Academy, Orlando, Fla. First Tour guru to market himself into a multimillion-dollar international teaching empire. The two Nicks—Faldo and Price—among his stable of high-profile students. Lessons: Two-day retreat, $3,500.

DAVID LEE, World Woods GC, Brooksville, Fla. Teaches "gravity golf" and promises "Tour-length" shots within 100 days. Method is based upon balance and some unusual drills. Works extensively with Lee Trevino and J. C. Snead. Lessons: $100 per hour.

CARL LOHREN, The Golf Club at Indigo Run, Hilton Head Island, S.C. Author of one of the game's best-selling instruction books, *One Move to Better Golf*. Believes in building best possible set-up to avoid problems once swing begins. Lessons: $65 per half-hour.

MICHAEL LOPUSZYNSKI, Doral Resort, Miami, Fla. Up-and-comer who spends most of his teaching time instructing at Jim McLean Golf Schools. Former Duke University golf captain. Relies on video analysis. Lessons: $100 per hour.

JACK LUMPKIN, Sea Island GC, St. Simons Island, Ga. The PGA's 1995 National Teacher of the Year instructs all phases of the game and all skill levels. Davis Love III and Donna

Andrews among his pupils. Long-time Golf Digest Schools instructor. Lessons: $125 per hour.

BILL MADONNA, Timonium, Md. Has established a learning center and coaching atmosphere at his club. Has copyrighted his own "Short Game Exam." Uses state-of-the-art video system and many teaching aids and drills. Lessons: $100 per hour.

TIMOTHY P. MAHONEY, Troon North, Scottsdale, Ariz. At 33, one of youngest on this list. Involved in original swing research projects. Golf Digest Schools instructor. Works with Billy Mayfair. Lessons: $100 for 45 minutes.

MIKE MALASKA, Salt Lake City, Utah. Teaches for Nicklaus/Flick Golf Schools. Believes in a balanced approach to game, including proper swing technique, course management, mental preparation, fitness, and nutrition. Well known in Japan. Lessons: $75 per hour.

PAUL MARCHAND, Houston CC, Houston, Tex. Coach to Fred Couples. Believes in video and visual teaching. Will teach nonmembers sponsored by a member. Lessons: $100 per hour for members; $150 for nonmembers.

LYNN MARRIOTT, ASU Karsten GC, Tempe, Ariz. LPGA's 1992 National Teacher of the Year prefers teaching better players, but works with all skill levels. Instructs many ASU team members and plenty of juniors. Lessons: $125 per hour. Lower rate for juniors.

RICK MCCORD, Orange Lake CC, Kissimmee, Fla. Teaches Swing's the Thing Golf Schools with Dick Farley (see above). Book based on school's methods in press. Has taught around the world. Lessons: $100 per hour.

GERALD MCCULLAGH, Rush Creek Golf Academy, Maple Grove, Minn. British PGA member from Belfast, Ireland, who can play well left- or right-handed. Lessons: $75 per hour.

MIKE MCGETRICK, Meridian Golf Learning Center, Englewood, Colo. Addresses all areas of the game, including course management and mental preparation. Meg Mallon and Lauri Merten are students. Author of numerous instruction articles. Lessons: $120 per hour.

PATTI MCGOWAN, David Leadbetter Golf Academy, Orlando, Fla. Spends most of her time teaching full-swing mechanics. Trains instructors for The David Leadbetter Golf Academies. Swing coach to Mike Hulbert and John Morse. Lessons: $125 per hour.

BOB MCIVER, Farmington CC, Charlottesville, Va. Considers clubfitting an integral part of teaching. Well known for developing juniors. Taught Scott Verplank as a youngster. Lessons: $50 per hour for members, $100 for nonmembers.

JIM MCLEAN, Doral Resort, Miami, Fla. PGA's 1994 National Teacher of the Year and author of four books, including *The*

Eight-Step Swing. Helps students identify what they are doing, what they should be doing, and how to make changes. Lessons: $200 per hour.

EDDIE MERRINS, Bel-Air CC, Los Angeles, Cal. Former head coach at UCLA developed many of his charges into Tour stars, including Corey Pavin. Author of *Swing the Handle, Not the Clubhead*. Lessons: $100 per hour.

BILL MORETTI, Academy of Golf Dynamics, Austin, Tex. All-around instructor, holds 70 golf schools annually. Conducts thorough interview and evaluation before instructing. Teaches Russ Cochran and Fred Funk. Lessons: $120 per hour.

JERRY MOWLDS, Pumpkin Ridge GC, Cornelius, Ore. Concentrates full-swing instruction on four power sources: Arms, wrists, upper body rotation, and weight shift. Also a talented short-game teacher. Offers golf schools at Pumpkin Ridge. Lessons: $75 per hour.

JOHNNY MYERS, Muny GC, Monroe, La. Has spent decades analyzing the great players to find common components he can teach amateurs. A favorite with juniors. Also teaches at Culver Golf Camp in Culver, Ind. Lessons: $60 per hour.

ED OLDFIELD, Merit Club, Libertyville, Ill. During a 43-year career has become a guru to many LPGA stars, including Betsy King and Jan Stephenson. Does not use drills. Lessons: $130 per hour for members, $200 for nonmembers.

DR. DEDE OWENS, Carlsbad, Calif. Two-time LPGA National Teacher of the Year and author of six books and dozens of magazine articles. Teaches nearly 80 hours per week. President of LPGA Teaching and Club Professional Division. Lessons: $100 per hour.

DAN PASQUARIELLO, Mishawaka, Ind. Three-time PGA Aloha Section Teacher of the Year. Promotes short-game lessons as fastest way to lower scores. Offers 90-day program, including 24 hours of instruction, for $1,000. Lessons: $80 per hour.

DAVE PELZ, Austin, Tex. Former NASA scientist now undisputed favorite short-game instructor to the pros, including Peter Jacobsen and Steve Elkington. Instruction at Pelz's schools is based upon 20 years of intensive research. Lessons: Price varies by school location and schedule.

VERNE PERRY, Pumpkin Ridge GC, Cornelius, Ore. Golf historian who teaches all phases of golf, including proper attitude and positive self-esteem. Entertaining instructor who believes better swings are rooted in better preshot routine. Lessons: $60 per hour.

GALE PETERSON, Sea Island GC, St. Simons Island, Ga. Uses video extensively. A favorite with juniors and an excellent communicator. Develops improvement program based upon students' time constraints and skill level. Instructor with Golf Digest Schools. Lessons: $90 per hour.

JIM PETRALIA, San Gabriel CC, San Gabriel, Cal. Former high school physical education teacher has taught since 1966. Produced "Strategic Golf" video with star student Steve Pate. Lessons: $80 per hour.

KIP PUTERBAUGH, Aviara GC, Carlsbad, Cal. Was started in golf at age 11 by short-game wizard Paul Runyan, which may explain emphasis on short game. Full-swing instruction keys on grip, stance, and posture. Uses video extensively. Lessons: $120 per hour.

DANA RADER, Charlotte, N.C. LPGA's 1990 National Teacher of the Year is a 15-year veteran of the lesson tee. Rader builds swing to match individual body type. Produced "Back to Basics" video. Lessons: $80 per hour.

JOHN REDMAN, Winter Park, Fla. Forty-year career began as apprentice to Tommy Armour and Sam Snead. Paul Azinger's tutor. Believes proper tempo and balance are major keys to improvement. Lessons: $200 per hour.

CONRAD H. REHLING, Tuscaloosa, Ala. Long-time college coach very active teaching Special Olympians. Instructor to Bob Murphy and Jerry Pate. Teaches by progression from green back to tee. Original inductee, NCAA Golf Coaches Hall of Fame. Lessons: $50 per hour.

DEAN REINMUTH, San Diego, Cal. Teaches students to minimize muscle tension during their swing. The free-flowing results can be seen in Phil Mickelson, his star pupil. Has own schools and does many corporate schools. Lessons: $300 per hour.

JOHN RHODES, Progressive Golf Institute, Fort Worth, Tex. Aims for "Total Balanced Performance" in his students. His 35-year career has included work with a dozen Tour pros. Lessons: $100 per hour.

PHIL RITSON, Windermere, Fla. One of the most experienced teachers in the world. Exponent of using the "big muscles" to control the swing. One of his former pupils is David Leadbetter. Lessons: $200 per hour.

RINA RITSON, Rina Ritson Golf Schools, Orlando, Fla. Full-swing specialist who teaches both schools and individual lessons. Develops maximum clubhead speed through proper sequence of motion. LPGA's 1993 National Teacher of the Year. Lessons: $120 per hour.

PHIL RODGERS, La Jolla, Cal. Former winner on both PGA and Senior PGA Tours. Well known for rebuilding Jack Nicklaus's short game in early 1980s. Wrote *How to Play Lower Handicap Golf*. Also teaches at Grand Cypress Resort in Orlando, Fla. Lessons: $250 per hour.

PAUL RUNYAN, Pasadena, Cal. Two-time PGA champion and owner of world-renowned short game. Has given 145,000 lessons over 70-year teaching career. Short-game guru with unique teaching system. Member PGA World Golf Hall of Fame. Lessons: $100 per hour.

CHUCK SCALLY SR., Scally's Golf Center, Moon Township, Pa. Named PGA Tri-State Section Teacher of the Year four times over 48-year career. Instructs former U.S. Women's Amateur champion Carol Semple Thompson. Lessons: $80 per hour.

CRAIG SHANKLAND, Ocean Palm GC, Flagler Beach, Fla. Popular PGA seminar speaker who espouses "keep it simple" instruction style: Aim the face, hold the handle, aim yourself, make a swing. Beth Daniel's long-time coach. Lessons: $75 per hour, lower rates for juniors.

LAIRD SMALL, Pebble Beach, Cal. Recently opened Pebble Beach Golf Academy for swing instruction plus nutrition, psychology, club fitting, and fitness information. Also teaches at Nicklaus/Flick Golf Schools. Lessons: $80 per hour.

GARY J. SMITH, Isleworth CC, Windermere, Fla. Focuses on improving student's ball-flight characteristics. Believes many teachers are guilty of overcoaching, tries to keep instructions simple. Lessons: Fees vary based on format.

RICK SMITH, Treetops Sylvan Resort, Gaylord, Mich. Swing mentor to Lee Janzen and Billy Andrade. Consulted by Jack Nicklaus on regular basis. Best known for full-swing theories. Also designs golf courses. Lessons: $550 per person for 3½-hour foursome clinic.

TODD A. SONES, The Vintage Club, Indian Wells, Cal. Illinois PGA's 1994 Teacher of the Year. Simplicity and focusing on the root problem are his teaching philosophy. Robert Gamez solicits his help. Lessons: $100 per hour.

CHARLES SORRELL, Golf Meadows, Stockbridge, Ga. Uses rhymes to help students remember swing keys, plus video and learning aids. Also offers schools. PGA's 1990 National Teacher of the Year. Lessons: $125 per hour.

MITCHELL SPEARMAN, David Leadbetter Golf Academy, Orlando, Fla. Leadbetter protégé and full-swing specialist who breaks swing down into three "P's": posture, pivot, and positioning of club. Lessons: $400 for two hours.

BILL STRAUSBAUGH JR., Columbia CC, Chevy Chase, Md. PGA's 1992 National Teacher of the Year, now in his 50th season. Highly respected by his peers. Also teaches winter schools in Vero Beach, Fla. Lessons: $50 per hour for members, $100 for nonmembers.

DR. JIM SUTTIE, Cog Hill G&CC, Lemont, Ill. Biomechanics expert who spent 10 years studying high-speed film of Tour pros' swings. Averages 70 lessons per week. Visited by numerous pros, including Loren Roberts. Lessons: $125 per hour.

STAN THIRSK, Blue Hills CC, Kansas City, Mo. Best known as Tom Watson's coach, also teaches in Nicklaus/Flick Golf Schools. Wants students to swing the weight of the clubhead with the hands, wrists, and arms. Lessons: $85 per hour.

DICK TIDDY, Arnold Palmer Golf Academy, Orlando, Fla. All-around instructor with 42 years' experience. Focuses on fundamentals of the set-up and mechanics that create acceleration through the hitting zone. Scott Hoch is a pupil. Lessons: $75 per hour.

BOB TOSKI, Boca Raton, Fla. One of America's best-known instructors for 25 years. Elevated profession through numerous television appearances and magazine covers. Great communicator who stresses that students must learn how a good swing feels. Lessons: $100 per hour.

DON TRAHAN, Links O'Tryon, Campobello, S.C. All-around instructor and student of physics and biomechanics. Teaches three-quarter backswing for longer, straighter shots with minimal strain on the body. Wrote *Golf: Plain and Simple.* Lessons: $90 per hour.

J. D. TURNER, Brooks GC, Okoboji, Iowa. Produced six videos and has own syndicated television instruction show. Emphasizes driving and putting in no-nonsense style. Five-time Iowa Open champion. Lessons: $100 per hour.

KEVIN WALKER, Nantucket GC, Siasconset, Mass. Versatile teacher who uses video and computer analyses to speed learning. "Holistic approach" includes fitness and nutrition. Colorado PGA's 1995 Teacher of the Year. Lessons: $125 per hour.

JEFF WARNE, Doral Resort, Miami, Fla. Creative lead instructor with Jim McLean's Golf Schools, Warne focuses on creating proper impact position in the full swing. Relies heavily on video analysis. Lessons: $100 per hour.

CARL WELTY, Carlsbad, Cal. All-around instructor, identifies problems by videotaping on-course play and determining student's clubface impact with face tape. Wants to know what student does on the course, not on the practice tee. Lessons: $600 per day for two people.

DR. GARY WIREN, PGA National GC &R, Palm Beach Gardens, Fla. American ambassador of golf instruction, has lectured and taught more than 200,000 people to play golf around the world. Author of the *PGA of America's Teaching Manual.* Lessons: $150 per hour.

RICK WHITFIELD, Loblolly Pines GC, Hobe Sound, Fla. Imaginative teacher helps students learn by creating clear visual imagery of how the body should move. Teaches former U.S. Mid-Amateur champ Jim Taylor. Lessons: $70 per hour.

BIBLIOGRAPHY

Allen, Frank Kenyon, et al. *The Golfer's Bible.* Doubleday: New York, 1989.

Alliss, Peter. *The Who's Who of Golf.* Prentice-Hall: Englewood Cliffs, N.J., 1983.

Armour, Tommy. *How to Play Your Best Golf All the Time.* Simon & Schuster: New York, 1953.

Aultman, Dick, with Ken Bowden. *The Masters of Golf.* Macmillan: New York, 1975.

Ballard, Jimmy, with Brennan Quinn. *How to Perfect Your Golf Swing.* Golf Digest, Inc.: Norwalk, Conn., 1979.

Ballesteros, Seve, with John Andrisani. *Natural Golf.* Macmillan: New York, 1988.

Ballingall, Peter. *The Pocket Guide to Golf Practice Drills.* Dorling Kindersley: New York, 1995.

Barnes, Jim. *Picture Analysis of Golf Strokes.* J.B. Lippincott: Philadelphia and London, 1919.

Beldam, George. *Great Golfers: Their Methods at a Glance.* McMillan: London, 1904.

Boomer, Percy. *On Learning Golf.* Alfred A. Knopf, Inc.: New York, 1946.

Browning, Robert. *A History of Golf (Classics of Golf Edition).* Ailsa, Inc: New York, n.d.

Bunker, Linda K., and DeDe Owens. *Golf—Better Practice For Better Play.* Leisure Press: New York, 1984.

Burke, Jack. *The Natural Way to Better Golf.* Hanover House: Garden City, N.Y., 1954.

Campbell, Malcolm. *Ultimate Golf Techniques.* Dorling Kindersley Ltd.: London, 1996.

Casper, Billy. *My Million-Dollar Shots.* Bantam Books: New York, 1971.

Clark, R. *Golf: A Royal and Ancient Game.* EP Publishing: London, 1975.

Cochran, A. J., ed. *Science and Golf.* E. & F.N. Spon: London, 1990.

——. *Science and Golf II.* E. & F.N. Spon: London, 1994.

——. *Golf the Scientific Way,* Aston Publishing Group: Hertfordshire, U.K., 1995.

——, and John Stobbs. *Search for the Perfect Swing.* Lippincott: Philadelphia: 1968.

Cohn, Dr. Patrick J. *The Mental Game of Golf, A Guide to Peak Performance.* Diamond Communications: South Bend, Ind., 1994.

——, and Robert K. Winters. *The Mental Art of Putting: Using Your Mind to Putt Your Best.* Diamond Communications: South Bend, Ind., 1995.

Coop, Dr. Richard H. *Mind Over Golf.* Macmillan: New York, 1993.

Cornish, Geoffrey S., and Ronald E. Whitten. *The Architects of Golf.* Harper Collins: New York, 1993.

Cotton, Henry. *A History of Golf Illustrated.* J.B. Lippincott: New York, 1975.

Couples, Fred, with John Andrisani. *Total Shotmaking.* Harper Collins: New York, 1994.

Cranford, Dr. Peter G. *The Winning Touch in Golf.* Herbert Jenkins, Ltd.: London, 1962.

Daly, John, with John Andrisani. *Grip It and Rip It!* Harper Collins: New York, 1992.

Dante, Jim, and Leo Diegel. *The Nine Bad Shots of Golf.* McGraw Hill: New York, 1947.

Davies, Peter. *Davies' Dictionary of Golfing Terms.* Simon & Schuster: New York, 1980.

Davis, Martin, ed. *The Hogan Mystique.* The American Golfer, Inc.: Greenwich, Conn., 1994.

Demaret, Jimmy, et al. *GOLF Magazine's Your Short Game.* Harper & Row: New York, 1962.

Doak, Tom. *The Anatomy of a Golf Course.* Lyons & Burford: New York, 1992.

Dunaway, Mike, with John Andrisani. *Hit It Hard!* Simon & Schuster: New York, 1992.

Dunn, Seymour. *Golf Fundamentals.* Privately printed, 1922.

Fabian-Baddiel, Sarah. *Miller's Golf Memorabilia.* Miller's: London, 1994.

Fishman, Lew, ed. *GOLF Magazine's Shortcuts to Better Golf.* Bristol Park Books: New York, 1979.

Floyd, Ray, with Larry Dennis. *From 60 Yards In.* Harper & Row: New York, 1989.

Frank, James A. *Golf Secrets.* Lyons & Burford: New York, 1994.

Gallwey, W. Timothy. *The Inner Game of Golf.* Random House: New York, 1979.

GOLF Magazine Editors. *GOLF Magazine's Handbook of Putting.* Pelham Books: London, 1975.

Harmon, Claude. Jr., with John Andrisani. *The Four Cornerstones of Winning Golf.* Simon & Schuster: New York, 1996.

Haultain, Arnold. *The Mystery of Golf.* Houghton Mifflin: New York, 1908.

Hobbs, Michael. *Golf: A Visual History.* Crescent Books: New York, 1992.

Hogan, Ben, with Herbert Warren Wind. *Five Lessons: The Modern Fundamentals of Golf.* A.S. Barnes: New York, 1957.

Hogan, Charles. *Five Days to Golfing Excellence.* Lake Oswego, Ore., 1986.

——, *Practicing Golf: A System for Generating the Best Golf You Can Play.* Sedona, Ariz., n.d.

How to Solve Your Golf Problems. Golf Digest: South Norwalk, Conn., 1963.

Hunter, Robert. *The Links.* Charles Scribner's Sons: New York, 1926.

Hutchinson, Horace G. *The Badminton Library: Golf.* Longmans, Green: London, 1890.

Improve Your Golf. Willow Books: London, 1986.

Jacobs, John. *Play Better Golf.* Arco Publishing: New York, 1972.

——. *The Golf Swing Simplified.* Lyons & Burford: New York, 1994.

——, with Ken Bowden. *Practical Golf.* Quadrangle Press: New York, 1972.

Janello, Amy, and Brennon Jones, eds. *Golf: The Greatest Game.* Harper Collins: New York, 1994.

Johnson, Hank. *How to Win the Three Games of Golf.* NYT Special Services, Inc.: Trumbull, Conn.,1993.

Jones, Robert Trent, Jr. *Golf by Design.* Little, Brown and Company: Boston, 1993.

Jones, Robert Tyre. *Bobby Jones on Golf.* Doubleday and Co.: New York, 1966.

——. *Down the Fairway: The Golf Life and Play of Robert T. Jones, Jr.* Minton, Balch & Co.: New York, 1927.

——, and O. B. Keeler. *Down The Fairway (Classics of Golf Edition).* Ailsa, Inc.: New York, 1985.

Kaplan, Jim, ed. *Wilson Golf History—Catalogs.* Vintage Golf: Glencoe, Ill., 1981.

Kelley, Homer. *The Golfing Machine.* Star System Press: Seattle, Wash., 1969.

Kite, Tom, and Larry Dennis. *How to Play Consistent Golf.* Golf Digest/Tennis, Inc.: Trumbull, Conn., 1990.

Lawless, Peter. *The Golfer's Companion.* J.M. Dent & Sons, Ltd.: London, 1937.

Leadbetter, David. *David Leadbetter's Faults and Fixes.* Harper Collins: New York, 1993.

——. *The Golf Swing.* The Stephen Greene Press: New York, 1990.

Locke, Arthur d'Arcy. *Bobby Locke on Golf,* Country Life Ltd.: London, 1953

Loehr, Dr. James E. *The New Toughness Training for Sports.* Penguin: New York, 1994.

——, and Peter J. McLaughlin. *Mentally Tough.* M. Evans and Co.: New York, 1986.

Lohren, Carl. *Getting Set for Golf.* Penguin Books: New York, 1995.

——, with Larry Dennis. *One Move to Better Golf.* Quadrangle Press: New York, 1975.

Longhurst, Henry. *Golf.* J.M. Dent and Sons: London, 1937.

Lupo, Maxine Van Evera. *How to Master a Good Golf Swing.* Contemporary Books: Chicago, 1992.

Maltz, Dr. Maxwell. *Psycho-Cybernetics.* Prentice-Hall: Englewood Cliffs, N.J., 1960.

McLean, Jim. *Golf Digest's Book of Drills.* Golf Digest/Tennis, Inc.: Trumbull, Conn., 1990.

——. *The Eight-Step Swing.* Harper Collins: New York, 1994.

Meyer, D. Swing. *The Method: A Golf Success Strategy.* Acorn Press: Columbia, S.C., 1981.

Michael, Tom, ed. *Golfer's Digest.* Golfer's Digest Association: Chicago, 1968.

Middlecoff, Cary. *Master Guide to Golf.* Prentice-Hall: Englewood Cliffs, N.J., 1960.

Miller, Johnny, with Dale Shankland. *Pure Golf.* Doubleday & Co, Inc.: New York, 1976.

Murphy, Michael. *Golf in the Kingdom.* Penguin: New York, 1972.

Nelson, Byron. *Shape Your Swing the Modern Way.* Golf Digest, Inc.: Norwalk, Conn., 1976.

——. *Winning Golf,* Taylor: Dallas, Tex., n.d.

Nicklaus, Jack. *Jack Nicklaus' Lesson Tee.* Simon & Schuster: New York, 1972.

——. *Jack Nicklaus' Playing Lessons.* Golf Digest/Tennis, Inc.: Norwalk, Conn., 1976.

———. *My 55 Ways to Lower Your Score*. Simon & Schuster: New York, 1964.

———, with Ken Bowden. *Golf My Way*. Simon & Schuster: New York, 1974.

Norman, Greg. *Greg Norman Advanced Golf*. Charles E. Tuttle Co.: Rutland, Vt., 1995.

———, with George Peper. *Greg Norman's Instant Lessons*. Simon & Schuster: New York, 1993.

———. *Shark Attack!* Simon & Schuster: New York, 1988.

Olman, John M. and Morton W. *Olmans' Guide to Golf Antiques*. Market Street Press: Cincinnati, Ohio, 1991.

Palmer, Arnold. *Arnold Palmer's Golf Book*. The Ronald Press Company: New York, 1961.

———, and Peter Dobereiner. *Arnold Palmer's Complete Book of Putting*. Atheneum: New York, 1986.

———, with William Barry Furlong. *Go For Broke*. Simon & Schuster: New York, 1973.

Pavin, Corey. *Corey Pavin's Shotmaking*. NYT Special Services, Inc.: Trumbull, Conn.,1996.

Pelz, Dave, with Nick Mastroni. *Putt Like The Pros*. Harper & Row: New York, 1989.

Penick, Harvey, with Bud Shrake. *Harvey Penick's Little Red Book*. Simon & Schuster: New York, 1992.

Peper, George. *Scrambling Golf*. Prentice-Hall: Englewood Cliffs, N.J., 1977.

———, and The Editors of *GOLF Magazine*. *Golf in America: The First One Hundred Years*. Harry N. Abrams: New York, 1988.

PGA Teaching Manual. *The Art and Science of Golf Instruction*. PGA of America: Palm Beach Gardens, Fla., 1990.

Puckett, Earl, ed. *Golfer's Digest*. Golfer's Digest Books: Chicago, 1974.

Rees, Dai. *Dai Rees on Golf*. Gerald Duckworth & Co.: London, 1959.

Ritson, Phil, with John Andrisani. *Golf Your Way*. Harper Collins: New York, 1992.

Rodriguez, Chi Chi, with John Andrisani. *101 Super Shots*. Harper & Row: New York, 1990.

Rosburg, Bob. *The Putter Book*. Cornerstone Library: New York, 1967.

Rotella, Dr. Robert J. *Golf Is Not a Game of Perfect*. Simon & Schuster: New York, 1995.

———, and Linda K. Bunker. *Mind Mastery for Winning Golf*. Prentice-Hall: Englewood Cliffs, N.J., 1981.

Sampson, Curt. *Hogan*. Rutledge Hill Press: Nashville, Tenn., 1996.

Sarazen, Gene. *Thirty Years of Championship Golf (Classics of Golf Edition)*. Ailsa, Inc.: New York, 1987.

Saunders, Vivien. *The Complete Book of Golf Practice*. Stanley Paul & Co.: North Pomfret, Vt., 1988.

———. *The Golf Handbook*. Pan Books: London, 1989.

———. *The Golfing Mind*. Atheneum: New York, 1988.

Scharff, Robert, and The Editors of *GOLF Magazine, GOLF Magazine's Handbook of Golf Strategy*. Harper & Row: New York, 1959.

Schlee, John. *Maximum Golf*. Acorn Press: Columbia, S.C., 1986.

Scott, Tom, and Geoffrey Cousins. *Golf Secrets of the Masters*. Stanely Paul: London, 1968.

Shapiro, Mel, et al. *Golf: A Turn-of-the-Century Treasury*. Castle: Secaucus, N.J., 1986.

Simek, Thomas C., and Dr. Richard M. O'Brien. *Total Golf: A Behavioral Approach to Lowering Your Score and Getting More Out of Your Game*. Doubleday: Garden City, N.Y., 1981.

Smith, Garden. *The World of Golf*. A.D. Innes & Company: London, 1898.

Snead, Sam. *How to Play Golf*. Garden City Books: Garden City, N.Y., 1952.

———. *Sam Snead on Golf*. Prentice-Hall: Englewood Cliffs, N.J., 1961.

Steel, Donald. *Classic Golf Links of Great Briatin and Ireland*. Chapmans: London, England, 1992.

———, and Peter Ryde, eds. *The Encyclopedia of Golf*. Viking Press: New York, 1975.

Strange, Curtis, with Kenneth Van Kampen. *Win and Win Again!* Contemporary Books: Chicago, 1990.

The Game of Golf: The Lonsdale Library. London: Seeley Service & Co., 1931., 1980.

Thompson, Kenneth R. *The Mental Side of Golf*. Funk & Wagnalls: London and New York, 1939.

Toski, Bob, and Davis Love, Jr. *How to Feel a Real Golf Swing*. Golf Digest/Tennis, Inc.: Trumbull, Conn., 1988.

Travers, Jerome D. *Travers' Golf Book*. Macmillan: New York, 1913.

Vardon, Harry. *The Complete Golfer*. Methuen & Co.: London, 1921.

Venturi, Ken, with Al Barkow. *The Venturi Analysis (Classics of Golf Edition)*. Ailsa, Inc.: New York, 1985.

Ward-Thomas, Pat. *The Royal and Ancient.* Scottish Academic Press: Edinburgh

——, ed. *The World Atlas of Golf.* Gallery Books: New York, 1991.

Watson, Tom. *Tom Watson's Strategic Golf.* NYT Special Services: Trumbull, Conn., 1993.

——, with Nick Seitz. *Getting Up and Down.* Random House: New York, 1983.

Whigham, H. J. *How to Play Golf.* Herbert S. Stone: Chicago and New York, 1897.

Wind, Herbert Warren. *The Story of American Golf.* Simon & Schuster: New York, 1956.

——, and Robert Macdonald, eds. *Vardon on Golf.* Ailsa, Inc.: Stamford, Conn., 1989.

——, ed. *The Complete Golfer.* William Heinemann, Ltd.: London, 1954.

Wiren, Gary. *The PGA Manual of Golf.* Macmillan: New York, 1991.

——, and Dr. Richard Coop. *The New Golf Mind.* Simon & Schuster: New York, 1978.

MAGAZINES:

The American Golfer

Golf Digest

Golf Illustrated

GOLF Magazine

Golf Shop Operations

Golf World

Orlando Magazine

Sports Illustrated

The Golfer

INDEX

PHOTOGRAPH CREDITS